Math Chess Sudoku Puzzles

Frankho ChessDoku

何数棋谜算独

IQ and Chess Puzzles for Juniors

青少年益智及棋芸健腦題

Frank Ho   Amanda Ho

何数棋谜 培训

Ho Math Chess Learning Centre

Math Chess Sudoku Puzzles －青少年益智棋芸健脑

Frankho ChessDoku － 何数棋谜算独

© 2007 － 2020   Frank Ho, Amanda Ho   All rights reserved.   www.homathchess.com

Student's name _____ Date _____

Table of Contents

Preface 10

What are specials about Frankho ChessDoku™ puzzles? 11

Why children like Frankho ChessDoku™? 12

Ho Math Chess workbooks are good for children. 13

Ho Math Chess worksheet simulating an internet screen 14

Traditional chess setup and Ho Math Chess setup 15

Ho Math Chess pieces moves 17

Knight moves 18

Row and column 54

3 by 3 Sudoku 55

Partition of a sum 61

How to solve Frankho ChessDoku ™ 64

Frankho ChessDoku™ # 8 68

Frankho ChessDoku™ # 9 69

Part 1 Frankho ChessDoku 3 by 3 70

Frankho ChessDoku™ # 1 70

Frankho ChessDoku™ # 2 71

Frankho ChessDoku™ # 3 72

Frankho ChessDoku™ # 4 73

Frankho ChessDoku™ # 5 74

Frankho ChessDoku™ # 6 75

***** Part 1 Frankho ChessDoku 3 by 3 ***** 76

Frankho ChessDoku™ # 1 76

Frankho ChessDoku™ # 2 77

Frankho ChessDoku™ # 3 78

Frankho ChessDoku™ # 4 79

Frankho ChessDoku™ # 5 80

Frankho ChessDoku™ # 6 81

Frankho ChessDoku™ # 7 82

Frankho ChessDoku™ # 8 83

Frankho ChessDoku™ # 9 84

Frankho ChessDoku™ # 10 85

Math Chess Sudoku Puzzles 一青少年益智棋芸健脑	
Frankho ChessDoku 一 何数棋谜算独	
© 2007 一 2020　Frank Ho, Amanda Ho　　All rights reserved.　www.homathchess.com	
Student's name _____Date _____	

Frankho ChessDoku™ # 11..86
Frankho ChessDoku™ # 12..87
Frankho ChessDoku™ # 13..88
Frankho ChessDoku™ # 14..89
Frankho ChessDoku™ # 15..90
Frankho ChessDoku™ # 16..91
Frankho ChessDoku™ # 17..92
Frankho ChessDoku™ # 18..93
Frankho ChessDoku™ # 19..94
Frankho ChessDoku™ # 20..95
Frankho ChessDoku™ # 21..96
Frankho ChessDoku™ # 22..97
Frankho ChessDoku™ # 23..98
Frankho ChessDoku™ # 24..99
Frankho ChessDoku™ # 25..100
Frankho ChessDoku™ # 26..101
Frankho ChessDoku™ # 27..102
Frankho ChessDoku™ # 28..103
Frankho ChessDoku™ # 29..104
Frankho ChessDoku™ # 30..105
Frankho ChessDoku™ # 31..106
Frankho ChessDoku™ # 32..107
Frankho ChessDoku™ # 33..108
Frankho ChessDoku™ # 34..109
Frankho ChessDoku™ # 35..110
Frankho ChessDoku™ # 36..111
Frankho ChessDoku™ # 37..112
Frankho ChessDoku™ # 38..113
Frankho ChessDoku™ # 39..114
Frankho ChessDoku™ # 40..115
Frankho ChessDoku™ # 41..116
Frankho ChessDoku™ # 42..117
Frankho ChessDoku™ # 43..118
Frankho ChessDoku™ # 44..119

Math Chess Sudoku Puzzles — 青少年益智棋芸健脑	
Frankho ChessDoku — 何数棋谜算独	
© 2007 — 2020 Frank Ho, Amanda Ho All rights reserved. www.homathchess.com	
Student's name _____ Date _____	

Frankho ChessDoku™ # 45 120
Frankho ChessDoku™ # 46 121
Frankho ChessDoku™ # 47 122
Frankho ChessDoku™ # 48 123
Frankho ChessDoku™ # 49 124
Frankho ChessDoku™ # 50 125
Frankho ChessDoku™ # 51 126
Frankho ChessDoku™ # 52 127
Frankho ChessDoku™ # 53 128
Frankho ChessDoku™ # 54 129
Frankho ChessDoku™ # 55 130
Frankho ChessDoku™ # 56 131
Frankho ChessDoku™ # 57 132
Frankho ChessDoku™ # 58 133
Frankho ChessDoku™ # 59 134
Frankho ChessDoku™ # 60 135
Frankho ChessDoku™ # 61 136
Frankho ChessDoku™ # 62 137
Frankho ChessDoku™ # 63 138
Frankho ChessDoku™ # 64 139
Frankho ChessDoku™ # 65 140
Frankho ChessDoku™ # 66 141
Frankho ChessDoku™ # 67 142
Frankho ChessDoku™ # 68 143
Frankho ChessDoku™ # 69 144
Frankho ChessDoku™ # 70 145
Frankho ChessDoku™ # 71 146
Frankho ChessDoku™ # 72 147
Frankho ChessDoku™ # 73 148
Frankho ChessDoku™ # 74 149
Frankho ChessDoku™ # 75 150
Frankho ChessDoku™ # 76 151
Frankho ChessDoku™ # 77 152
Frankho ChessDoku™ # 78 153

Frankho ChessDoku™ # 79	154
Frankho ChessDoku™ # 80	155
Frankho ChessDoku™ # 81	156
Frankho ChessDoku™ # 82	157
Frankho ChessDoku™ # 83	158
Frankho ChessDoku™ # 84	159
Frankho ChessDoku™ # 85	160
Frankho ChessDoku™ # 86	161
Frankho ChessDoku™ # 87	162
Frankho ChessDoku™ # 88	163
Frankho ChessDoku™ # 89	164
Frankho ChessDoku™ # 90	165
Frankho ChessDoku™ # 91	166
Frankho ChessDoku™ # 92	167
Frankho ChessDoku™ # 93	168
Frankho ChessDoku™ # 94	169
Frankho ChessDoku™ # 95	170
Frankho ChessDoku™ # 96	171
Frankho ChessDoku™ # 97	172
Frankho ChessDoku™ # 98	173
Frankho ChessDoku™ # 99	174
Frankho ChessDoku™ # 100	175
Frankho ChessDoku™ # 101	176
Frankho ChessDoku™ # 102	177
Frankho ChessDoku™ # 103	178
Frankho ChessDoku™ # 104	179
Frankho ChessDoku™ # 105	180
Frankho ChessDoku™ # 106	181
Frankho ChessDoku™ # 107	182
Frankho ChessDoku™ # 108	183
Frankho ChessDoku™ # 109	184
Frankho ChessDoku™ # 110	185
Frankho ChessDoku™ # 111	186
Frankho ChessDoku™ # 112	187

Frankho ChessDoku™ # 113	188
Frankho ChessDoku™ # 114	189
Frankho ChessDoku™ # 115	190
Frankho ChessDoku™ # 116	191
Frankho ChessDoku™ # 117	192
Frankho ChessDoku™ # 118	193
Frankho ChessDoku™ # 119	194
Frankho ChessDoku™ # 120	195
Frankho ChessDoku™ # 121	196
Frankho ChessDoku™ # 122	197
Frankho ChessDoku™ # 123	198
Frankho ChessDoku™ # 124	199
Frankho ChessDoku™ # 125	200
Frankho ChessDoku™ # 126	201
Frankho ChessDoku™ # 127	202
Frankho ChessDoku™ # 128	203
Frankho ChessDoku™ # 129	204
Frankho ChessDoku™ # 130	205
Frankho ChessDoku™ # 131	206
Frankho ChessDoku™ # 132	207
Frankho ChessDoku™ # 133	208
Frankho ChessDoku™ # 134	209
Frankho ChessDoku™ # 135	210
Frankho ChessDoku™ # 136	211
Frankho ChessDoku™ # 137	212
Frankho ChessDoku™ # 138	213
Frankho ChessDoku™ # 139	214
Frankho ChessDoku™ # 140	215
Frankho ChessDoku™ # 141	216
Frankho ChessDoku™ # 142	217
Frankho ChessDoku™ # 143	218
Frankho ChessDoku™ # 144	219
Frankho ChessDoku™ # 145	220
Frankho ChessDoku™ # 146	221

Frankho ChessDoku™ # 147 222
Frankho ChessDoku™ # 148 223
Frankho ChessDoku™ # 149 224
Frankho ChessDoku™ # 150 225
Frankho ChessDoku™ # 151 226
Frankho ChessDoku™ # 152 227
***** Part 2 – 3 Dimensional Frankho ChessDoku ***** 228
3 Dimensional Frankho ChessDoku™ # 1 228
3 Dimensional Frankho ChessDoku™ # 2 229
3 Dimensional Frankho ChessDoku™ # 3 230
3 Dimensional Frankho ChessDoku™ # 4 231
3 Dimensional Frankho ChessDoku™ # 5 232
3 Dimensional Frankho ChessDoku™ # 6 233
3 Dimensional Frankho ChessDoku™ # 7 234
3 Dimensional Frankho ChessDoku™ # 8 235
3 Dimensional Frankho ChessDoku™ # 9 236
3 Dimensional Frankho ChessDoku™ # 10 237
3 Dimensional Frankho ChessDoku™ # 11 238
3 Dimensional Frankho ChessDoku™ # 12 239
3 Dimensional Frankho ChessDoku™ # 13 240
3 Dimensional Frankho ChessDoku™ # 14 241
3 Dimensional Frankho ChessDoku™ # 15 242
3 Dimensional Frankho ChessDoku™ # 16 243
3 Dimensional Frankho ChessDoku™ # 17 244
3 Dimensional Frankho ChessDoku™ # 18 245
3 Dimensional Frankho ChessDoku™ # 19 246
3 Dimensional Frankho ChessDoku™ # 20 247
3 Dimensional Frankho ChessDoku™ # 21 248
3 Dimensional Frankho ChessDoku™ # 22 249
3 Dimensional Frankho ChessDoku™ # 23 250
3 Dimensional Frankho ChessDoku™ # 24 251
3 Dimensional Frankho ChessDoku™ # 25 252
3 Dimensional Frankho ChessDoku™ # 26 253
3 Dimensional Frankho ChessDoku™ # 27 254

3 Dimensional Frankho ChessDoku™ # 28 255
3 Dimensional Frankho ChessDoku™ # 29 256
3 Dimensional Frankho ChessDoku™ # 30 257
3 Dimensional Frankho ChessDoku™ # 31 258
3 Dimensional Frankho ChessDoku™ # 32 259
3 Dimensional Frankho ChessDoku™ # 33 260
3 Dimensional Frankho ChessDoku™ # 34 261
3 Dimensional Frankho ChessDoku™ # 35 262
3 Dimensional Frankho ChessDoku™ # 36 263
3 Dimensional Frankho ChessDoku™ # 37 264
3 Dimensional Frankho ChessDoku™ # 38 265
3 Dimensional Frankho ChessDoku™ # 39 266
3 Dimensional Frankho ChessDoku™ # 40 267
3 Dimensional Frankho ChessDoku™ # 41 268
3 Dimensional Frankho ChessDoku™ # 42 269
3 Dimensional Frankho ChessDoku™ # 43 270
3 Dimensional Frankho ChessDoku™ # 44 271
3 Dimensional Frankho ChessDoku™ # 45 272
3 Dimensional Frankho ChessDoku™ # 46 273
3 Dimensional Frankho ChessDoku™ # 47 274
3 Dimensional Frankho ChessDoku™ # 48 275
3 Dimensional Frankho ChessDoku™ # 49 276
3 Dimensional Frankho ChessDoku™ # 50 277
3 Dimensional Frankho ChessDoku™ # 51 278

Comparing Frankho ChessDoku and CalcuDoku 279

Introduction of Frankho ChessDoku © 279

Introduction of CalcuDoku 280

Comparisons 280

Example 1 281

Example 2 282

Example 3 283

Commutative law 285

Chess strategy and *Frankho ChessDoku* strategy 286

Triangular solving strategy for 3 by 3 grid 287

Math Chess Sudoku Puzzles 一青少年益智棋芸健脑

Frankho ChessDoku 一 何数棋谜算独

© 2007 一 2020   Frank Ho, Amanda Ho   All rights reserved.   www.homathchess.com

Student's name _____ Date _____

References 288

Preface

Frankho ChessDoku™ puzzles were invented by Mr. Frank Ho, a Canadian math teacher and the founder of Ho Math Chess Tutor Franchise Learning Centre. The puzzles included in this workbook were jointly created by Frank Ho and Amanda Ho.

The gameplay is an excellent way to inspire children's interest in learning math, and chess has proven to be effective as a learning tool. Frankho ChessDoku™ is a collection of a special kind of math puzzles that are solved by using addition, subtraction, multiplication, division, or number factoring by following chess moves, logic, and backwards thinking strategy. Frankho ChessDoku™ is a one-of-a-kind puzzle that can help children improve their computing, logic, and chess abilities all in one workbook and at the same time.

Since most children like puzzles and games, so for children working on Frankho ChessDoku™ is a good alternative for them to learn math computation skills, whether they are interested in playing chess or not. There is no chess knowledge required at all when working on Frankho ChessDoku™ because children could simply follow the directions as indicated by the darker lines. The numbers involved in the computations are all just one-digit numbers.

Frankho ChessDoku™ puzzles were created by using the following Frank's invented and trademarked Geometric Chess Symbols, which are also used for Ho Math Chess Teaching Set. A child as young as four years old can play chess almost instantly by learning this chess set.

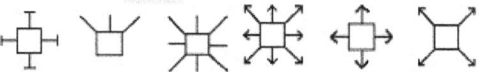

(Canada copyright 1069744, trademark TMA 771400)

When working on Frankho ChessDoku™ puzzles, children explore the calculation pathways by using clues such as common squares intersected by chess moves. This logical thinking process adds a fun element to the learning of basic number facts.

What makes Frankho ChessDoku™ intriguing is that it teaches children logic and the decision-making process. Even though there is only one final answer, the immediate answers in the process of calculating may be more than one. Many math concepts, such as operations of intersections and reversing order of operations such as finding addends of a given sum, are often included in the thinking process. Children also are taught the concepts of line interactions (chess moves) and logic while having fun following chess moves.

Frankho ChessDoku™ puzzles are educational, fun, and addictive.

For more details, please contact Ho Math Chess at homathchess@outlook.com.

Frank Ho
Amanda Ho

October 2008

What are specials about Frankho ChessDoku™ puzzles?

- They are unique math puzzles (over 200) combining with math, chess, Sudoku, and logic.

- They do not require any high-level math skills other than addition, subtraction, multiplication, division, factoring, comparisons, and visualization.

- The chess skills required are very elementary. Students are only required to know how each chess piece moves and how it is represented by a corresponding Geometric Chess Symbol – invented and trademarked by Frank Ho.

- All the puzzles can be solved by students with minimum teacher's guidance.

- The puzzles train students to be patient and provide opportunities to use their problem-solving abilities. They are fun and addictive.

- The abilities learned by doing the puzzles can be applied to help students succeed in their day school math courses.

Ho Math Chess = A Cool and Fun Way to Learn Math!™

Math Chess Sudoku Puzzles 一青少年益智棋芸健脑

Frankho ChessDoku 一 何数棋谜算独

© 2007 — 2020   Frank Ho, Amanda Ho   All rights reserved.   www.homathchess.com

Student's name_____ Date_____

Why children like Frankho ChessDoku™?

One question puzzled me when I observed that our children's likeness of Frankho ChessDoku exceeding our expectations. Why? I started to look into the reasons and also did a little experiment to verify if our children like Frankho ChessDoku and the following is my report.

Frankho ChessDoku is a great invention for being used as a fun supplemental basic number facts training material. We have tested this product in our own Vancouver learning centre since the year 2008 and discovered Frankho ChessDoku 3 by 3 has always been the most favourite workbook for primary students, and this can be testified by students when they were asked to choose the most liked workbook out of their workbooks. Some parents even told me that their kids would voluntarily to work on Frankho ChessDoku on their own without being asked to do so,

Why our students like Frankho ChessDoku workbook? What is the secret?

1. It benefits children, and they know it. Not only Frankho ChessDoku improves a child's basic number facts computation ability, but it can also improve their logical thinking and visualization skills and even chess playability because children are trained to watch for the intersections of chess moves while working on Frankho ChessDoku.

2. Frankho ChessDoku is not dull because every problem is different. The problem presents a mystery to children and makes them want to solve it simply it is not too difficult, yet it is also challenging for them, and the chess moves encourage them to solve the puzzle one step at a time.

3. There are no lengthy English sentences to comprehend before they could solve the problem. Many times, they face multiple answers but not sure which one is right, so they have to put on their logic thinking hat to try to identify the correct answer. While they are working on arithmetic problems, it is not straightforward to find the answer 2 + 3. Instead, it is what numbers would make 3 by using some kind of arithmetic operations, so that is why they do not feel bored.

4. Often children feel bored when working on word problems because most of the time when they get stuck when they feel hopeless to continue, but this kind of feeling does not exist in Frankho ChessDoku because they could tackle the same problem from different directions by following chess moves and try to find the answer.

5. Often children feel bored when working on pure computation worksheets because they constantly have to do arithmetic sheets after sheets, and they do not like those multiple-digit numbers. With Frankho ChessDoku, children only using numbers 1, 2, 3, so the calculations are not so difficult, and even a kindergarten could work on Frankho ChessDoku problems.

6. The final result always follows the Sudoku rule so children could check on their answers to see if the result is correct or not. The entire learning process also trains children to be a self-learner form the beginning to the end. Teacher's or parent's guidance is kept to minimal.

7. After finishing Frankho ChessDoku, there is no messy room to be cleaned up and no scattered manipulative to be collected. Students get a good brain workout by only using a pencil and an eraser. Both teachers and children feel happy in this kind of organized environment.

8. Students could even help each other to have a good team spirit when working on Frankho ChessDoku.

9. Even though Frankho ChessDoku involves chess, it does not require students to know how to play chess because students simply follow the directions of lines.

| Math Chess Sudoku Puzzles 一青少年益智棋芸健脑 |
| Frankho ChessDoku — 何数棋谜算独 |
| © 2007 — 2020 Frank Ho, Amanda Ho   All rights reserved.   www.homathchess.com |
| Student's name_____Date_____ |

Ho Math Chess workbooks are good for children.

使用何数棋谜教材的好处

加拿大 何数棋谜 培训中心
創辦人何数棋 (Frank Ho)
www.mathandchess.com

今天儿童面对的世界是学习如何处理数字,图形,资料搜寻,音影上下载,资讯比较,分类等资讯.这些活动实际已成為儿童生活的一部份.所以如果说学数学就是计算数字就错了.学数学的另一个目的就是学习如何利用数字资讯去解决问题及培养创造力.但是**传统式数学的计算练习题却完全没跟上科研已经改变了儿童面对的世界.**

儿童想要的计算题已经不是单纯的从上到下,从左到右的纯计算.**儿童需要的是他们情愿的而又快乐地做不枯燥的计算题.**所以如何将传统式数学计算题变得有趣而且又好玩,并且还可以增强儿童的计算及解决问题能力及培养创造力,同时还可以增进儿童记忆的能力达到全脑开发的目的?

何数棋谜首创巳申情商标的几何棋艺符号并利用此符号发明了世界第一無二的何数棋迷教材及教学棋具.何数棋谜教材让儿童能利用几何棋艺符号进行数学的运算.

何数棋谜与传统式,数学教材不同的是小朋友不但要发掘题目,而且还要依国际象棋棋子的走法去发掘谜题与计算题（見下圖）及答案. 只见棋谜不见题   劝君迷路不哭涕   数学象棋加谜题   健脑思维真神奇

何数棋谜是将国际象棋融入数学以达到寓教於乐的教学理念.学生不但可以增强计算能力并且逻可以增强解题能力及培养全脑开发创造力.

详细资料请上网查询 www.homathchess.com.

Ho Math Chess worksheet simulating an internet screen

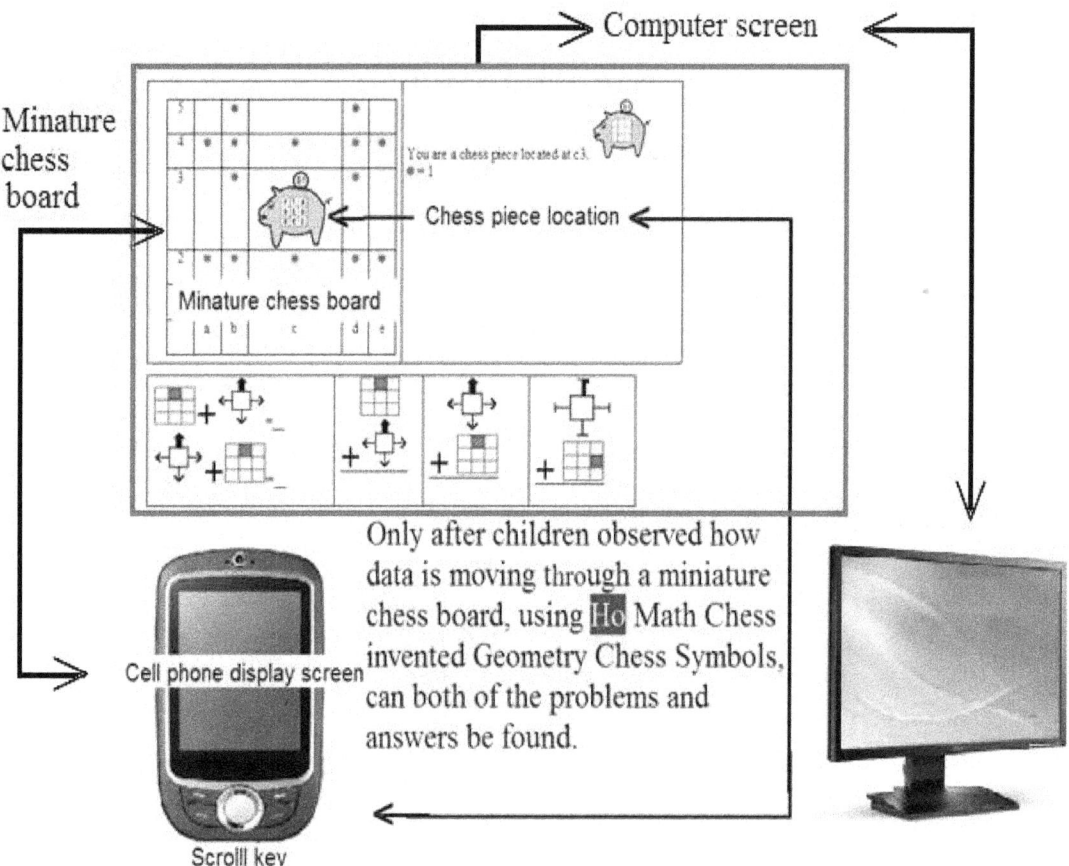

Traditional chess setup and Ho Math Chess setup

Frank Ho said, "Chess is a hands-on brain work using directions."
Frank Ho said, "Chess move is decided by visualizing how lines intersect to each other."

Ho Math Chess Training Set is designed to train children how to play chess using geometry concepts of lines and line segments. For details, please see www.homathchess.com

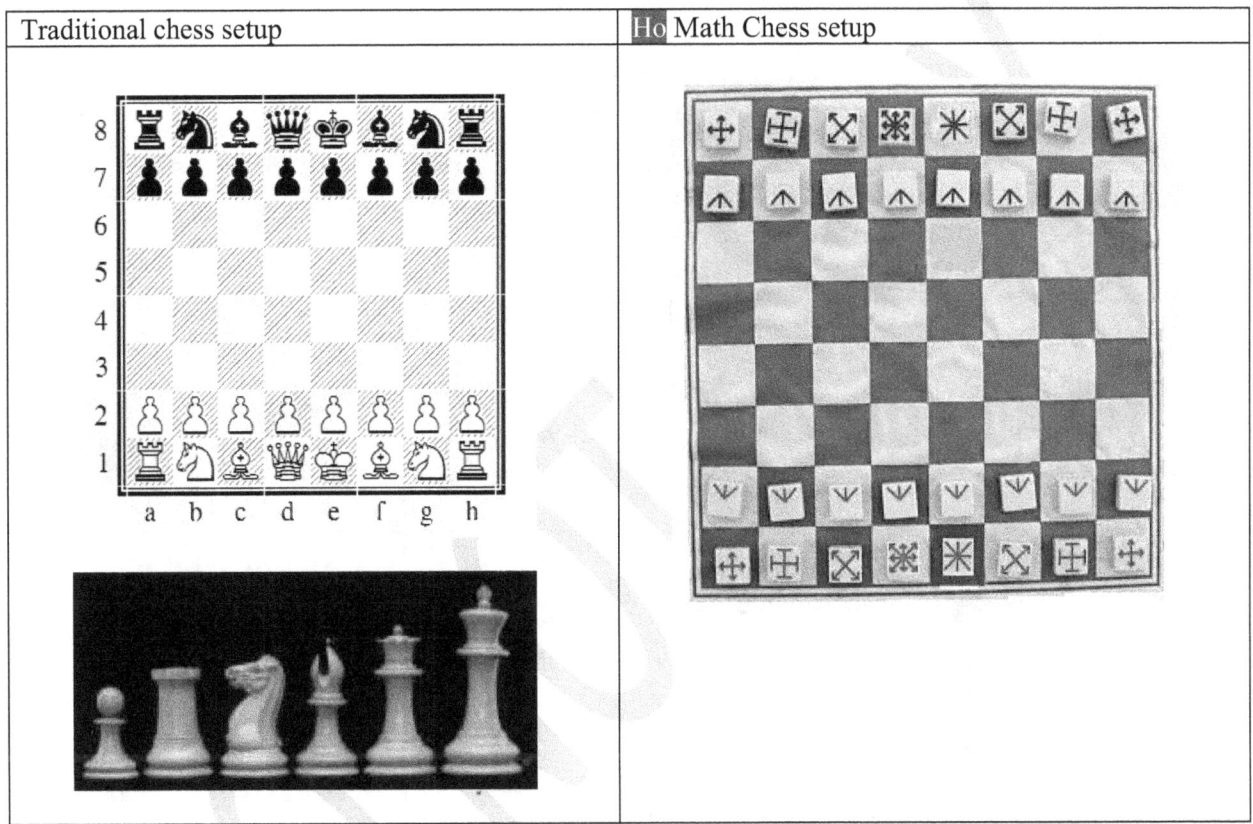

Ho Math Chess chessboard setup

How many chess pieces are there for each of the following symbols (Black)?

✠	✢	✣	✱	✺	⋎
2	2	2	1	1	8

How many chess pieces are there for each of the following symbols (White)?

✠	✢	✣	⋎	✺	✱
2	2	2	8	1	1

Math Chess Sudoku Puzzles 一青少年益智棋芸健脑

Frankho ChessDoku 一 何数棋谜算独

© 2007 － 2020   Frank Ho, Amanda Ho   All rights reserved.   www.homathchess.com

Student's name _____ Date _____

Ho Math Chess pieces moves

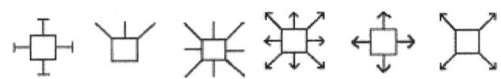

(Canada copyright 1069744, Trademark TMA771400)

Ho Math Chess Teaching Set	Traditional chess set	English name
		Pawn
		Knight
		Bishop
		Rook
		Queen
		King

Knight moves

Mark an "X" on a square to show where each (knight) can move to.

The knight moves straight in 2 squares, then turns one square like an English L letter. The knight's move follows the "1, 2, and turn" direction.

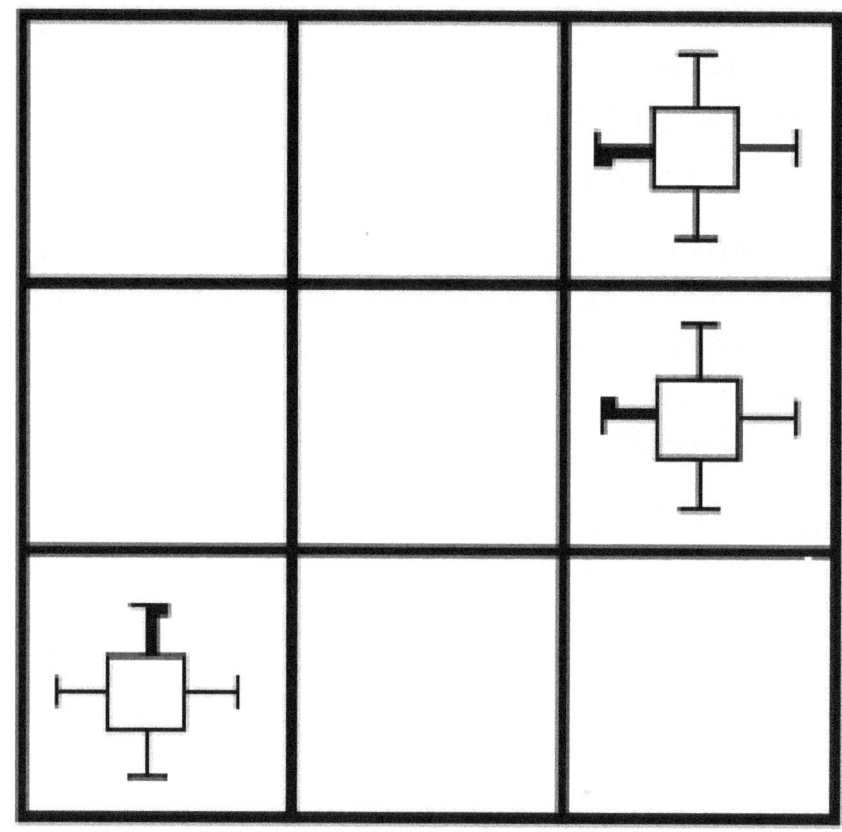

answer

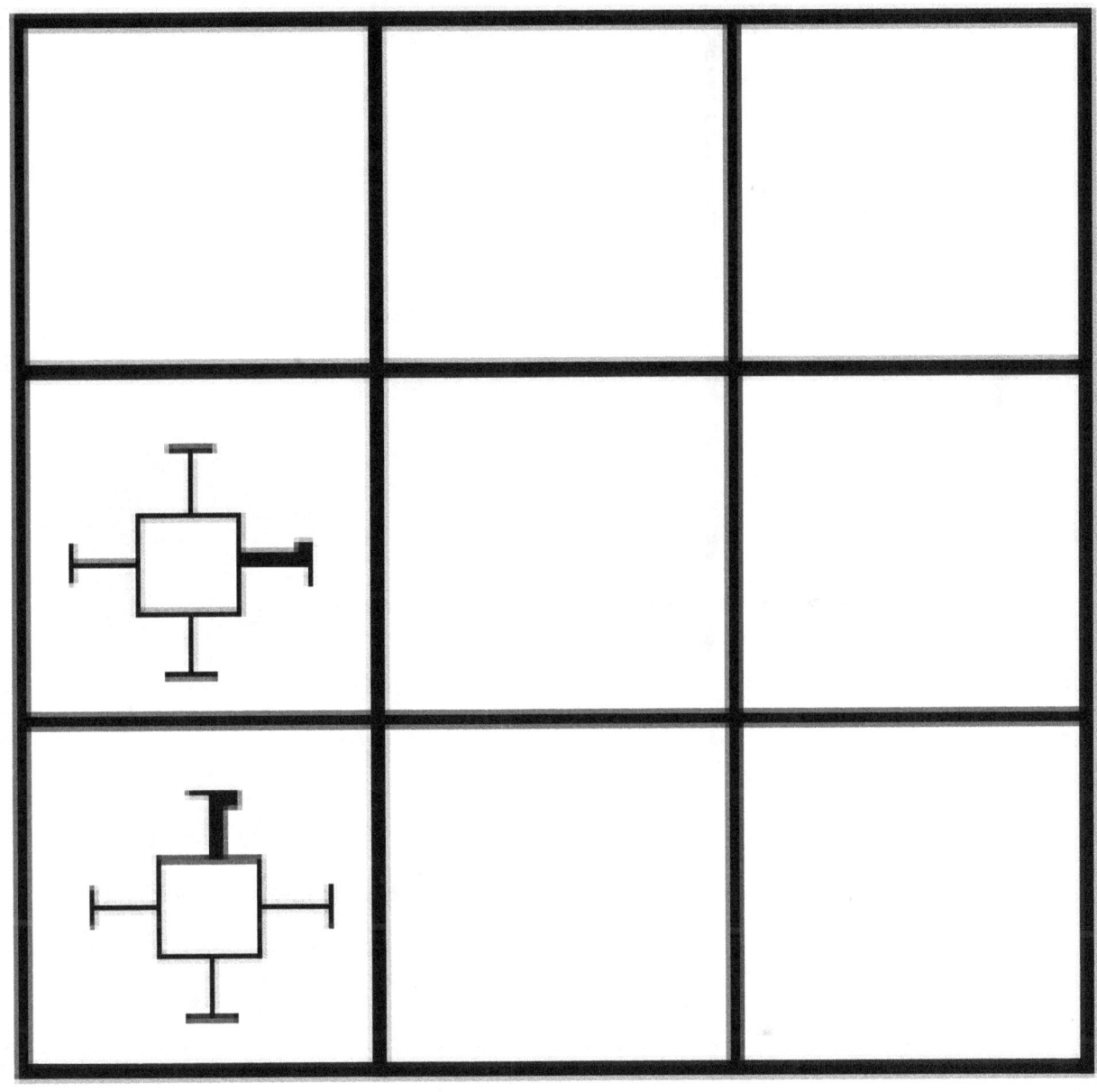

Math Chess Sudoku Puzzles 一 青少年益智棋芸健脑

Frankho ChessDoku 一 何数棋谜算独

© 2007 一 2020 Frank Ho, Amanda Ho   All rights reserved.   www.homathchess.com

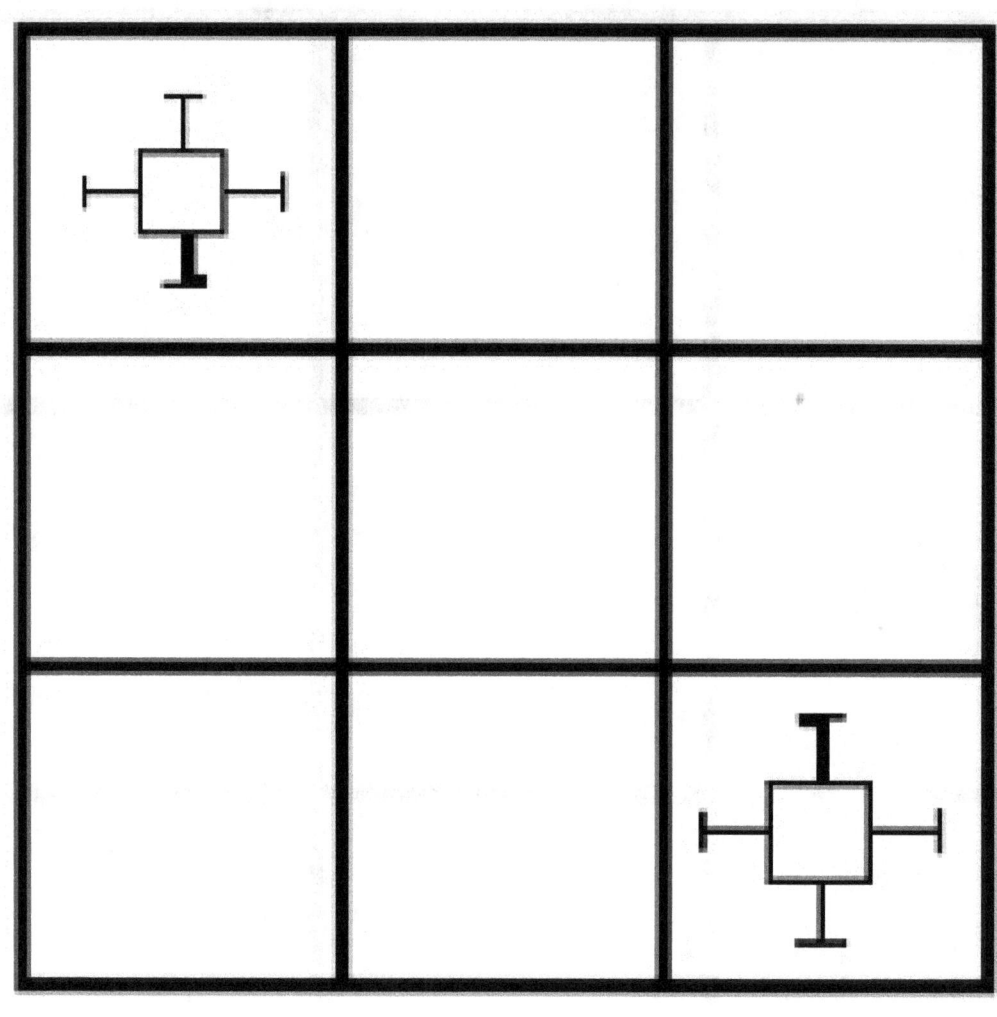

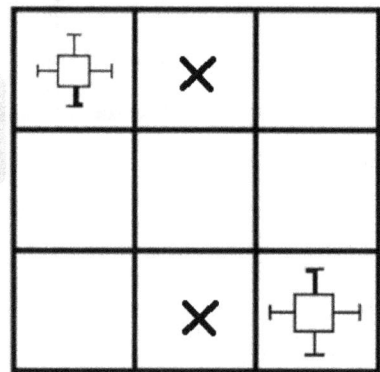 answer

Math Chess Sudoku Puzzles －青少年益智棋芸健脑

Frankho ChessDoku － 何数棋谜算独

© 2007 － 2020 Frank Ho, Amanda Ho   All rights reserved.   www.homathchess.com

Student's name _____ Date _____

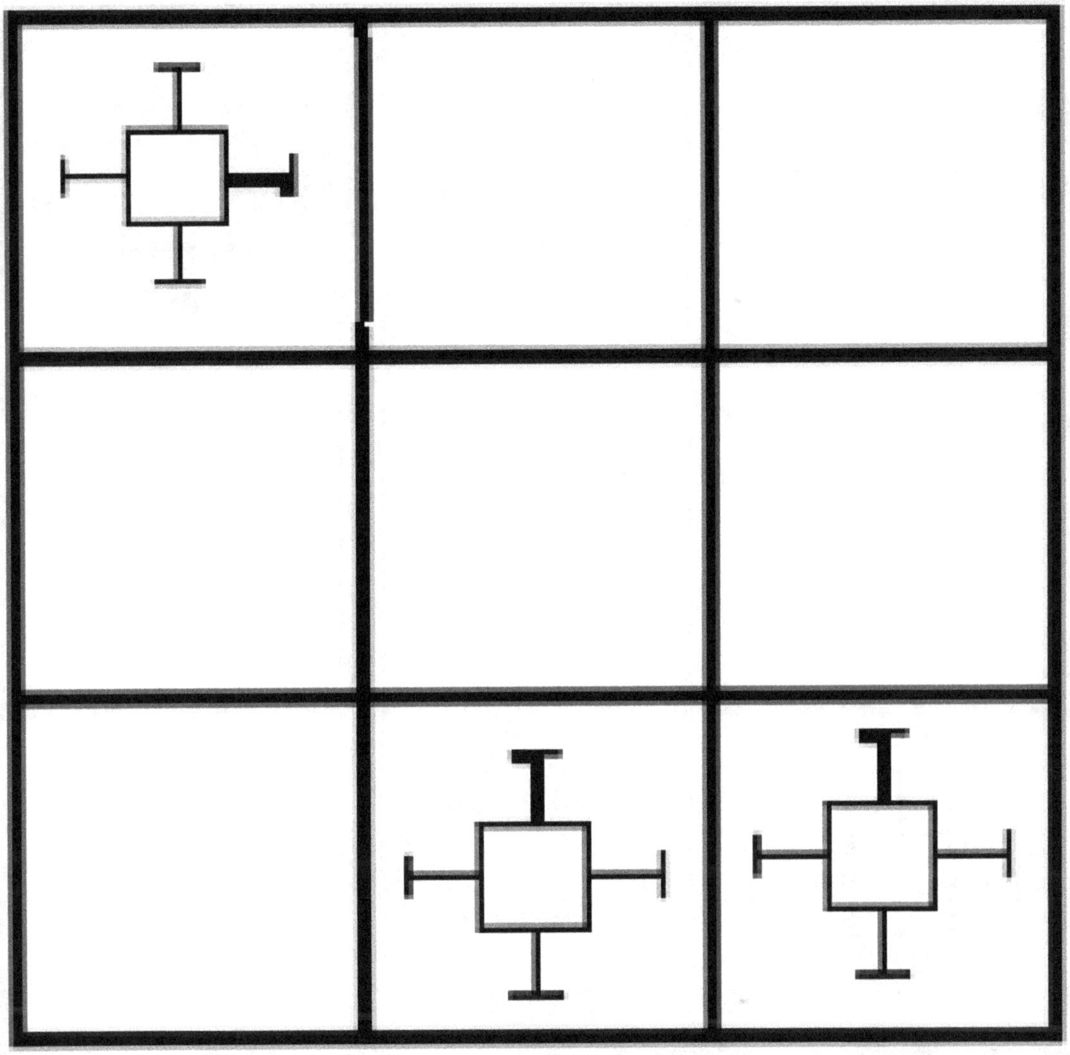

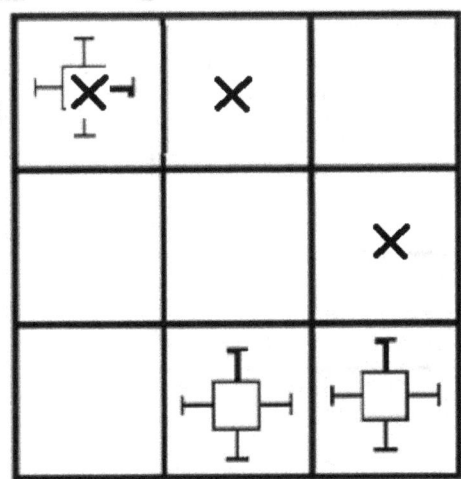
answer

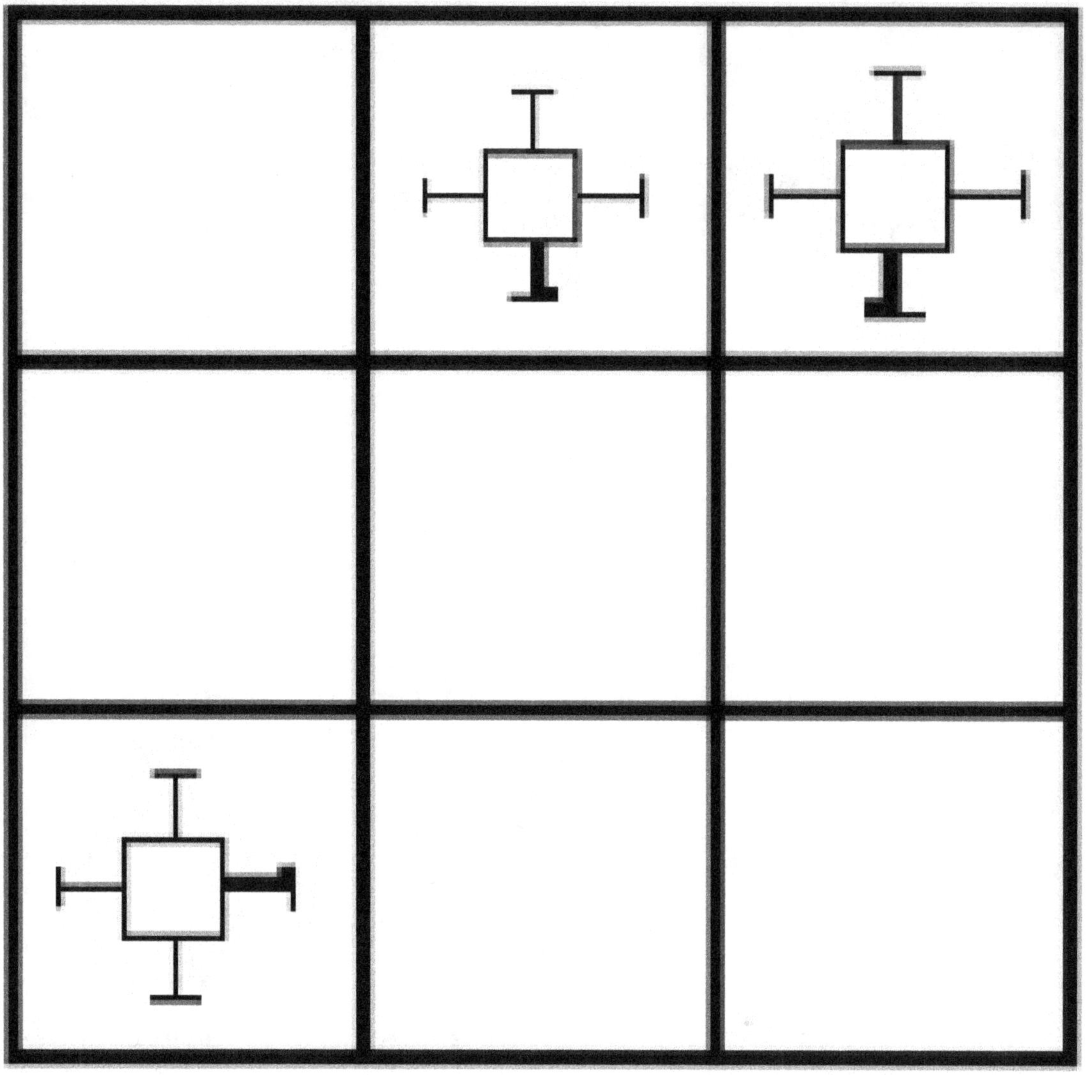

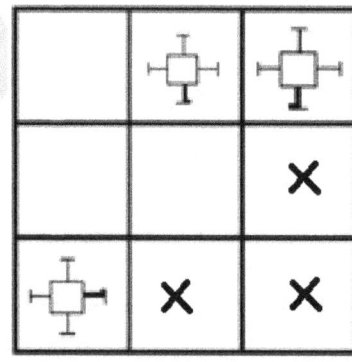

Math Chess Sudoku Puzzles 一青少年益智棋芸健脑

Frankho ChessDoku 一 何数棋谜算独

© 2007 — 2020 Frank Ho, Amanda Ho   All rights reserved.   www.homathchess.com

Student's name _____ Date _____

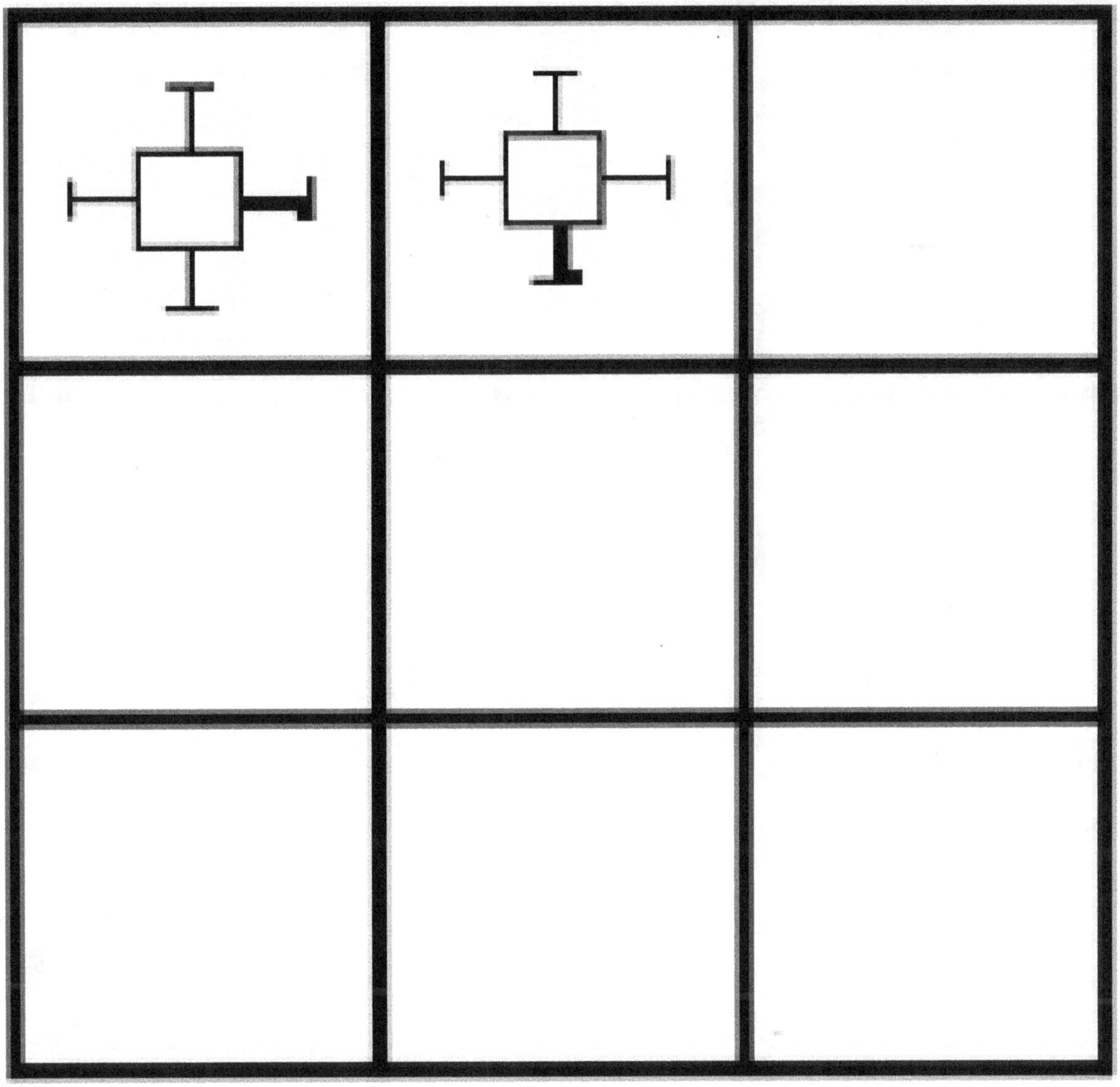

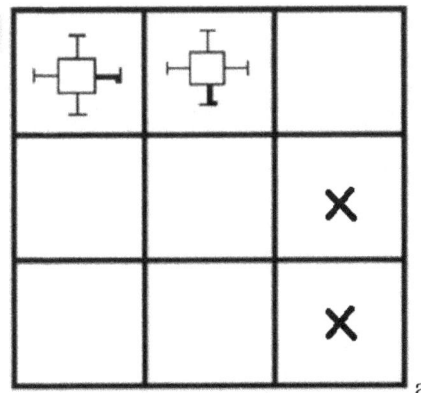
answer

Page 23 of 288

Math Chess Sudoku Puzzles －青少年益智棋芸健脑

Frankho ChessDoku － 何数棋谜算独

© 2007 － 2020   Frank Ho, Amanda Ho   All rights reserved.   www.homathchess.com

Student's name_____ Date_____

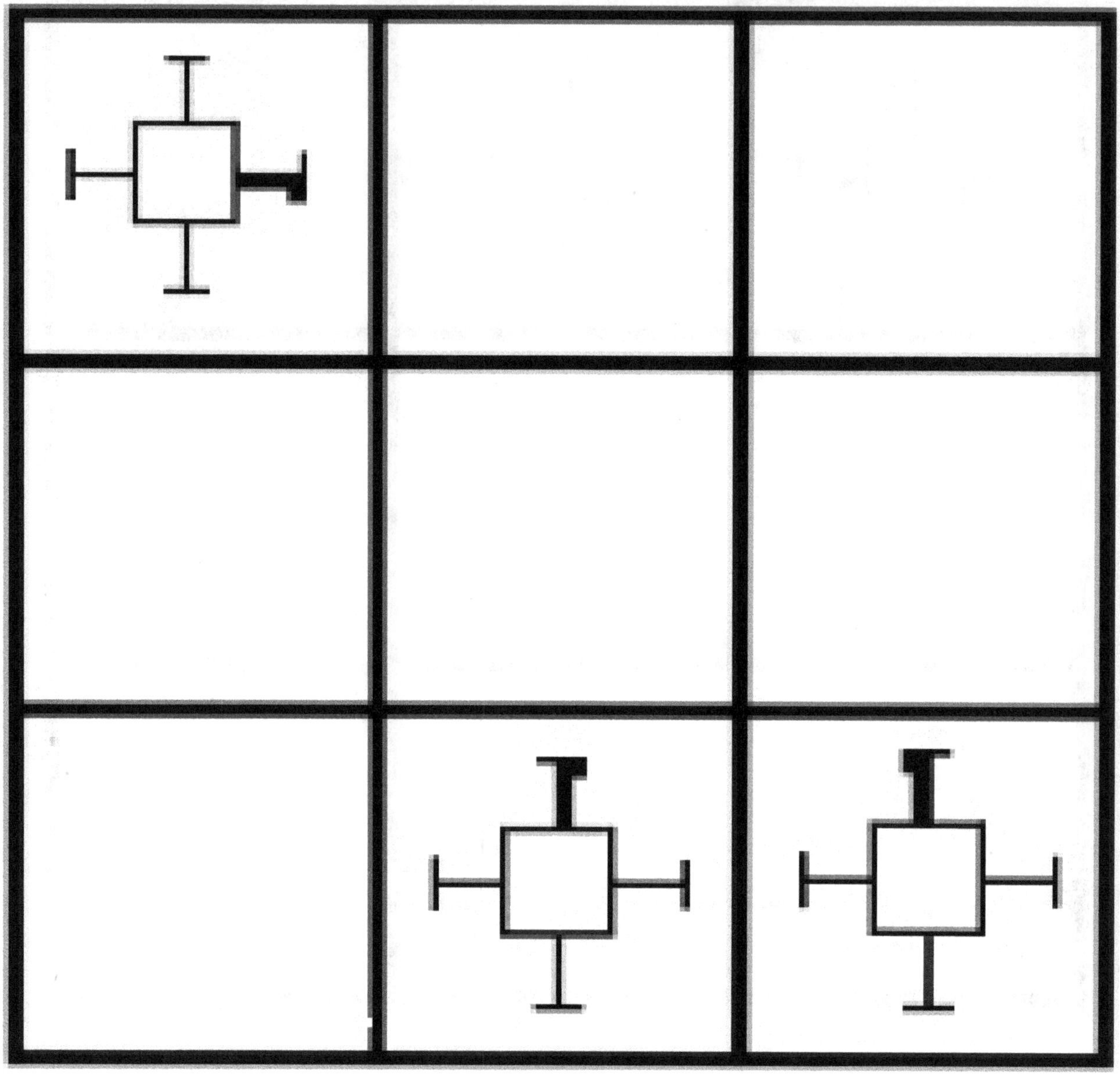

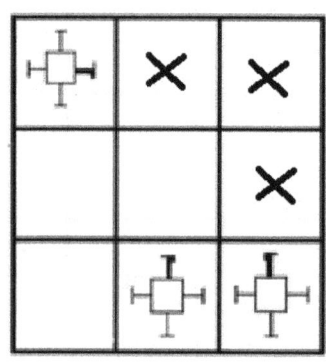

answer

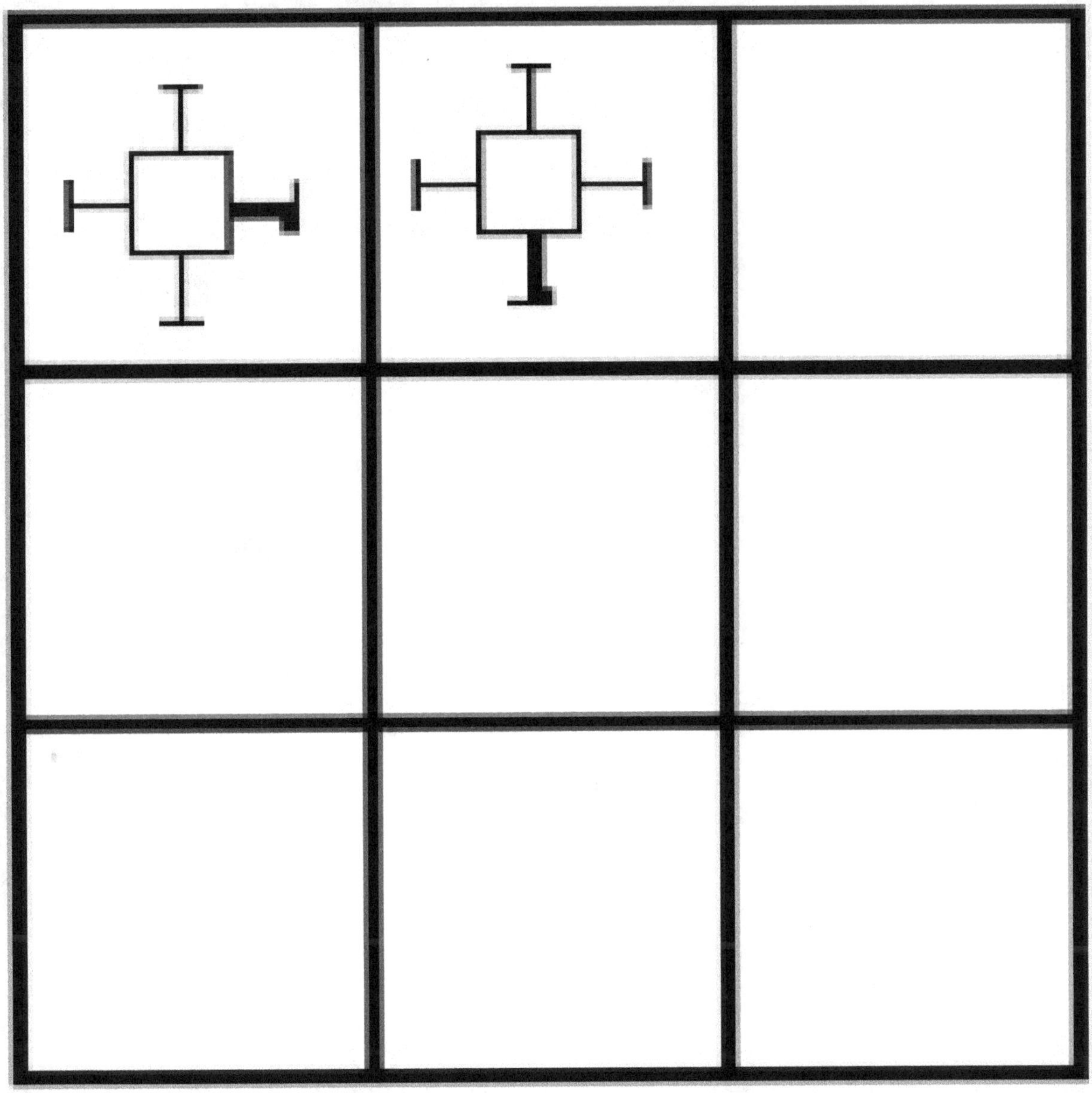

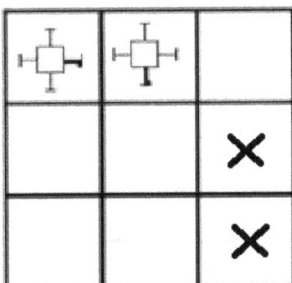
answer

Math Chess Sudoku Puzzles 一青少年益智棋芸健脑

Frankho ChessDoku 一 何数棋谜算独

© 2007 一 2020   Frank Ho, Amanda Ho   All rights reserved.   www.homathchess.com

Student's name _____ Date _____

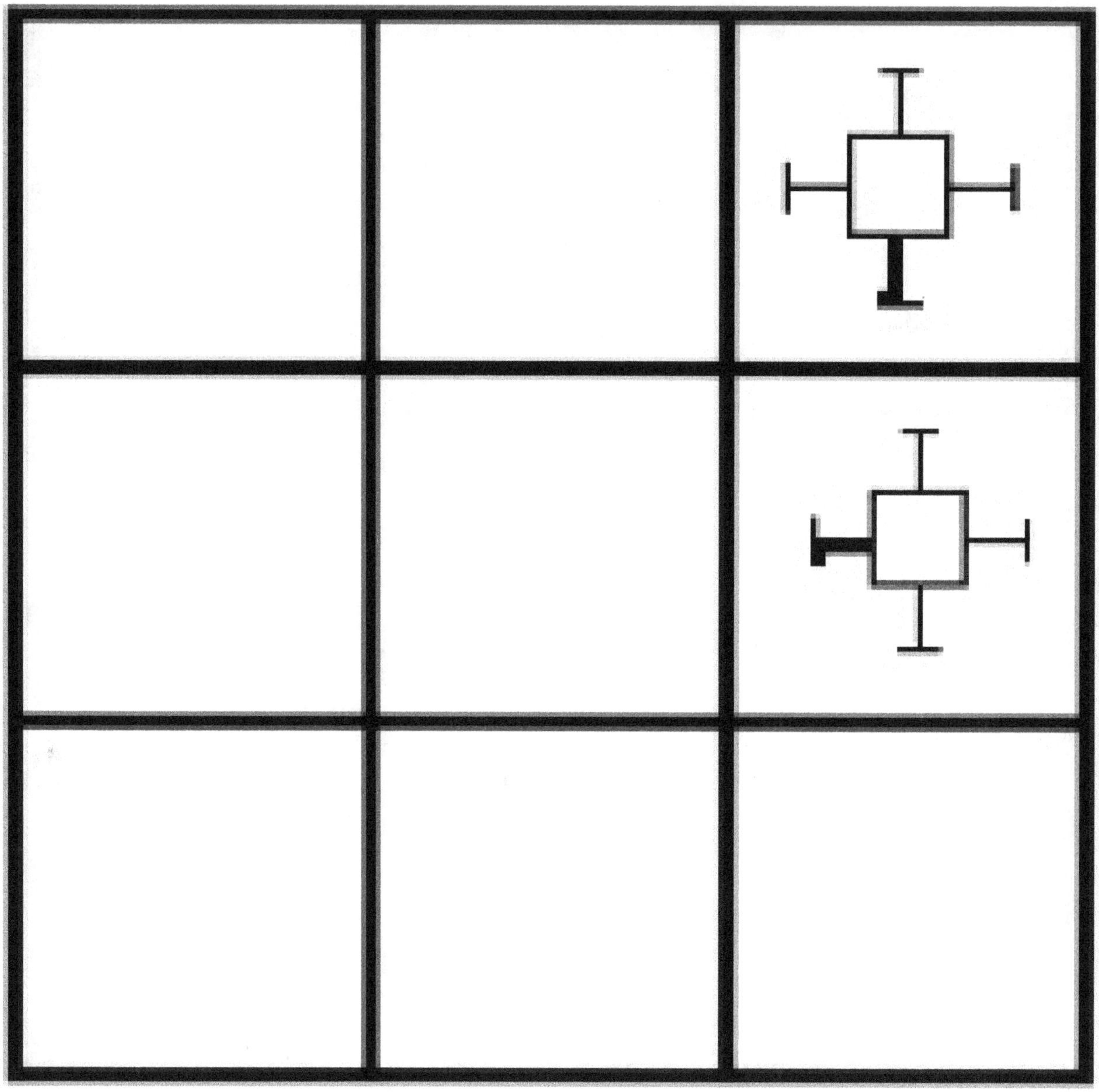

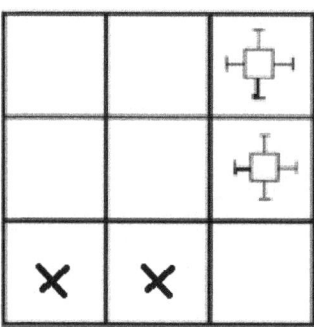
answer

Math Chess Sudoku Puzzles 一青少年益智棋芸健脑

Frankho ChessDoku 一 何数棋谜算独

© 2007 一 2020   Frank Ho, Amanda Ho   All rights reserved.   www.homathchess.com

Student's name _____ Date _____

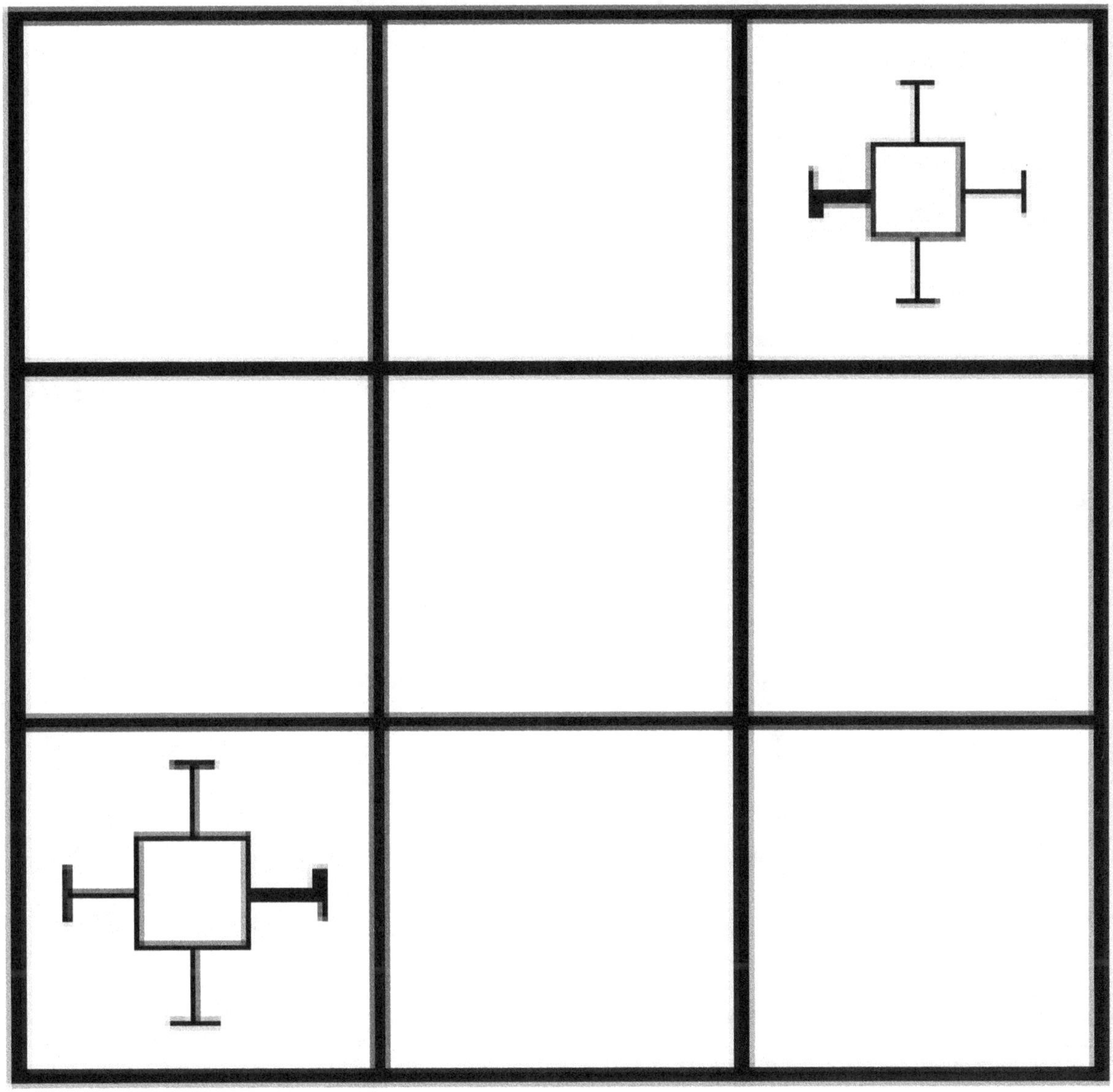

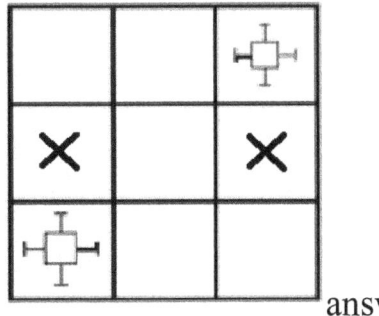

answer

Math Chess Sudoku Puzzles 一青少年益智棋芸健脑

Frankho ChessDoku 一 何数棋谜算独

© 2007 — 2020 Frank Ho, Amanda Ho   All rights reserved.   www.homathchess.com

Student's name_____Date_____

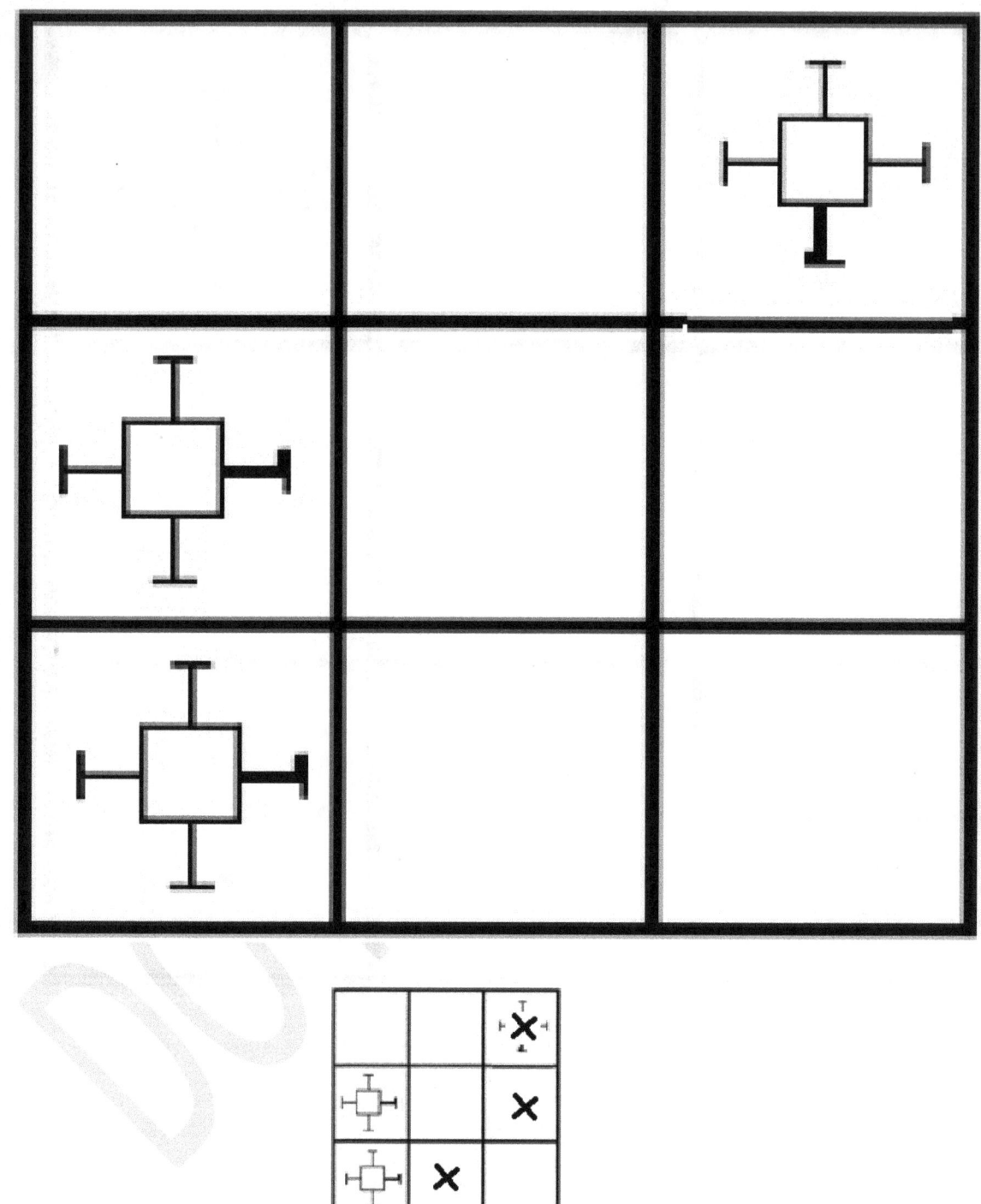

answer

Math Chess Sudoku Puzzles －青少年益智棋芸健脑

Frankho ChessDoku － 何数棋谜算独

© 2007 － 2020   Frank Ho, Amanda Ho   All rights reserved.   www.homathchess.com

Student's name _____Date_____

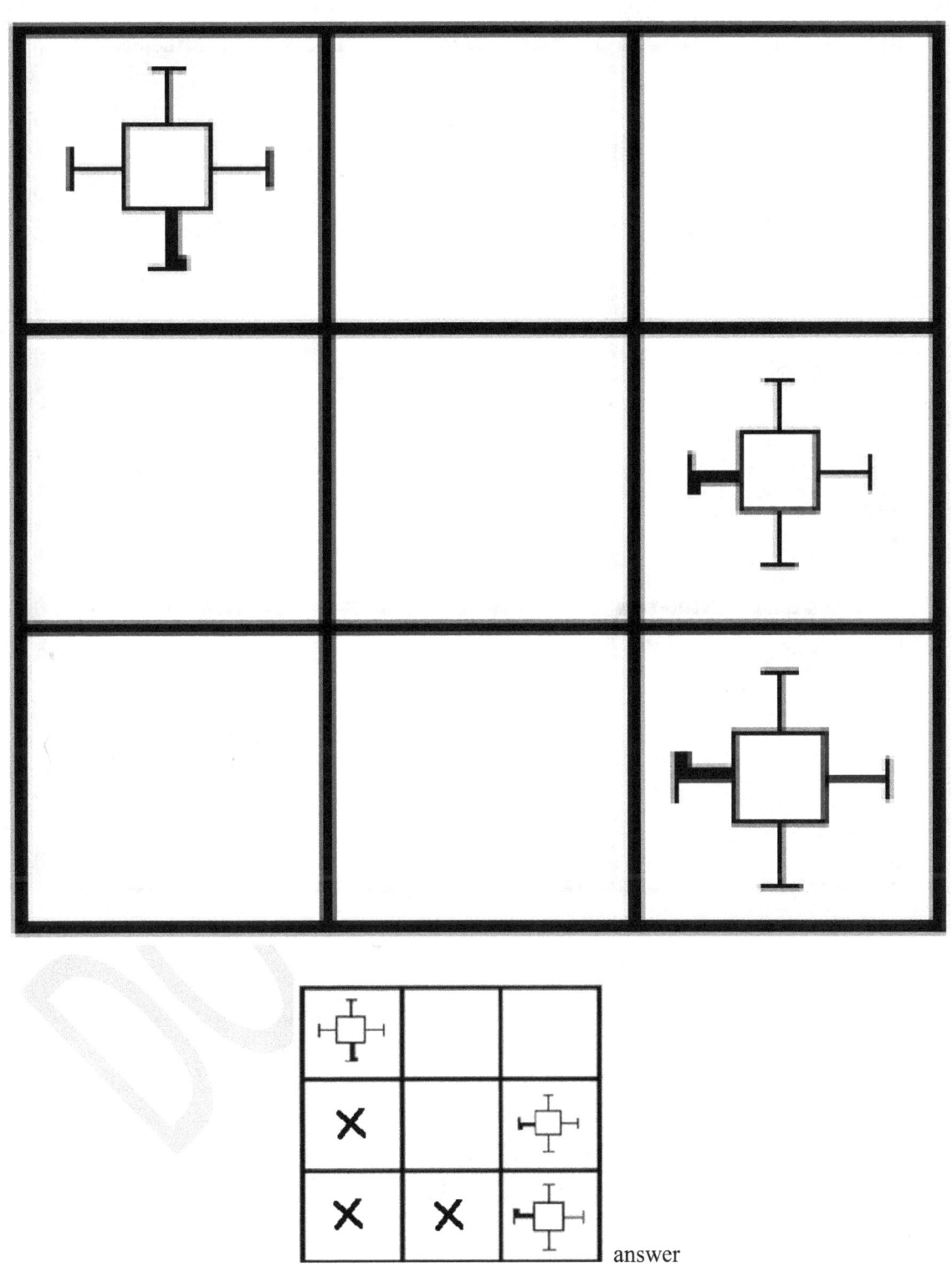

Math Chess Sudoku Puzzles 一 青少年益智棋芸健脑

Frankho ChessDoku 一 何数棋谜算独

© 2007 — 2020 Frank Ho, Amanda Ho   All rights reserved.   www.homathchess.com

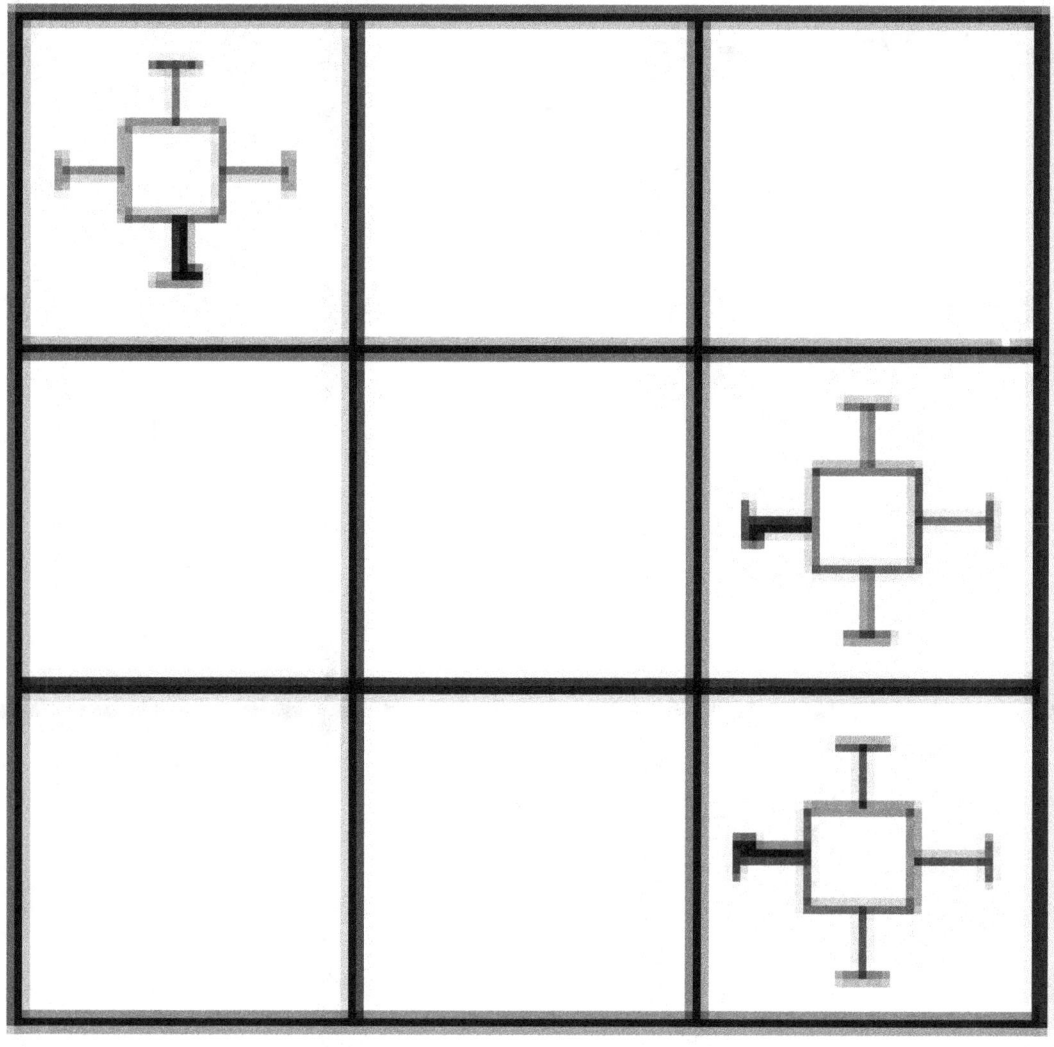

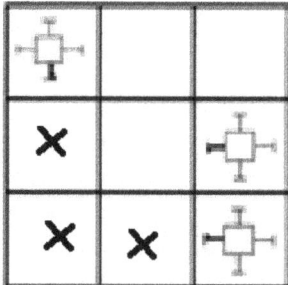 answer

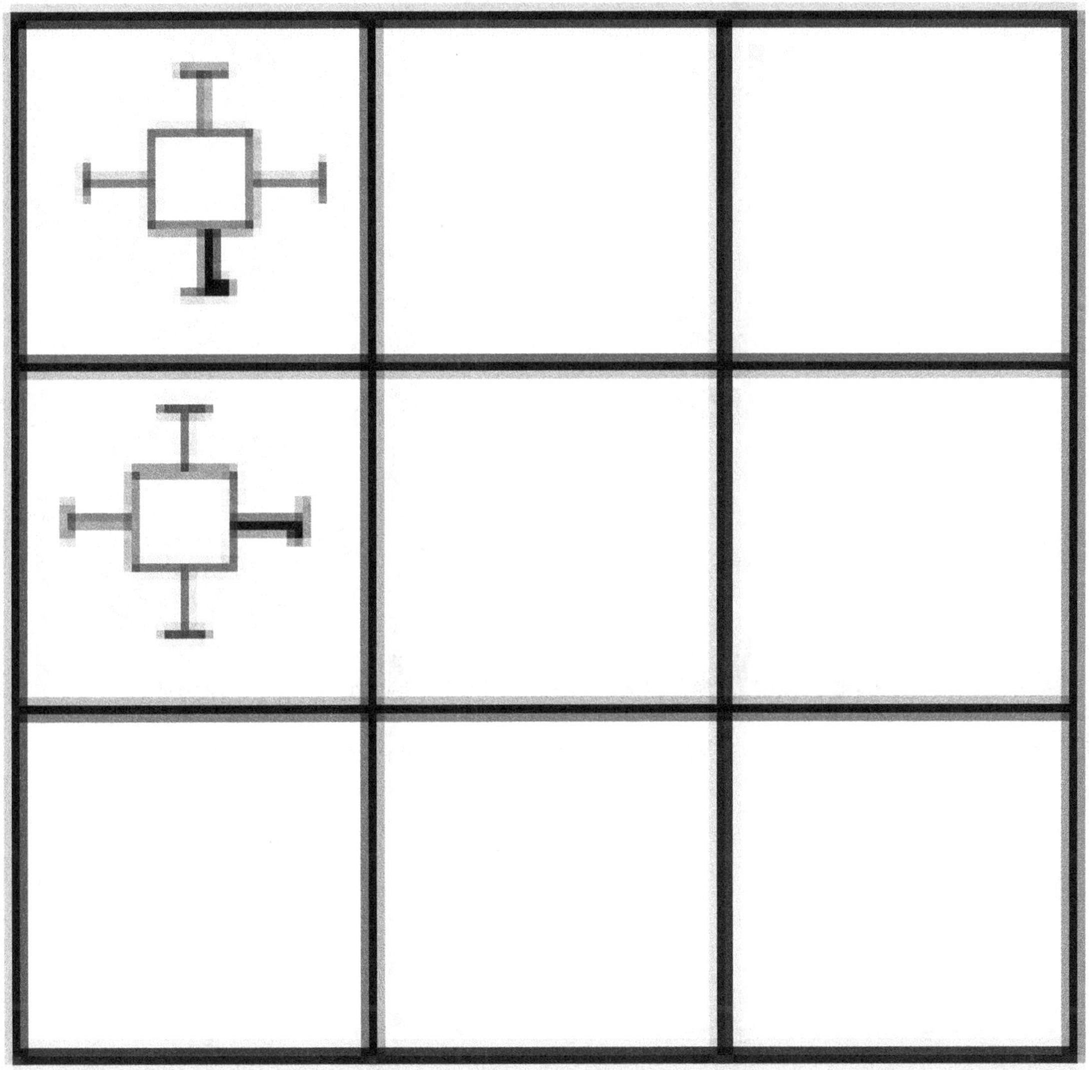

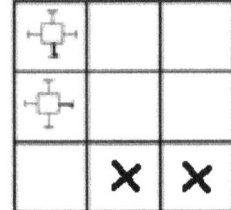
answer

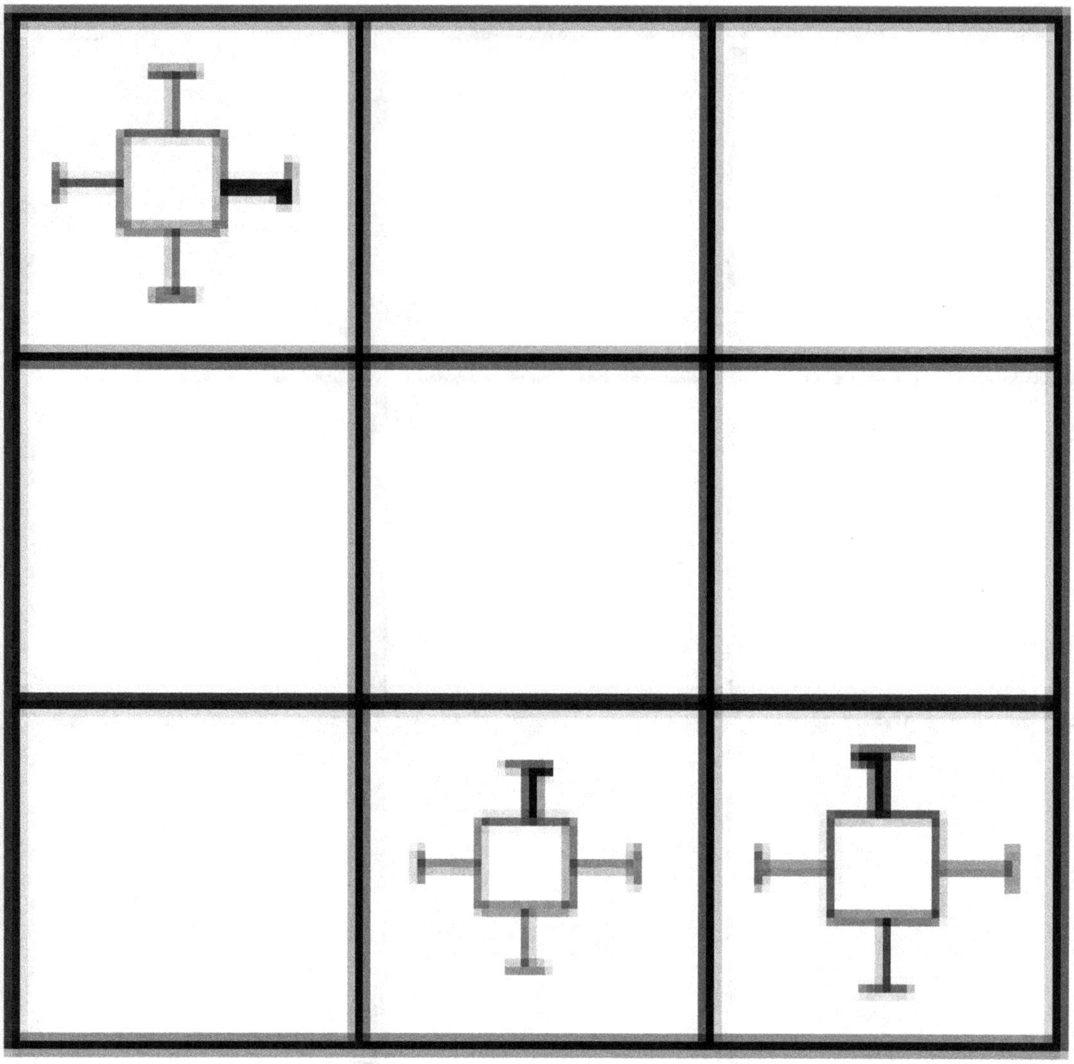

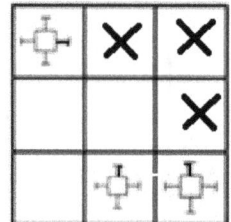

Math Chess Sudoku Puzzles －青少年益智棋芸健腦

Frankho ChessDoku － 何數棋謎算獨

© 2007 － 2020 Frank Ho, Amanda Ho   All rights reserved.   www.homathchess.com

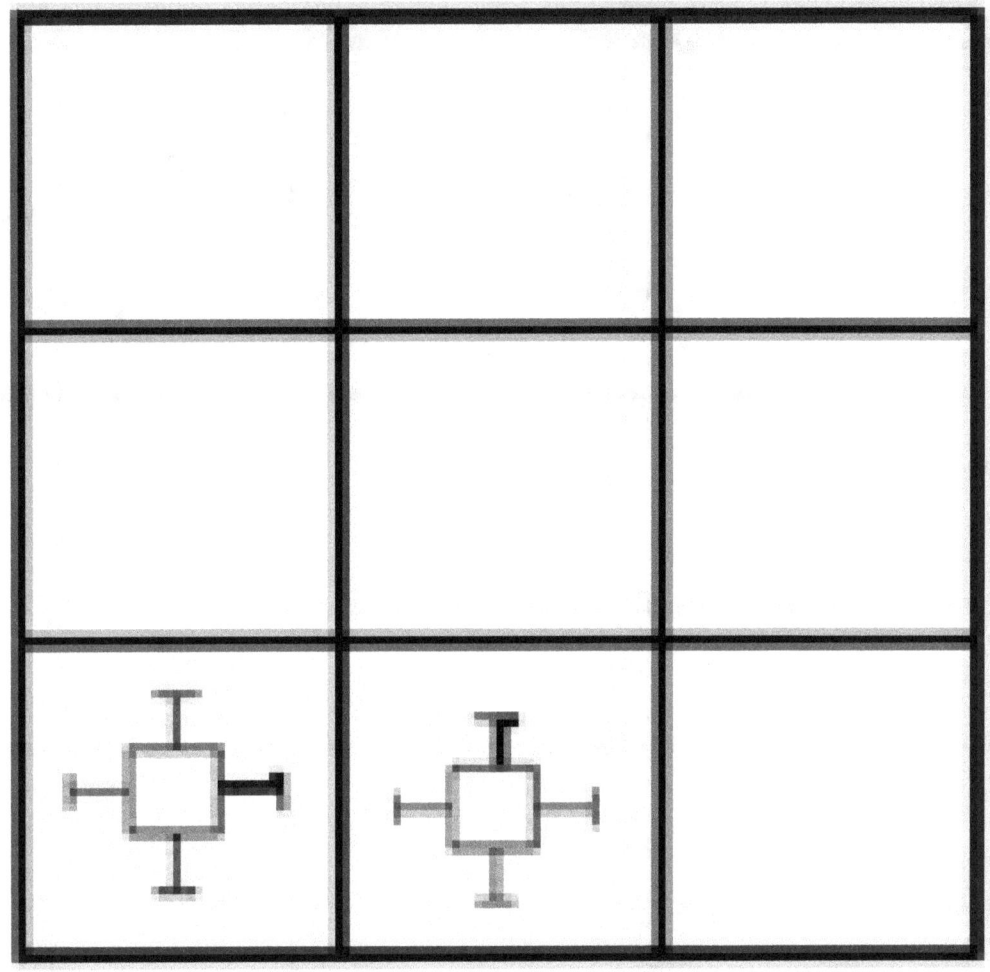

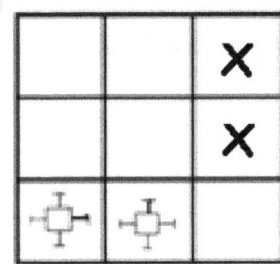
answer

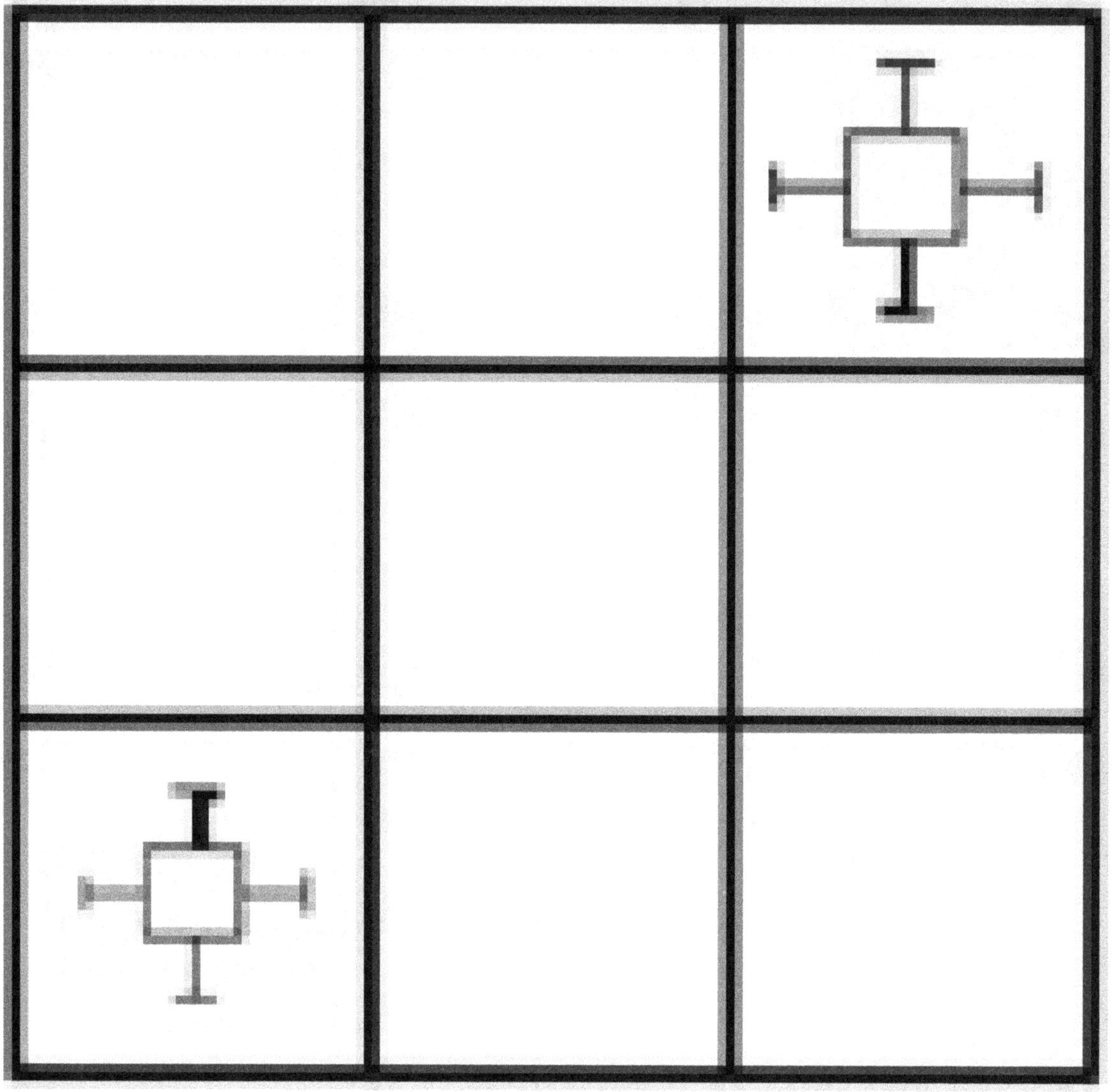

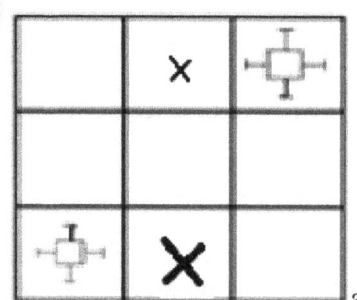
answer

Math Chess Sudoku Puzzles －青少年益智棋芸健脑

Frankho ChessDoku － 何数棋谜算独

© 2007 － 2020 Frank Ho, Amanda Ho   All rights reserved.   www.homathchess.com

Student's name _____   Date_____

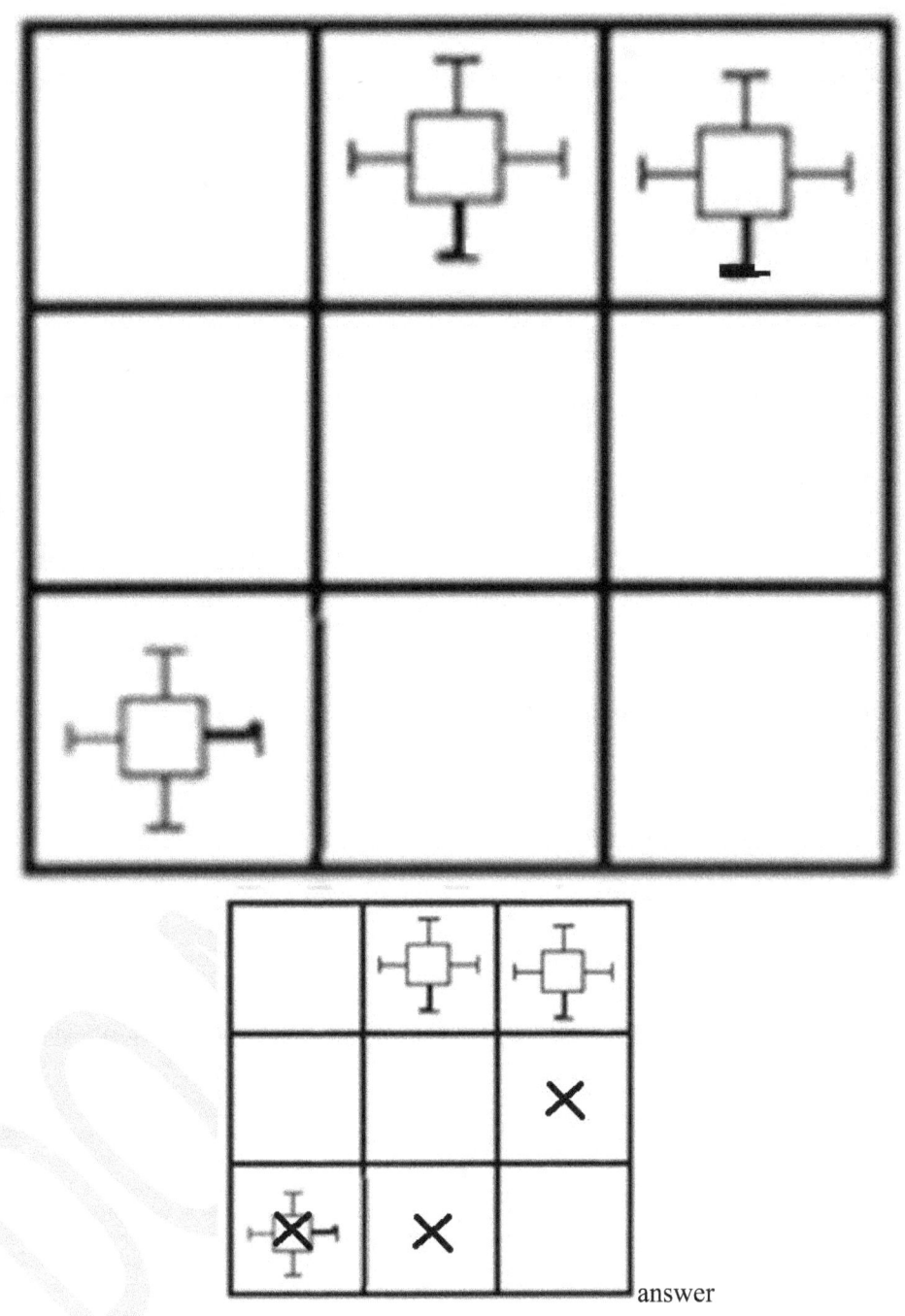

answer

Math Chess Sudoku Puzzles －青少年益智棋芸健脑

Frankho ChessDoku － 何数棋谜算独

© 2007 － 2020 Frank Ho, Amanda Ho   All rights reserved.   www.homathchess.com

Student's name _____ Date _____

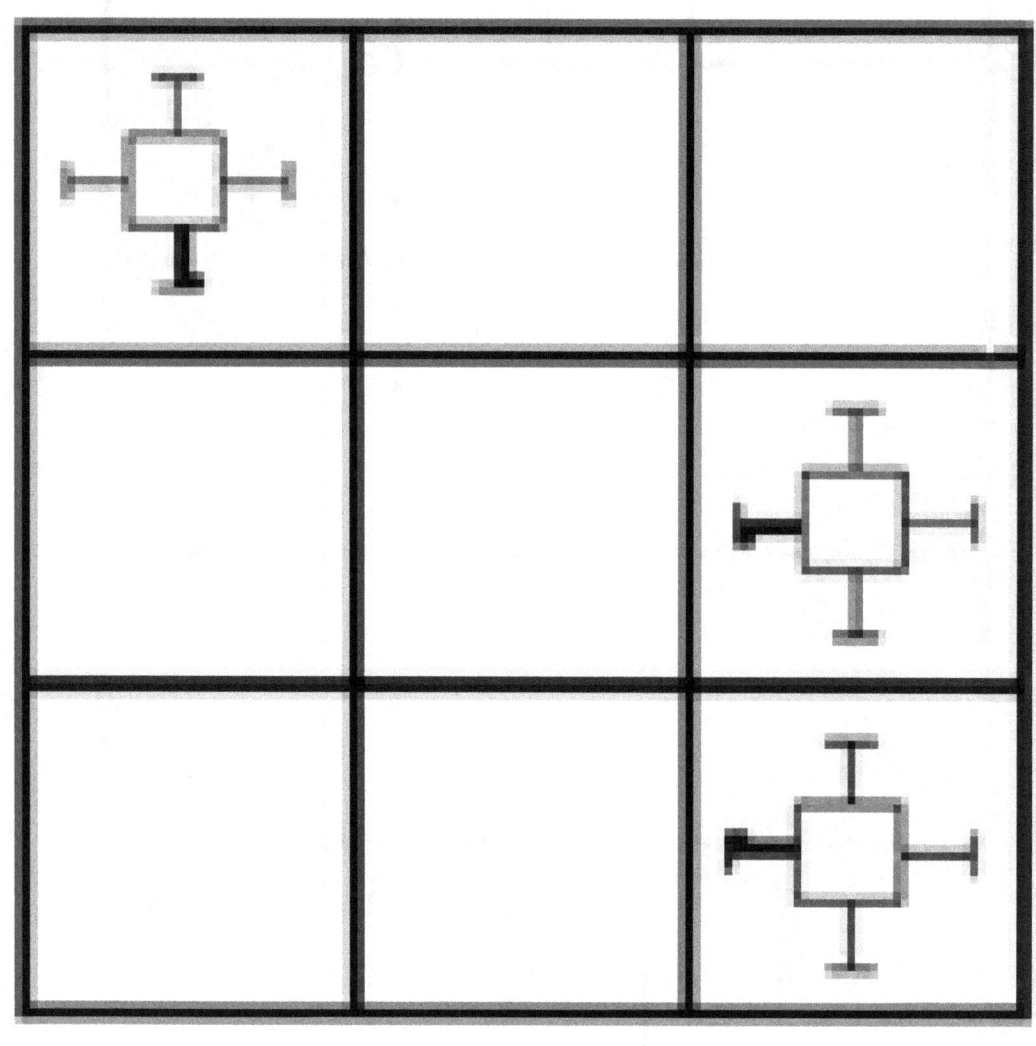

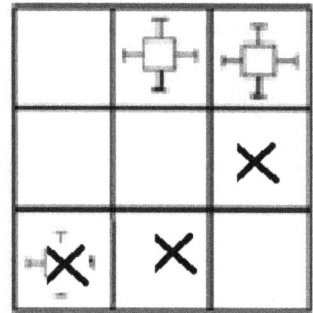

answer

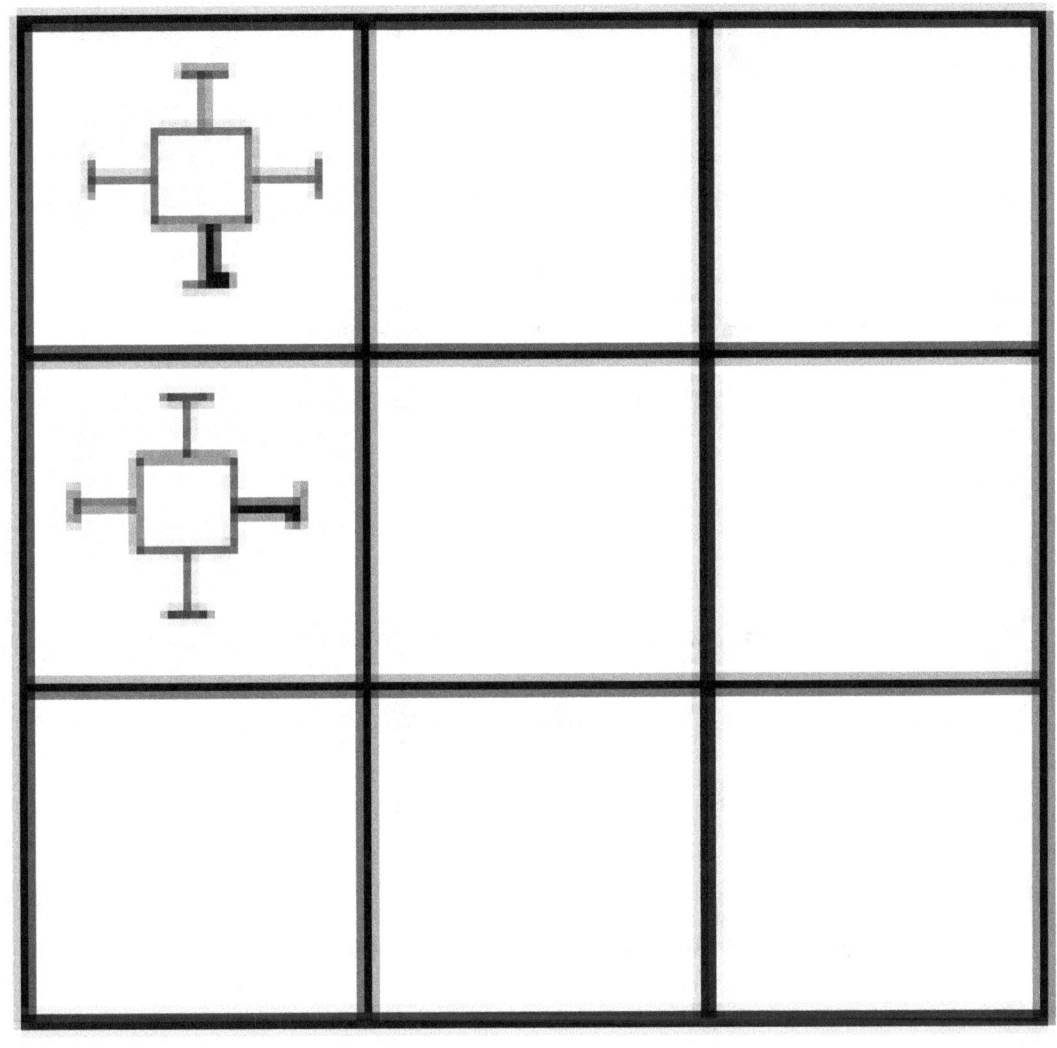
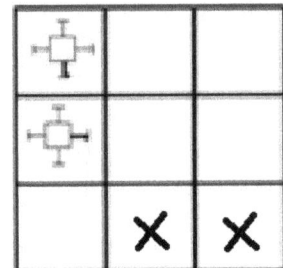
answer

Math Chess Sudoku Puzzles 一青少年益智棋芸健脑
Frankho ChessDoku 一 何数棋谜算独

© 2007 一 2020 Frank Ho, Amanda Ho   All rights reserved.   www.homathchess.com

Student's name_____   Date_____

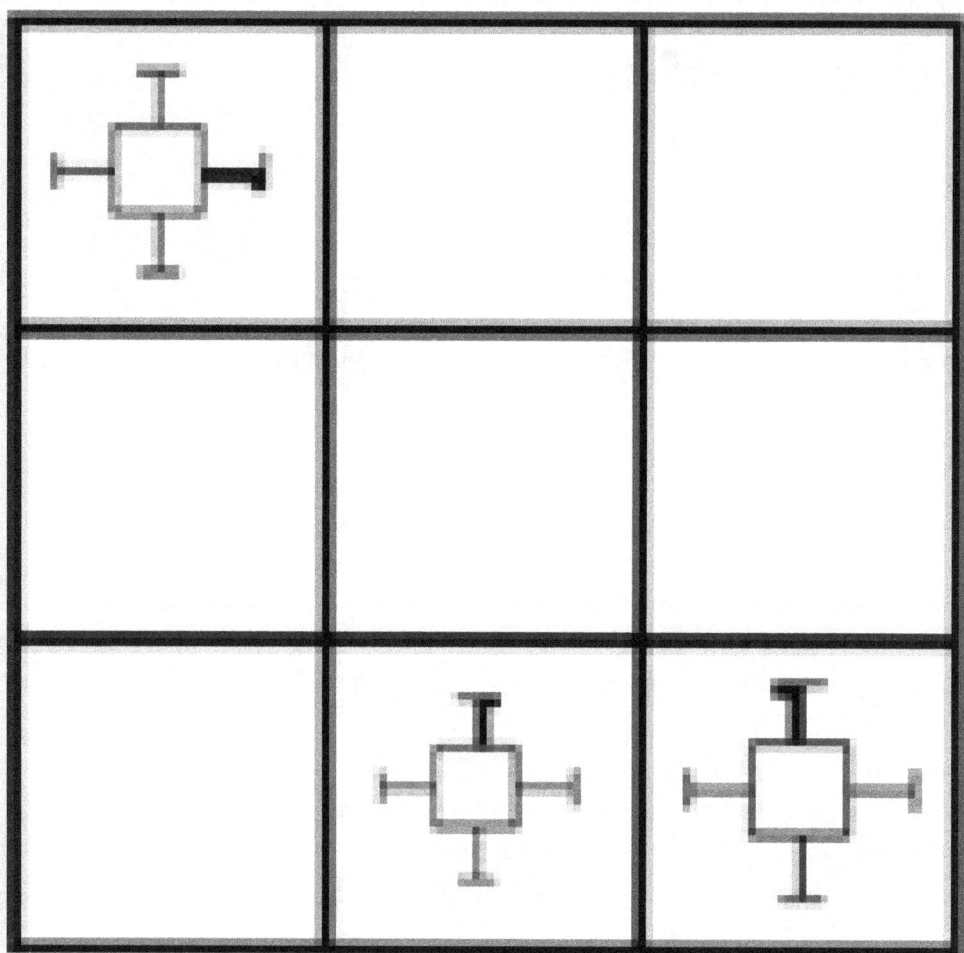

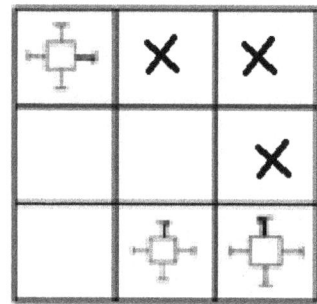 answer

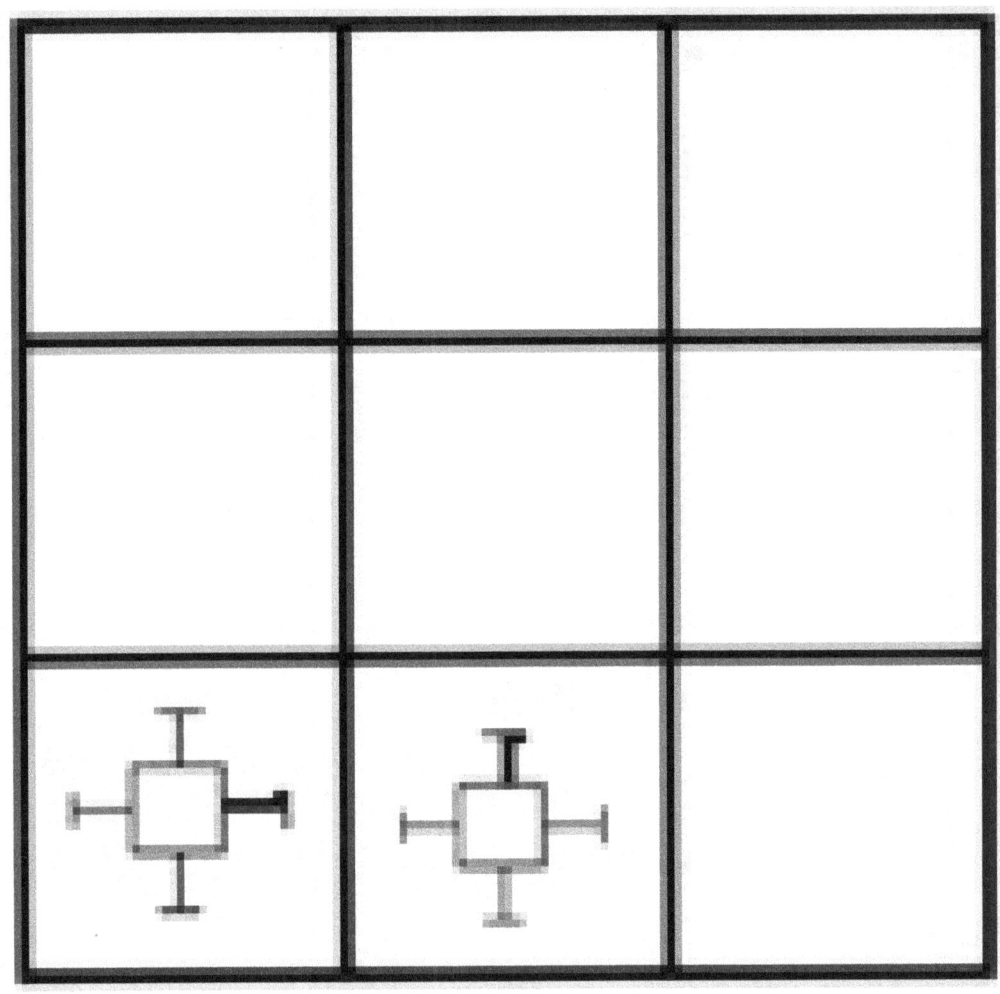

c2, c3

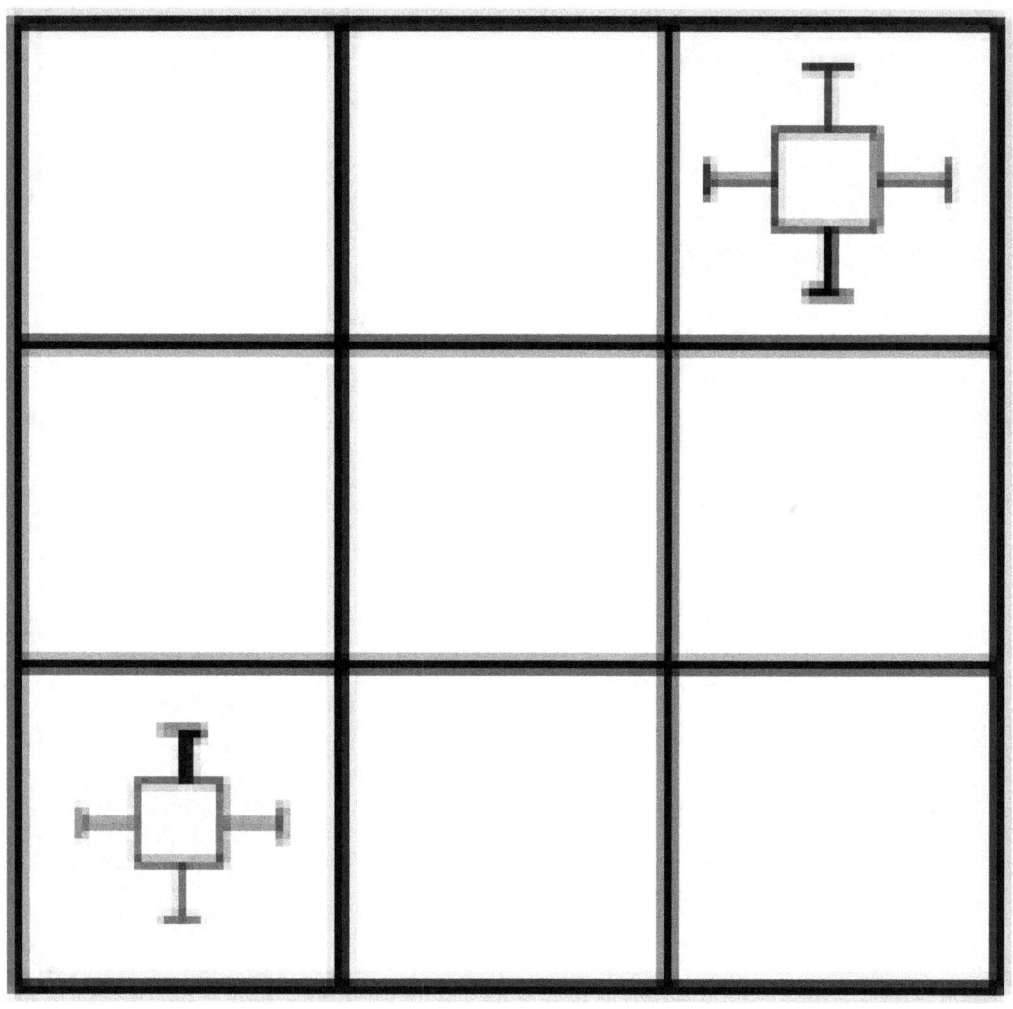

a2, b3

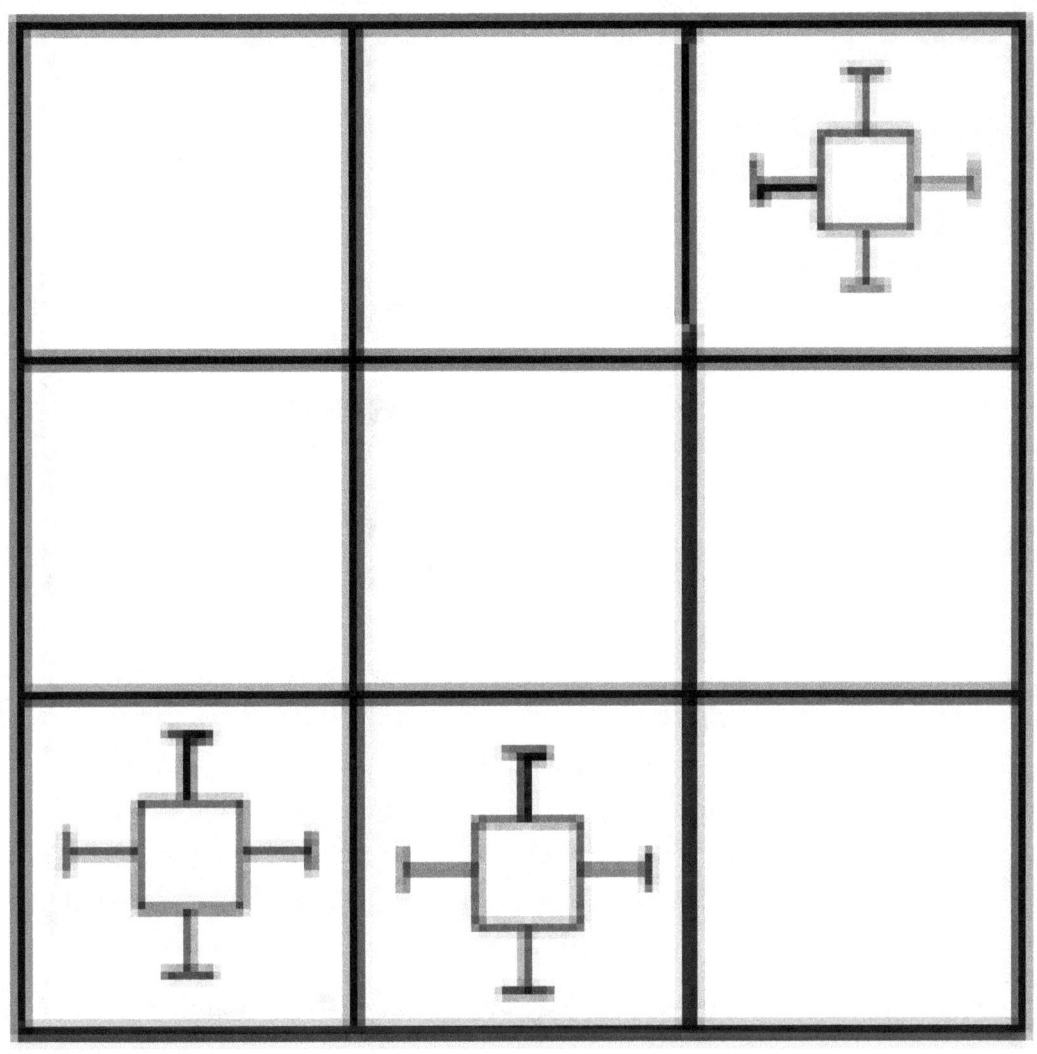

a2, b3, c3

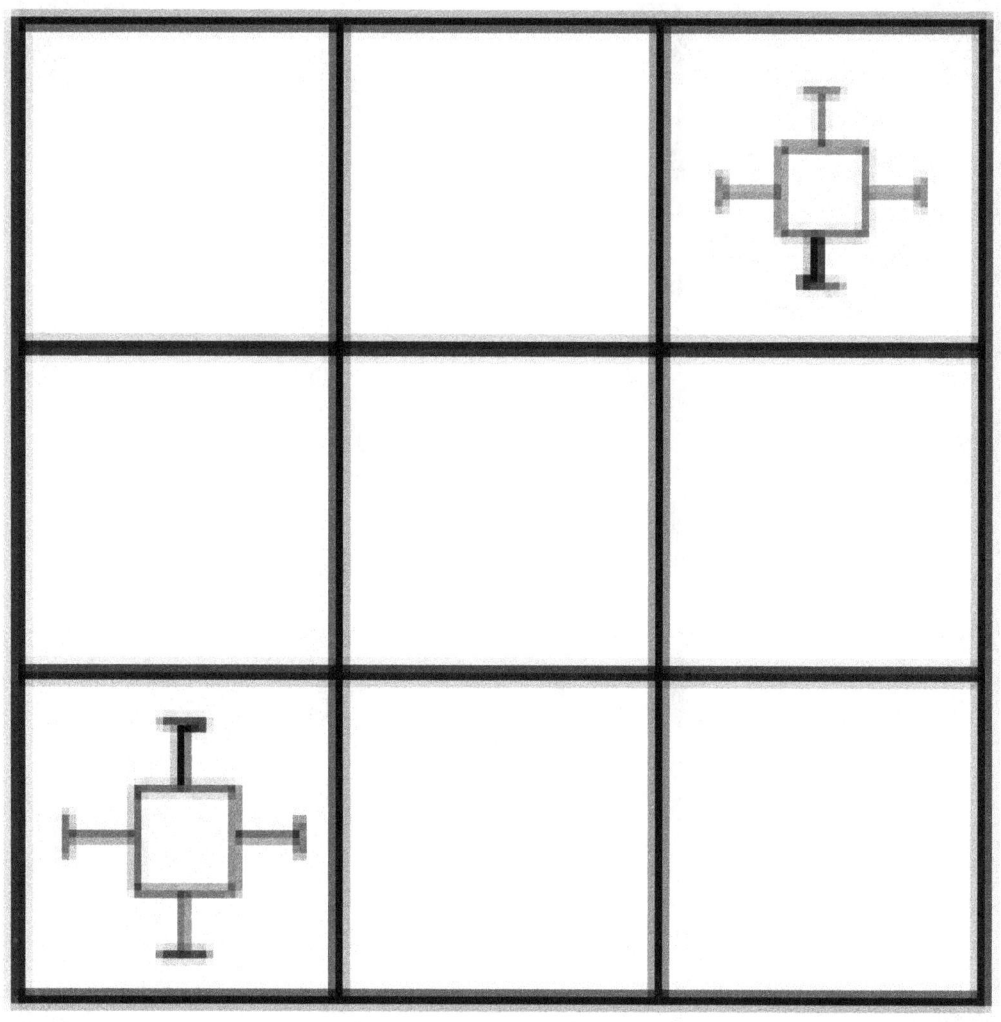

b1, b3

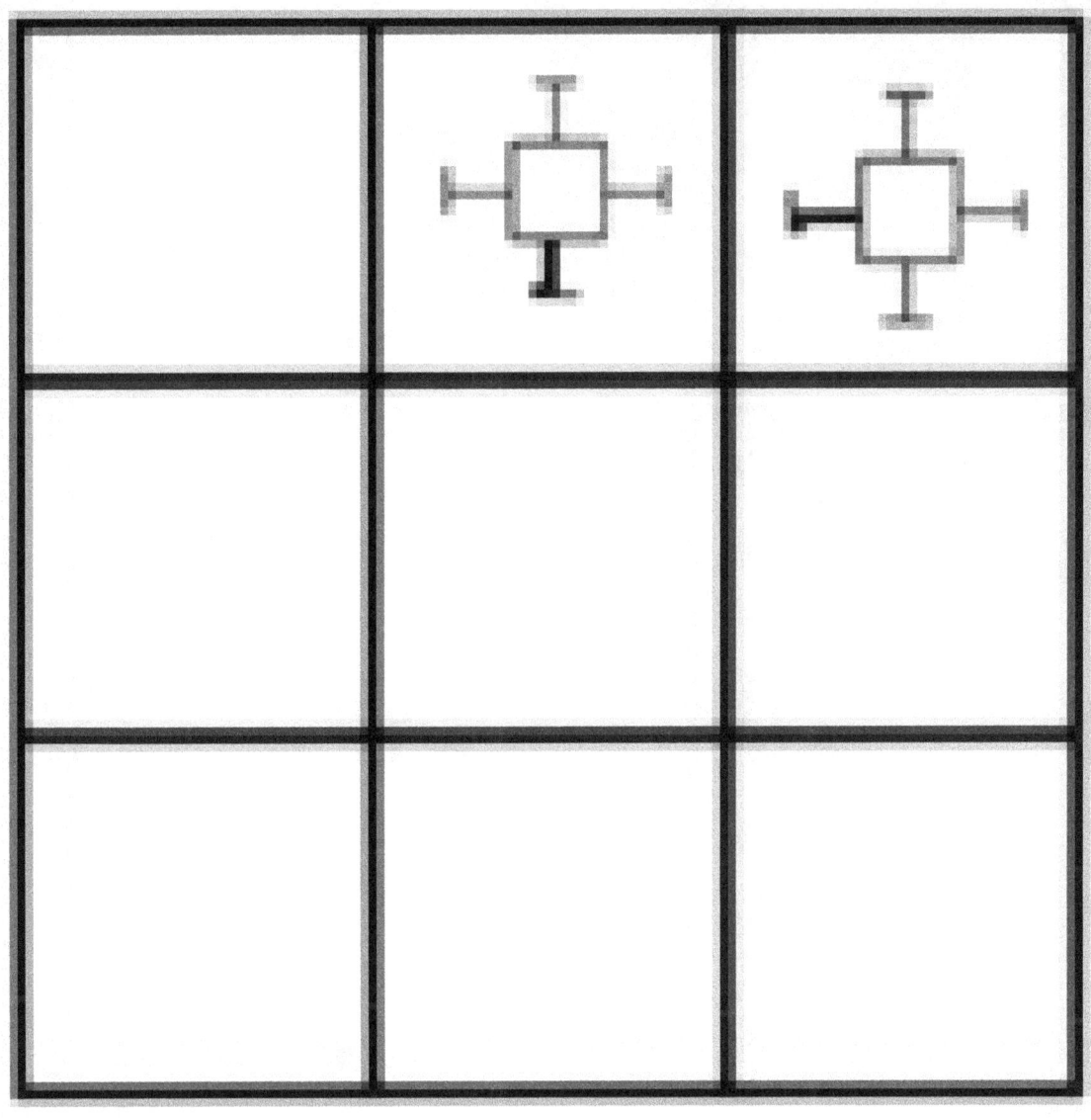

a1, a2

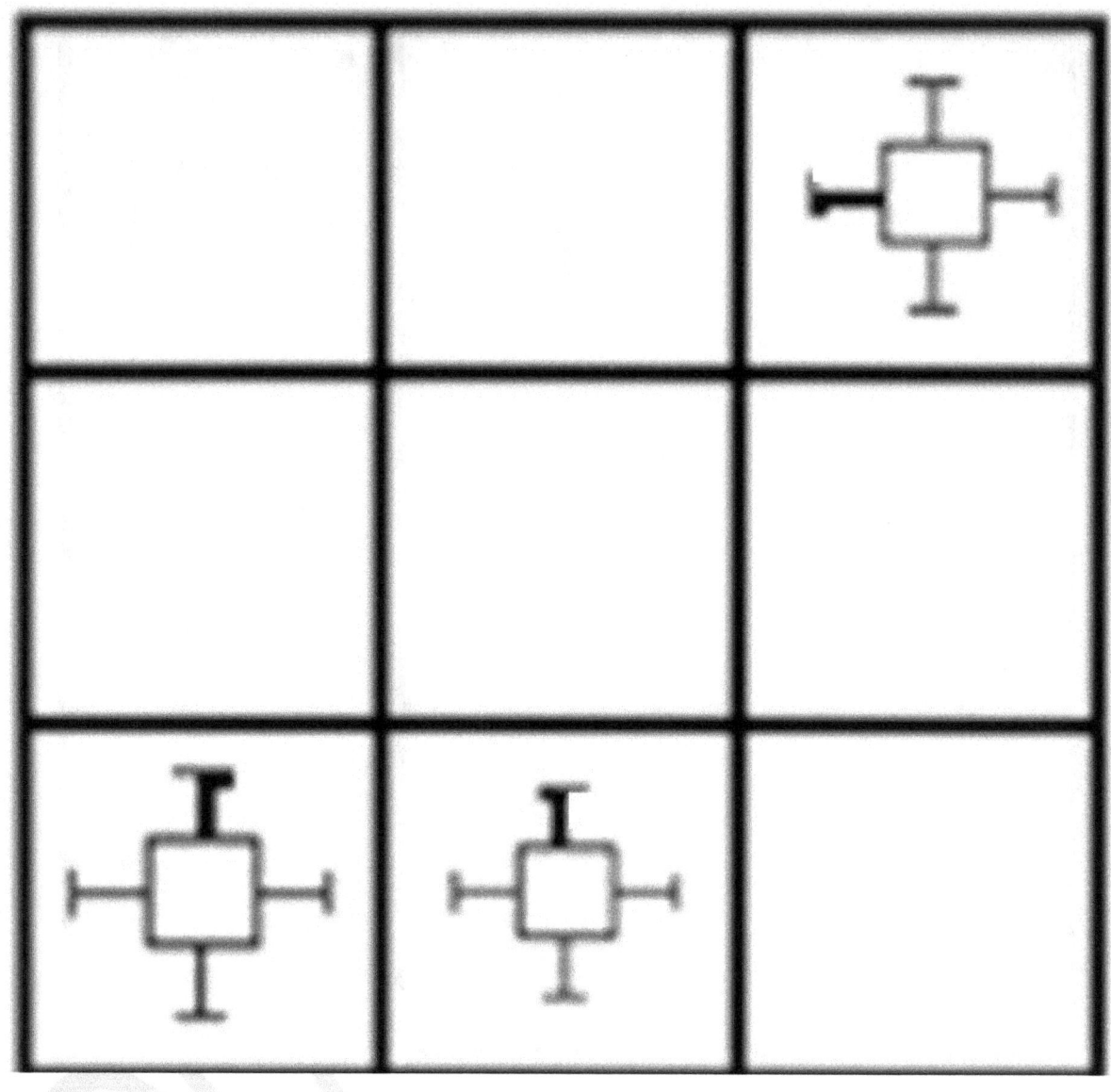

a2, a3, b3

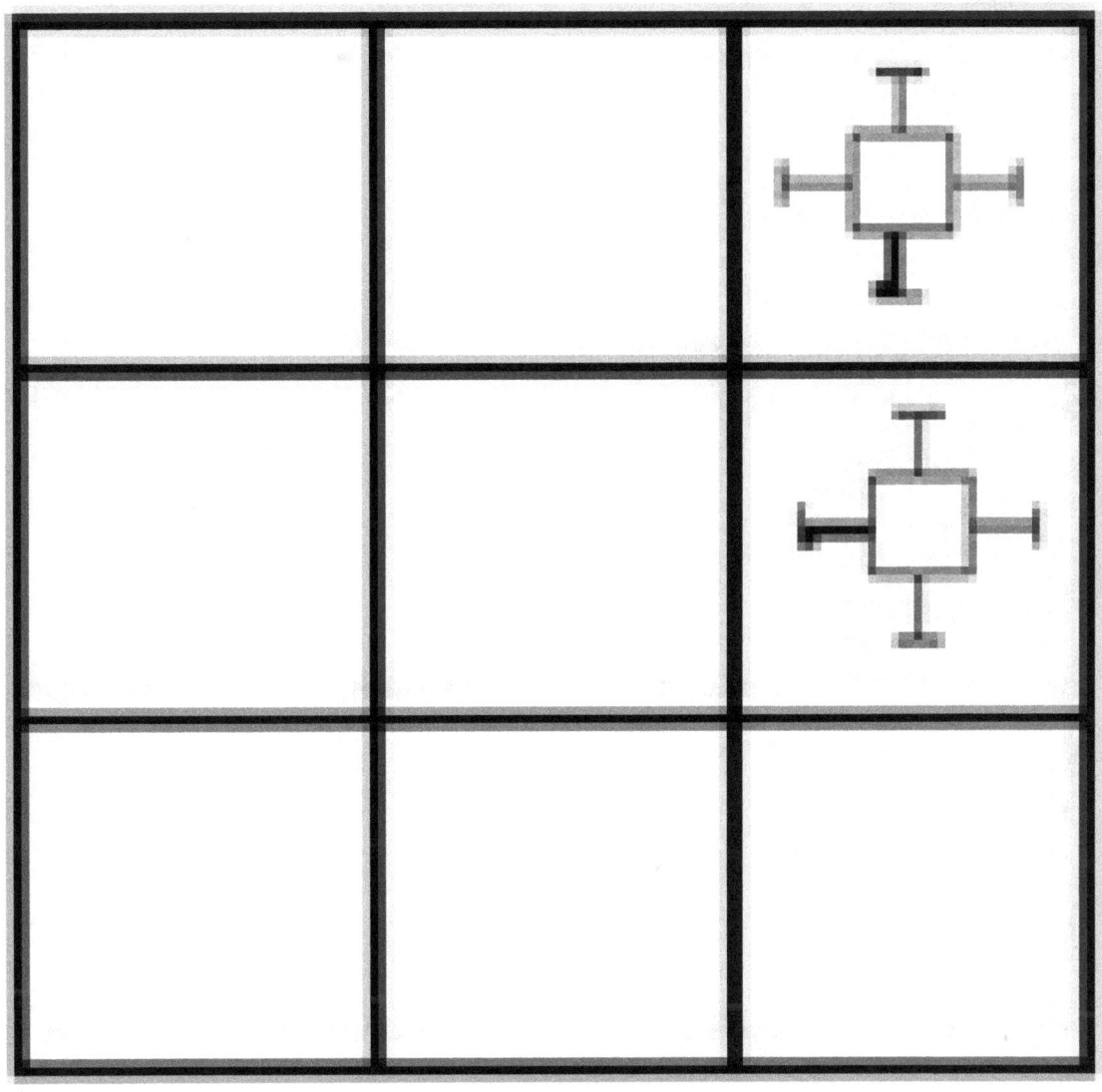

a1, b1

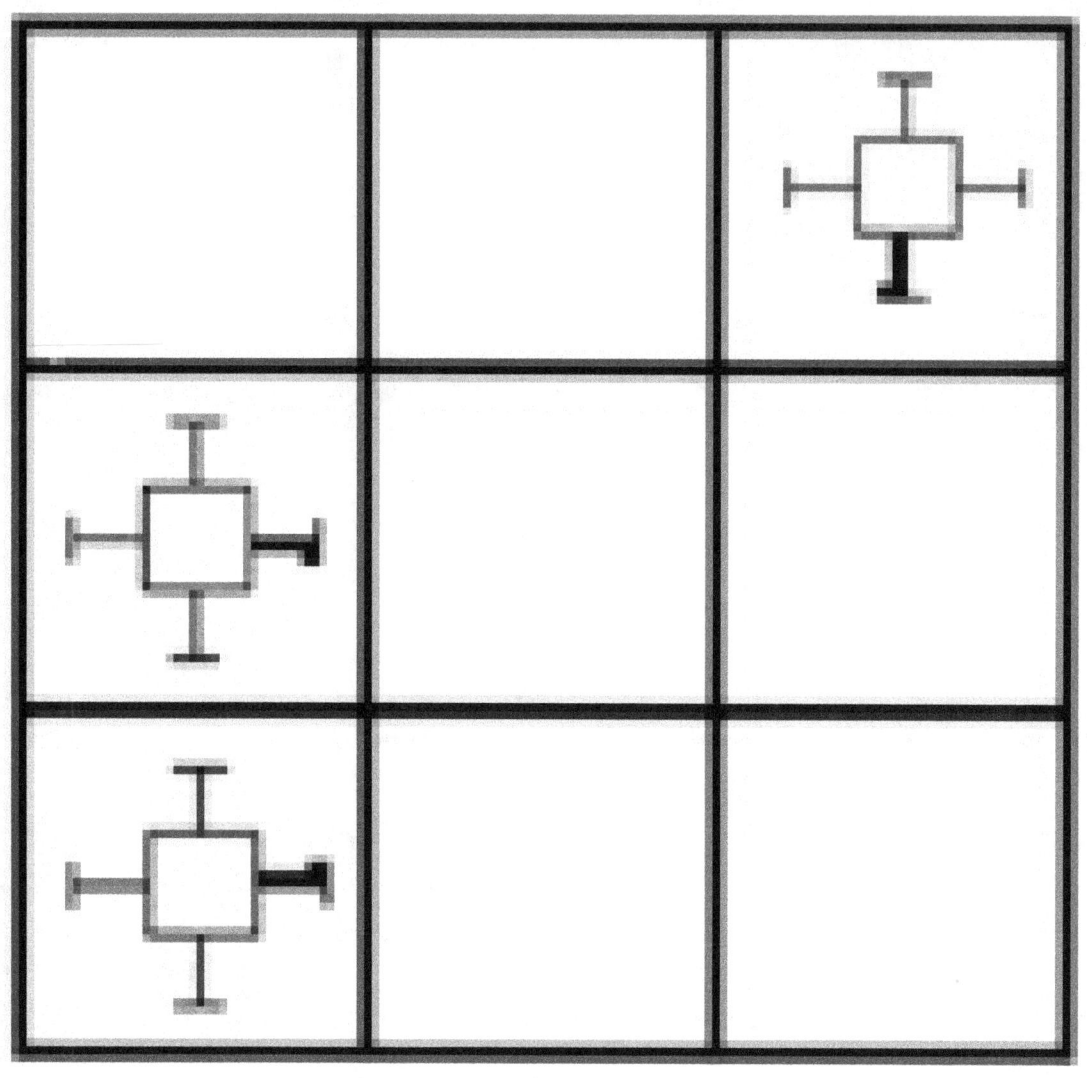

b1, c1, c2

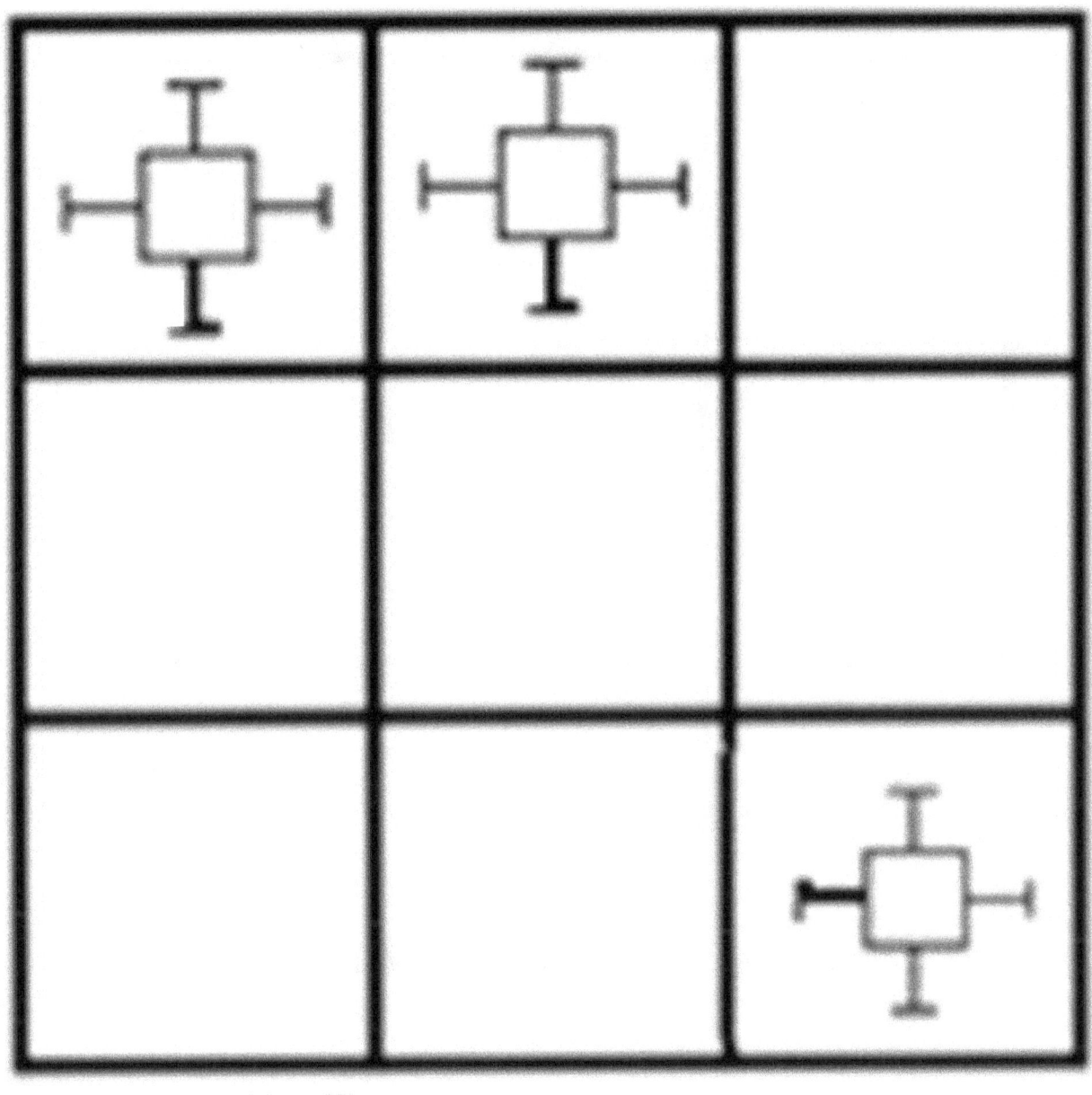

a2, b1, c1

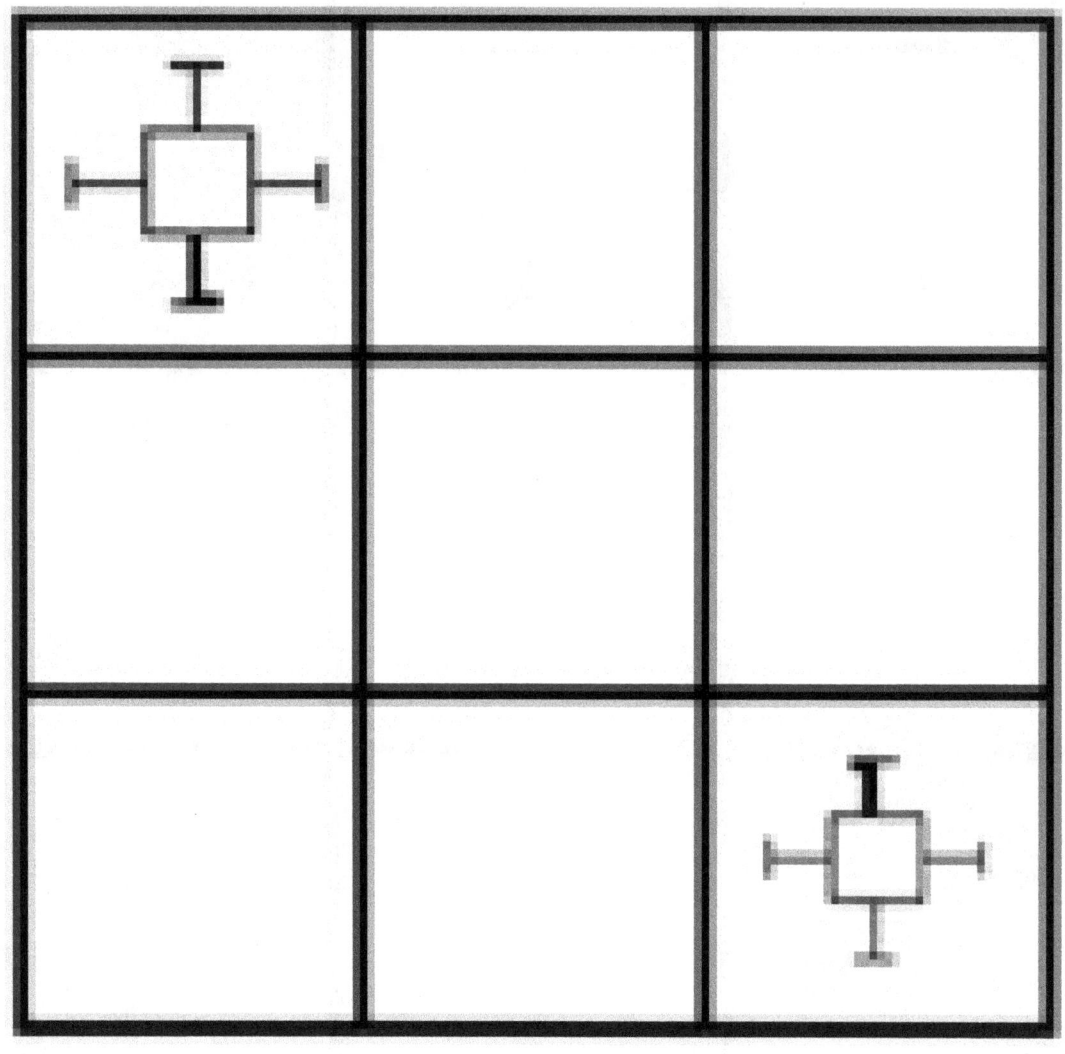

b1, b3

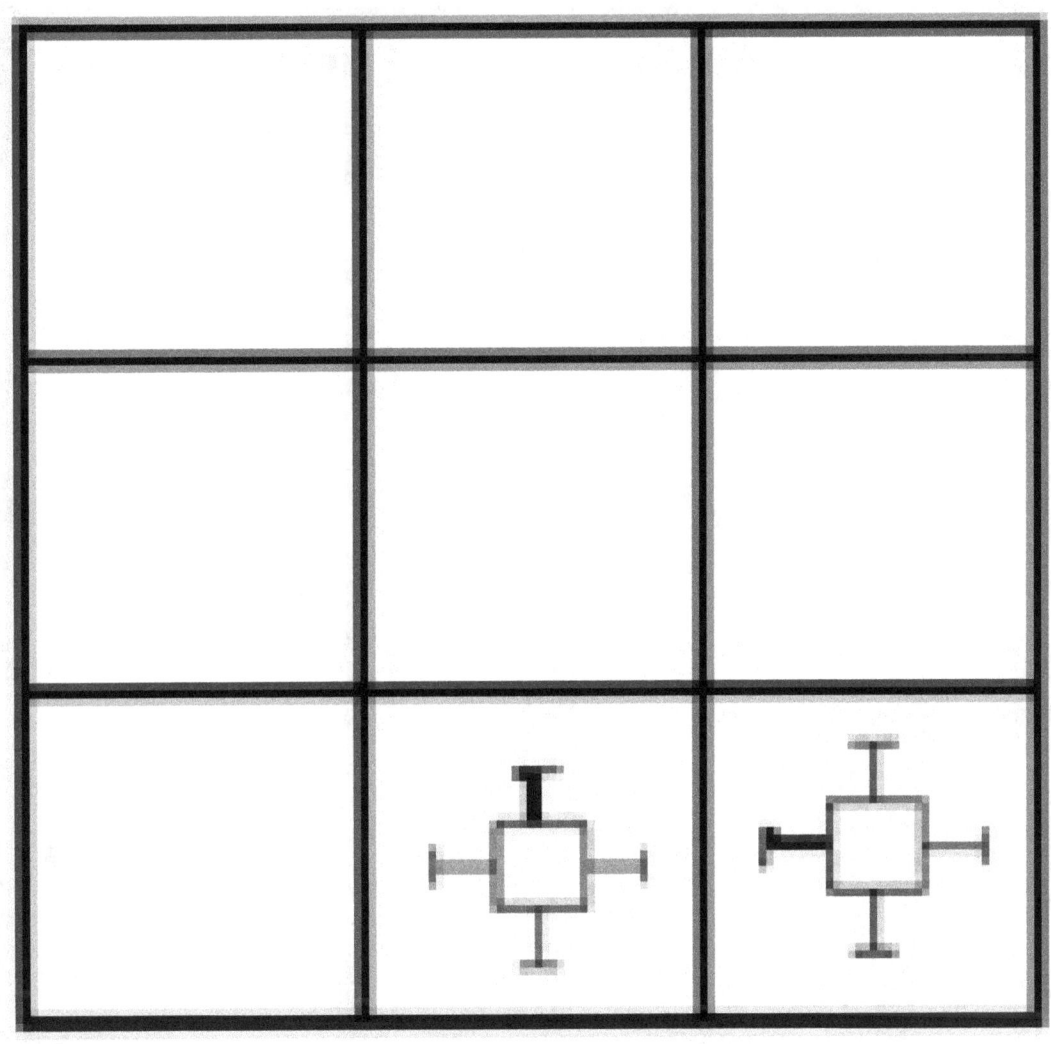

a2, a3

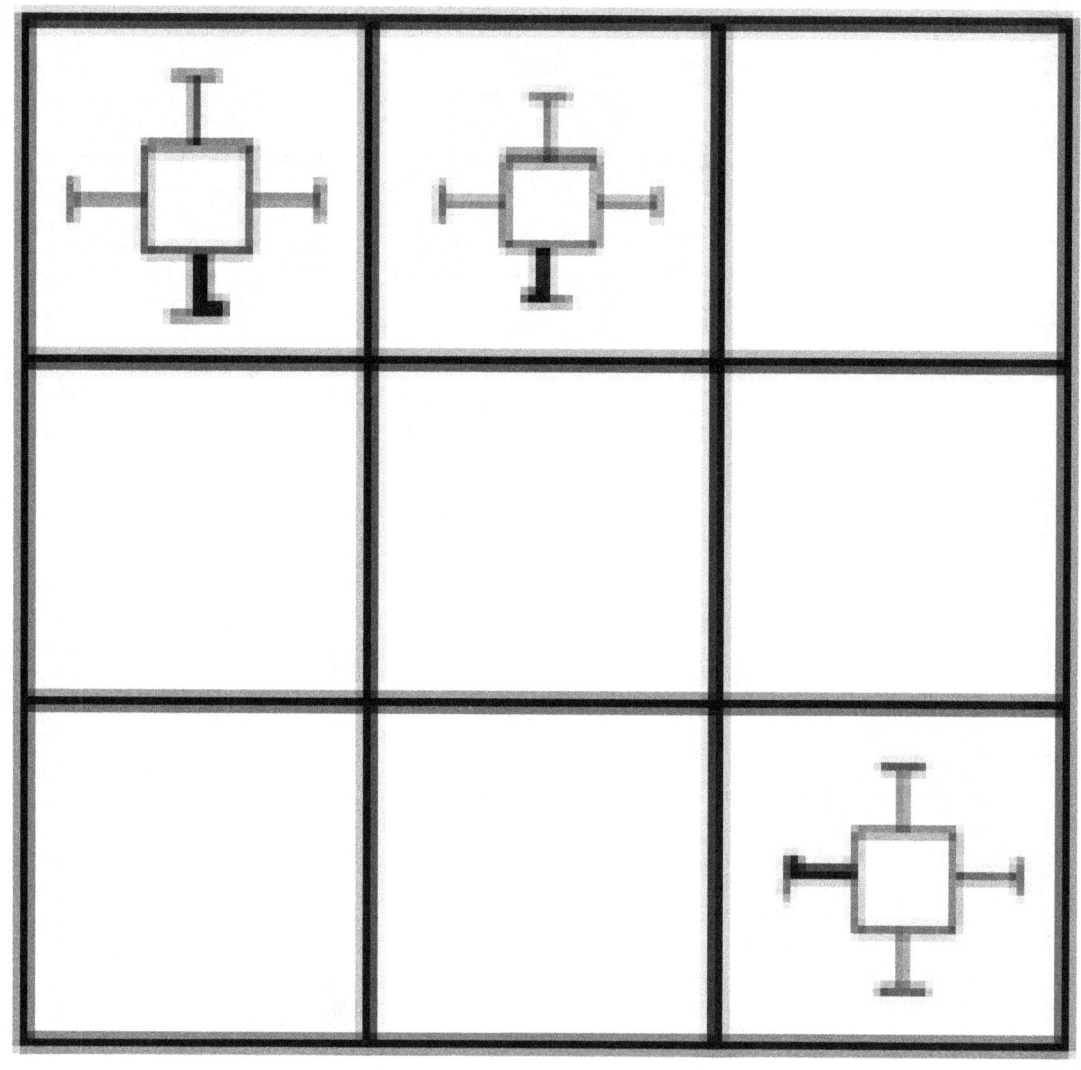

a1, a2, b1

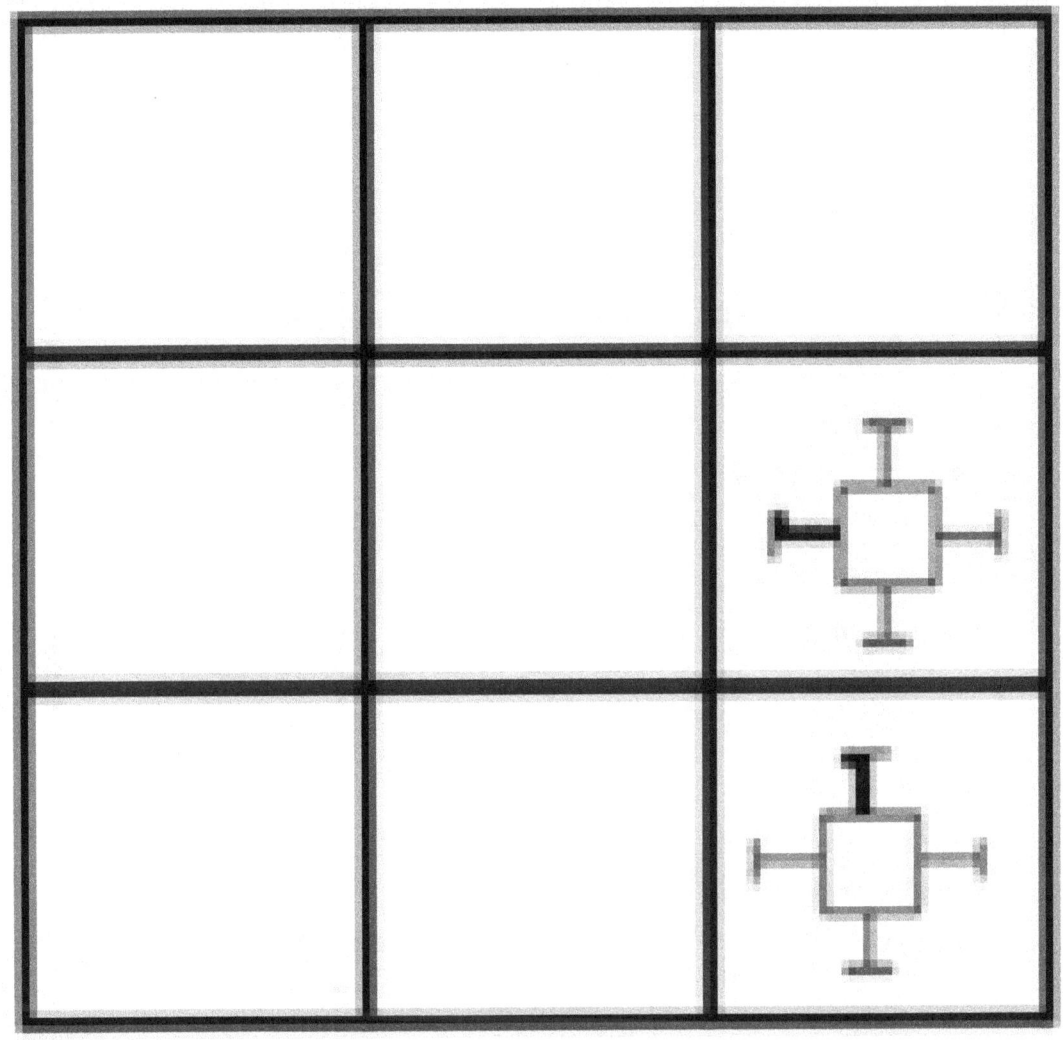

a3, b3

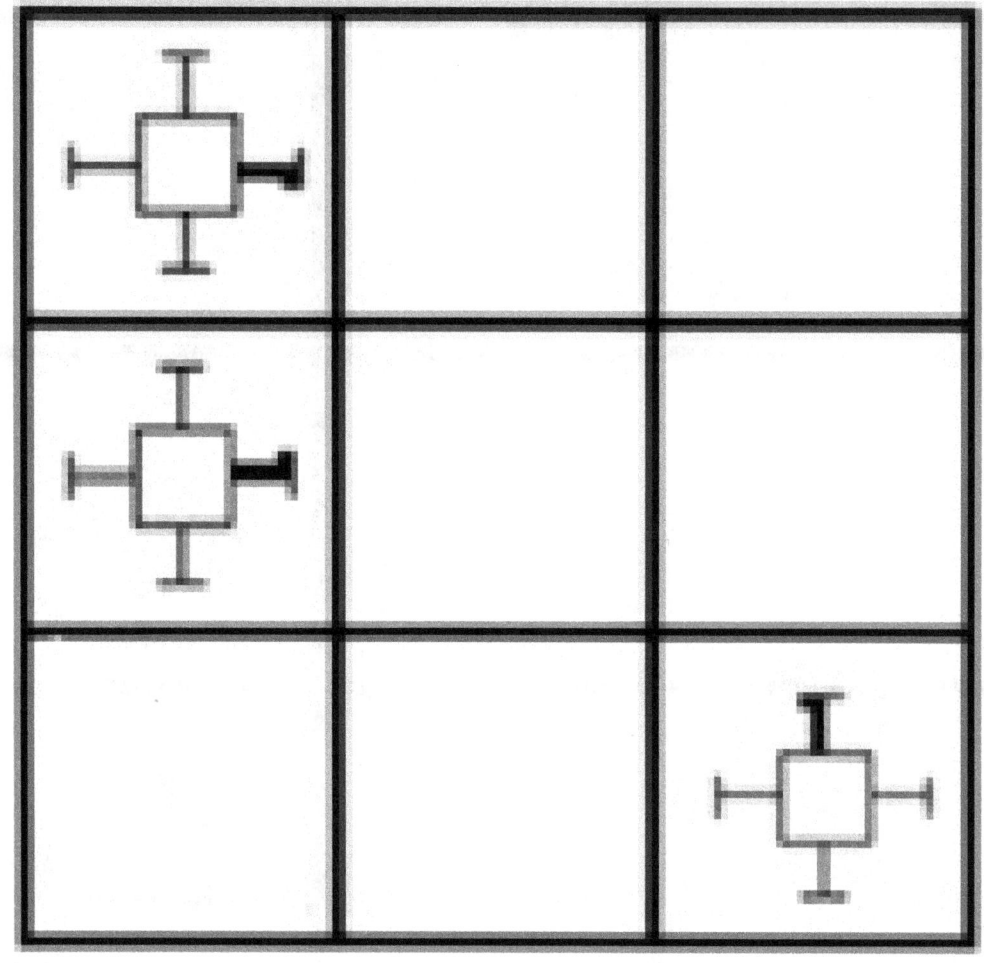

C2, c3, b3

Knight move

The knight is located at c3, and the sequence of knight moves are as follows:
Follow the colours of the knight moves in the following mini-chessboard and write the chess notation of its final square _____ _____. a2 – c1 – b3. The answer is b3.

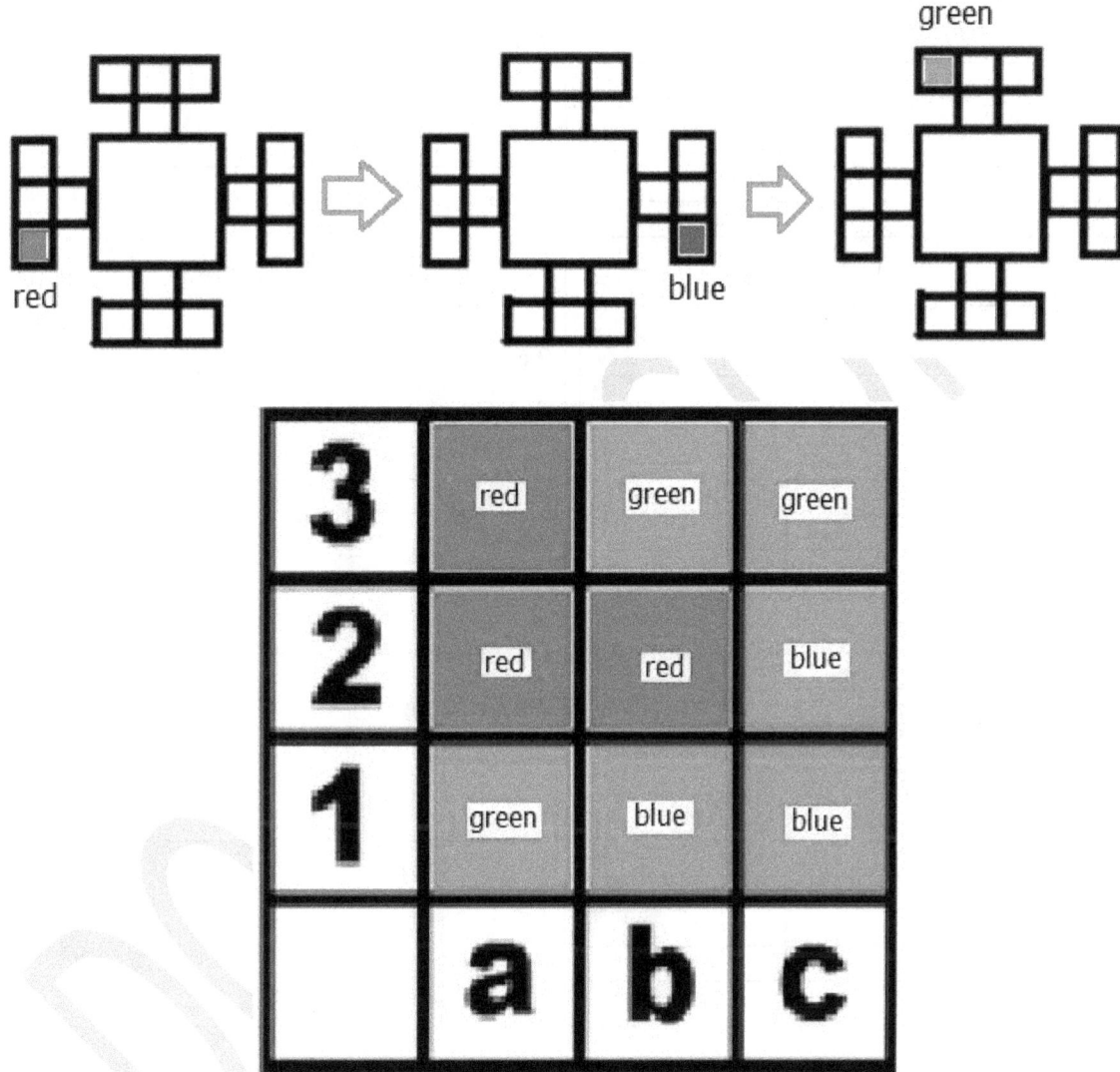

Row and column

Table	
	Rows are horizontal cells, and columns are vertical cells. How many rows and columns are on the left table?
	2 rows 1 column
	2 c 1 r
	2 c 2 r
	3 c 2 r
	2 c 3 r
	3 r 3 c

3 by 3 Sudoku

Every number from 1 to 3 shall appear only once in every row and column of the following 3 by 3 large square.

123 231 213
312 312 321
231 123 132

132 312 231
213 231 312
321 123 123

231 213 312
123 321 123
312 132 231

3 by 3 Sudoku

Every number from 1 to 3 shall appear only once in every row and column of the following 3 by 3 large square.

231 231 213
312 123 321
123 312 132

312 123 231
231 231 312
123 312 123

321 312 132
213 231 321
132 123 213

3 by 3 Sudoku

Every number from 1 to 3 shall appear only once in every row and column of the following 3 by 3 large square.

213 132 213
132 213 321
321 321 132

　　　132 132 132
　　　213 321 213
　　　321 213 321

　　　321 312 312
　　　213 231 231
　　　132 123 123

3 by 3 Sudoku

Every number from 1 to 3 shall appear only once in every row and column of the following 3 by 3 large square.

		3
2		

		1
2		

		3
2		

1		
	2	

	3	
1		

2		
		1

	2	
3	2	

	1	
		2

		3
	2	

123 321 123
231 132 312
312 213 231

132 312 231
213 231 312
321 123 123

123 213 132
231 321 213
312 132 321

Fill in the missing number using 1, 2, and 3.

Every number from 1 to 3 shall appear only once in every row.

1	2	☐	☐	2	1	3	☐	1
☐	2	1	3	☐	1	1	2	☐
3	☐	1	☐	2	1	1	2	☐
☐	2	1	1	2	☐	3	☐	1

Every number from 1 to 3 shall appear only once in every column.

Col1	Col2	Col3	Col4
1, 2, ☐	3, ☐, 2	1, 3, ☐	2, ☐, 1
☐, 3, 2	☐, 1, 2	3, 1, ☐	1, 2, ☐

Partition of a sum

Choose 2 digits out of 1, 2, and 3 digits such that the sum of these digits is 2. 1+1=2
Choose 2 digits out of 1, 2, and 3 digits such that the sum of these digits is 3. 2+1=2; 2+1
Choose 2 digits out of 1, 2, and 3 digits such that the sum of these digits is 4. 2+2; 1+3; 3+1
Choose 2 digits out of 1, 2, and 3 digits such that the sum of these digits is 5. 3+2; 2+3
Choose 2 digits out of 1, 2, and 3 digits such that the sum of these digits is 6. 3+3
Choose 3 digits out of 1, 2, and 3 digits such that the sum of these digits is 3. 1+1+1=3
Choose 3 digits out of 1, 2, and 3 digits such that the sum of these digits is 4. 2+1+1=4; 1+2+1; 1+1+2=4
Choose 3 digits out of 1, 2, and 3 digits such that the sum of these digits is 5. 3+1+1=5; 1+3+1=5; 1+1+3=5; 2+2+1=5; 1+2+2=5; 2+1+2=5; 3+1+1=5; 1+3+1=5; 1+1+3=5
Choose 3 digits out of 1, 2, and 3 digits such that the sum of these digits is 6. 2+2+2=6; 1+2+3=6; 1+3+2=6; 2+1+3=6; 2+3+1=6; 3+1+2=6; 3+2+1=6
Choose 3 digits out of 1, 2, and 3 digits such that the sum of these digits is 7. 3+3+1=7; 3+1+3=7; 1+3+3=7; 3+2+2=7; 2+3+2=7; 2+2+3=7
Choose 3 digits out of 1, 2, and 3 digits such that the sum of these digits is 8. 3+3+2=8; 3+2+3=8; 2+3+3=8
Choose 3 digits out of 1, 2, and 3 digits such that the sum of these digits is 9. 3+3+3=9
Choose 4 digits out of 1, 2, and 3 digits such that the sum of these digits is 4. 1+1+1+1=4
Choose 4 digits out of 1, 2, and 3 digits such that the sum of these digits is 5. 2+1+1+1=5; 1+2+1+1; 1+1+2+1; 1+1+1+2
Choose 4 digits out of 1, 2, and 3 digits such that the sum of these digits is 6. 3111 1311 1113 2211 2121 2112 1122 1212 1221

Choose 4 digits out of 1, 2, and 3 digits such that the sum of these digits is 7.
3211 3121 3112 3121 2311 2221 2212 2122 1222 2131
2113
1132
1123
1231
1213
1321
1312

Choose 4 digits out of 1, 2, and 3 digits such that the sum of 8.
3311
3131
3113
2222

Choose 4 digits out of 1, 2, and 3 digits such that the sum of these digits is 9.
3321
3312
3231
3213
2331
2313
2133
1332
1323
1233

Choose 4 digits out of 1, 2, and 3 digits such that the sum of these digits is 10.
3331
3313
3133
1333
3322
3232
2332
2323
2233

Choose four digits out of 1, 2, and 3 digits such that the sum of these digits is 11.
3332
3323
3233
2333

Choose four digits out of 1, 2, and 3 digits such that the sum of these digits is 12.
3333

Math Chess Sudoku Puzzles －青少年益智棋芸健脑

Frankho ChessDoku － 何数棋谜算独

© 2007 － 2020   Frank Ho, Amanda Ho   All rights reserved.   www.homathchess.com

Student's name_____ Date_____

How to solve Frankho ChessDoku ™

Rule: The numbers 1, 2, 3 must appear only once in every row or column of the following ChessDoku problem.

Step 1: The squares with numbers in them shall be the ones we pay attention to first. The math strategy is to work backwards. These numbers are results of calculations according to some arithmetic operator(s) and chess moves(s) as indicated by the darker arrow(s).

Step 2: First, let us look at number 5 in the c3 square. The 5 is a result of chess piece Queen's move coming from the left, so let us think what two numbers add to 5? The answer is 2 + 3 or 3 + 2, but we are not sure which one to choose, so we now take a look at the number 6 in b2 square.

Step 3: The number 6 is the result of 3 + 3, and no other combination of two numbers (from the number choices of 1, 2, and 3) can be added to have the result of 6. We then can conclude that the number 3, which we could not decide at Step 2, shall be in the c3 square.

Step 4: Now we have three squares figured out, they are 2 in b3, 3 in c3, and 3 in b2. By using the strategy of the rules of Sudoku (each number only appears once per row or column.), we know 1 must be placed in square a3 and also 1 must be placed in square b1.

Step 5: Now, we look at the square, which is intersected by two other squares having numbers written in them. For example, square c1 is intersected by square b1 (1) and c3 (3) (Note in this case 3 points b1, c1, and c3 forming a triangle so we can call it Triangle strategy). We know if the number 1 already appeared in row 1 and the number 3 already appeared in column c, then the square c3 must have the number 2. Continue to use the restriction of no same numbers that can be appeared on the same row and column. We can figure out all the other numbers.

To watch Frank Ho's video presentation explaining the following problem, go to
https://youtu.be/Ksjc7Ta7gCI

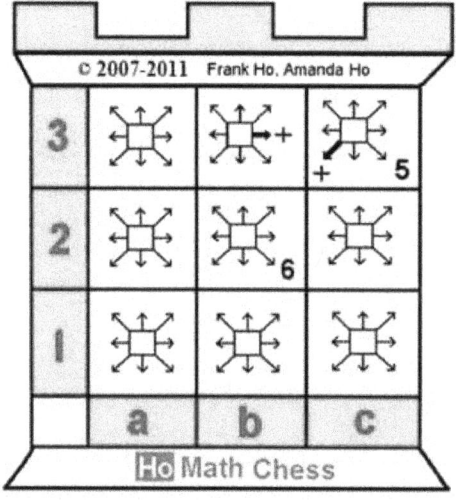

Line and one point

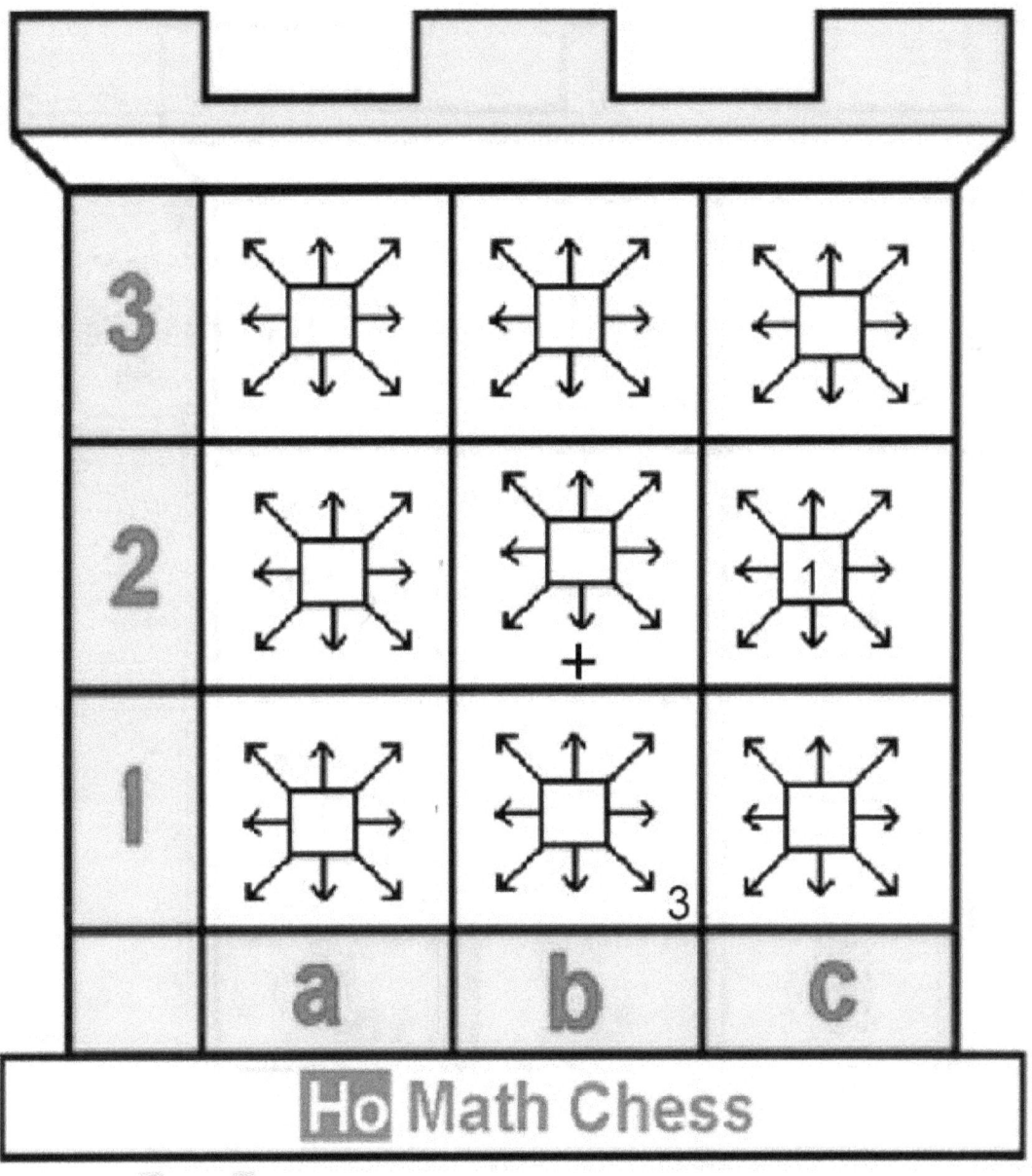

Line and one point

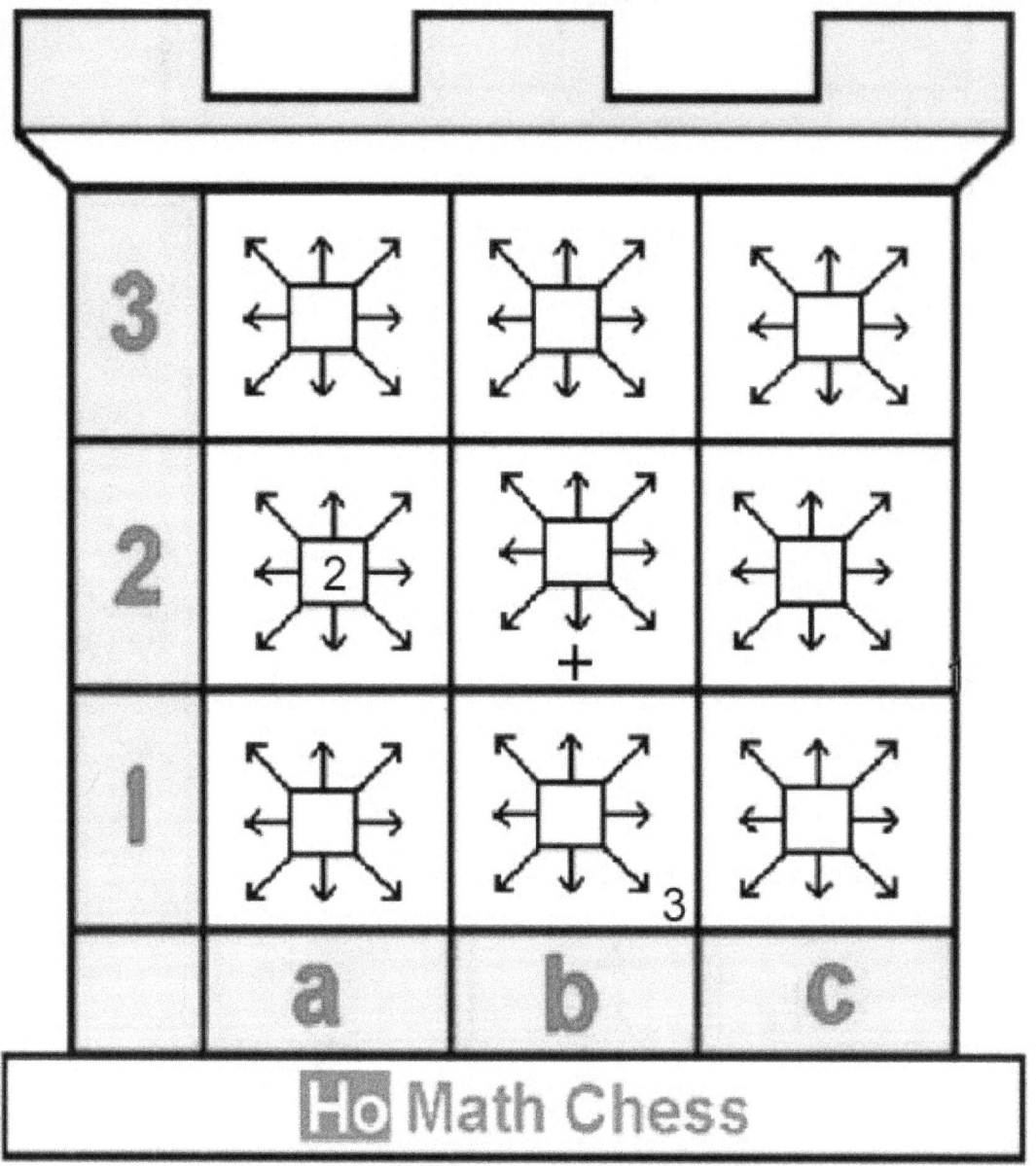

Line and one point

ChessDoku™ is solved by using one or more operators of addition, subtraction, multiplication, or division after following chess moves and logic.

Rule All the digits 1 to 3 must appear exactly once in every row and column. The number appears in the bottom right-hand corner is the result calculated according to the arithmetic operator(s) and chess move(s) as indicated by the darker arrow(s).

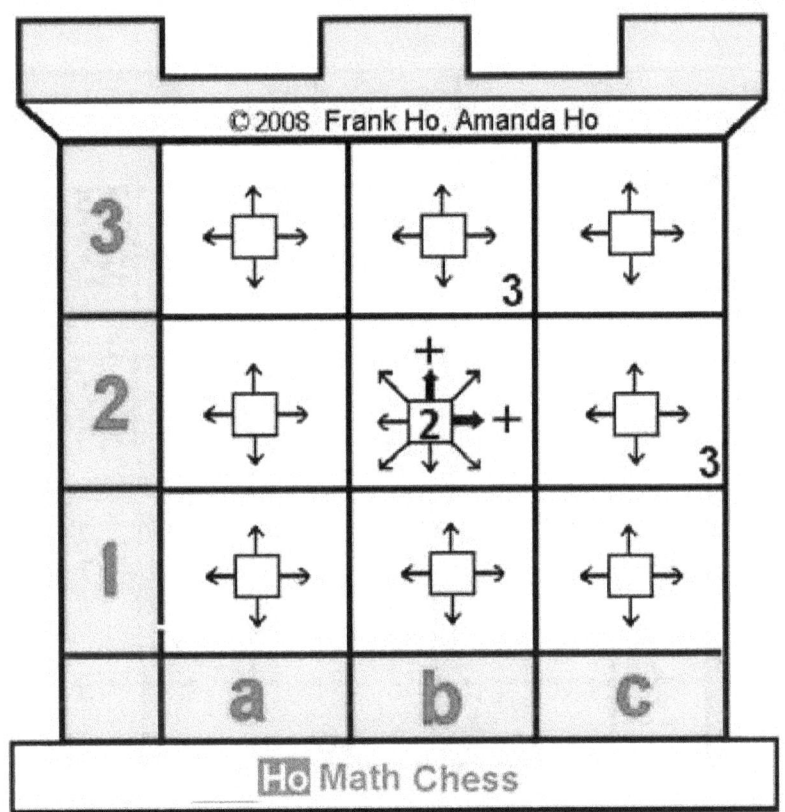

213
321
132

Frankho ChessDoku™ # 8

Movement + Calculation

Frankho ChessDoku™ is solved by using one or more operators of addition, subtraction, multiplication, or division after following chess moves and logic.

Rule All the digits 1 to 3 must appear exactly once in every row and column. The number appears in the bottom right-hand corner is the result calculated according to the arithmetic operator(s) and chess move(s) as indicated by the darker arrow(s).

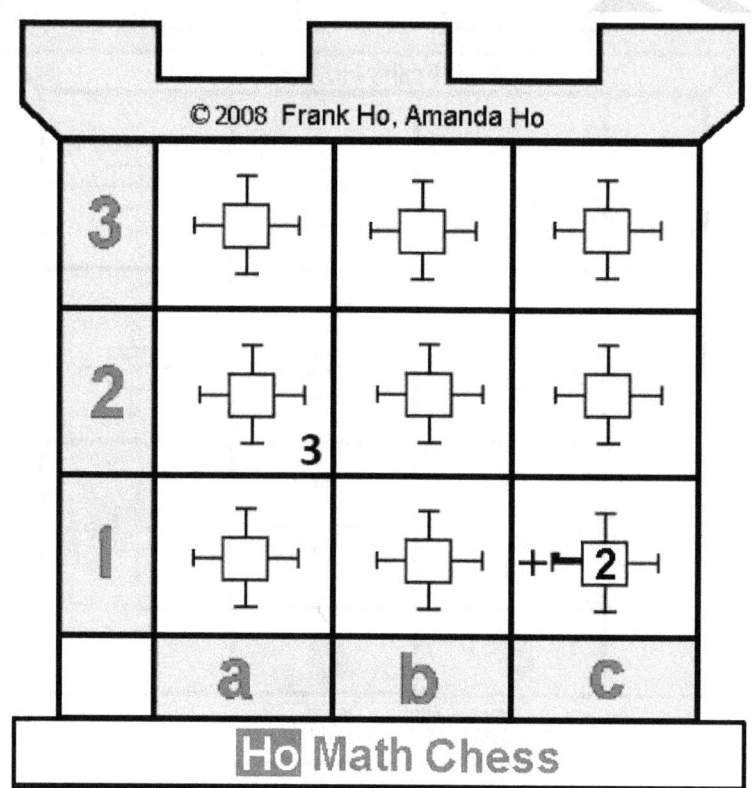

231
123
312

Frankho ChessDoku™ # 9

Movement + Calculation

Frankho ChessDoku™ is solved by using one or more operators of addition, subtraction, multiplication, or division after following chess moves and logic.

Rule All the digits 1 to 3 must appear exactly once in every row and column. The number appears in the bottom right-hand corner is the result calculated according to the arithmetic operator(s) and chess move(s) as indicated by the darker arrow(s).

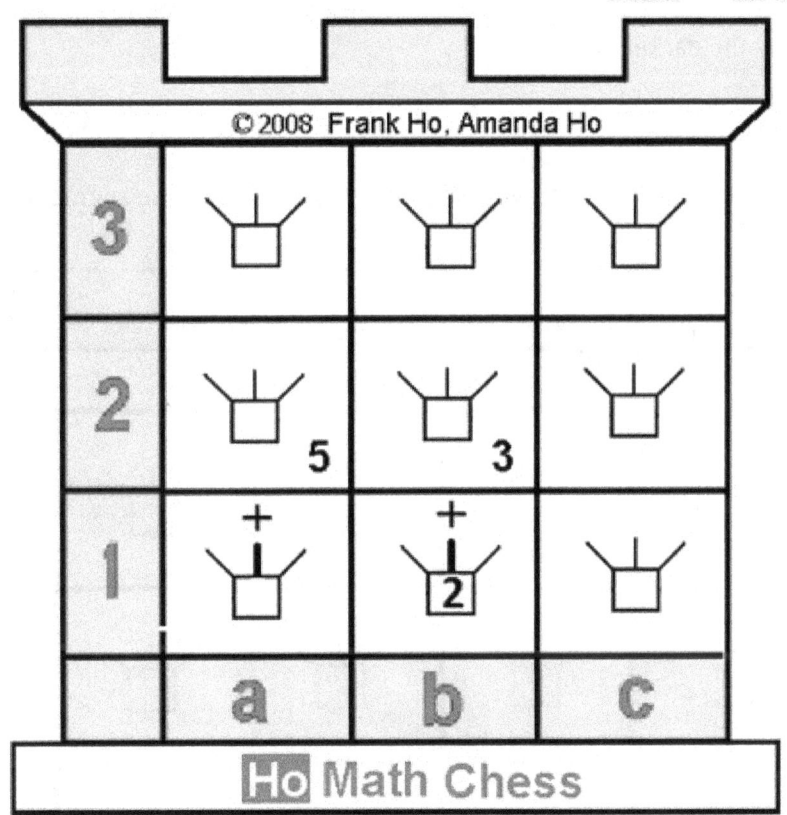

132
213
321

Part 1 Frankho ChessDoku 3 by 3

Frankho ChessDoku™ # 1

Movement

Frankho ChessDoku™ is solved by using one or more operators of addition, subtraction, multiplication, or division after following chess moves and logic.

Rule All the digits 1 to 3 must appear exactly once in every row and column. The number appears in the bottom right-hand corner is the result calculated according to the arithmetic operator(s) and chess move(s) as indicated by the darker arrow(s).

Pawn

The following figure shows how pawn moves by following its darker line segment(s).

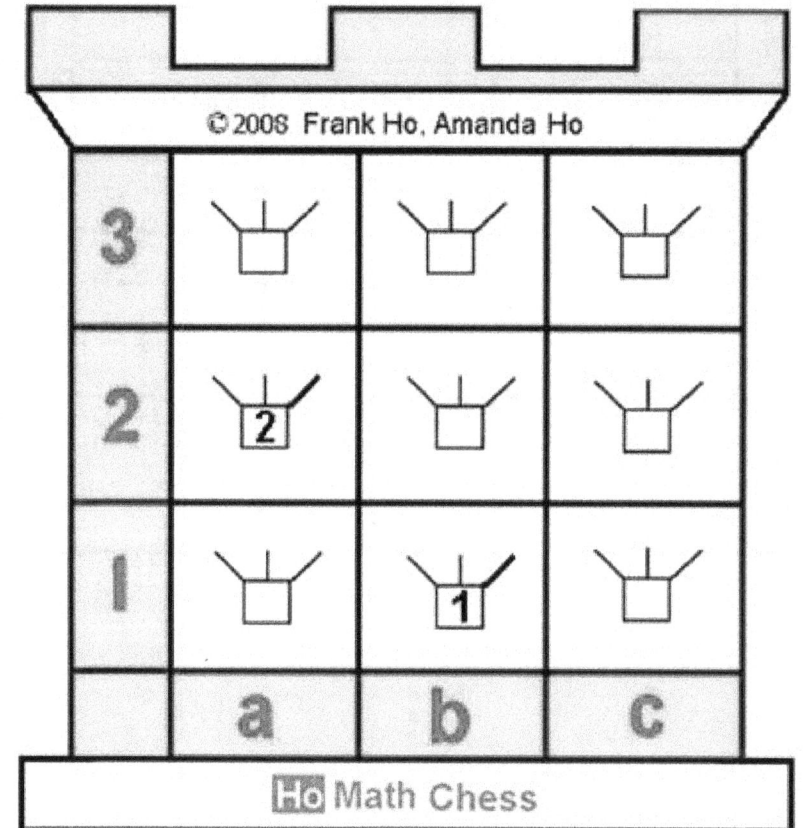

123
231
312

Frankho ChessDoku™ # 2

Movement

Frankho ChessDoku™ is solved by using one or more operators of addition, subtraction, multiplication, or division after following chess moves and logic.

Rule All the digits 1 to 3 must appear exactly once in every row and column. The number appears in the bottom right-hand corner is the result calculated according to the arithmetic operator(s) and chess move(s) as indicated by the darker arrow(s).

Bishop

The following figure shows how the bishop moves by following its darker line segment(s).

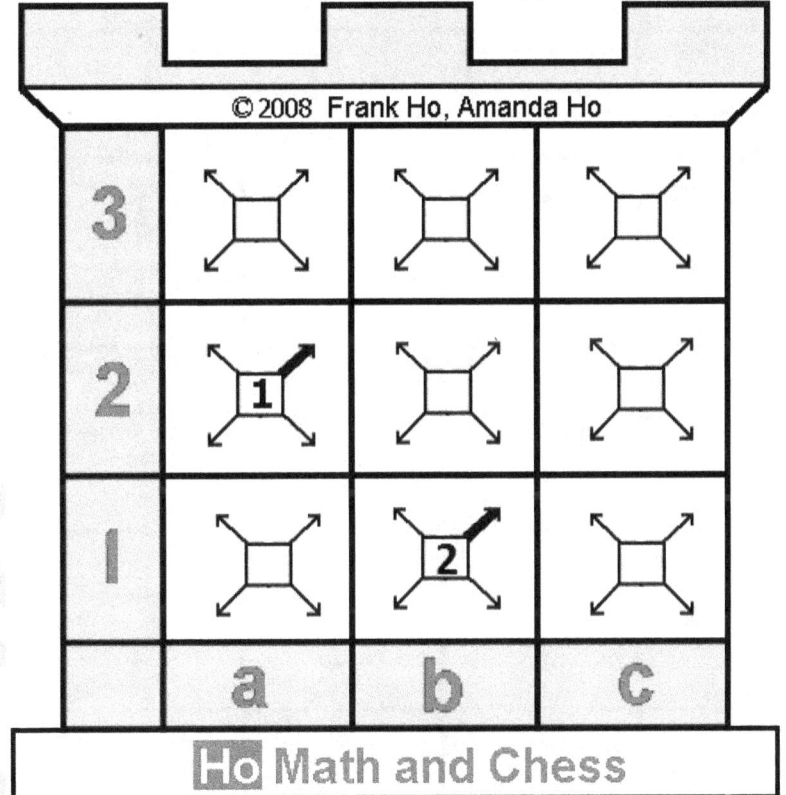

213
132
321

Math Chess Sudoku Puzzles 一青少年益智棋芸健脑

Frankho ChessDoku 一 何数棋谜算独

© 2007 一 2020 Frank Ho, Amanda Ho   All rights reserved.   www.homathchess.com

Student's name_____Date_____

Frankho ChessDoku™ # 3

Movement + Calculation

Frankho ChessDoku™ is solved by using one or more operators of addition, subtraction, multiplication, or division after following chess moves and logic.

Rule All the digits 1 to 3 must appear exactly once in every row and column. The number appears in the bottom right-hand corner is the result calculated according to the arithmetic operator(s) and chess move(s) as indicated by the darker arrow(s).

Rook

The following figure shows how rook moves by following its darker line segment(s).

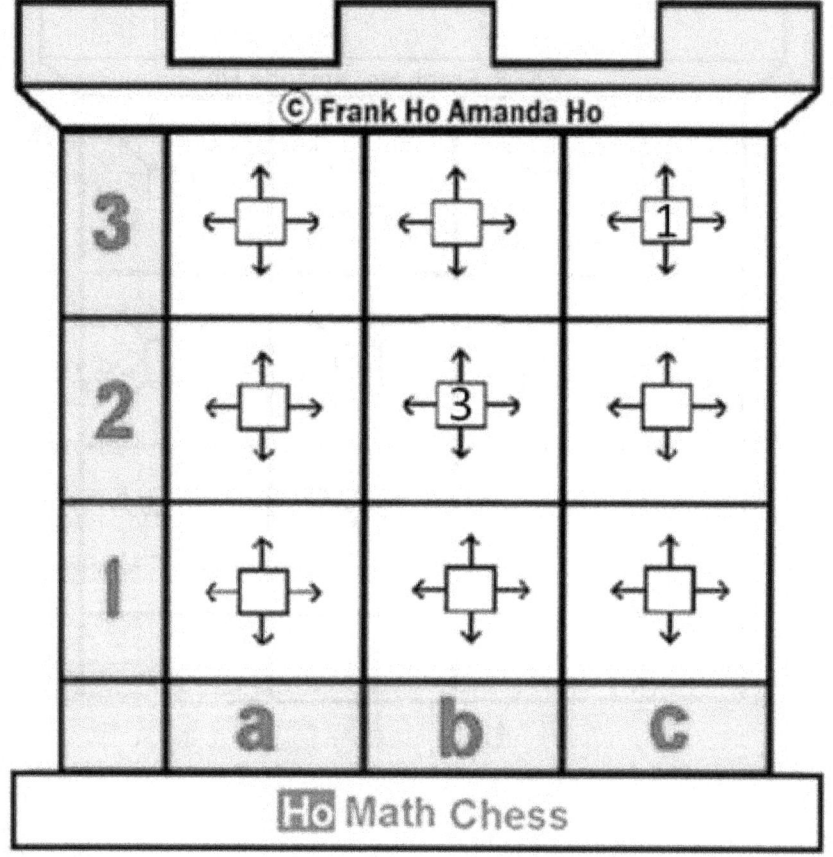

321
132
213

Frankho ChessDoku™ # 4

Movement

Frankho ChessDoku™ is solved by using one or more operators of addition, subtraction, multiplication, or division after following chess moves and logic.

Rule All the digits 1 to 3 must appear exactly once in every row and column. The number appears in the bottom right-hand corner is the result calculated according to the arithmetic operator(s) and chess move(s) as indicated by the darker arrow(s).

Knight

The following figure shows how the knight moves by following its darker line segment(s).

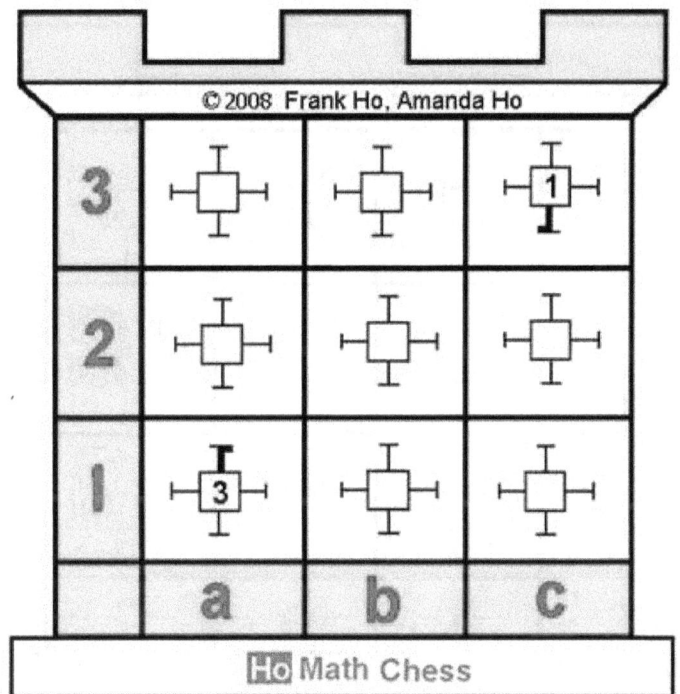

231
123
312

Frankho ChessDoku™ # 5

Movement

Frankho ChessDoku™ is solved by using one or more operators of addition, subtraction, multiplication, or division after following chess moves and logic.

Rule All the digits 1 to 3 must appear exactly once in every row and column. The number appears in the bottom right-hand corner is the result calculated according to the arithmetic operator(s) and chess move(s) as indicated by the darker arrow(s).

King

The following figure shows the king moves by following its darker line segment(s).

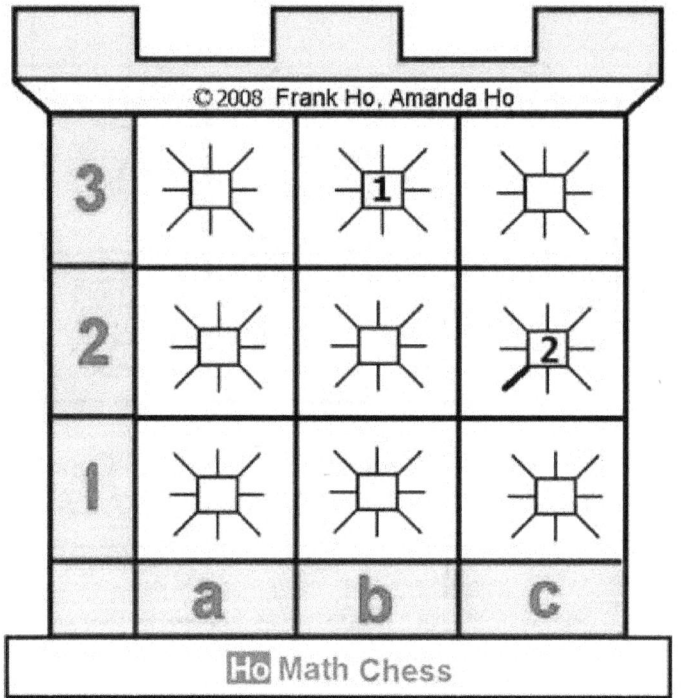

213
132
321

Frankho ChessDoku™ # 6

Movement

Frankho ChessDoku™ is solved by using one or more operators of addition, subtraction, multiplication, or division after following chess moves and logic.

Rule All the digits 1 to 3 must appear exactly once in every row and column. The number appears in the bottom right-hand corner is the result calculated according to the arithmetic operator(s) and chess move(s) as indicated by the darker arrow(s).

Queen

The following figure shows how the queen moves by following its darker line segment(s).

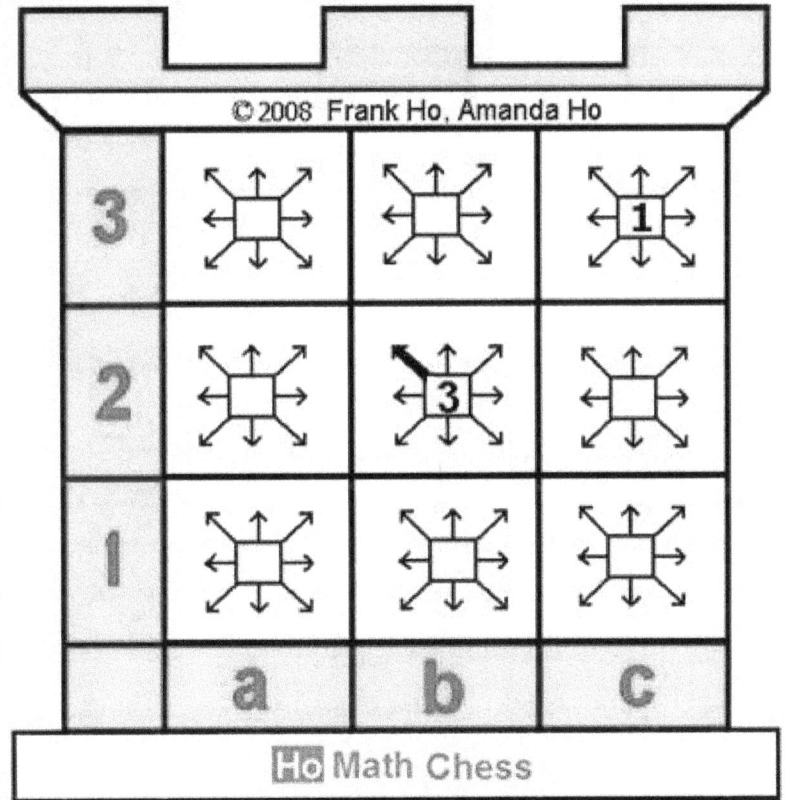

321
132
213

Math Chess Sudoku Puzzles 一青少年益智棋芸健脑

Frankho ChessDoku 一 何数棋谜算独

© 2007－2020   Frank Ho, Amanda Ho   All rights reserved.   www.homathchess.com

Student's name_____Date_____

***** Part 1 Frankho ChessDoku 3 by 3 *****
Frankho ChessDoku™ # 1

Frankho ChessDoku™ is solved by using one or more operators of addition, subtraction, multiplication, or division after following chess moves and logic.

Rule All the digits 1 to 3 must appear exactly once in every row and column. The number appears in the bottom right-hand corner is the result calculated according to the arithmetic operator(s) and chess move(s) as indicated by the darker arrow(s).

Pawn

The following figure shows how pawn moves by following its darker line segment(s).

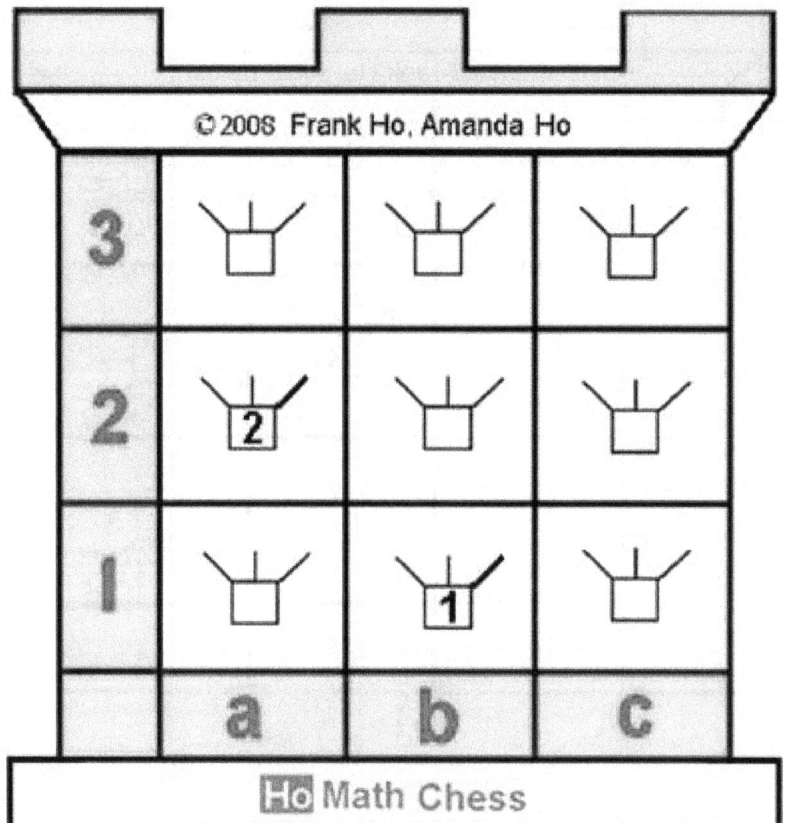

123
231
312

Frankho ChessDoku™ # 2

Frankho ChessDoku™ is solved by using one or more operators of addition, subtraction, multiplication, or division after following chess moves and logic.

Rule All the digits 1 to 3 must appear exactly once in every row and column. The number appears in the bottom right-hand corner is the result calculated according to the arithmetic operator(s) and chess move(s) as indicated by the darker arrow(s).

Bishop

The following figure shows how the bishop moves by following its darker line segment(s).

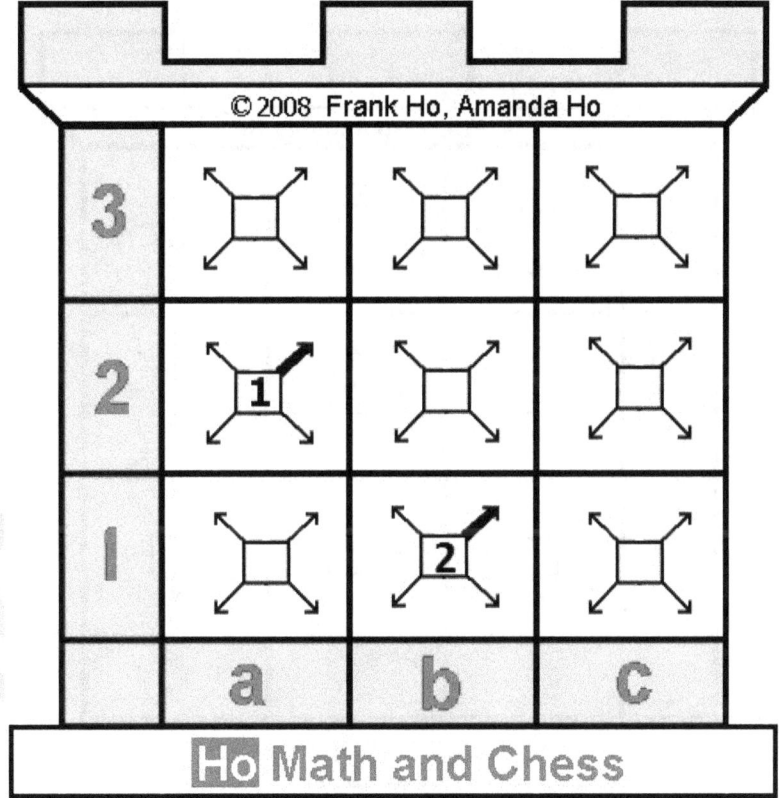

213
132
321

Math Chess Sudoku Puzzles — 青少年益智棋芸健脑

Frankho ChessDoku — 何数棋谜算独

© 2007 — 2020   Frank Ho, Amanda Ho   All rights reserved.   www.homathchess.com

Student's name_____ Date_____

Frankho ChessDoku™ # 3

Frankho ChessDoku™ is solved by using one or more operators of addition, subtraction, multiplication, or division after following chess moves and logic.

Rule All the digits 1 to 3 must appear exactly once in every row and column. The number appears in the bottom right-hand corner is the result calculated according to the arithmetic operator(s) and chess move(s) as indicated by the darker arrow(s).

Rook

The following figure shows how rook moves by following its darker line segment(s).

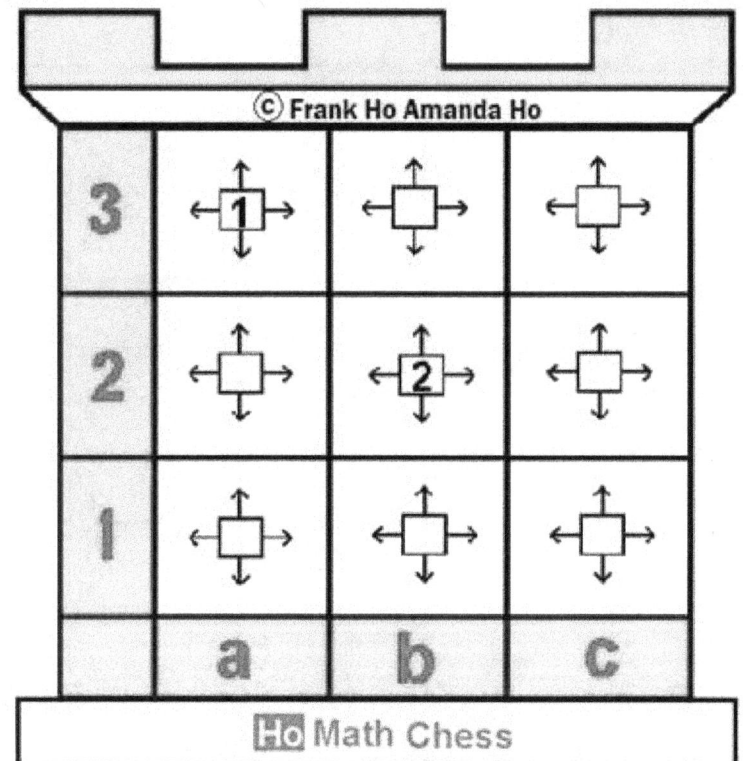

132
321
213

Frankho ChessDoku™ # 4

Frankho ChessDoku™ is solved by using one or more operators of addition, subtraction, multiplication, or division after following chess moves and logic.

Rule All the digits 1 to 3 must appear exactly once in every row and column. The number appears in the bottom right-hand corner is the result calculated according to the arithmetic operator(s) and chess move(s) as indicated by the darker arrow(s).

Knight

The following figure shows how the knight moves by following its darker line segment(s).

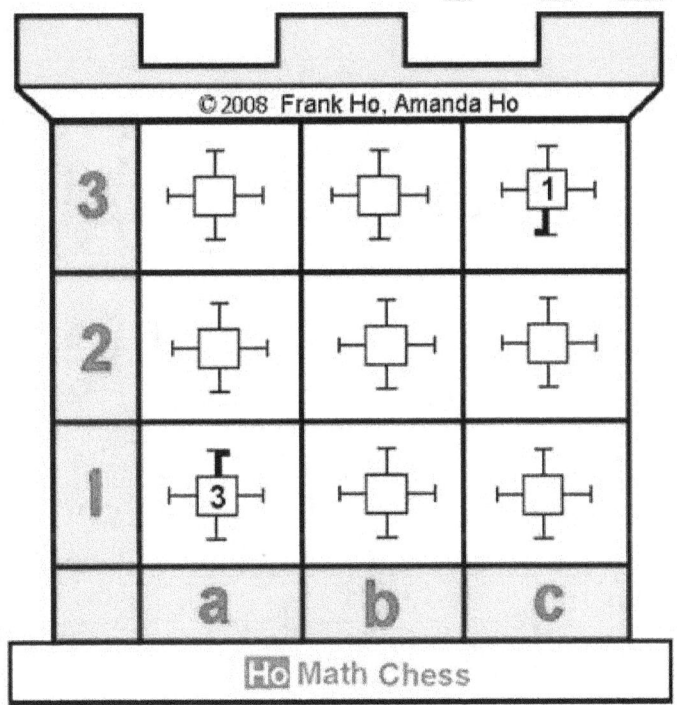

231
123
312

Frankho ChessDoku™ # 5

Frankho ChessDoku™ is solved by using one or more operators of addition, subtraction, multiplication, or division after following chess moves and logic.

Rule All the digits 1 to 3 must appear exactly once in every row and column. The number appears in the bottom right-hand corner is the result calculated according to the arithmetic operator(s) and chess move(s) as indicated by the darker arrow(s).

King

The following figure shows the king moves by following its darker line segment(s).

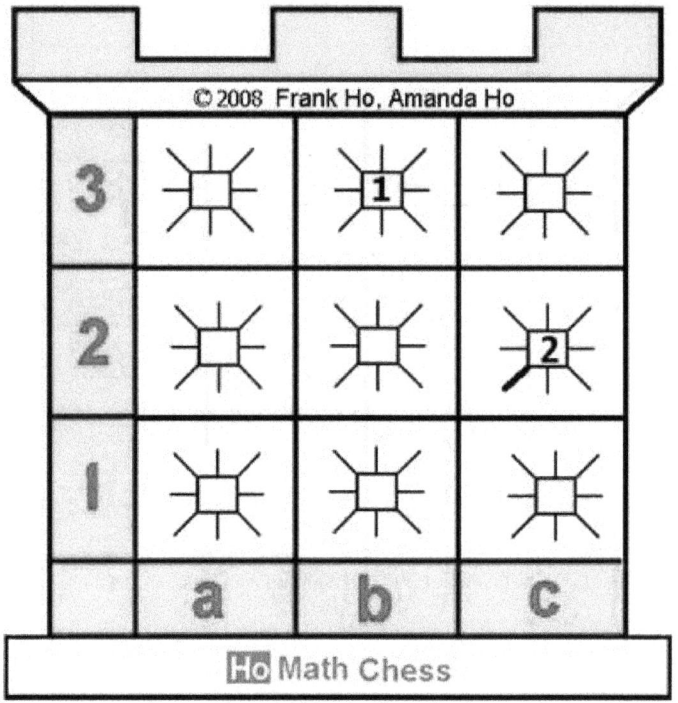

213
132
321

Math Chess Sudoku Puzzles 一青少年益智棋芸健脑

Frankho ChessDoku 一 何数棋谜算独

© 2007 － 2020   Frank Ho, Amanda Ho   All rights reserved.   www.homathchess.com

Student's name_____ Date_____

Frankho ChessDoku™ # 6

Frankho ChessDoku™ is solved by using one or more operators of addition, subtraction, multiplication, or division after following chess moves and logic.

Rule All the digits 1 to 3 must appear exactly once in every row and column. The number appears in the bottom right-hand corner is the result calculated according to the arithmetic operator(s) and chess move(s) as indicated by the darker arrow(s).

Queen

The following figure shows how the queen moves by following its darker line segment(s).

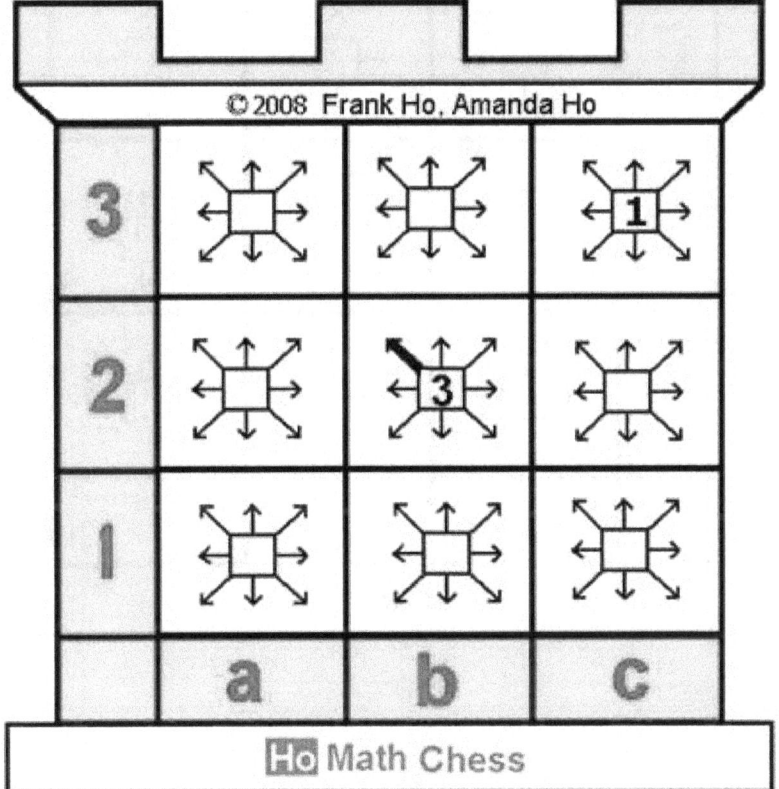

321
132
213

Frankho ChessDoku™ # 7

Frankho ChessDoku™ is solved by using one or more operators of addition, subtraction, multiplication, or division after following chess moves and logic.

Rule All the digits 1 to 3 must appear exactly once in every row and column. The number appears in the bottom right-hand corner is the result calculated according to the arithmetic operator(s) and chess move(s) as indicated by the darker arrow(s).

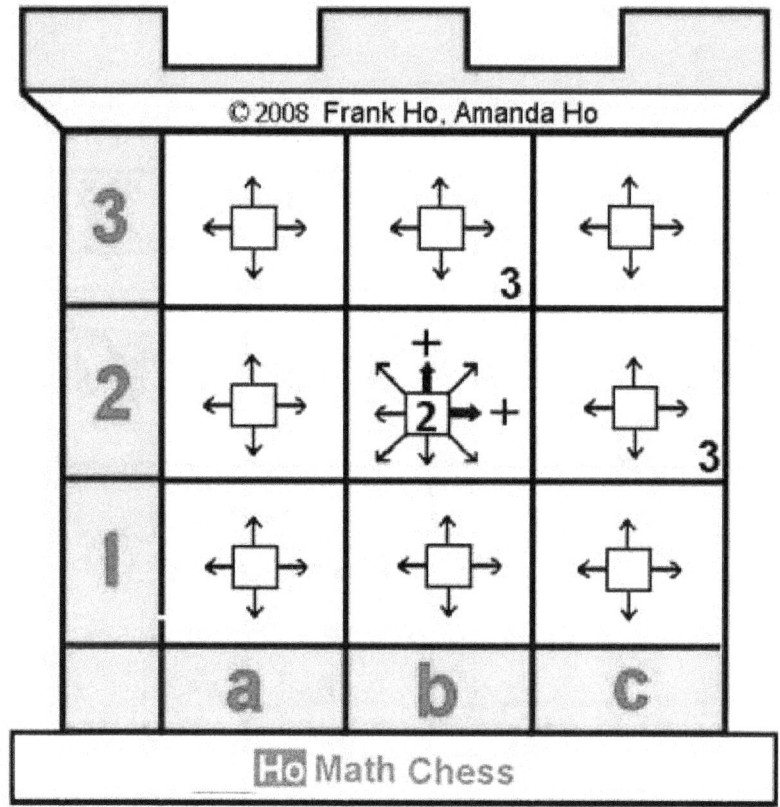

213
321
132

Frankho ChessDoku™ # 8

Frankho ChessDoku™ is solved by using one or more operators of addition, subtraction, multiplication, or division after following chess moves and logic.

Rule All the digits 1 to 3 must appear exactly once in every row and column. The number appears in the bottom right-hand corner is the result calculated according to the arithmetic operator(s) and chess move(s) as indicated by the darker arrow(s).

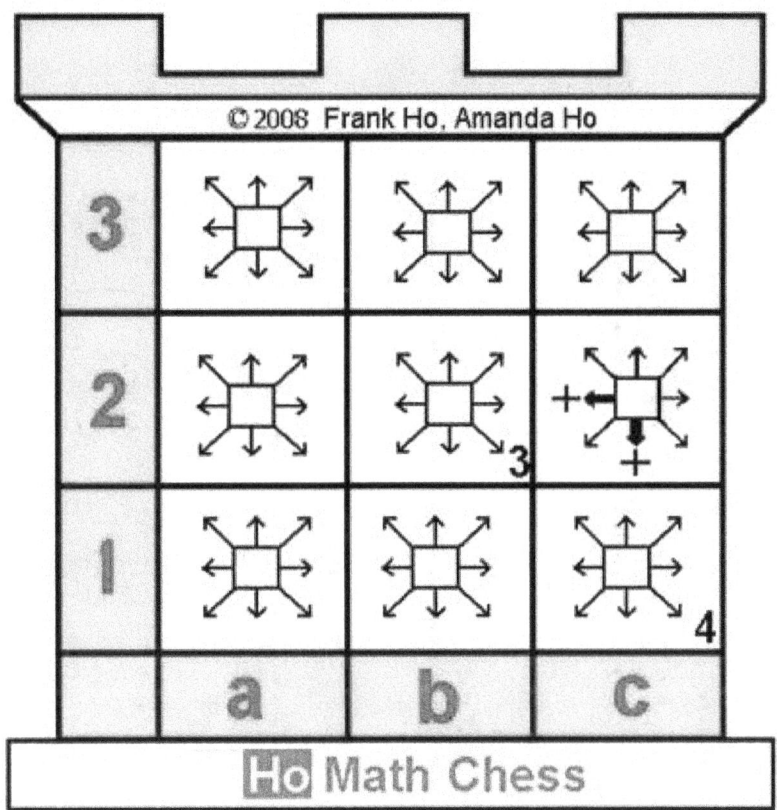

132
321
213

Frankho ChessDoku™ # 9

Frankho ChessDoku™ is solved by using one or more operators of addition, subtraction, multiplication, or division after following chess moves and logic.

Rule All the digits 1 to 3 must appear exactly once in every row and column. The number appears in the bottom right-hand corner is the result calculated according to the arithmetic operator(s) and chess move(s) as indicated by the darker arrow(s).

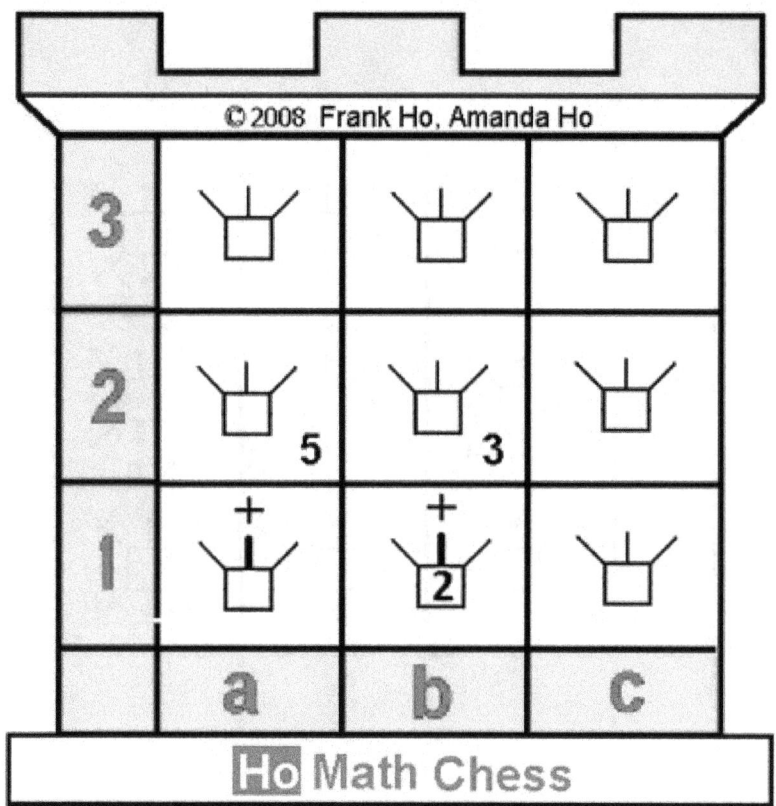

132
213
321

Frankho ChessDoku™ # 10

Frankho ChessDoku™ is solved by using one or more operators of addition, subtraction, multiplication, or division after following chess moves and logic.

Rule All the digits 1 to 3 must appear exactly once in every row and column. The number appears in the bottom right-hand corner is the result calculated according to the arithmetic operator(s) and chess move(s) as indicated by the darker arrow(s).

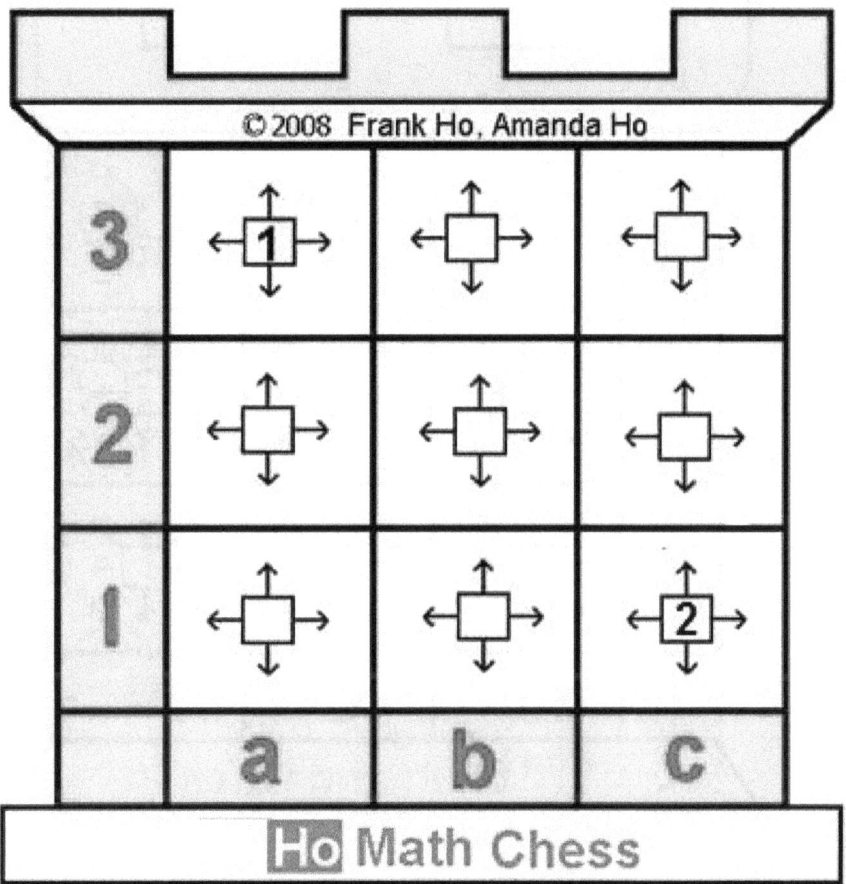

123
231
312

Frankho ChessDoku™ # 11

Frankho ChessDoku™ is solved by using addition, subtraction, multiplication, or division by following chess moves and logic.

Rule All the digits 1 to 3 must appear exactly once in every row and column. The number appears in the bottom right-hand corner is the result calculated according to the arithmetic operator(s) and chess move(s) as indicated by the darker arrow(s).

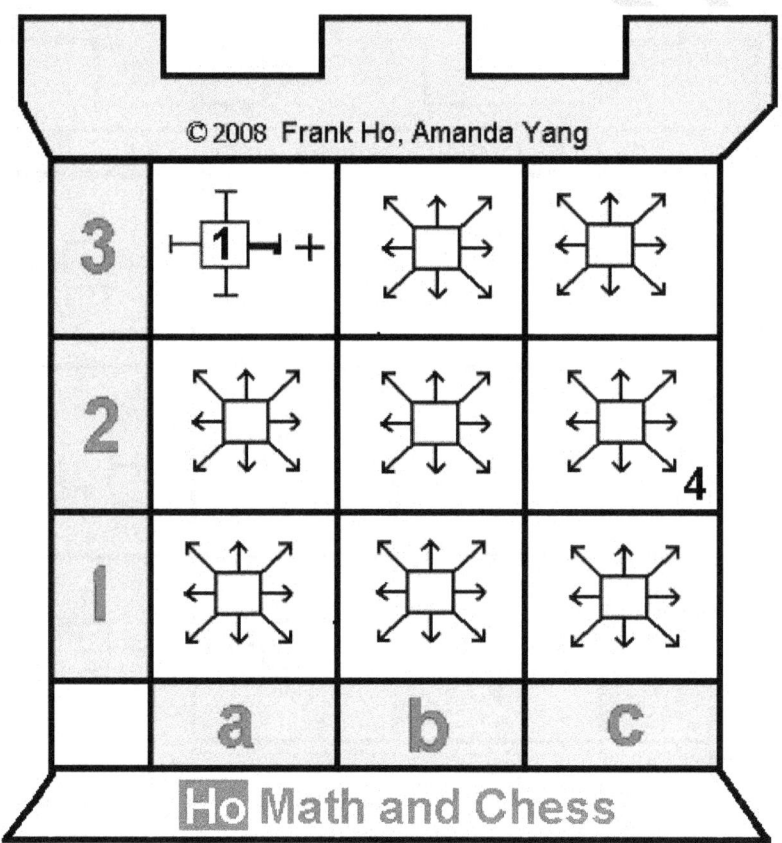

132
213
321

Frankho ChessDoku™ # 12

Frankho ChessDoku™ is solved by using addition, subtraction, multiplication, or division by following chess moves and logic.

Rule All the digits 1 to 3 must appear exactly once in every row and column. The number appears in the bottom right-hand corner is the result calculated according to the arithmetic operator(s) and chess move(s) as indicated by the darker arrow(s).

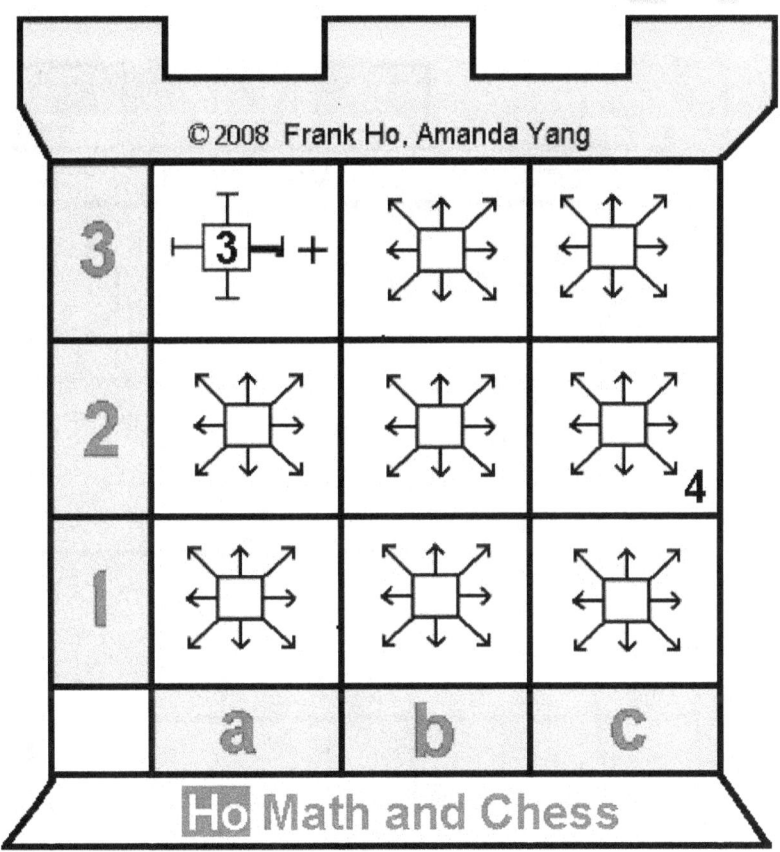

312
231
123

Frankho ChessDoku™ # 13

Frankho ChessDoku™ is solved by using addition, subtraction, multiplication, or division by following chess moves and logic.

Rule All the digits 1 to 3 must appear exactly once in every row and column. The number appears in the bottom right-hand corner is the result calculated according to the arithmetic operator(s) and chess move(s) as indicated by the darker arrow(s).

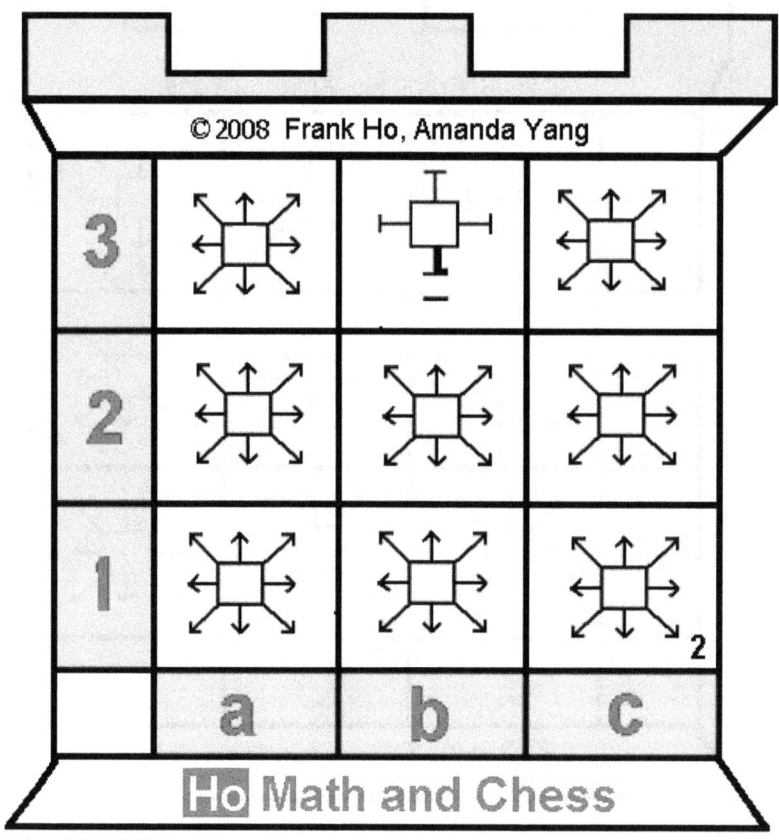

132
213
321

Frankho ChessDoku™ # 14

Frankho ChessDoku™ is solved by using addition, subtraction, multiplication, or division by following chess moves and logic.

Rule All the digits 1 to 3 must appear exactly once in every row and column. The number appears in the bottom right-hand corner is the result calculated according to the arithmetic operator(s) and chess move(s) as indicated by the darker arrow(s).

Knight

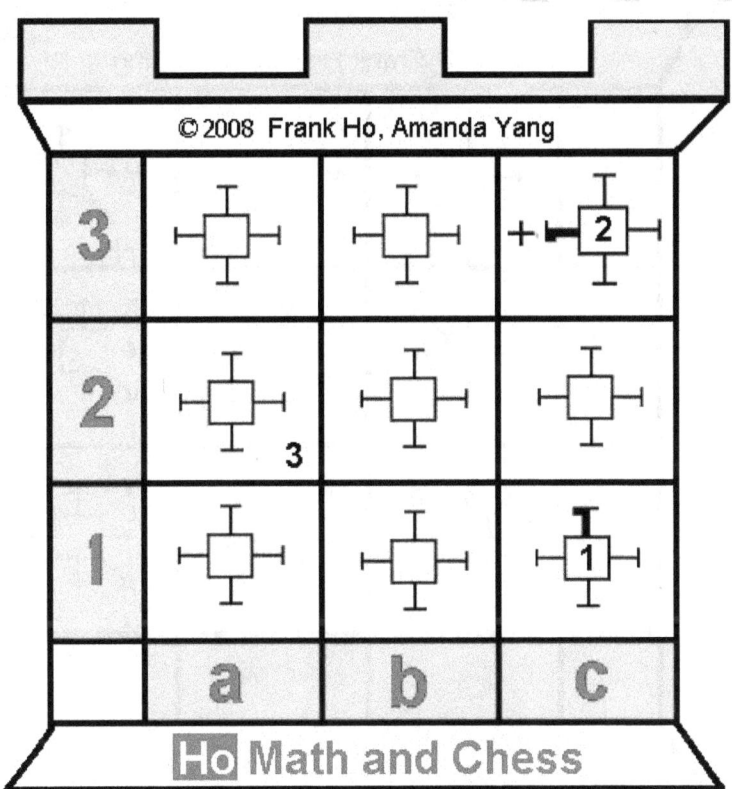

312
123
231

Frankho ChessDoku™ # 15

Frankho ChessDoku™ is solved by using addition, subtraction, multiplication, or division by following chess moves and logic.

Rule All the digits 1 to 3 must appear exactly once in every row and column. The number appears in the bottom right-hand corner is the result calculated according to the arithmetic operator(s) and chess move(s) as indicated by the darker arrow(s).

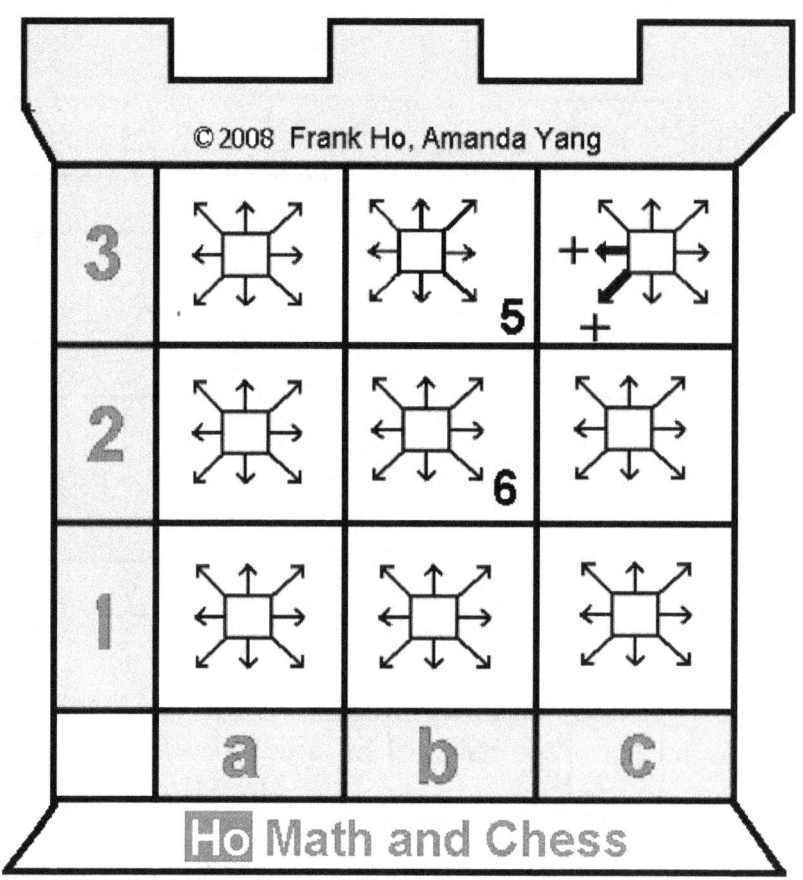

123
231
312

Frankho ChessDoku™ # 16

Frankho ChessDoku™ is solved by using addition, subtraction, multiplication, or division by following chess moves and logic.

Rule All the digits 1 to 3 must appear exactly once in every row and column. The number appears in the bottom right-hand corner is the result calculated according to the arithmetic operator(s) and chess move(s) as indicated by the darker arrow(s).

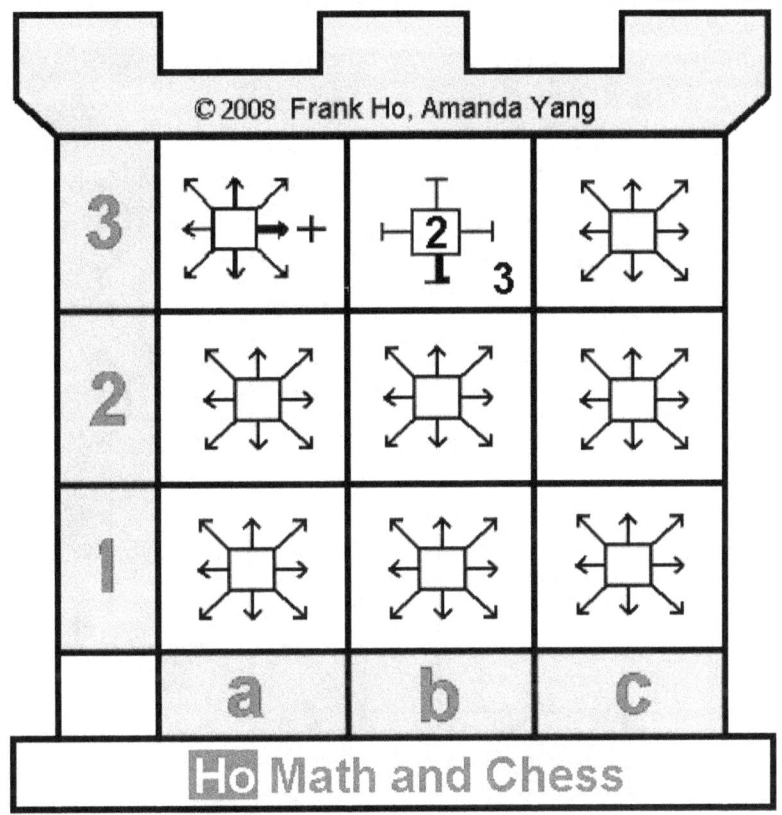

123
231
312

Frankho ChessDoku™ # 17

Frankho ChessDoku™ is solved by using addition, subtraction, multiplication, or division by following chess moves and logic.

Rule All the digits 1 to 3 must appear exactly once in every row and column. The number appears in the bottom right-hand corner is the result calculated according to the arithmetic operator(s) and chess move(s) as indicated by the darker arrow(s).

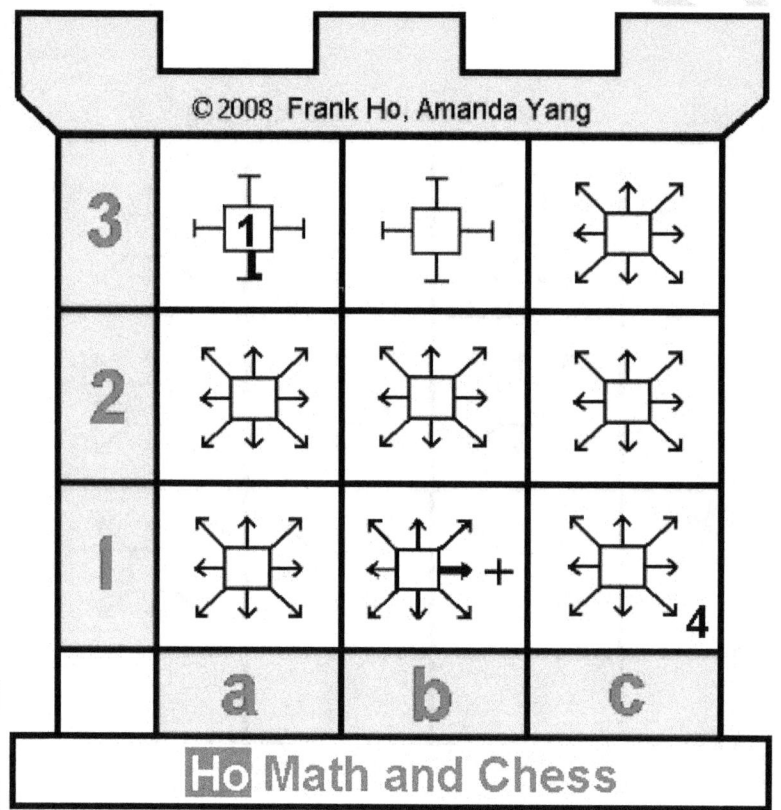

132
321
213

Frankho ChessDoku™ # 18

Frankho ChessDoku™ is solved by using addition, subtraction, multiplication, or division by following chess moves and logic.

Rule All the digits 1 to 3 must appear exactly once in every row and column. The number appears in the bottom right-hand corner is the result calculated according to the arithmetic operator(s) and chess move(s) as indicated by the darker arrow(s).

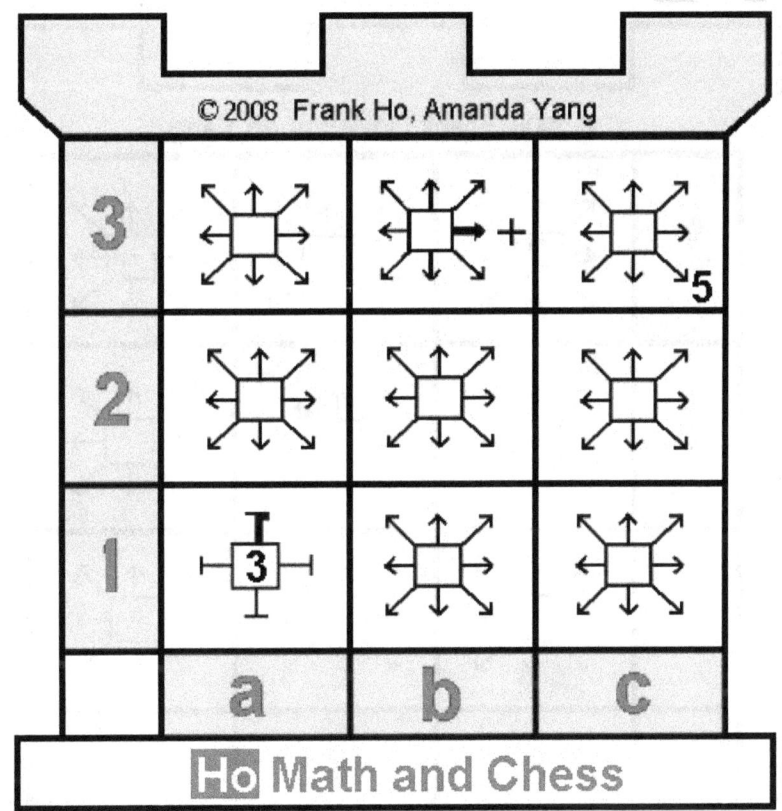

132
213
321

Frankho ChessDoku™ # 19

Frankho ChessDoku™ is solved by using addition, subtraction, multiplication, or division by following chess moves and logic.

Rule All the digits 1 to 3 must appear exactly once in every row and column. The number appears in the bottom right-hand corner is the result calculated according to the arithmetic operator(s) and chess move(s) as indicated by the darker arrow(s).

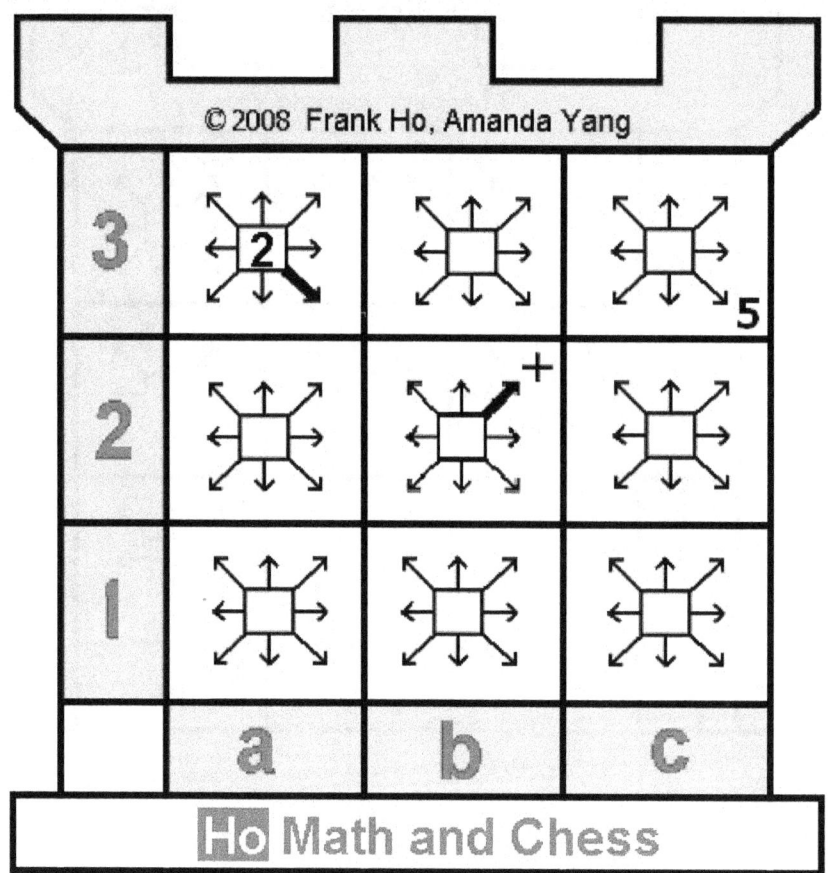

231
123
312

Frankho ChessDoku™ # 20

Frankho ChessDoku™ is solved by using addition, subtraction, multiplication, or division by following chess moves and logic.

Rule All the digits 1 to 3 must appear exactly once in every row and column. The number appears in the bottom right-hand corner is the result calculated according to the arithmetic operator(s) and chess move(s) as indicated by the darker arrow(s).

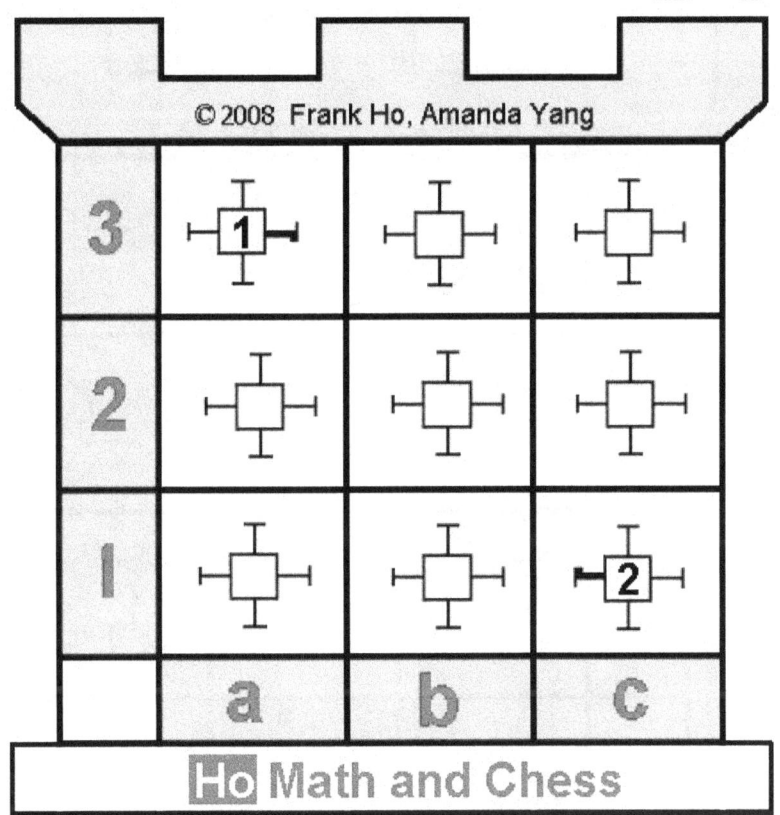

123
231
312

Frankho ChessDoku™ # 21

Frankho ChessDoku™ is solved by using addition, subtraction, multiplication, or division by following chess moves and logic.

Rule: All the digits 1 to 3 must appear exactly once in every row and column. The number appears in the bottom right-hand corner is the result calculated according to the arithmetic operator(s) and chess move(s) as indicated by the darker arrow(s).

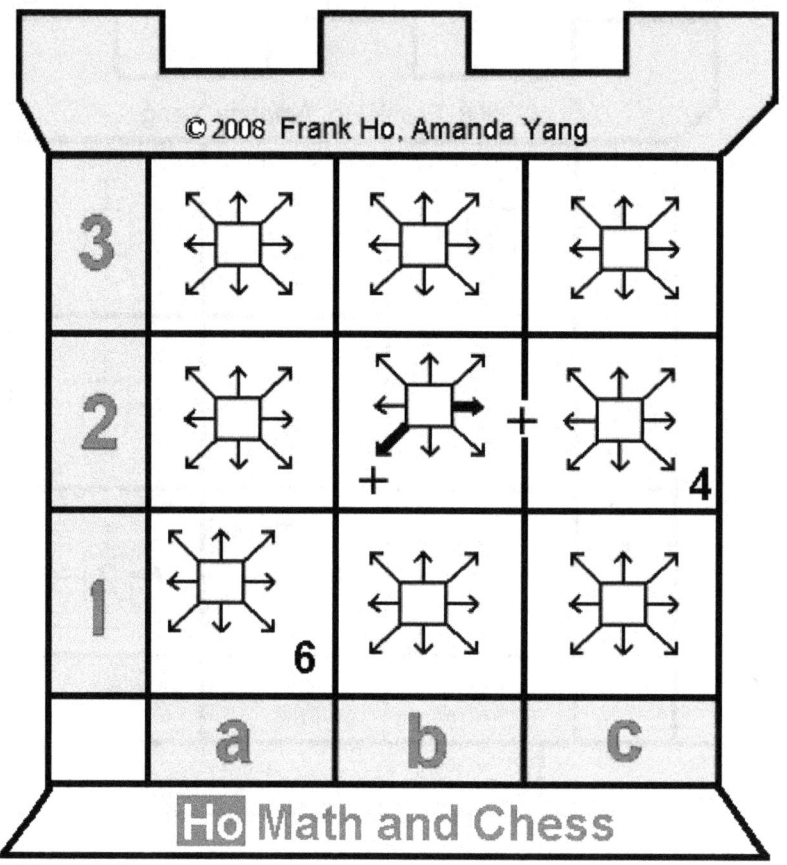

123
231
312

Frankho ChessDoku™ # 22

Frankho ChessDoku™ is solved by using addition, subtraction, multiplication, or division by following chess moves and logic.

Rule: All the digits 1 to 3 must appear exactly once in every row and column. The number appears in the bottom right-hand corner is the result calculated according to the arithmetic operator(s) and chess move(s) as indicated by the darker arrow(s).

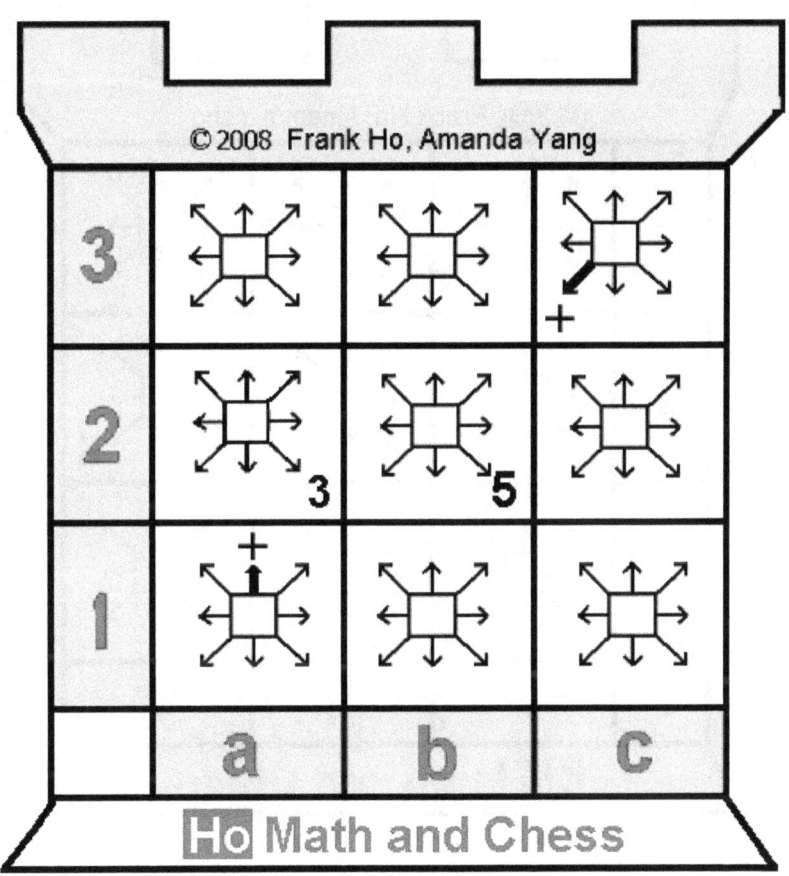

312
231
123

Frankho ChessDoku™ # 23

Frankho ChessDoku™ is solved by using addition, subtraction, multiplication, or division by following chess moves and logic.

Rule: All the digits 1 to 3 must appear exactly once in every row and column. The number appears in the bottom right-hand corner is the result calculated according to the arithmetic operator(s) and chess move(s) as indicated by the darker arrow(s).

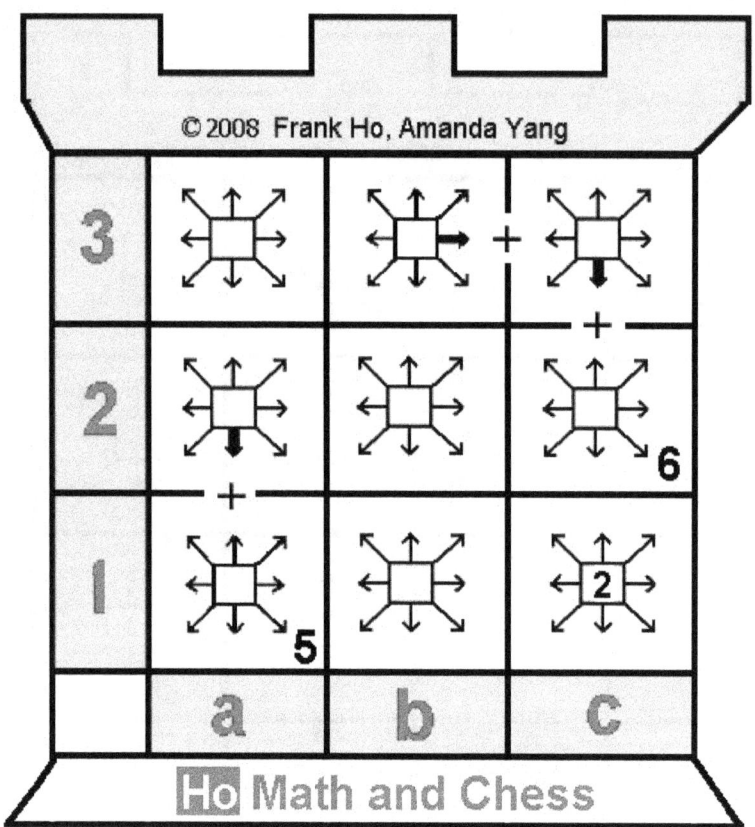

123
231
312

Frankho ChessDoku™ # 24

Frankho ChessDoku™ is solved by using addition, subtraction, multiplication, or division by following chess moves and logic.

Rule: All the digits 1 to 3 must appear exactly once in every row and column. The number appears in the bottom right-hand corner is the result calculated according to the arithmetic operator(s) and chess move(s) as indicated by the darker arrow(s).

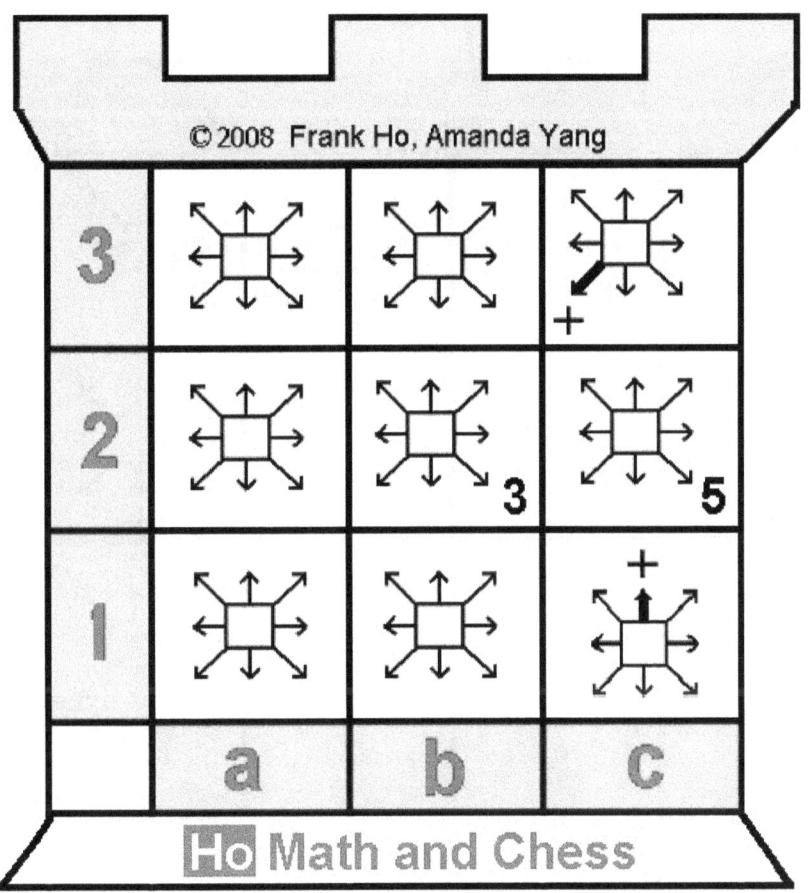

231
123
312

Frankho ChessDoku™ # 25

Frankho ChessDoku™ is solved by using addition, subtraction, multiplication, or division by following chess moves and logic.

Rule: All the digits 1 to 3 must appear exactly once in every row and column. The number appears in the bottom right-hand corner is the result calculated according to the arithmetic operator(s) and chess move(s) as indicated by the darker arrow(s).

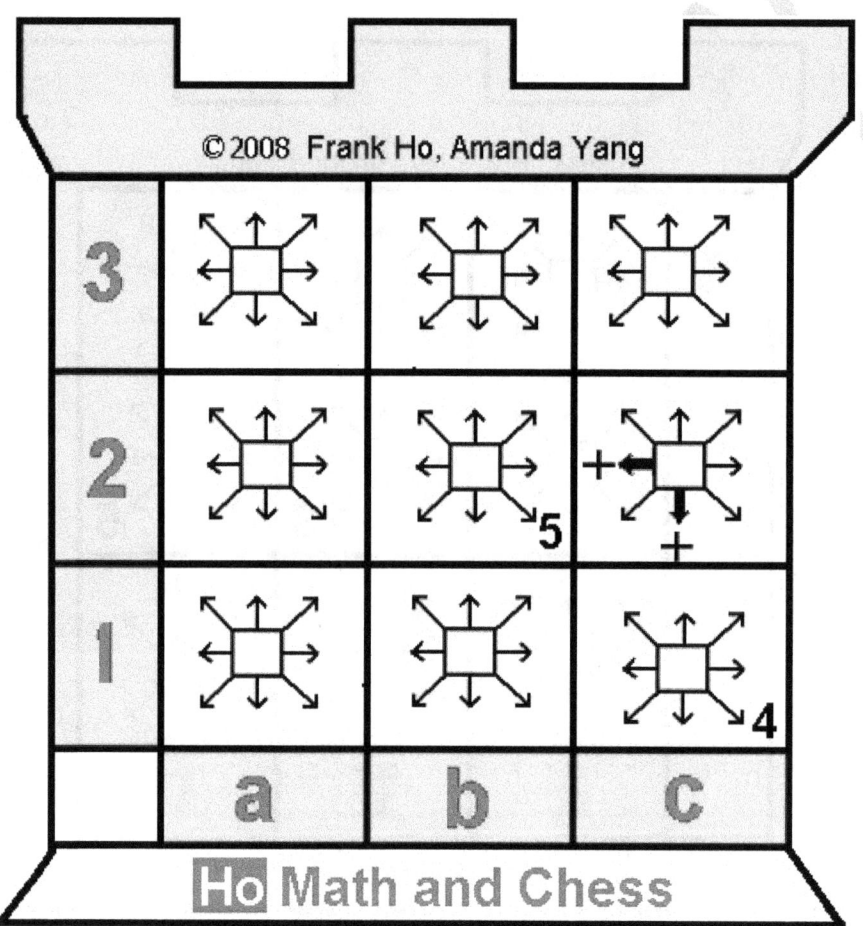

312
123
231

# Frankho ChessDoku™ # 26

Frankho ChessDoku™ is solved by using addition, subtraction, multiplication, or division by following chess moves and logic.

Rule: All the digits 1 to 3 must appear exactly once in every row and column. The number appears in the bottom right-hand corner is the result calculated according to the arithmetic operator(s) and chess move(s) as indicated by the darker arrow(s).

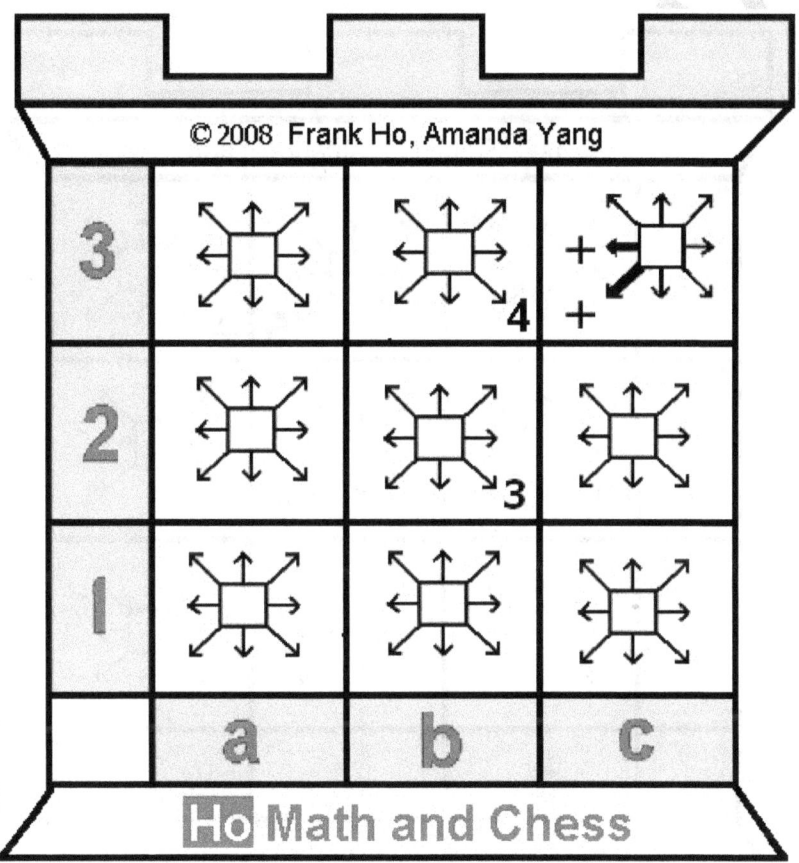

231
123
312

Frankho ChessDoku™ # 27

Frankho ChessDoku™ is solved by using addition, subtraction, multiplication, or division by following chess moves and logic.

Rule: All the digits 1 to 3 must appear exactly once in every row and column. The number appears in the bottom right-hand corner is the result calculated according to the arithmetic operator(s) and chess move(s) as indicated by the darker arrow(s).

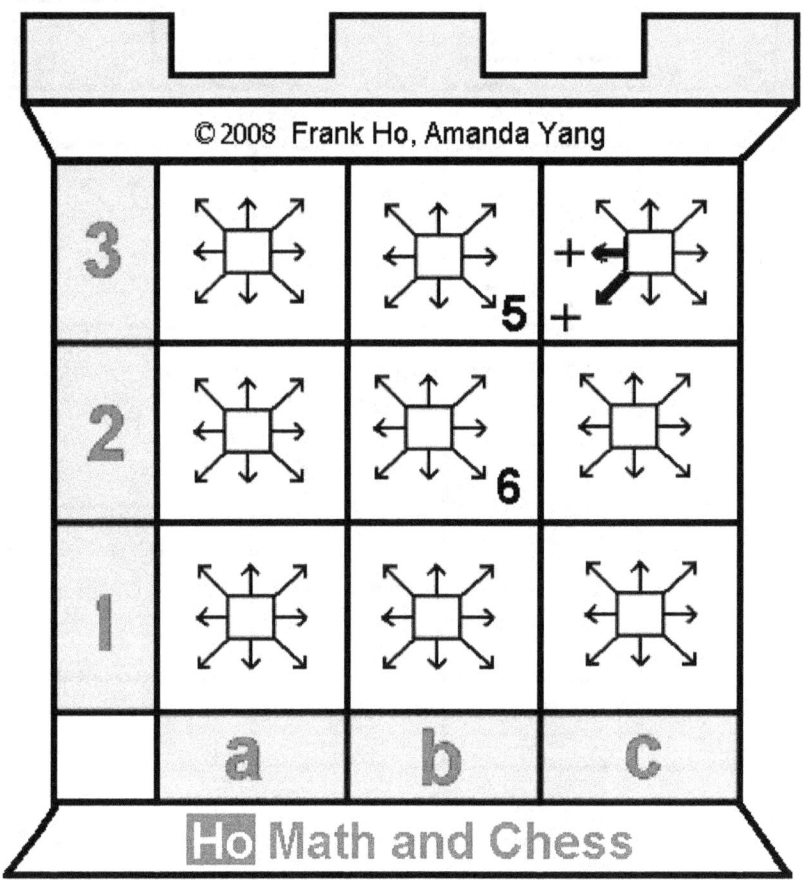

123
231
312

Math Chess Sudoku Puzzles 一青少年益智棋芸健脑

Frankho ChessDoku 一 何数棋谜算独

© 2007 — 2020 Frank Ho, Amanda Ho   All rights reserved.   www.homathchess.com

Student's name_____Date_____

Frankho ChessDoku™ # 28

Frankho ChessDoku™ is solved by using addition, subtraction, multiplication, or division by following chess moves and logic.

Rule All the digits 1 to 3 must appear exactly once in every row and column. The number appears in the bottom right-hand corner is the result calculated according to the arithmetic operator(s) and chess move(s) as indicated by the darker arrow(s).

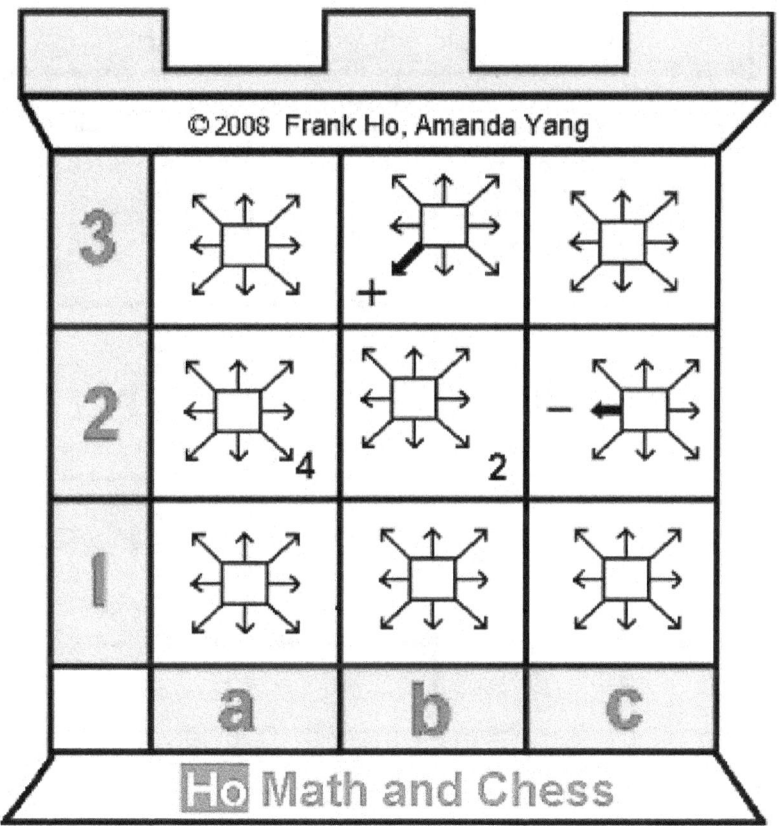

321
213
132

Frankho ChessDoku™ # 29

Frankho ChessDoku™ is solved by using addition, subtraction, multiplication, or division by following chess moves and logic.

Rule: All the digits 1 to 3 must appear exactly once in every row and column. The number appears in the bottom right-hand corner is the result calculated according to the arithmetic operator(s) and chess move(s) as indicated by the darker arrow(s).

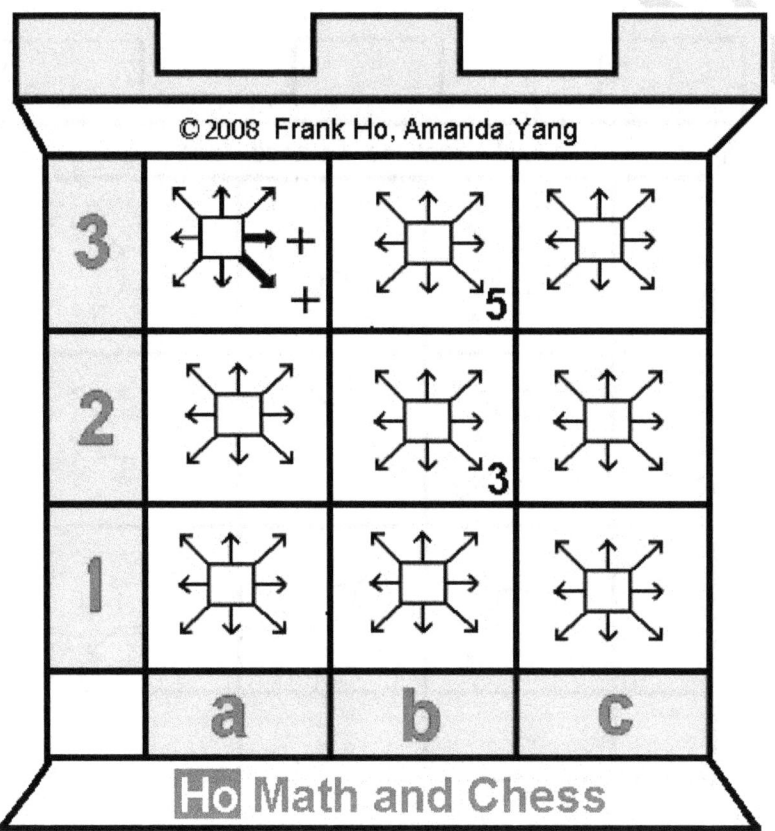

231
312
123

Frankho ChessDoku™ # 30

Frankho ChessDoku™ is solved by using addition, subtraction, multiplication, or division by following chess moves and logic.

Rule: All the digits 1 to 3 must appear exactly once in every row and column. The number appears in the bottom right-hand corner is the result calculated according to the arithmetic operator(s) and chess move(s) as indicated by the darker arrow(s).

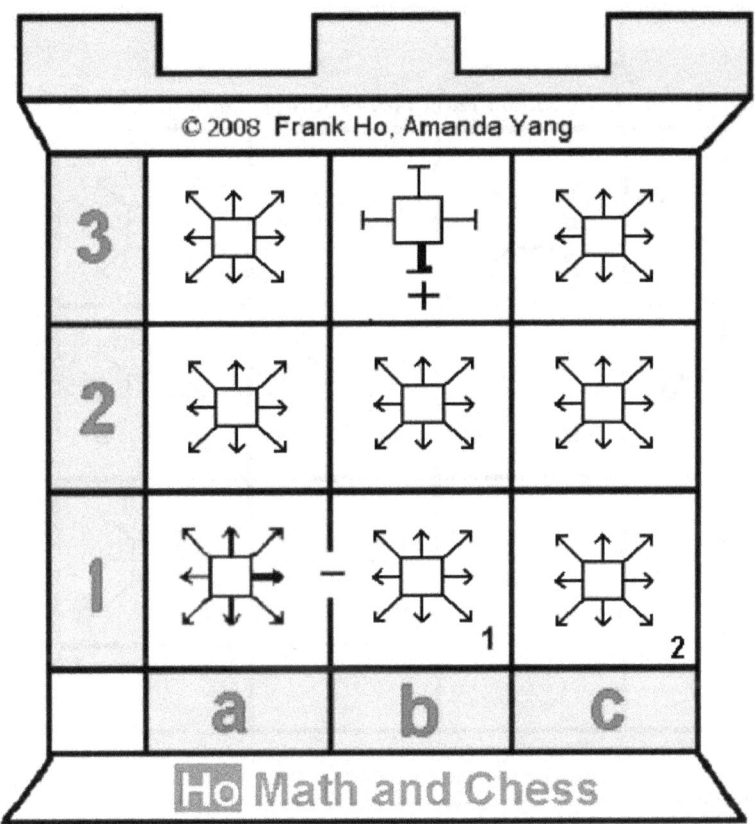

213
132
321

Frankho ChessDoku™ # 31

Frankho ChessDoku™ is solved by using addition, subtraction, multiplication, or division by following chess moves and logic.

Rule: All the digits 1 to 3 must appear exactly once in every row and column. The number appears in the bottom right-hand corner is the result calculated according to the arithmetic operator(s) and chess move(s) as indicated by the darker arrow(s).

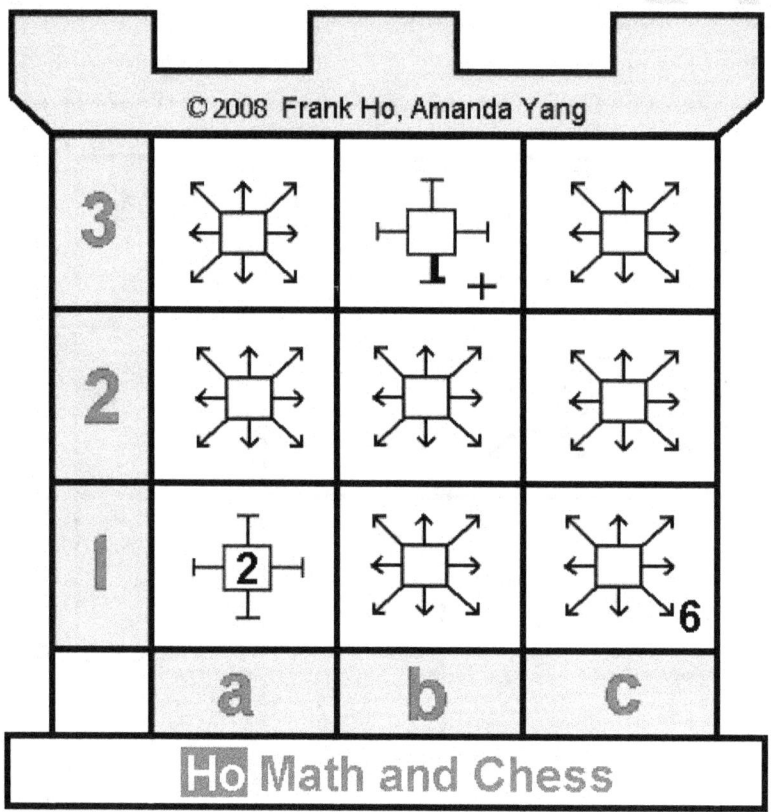

1323
321
213

Frankho ChessDoku™ # 32

Rule: All the digits 1 to 3 must appear exactly once in every row and column. The number appears in the bottom right-hand corner is the result calculated according to the arithmetic operator(s) and chess move(s) as indicated by the darker arrow(s).

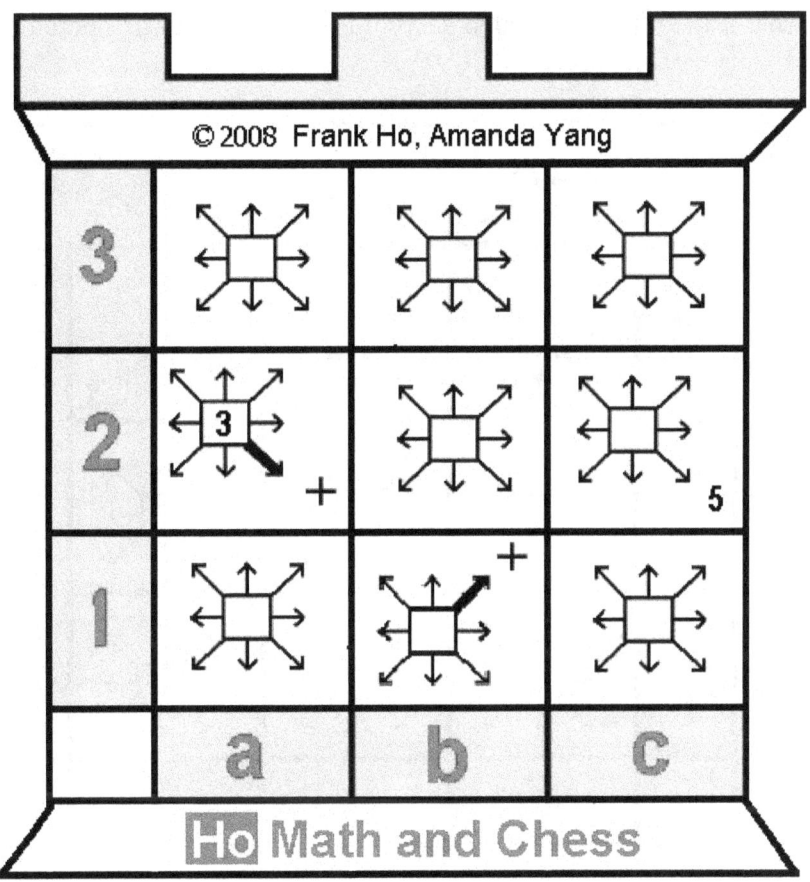

132
321
213

Frankho ChessDoku™ # 33

Frankho ChessDoku™ is solved by using addition, subtraction, multiplication, or division by following chess moves and logic.

Rule: All the digits 1 to 3 must appear exactly once in every row and column. The number appears in the bottom right-hand corner is the result calculated according to the arithmetic operator(s) and chess move(s) as indicated by the darker arrow(s).

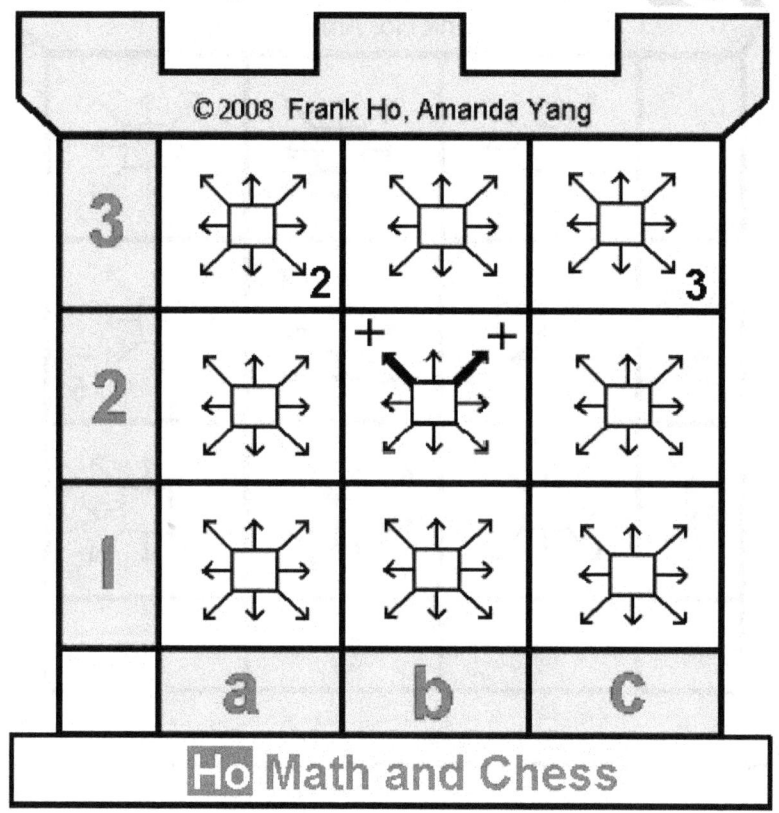

132
213
321

Math Chess Sudoku Puzzles 一青少年益智棋芸健脑

Frankho ChessDoku 一 何数棋谜算独

© 2007 — 2020   Frank Ho, Amanda Ho   All rights reserved.   www.homathchess.com

Student's name _____ Date _____

Frankho ChessDoku™ # 34

Frankho ChessDoku™ is solved by using addition, subtraction, multiplication, or division by following chess moves and logic.

Rule: All the digits 1 to 3 must appear exactly once in every row and column. The number appears in the bottom right-hand corner is the result calculated according to the arithmetic operator(s) and chess move(s) as indicated by the darker arrow(s).

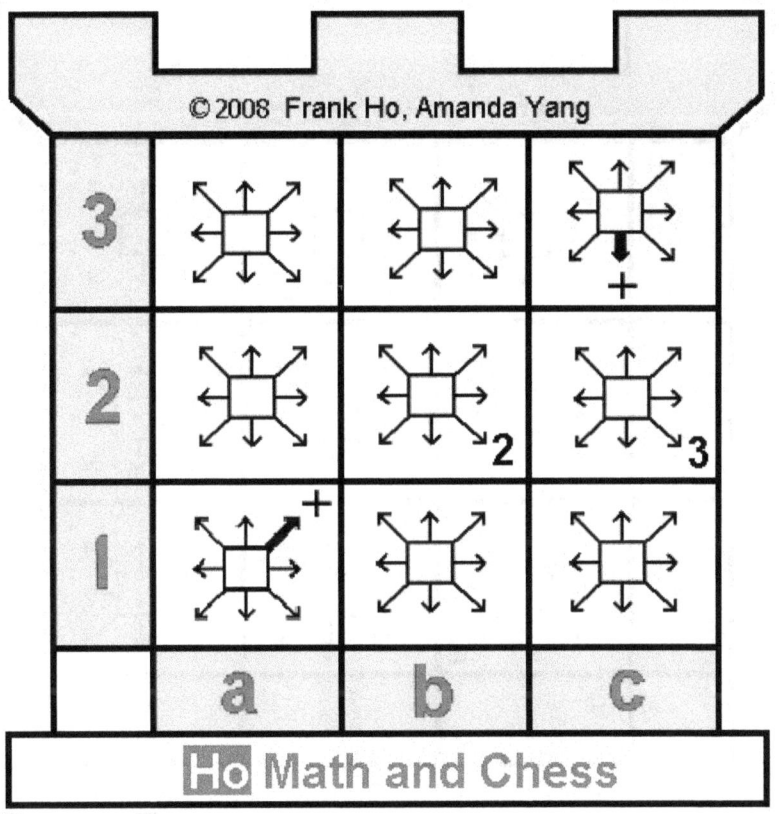

231
312
123

Frankho ChessDoku™ # 35

Frankho ChessDoku™ is solved by using addition, subtraction, multiplication, or division by following chess moves and logic.

Rule: All the digits 1 to 3 must appear exactly once in every row and column. The number appears in the bottom right-hand corner is the result calculated according to the arithmetic operator(s) and chess move(s) as indicated by the darker arrow(s).

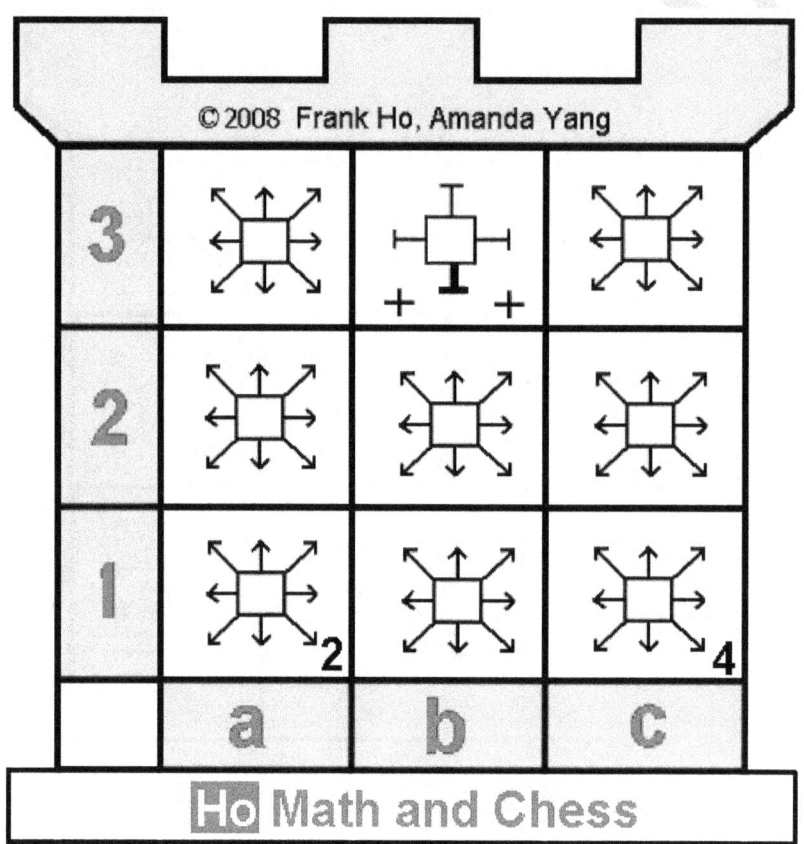

312
231
123

Frankho ChessDoku™ # 36

Frankho ChessDoku™ is solved by using addition, subtraction, multiplication, or division by following chess moves and logic.

Rule: All the digits 1 to 3 must appear exactly once in every row and column. The number appears in the bottom right-hand corner is the result calculated according to the arithmetic operator(s) and chess move(s) as indicated by the darker arrow(s).

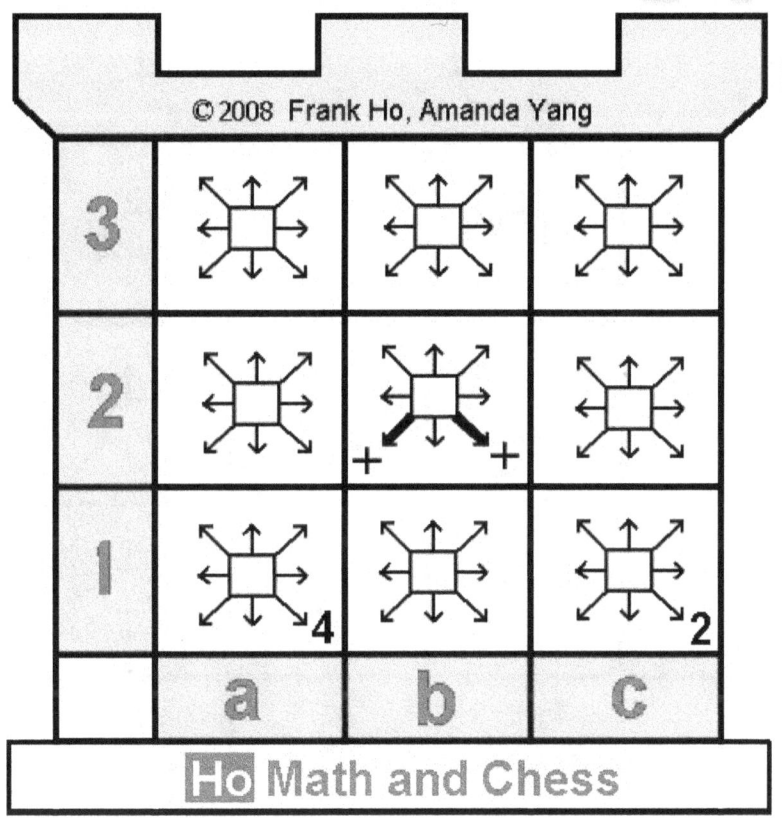

132
213
321

Frankho ChessDoku™ # 37

Frankho ChessDoku™ is solved by using addition, subtraction, multiplication, or division by following chess moves and logic.

Rule: All the digits 1 to 3 must appear exactly once in every row and column. The number appears in the bottom right-hand corner is the result calculated according to the arithmetic operator(s) and chess move(s) as indicated by the darker arrow(s).

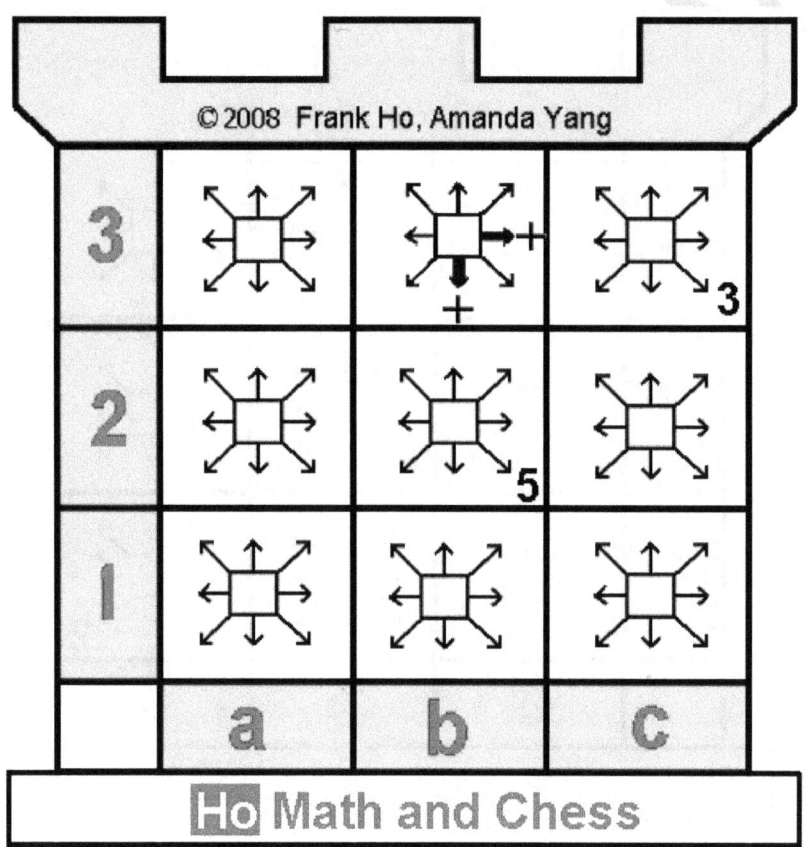

321
132
213

Frankho ChessDoku™ # 38

Frankho ChessDoku™ is solved by using addition, subtraction, multiplication, or division by following chess moves and logic.

Rule: All the digits 1 to 3 must appear exactly once in every row and column. The number appears in the bottom right-hand corner is the result calculated according to the arithmetic operator(s) and chess move(s) as indicated by the darker arrow(s).

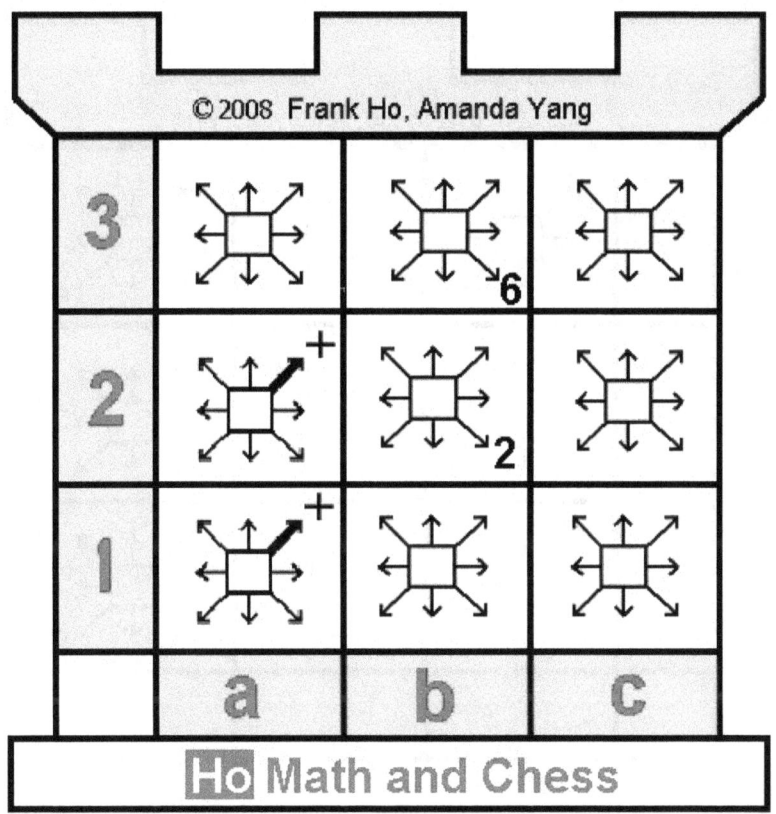

231
312
123

Frankho ChessDoku™ # 39

Frankho ChessDoku™ is solved by using addition, subtraction, multiplication, or division by following chess moves and logic.

Rule: All the digits 1 to 3 must appear exactly once in every row and column. The number appears in the bottom right-hand corner is the result calculated according to the arithmetic operator(s) and chess move(s) as indicated by the darker arrow(s).

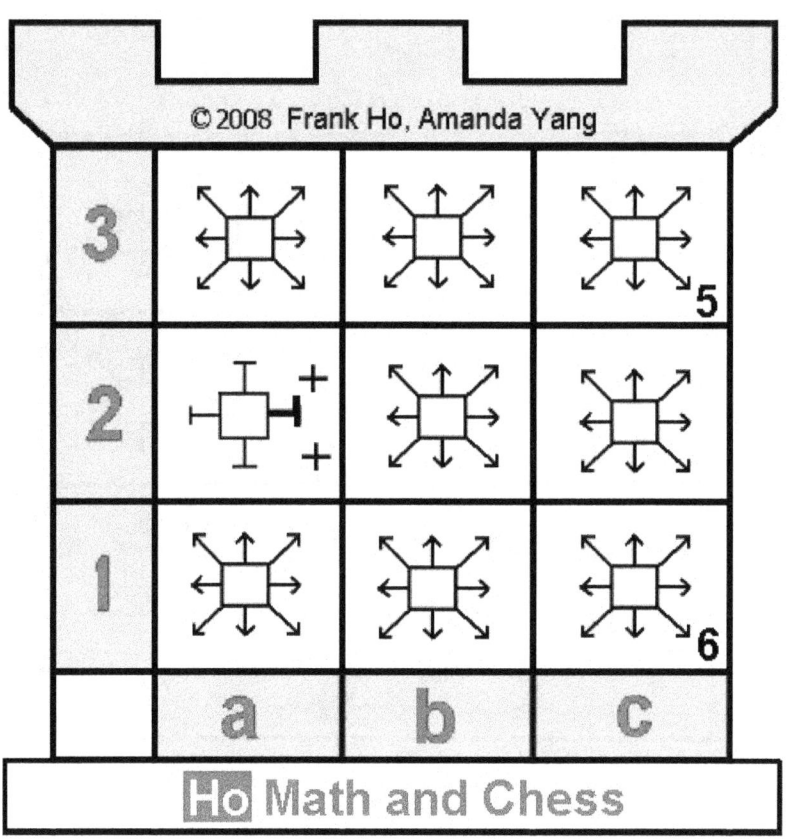

132
321
213

Frankho ChessDoku™ # 40

Frankho ChessDoku™ is solved by using addition, subtraction, multiplication, or division by following chess moves and logic.

Rule: All the digits 1 to 3 must appear exactly once in every row and column. The number appears in the bottom right-hand corner is the result calculated according to the arithmetic operator(s) and chess move(s) as indicated by the darker arrow(s).

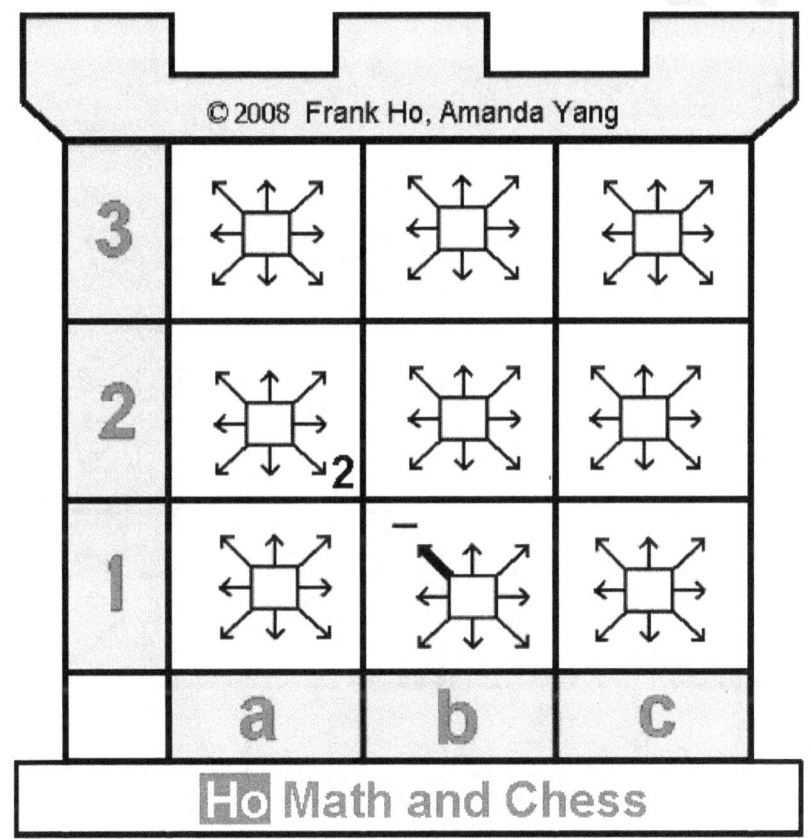

312
123
231

Frankho ChessDoku™ # 41

Frankho ChessDoku™ is solved by using addition, subtraction, multiplication, or division by following chess moves and logic.

Rule: All the digits 1 to 3 must appear exactly once in every row and column. The number appears in the bottom right-hand corner is the result calculated according to the arithmetic operator(s) and chess move(s) as indicated by the darker arrow(s).

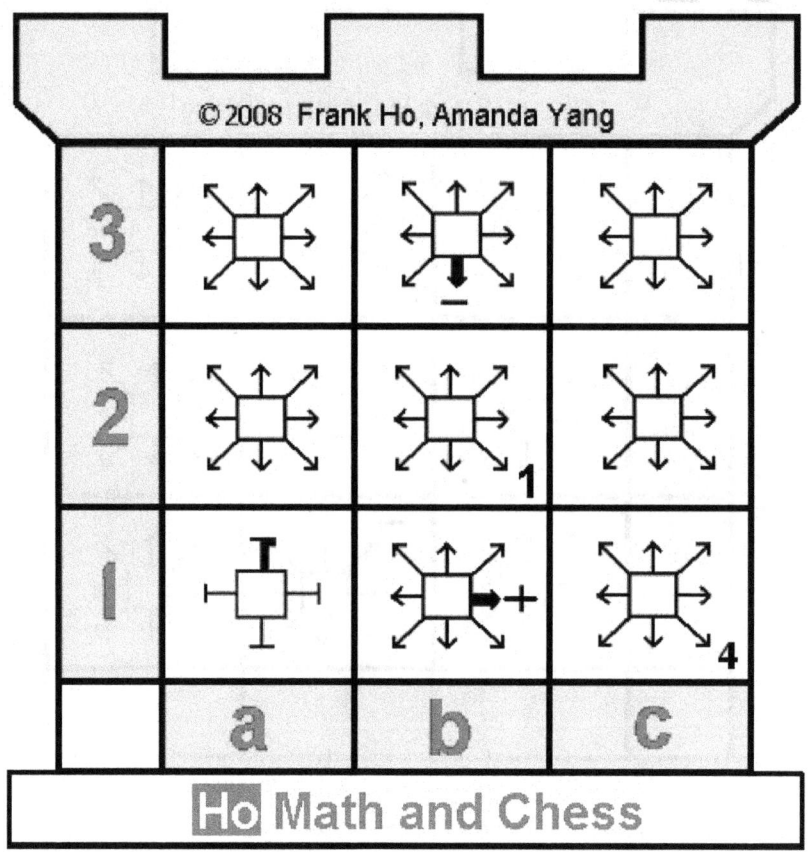

123
312
231

Frankho ChessDoku™ # 42

Frankho ChessDoku™ is solved by using addition, subtraction, multiplication, or division by following chess moves and logic.

Rule: All the digits 1 to 3 must appear exactly once in every row and column. The number appears in the bottom right-hand corner is the result calculated according to the arithmetic operator(s) and chess move(s) as indicated by the darker arrow(s).

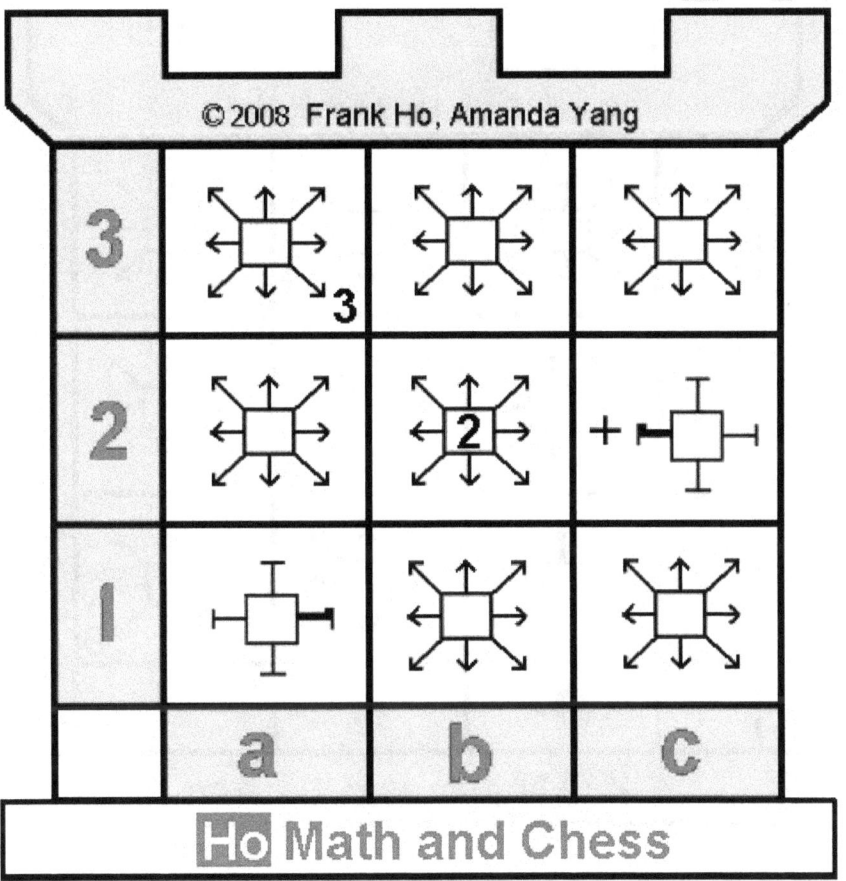

213
321
132

Frankho ChessDoku™ # 43

Frankho ChessDoku™ is solved by using addition, subtraction, multiplication, or division by following chess moves and logic.

Rule: All the digits 1 to 3 must appear exactly once in every row and column. The number appears in the bottom right-hand corner is the result calculated according to the arithmetic operator(s) and chess move(s) as indicated by the darker arrow(s).

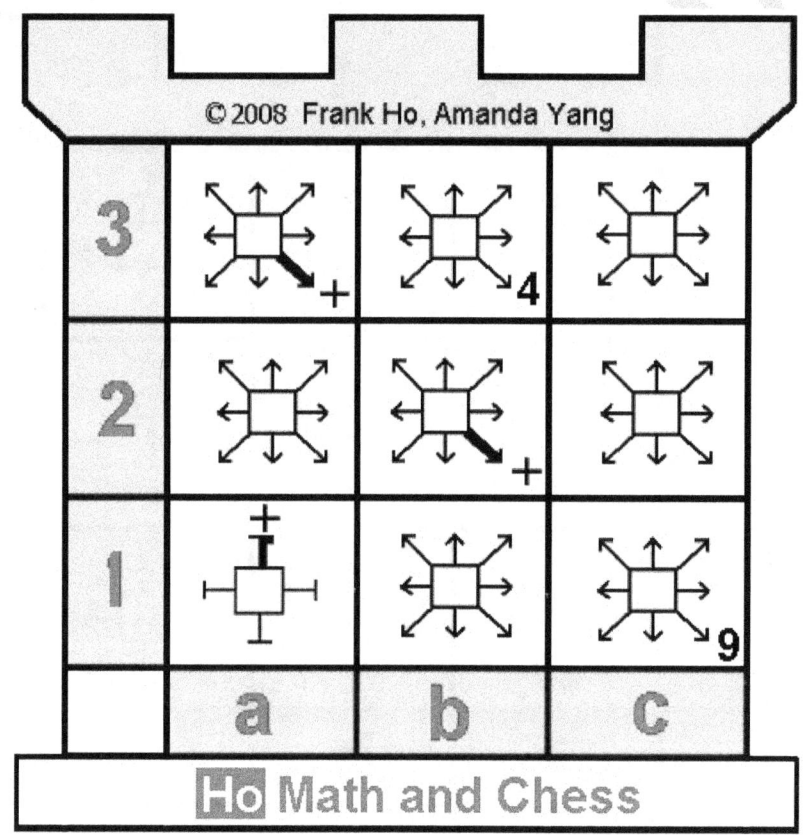

321
132
213

Frankho ChessDoku™ # 44

Frankho ChessDoku™ is solved by using addition, subtraction, multiplication, or division by following chess moves and logic.

Rule: All the digits 1 to 3 must appear exactly once in every row and column. The number appears in the bottom right-hand corner is the result calculated according to the arithmetic operator(s) and chess move(s) as indicated by the darker arrow(s).

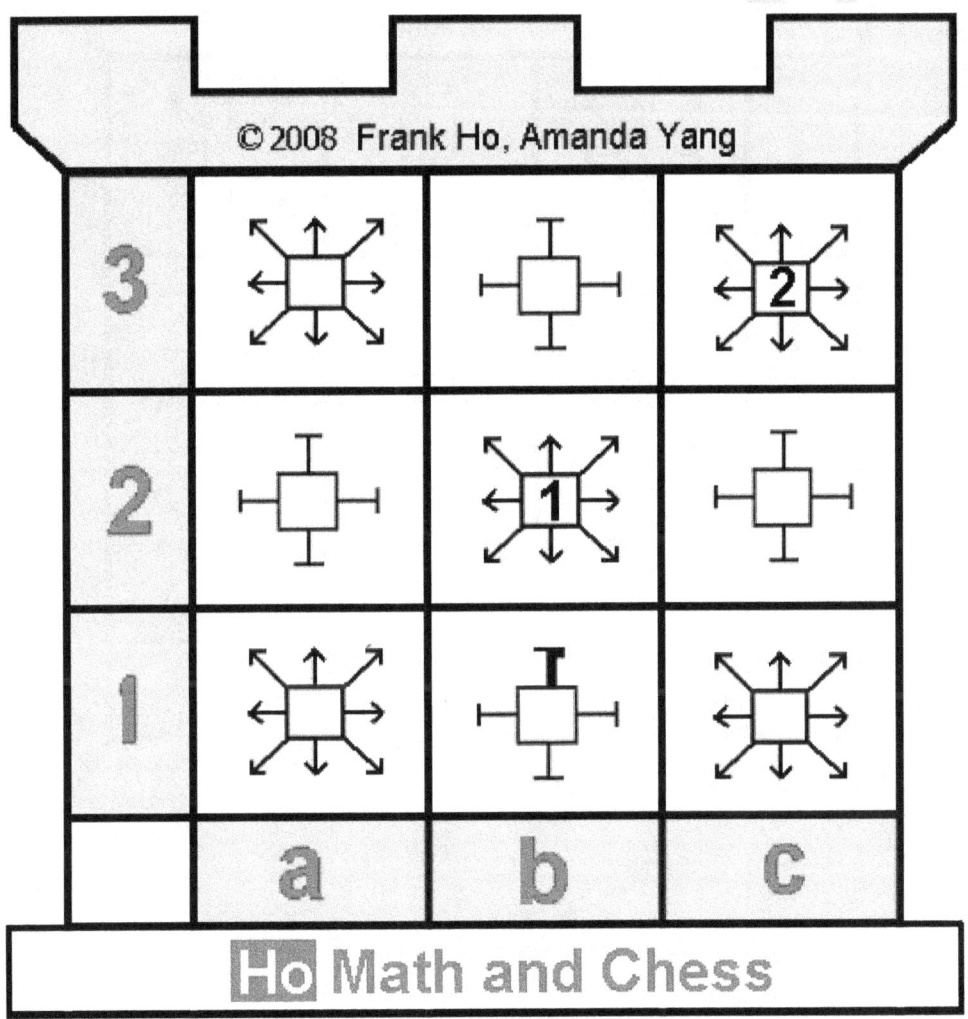

132
213
321

Frankho ChessDoku™ # 45

Rule: All the digits 1 to 3 must appear exactly once in every row and column. The number appears in the bottom right-hand corner is the result calculated according to the arithmetic operator(s) and chess move(s) as indicated by the darker arrow(s).

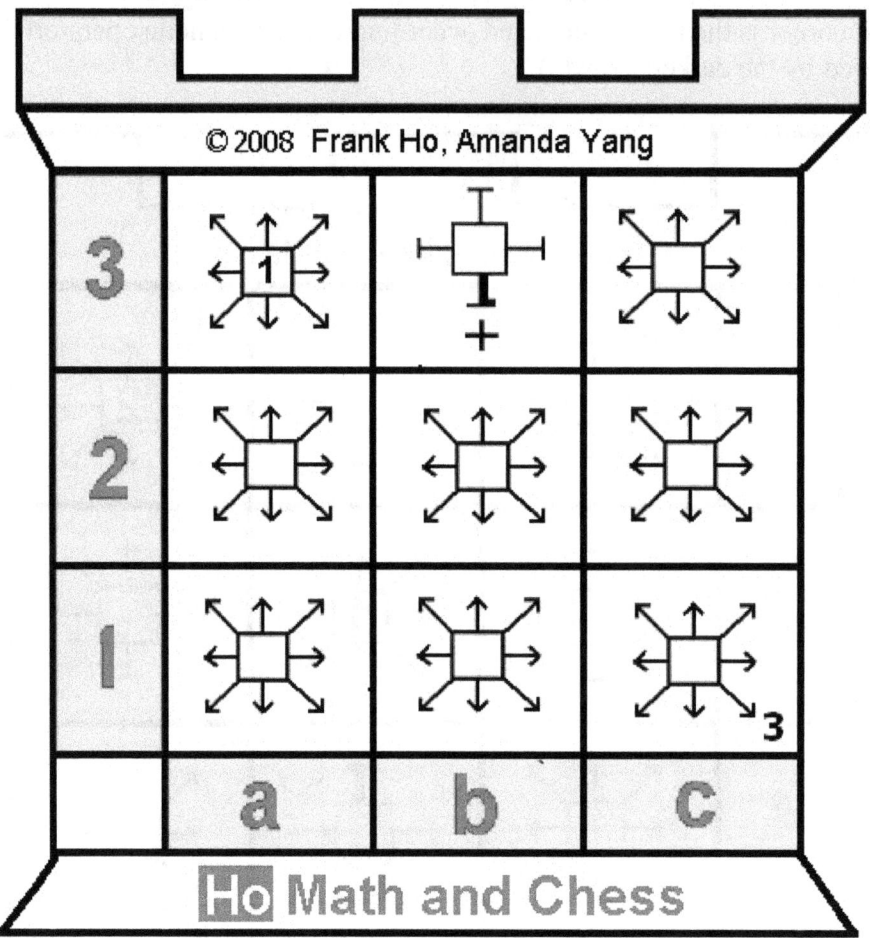

123
312
231

Frankho ChessDoku™ # 46

Frankho ChessDoku™ is solved by using addition, subtraction, multiplication, or division by following chess moves and logic.

Rule: All the digits 1 to 3 must appear exactly once in every row and column. The number appears in the bottom right-hand corner is the result calculated according to the arithmetic operator(s) and chess move(s) as indicated by the darker arrow(s).

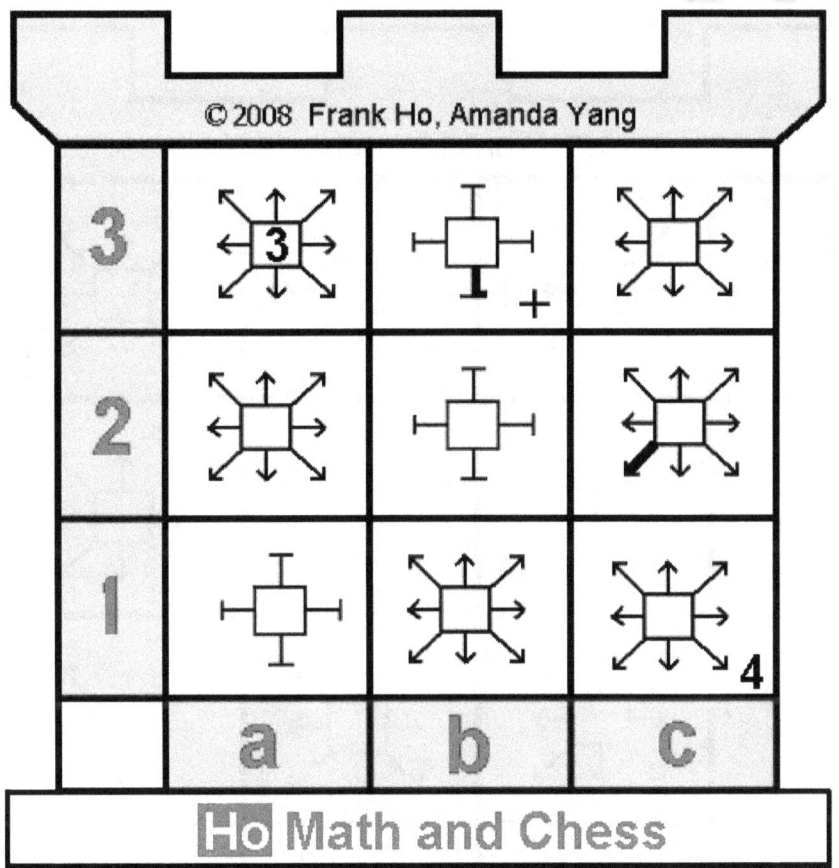

321
213
132

Frankho ChessDoku™ # 47

Frankho ChessDoku™ is solved by using addition, subtraction, multiplication, or division by following chess moves and logic.

Rule: All the digits 1 to 3 must appear exactly once in every row and column. The number appears in the bottom right-hand corner is the result calculated according to the arithmetic operator(s) and chess move(s) as indicated by the darker arrow(s).

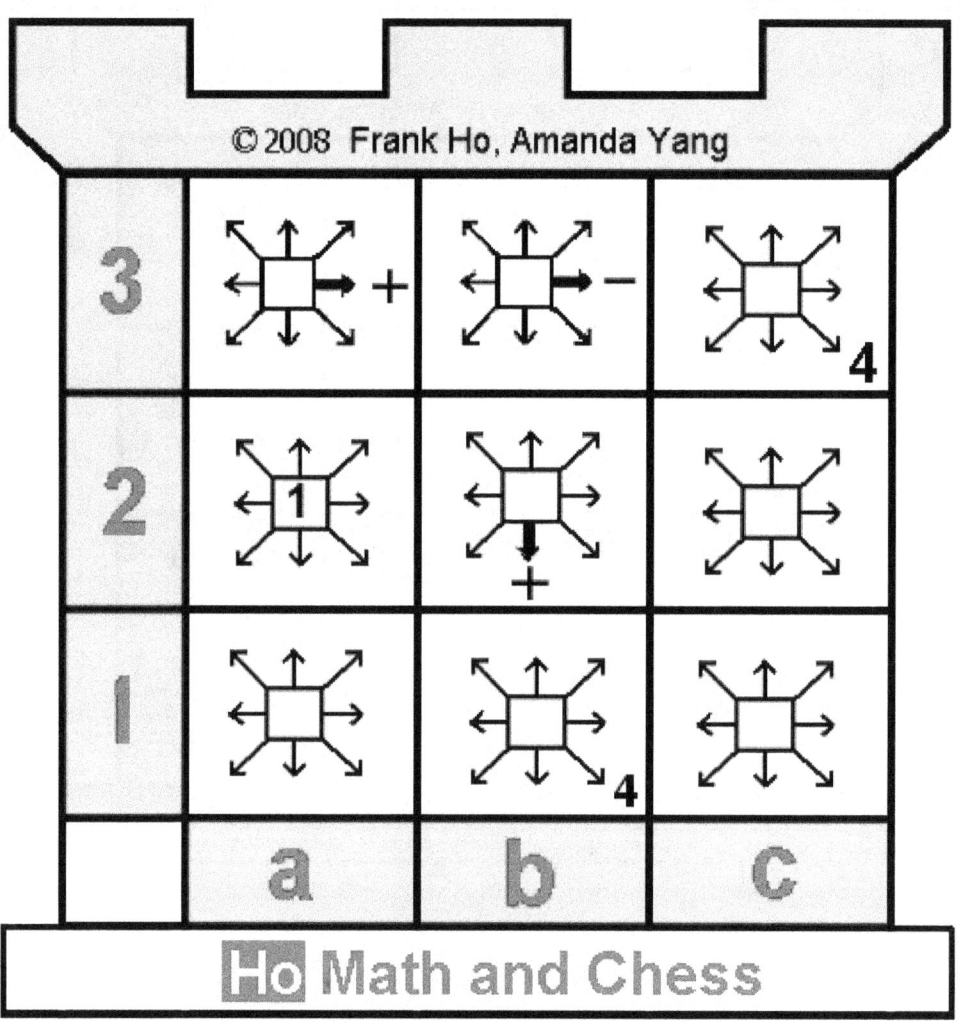

321
132
213

Math Chess Sudoku Puzzles 一青少年益智棋芸健脑

Frankho ChessDoku 一 何数棋谜算独

© 2007 — 2020   Frank Ho, Amanda Ho   All rights reserved.   www.homathchess.com

Student's name _____   Date _____

Frankho ChessDoku™ # 48

Frankho ChessDoku™ is solved by using addition, subtraction, multiplication, or division by following chess moves and logic.

Rule: All the digits 1 to 3 must appear exactly once in every row and column. The number appears in the bottom right-hand corner is the result calculated according to the arithmetic operator(s) and chess move(s) as indicated by the darker arrow(s).

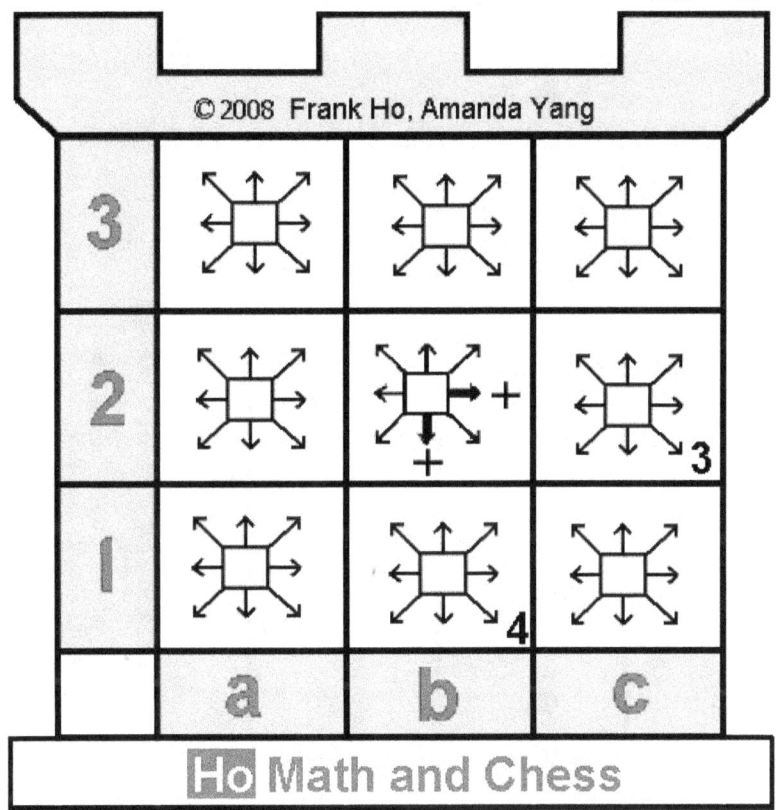

123
312
231

Frankho ChessDoku™ # 49

Frankho ChessDoku™ is solved by using addition, subtraction, multiplication, or division by following chess moves and logic.

Rule: All the digits 1 to 3 must appear exactly once in every row and column. The number appears in the bottom right-hand corner is the result calculated according to the arithmetic operator(s) and chess move(s) as indicated by the darker arrow(s).

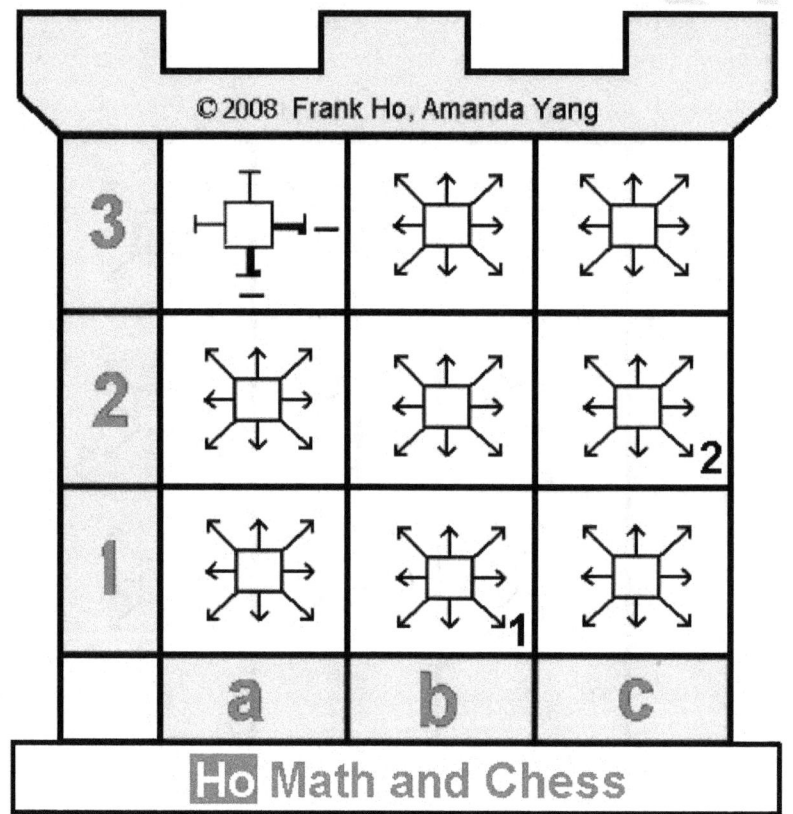

312
231
123

Frankho ChessDoku™ # 50

Frankho ChessDoku™ is solved by using addition, subtraction, multiplication, or division by following chess moves and logic.

Rule: All the digits 1 to 3 must appear exactly once in every row and column. The number appears in the bottom right-hand corner is the result calculated according to the arithmetic operator(s) and chess move(s) as indicated by the darker arrow(s).

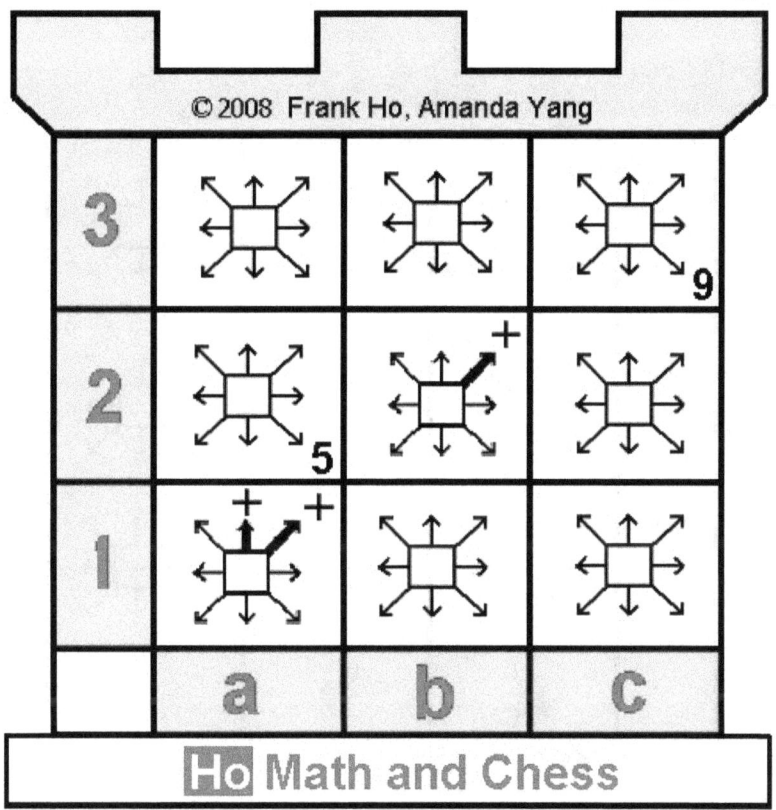

123
231
312

Frankho ChessDoku™ # 51

Frankho ChessDoku™ is solved by using addition, subtraction, multiplication, or division by following chess moves and logic.

Rule: All the digits 1 to 3 must appear exactly once in every row and column. The number appears in the bottom right-hand corner is the result calculated according to the arithmetic operator(s) and chess move(s) as indicated by the darker arrow(s).

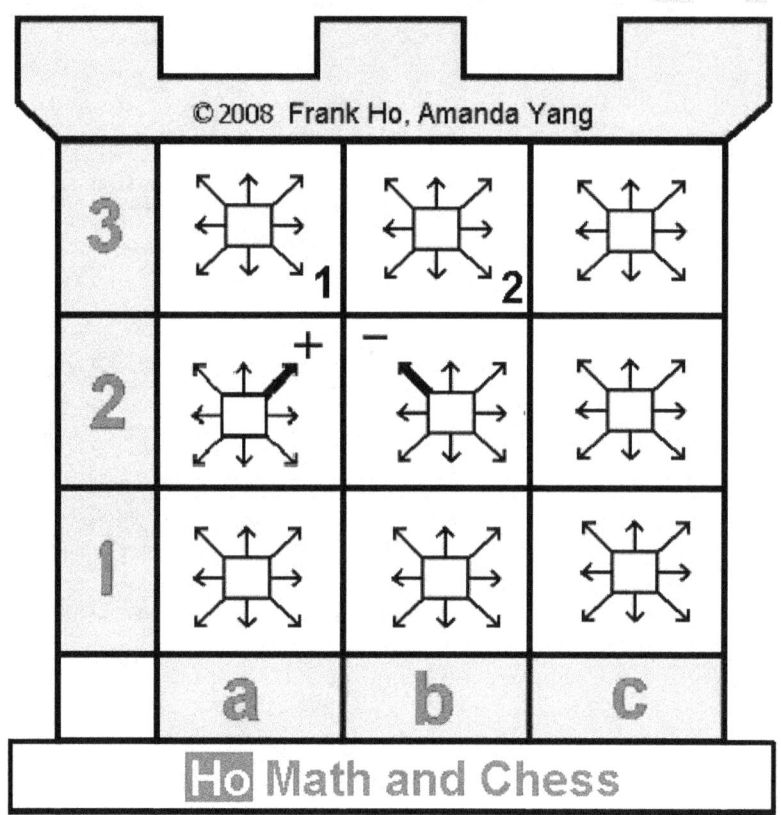

213
132
321

Frankho ChessDoku™ # 52

Frankho ChessDoku™ is solved by using addition, subtraction, multiplication, or division by following chess moves and logic.

Rule: All the digits 1 to 3 must appear exactly once in every row and column. The number appears in the bottom right-hand corner is the result calculated according to the arithmetic operator(s) and chess move(s) as indicated by the darker arrow(s).

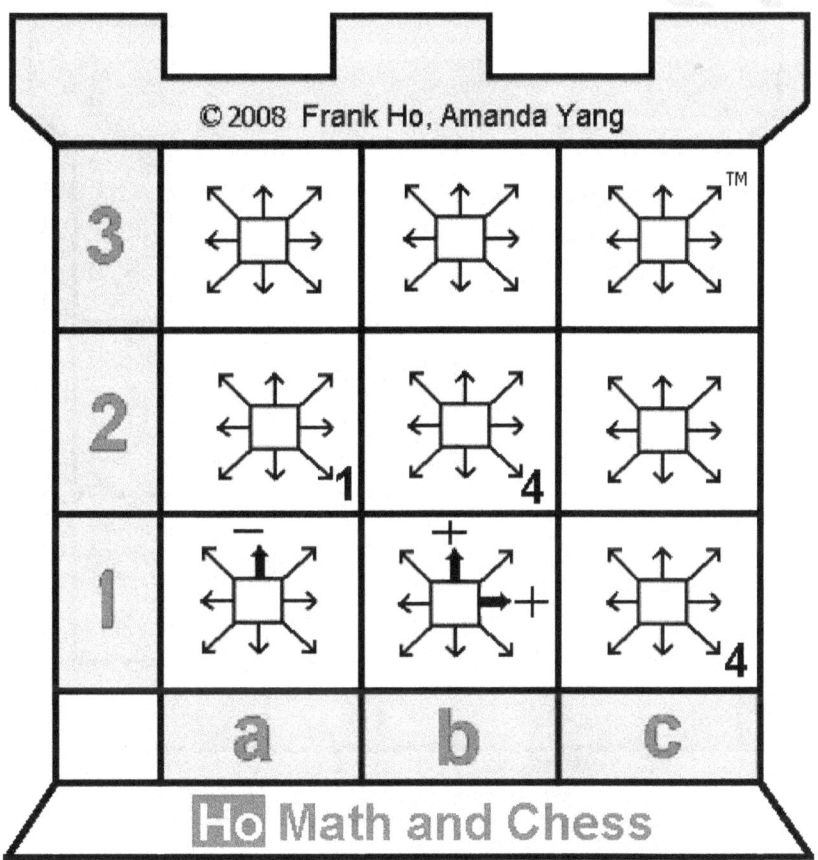

321
132
213

Frankho ChessDoku™ # 53

Frankho ChessDoku™ is solved by using addition, subtraction, multiplication, or division by following chess moves and logic.

Rule: All the digits 1 to 3 must appear exactly once in every row and column. The number appears in the bottom right-hand corner is the result calculated according to the arithmetic operator(s) and chess move(s) as indicated by the darker arrow(s).

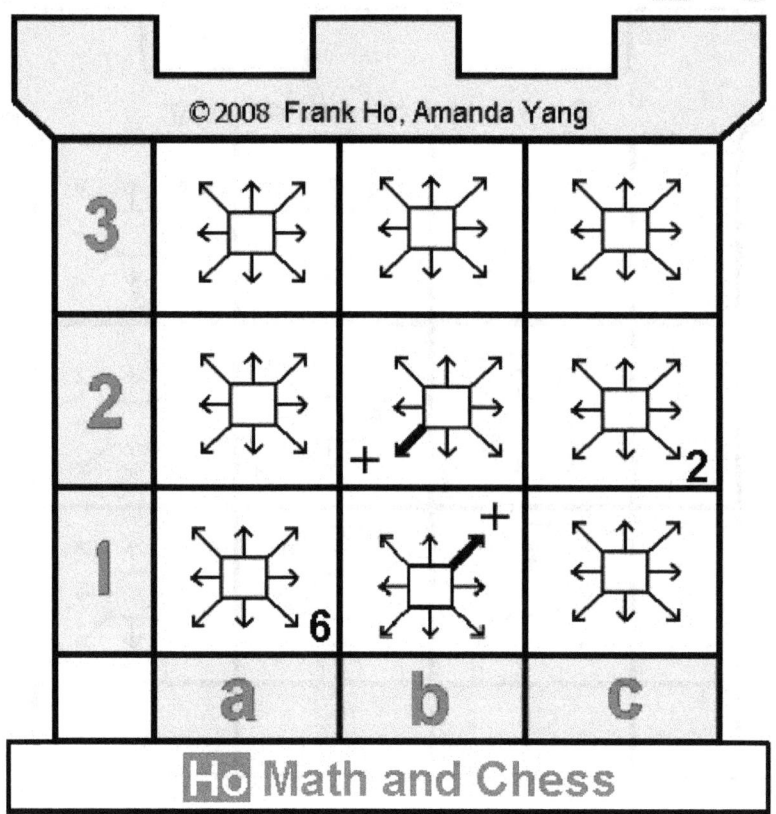

123
231
312

Frankho ChessDoku™ # 54

Frankho ChessDoku™ is solved by using addition, subtraction, multiplication, or division by following chess moves and logic.

Rule: All the digits 1 to 3 must appear exactly once in every row and column. The number appears in the bottom right-hand corner is the result calculated according to the arithmetic operator(s) and chess move(s) as indicated by the darker arrow(s).

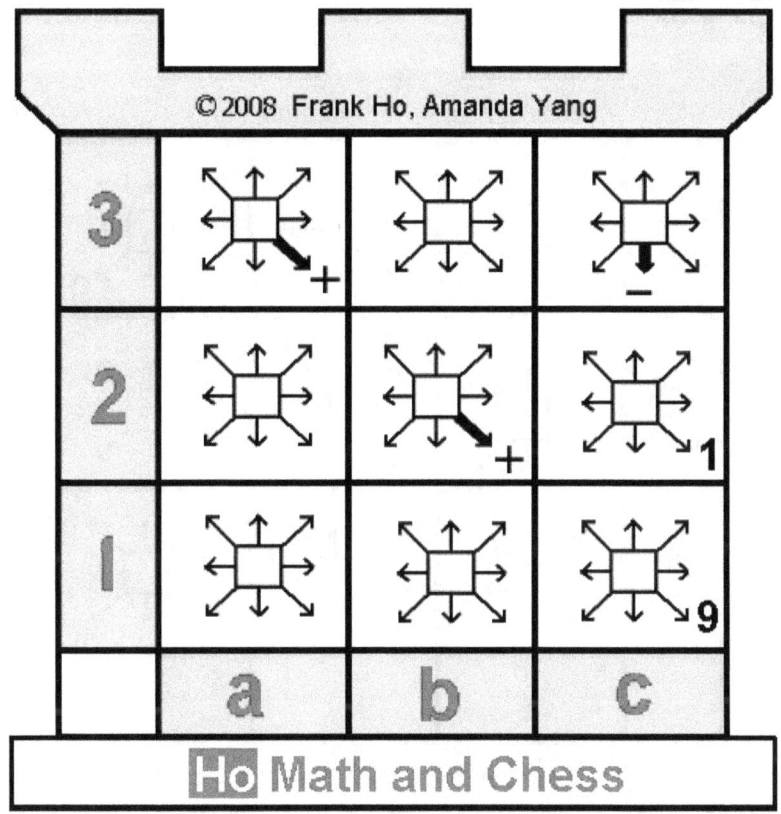

312
231
123

Frankho ChessDoku™ # 55

Frankho ChessDoku™ is solved by using addition, subtraction, multiplication, or division by following chess moves and logic.

Rule: All the digits 1 to 3 must appear exactly once in every row and column. The number appears in the bottom right-hand corner is the result calculated according to the arithmetic operator(s) and chess move(s) as indicated by the darker arrow(s).

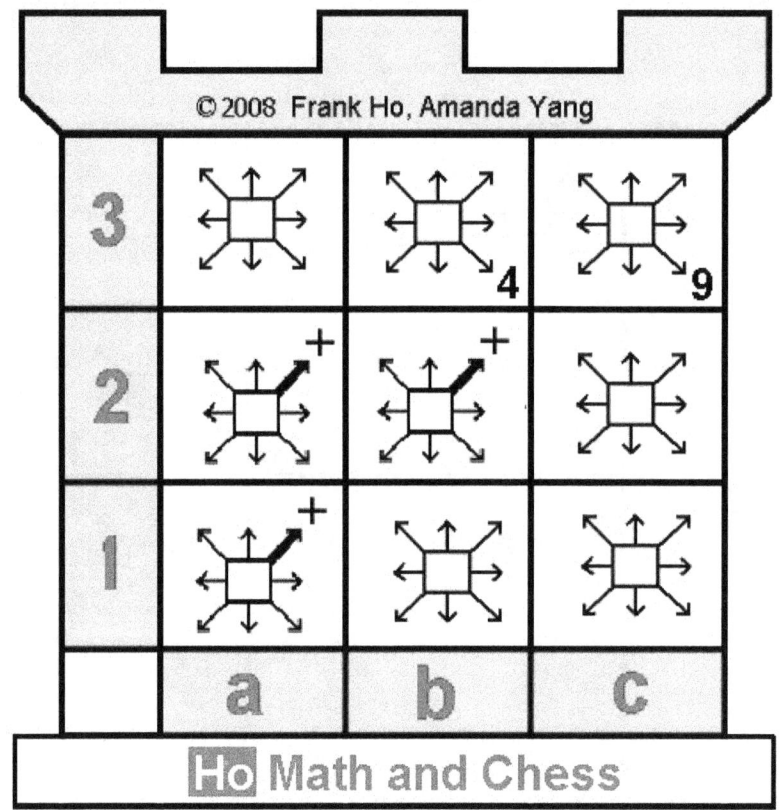

123
231
312

Frankho ChessDoku™ # 56

Frankho ChessDoku™ is solved by using addition, subtraction, multiplication, or division by following chess moves and logic.

Rule: All the digits 1 to 3 must appear exactly once in every row and column. The number appears in the bottom right-hand corner is the result calculated according to the arithmetic operator(s) and chess move(s) as indicated by the darker arrow(s).

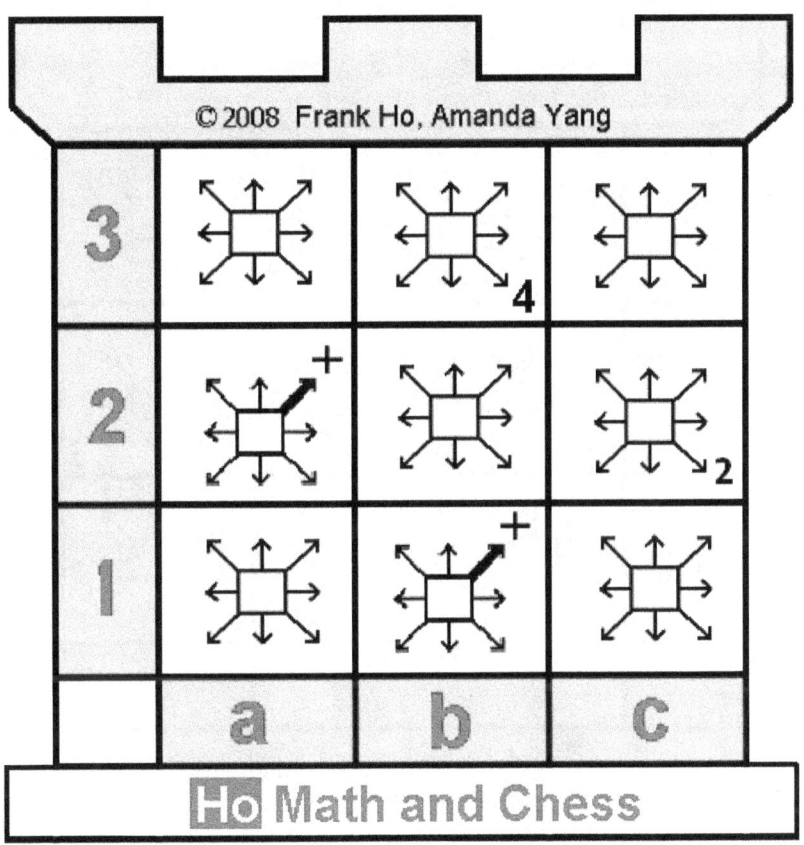

123
231
312

Frankho ChessDoku™ # 57

Frankho ChessDoku™ is solved by using addition, subtraction, multiplication, or division by following chess moves and logic.

Rule: All the digits 1 to 3 must appear exactly once in every row and column. The number appears in the bottom right-hand corner is the result calculated according to the arithmetic operator(s) and chess move(s) as indicated by the darker arrow(s).

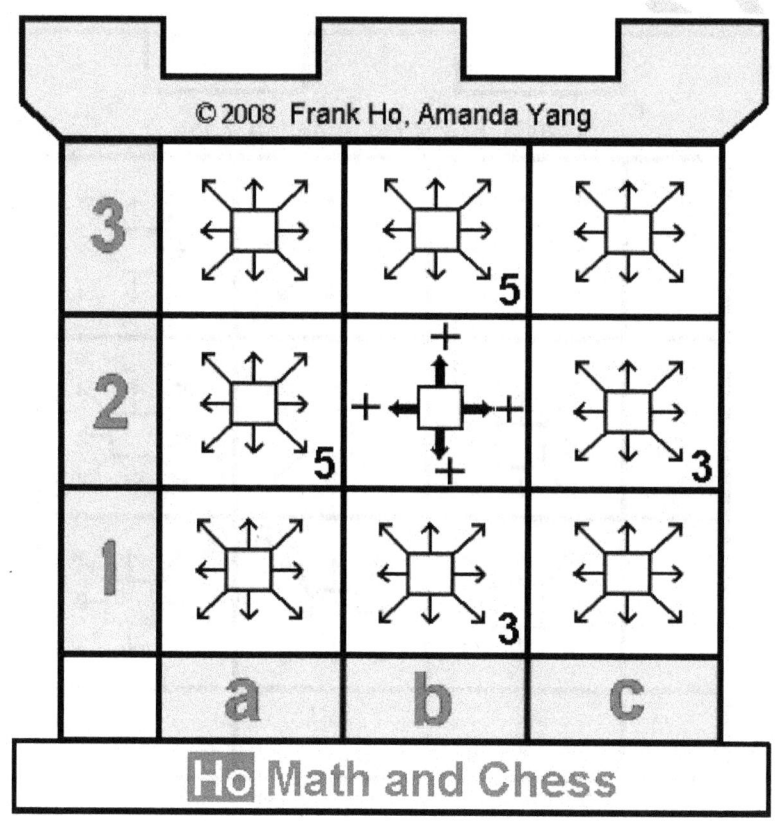

132
321
213

Frankho ChessDoku™ # 58

Frankho ChessDoku™ is solved by using addition, subtraction, multiplication, or division by following chess moves and logic.

Rule: All the digits 1 to 3 must appear exactly once in every row and column. The number appears in the bottom right-hand corner is the result calculated according to the arithmetic operator(s) and chess move(s) as indicated by the darker arrow(s).

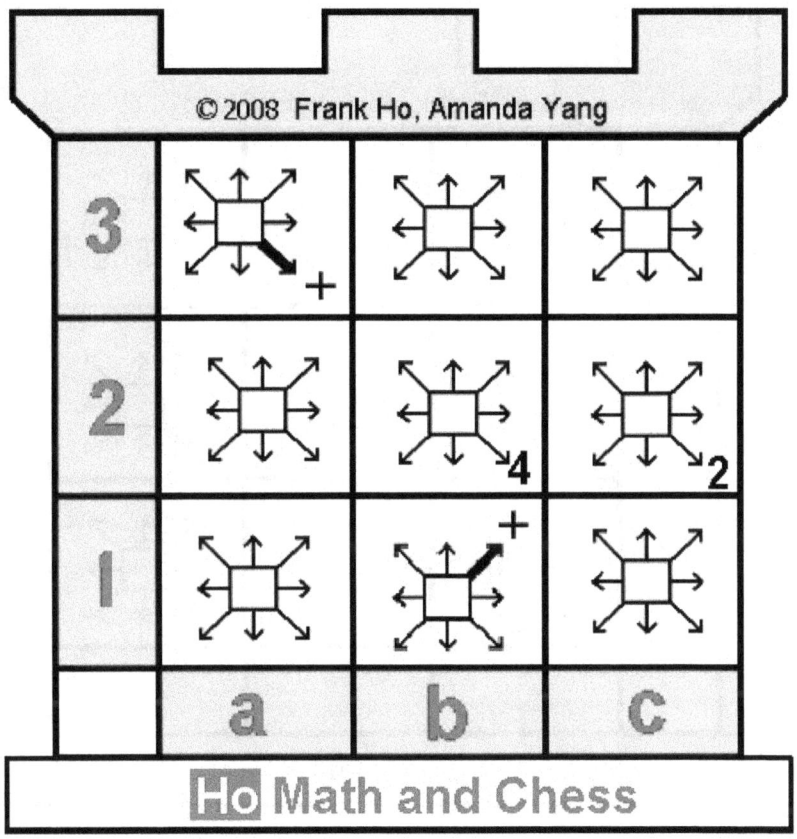

123
231
312

Frankho ChessDoku™ # 59

Frankho ChessDoku™ is solved by using addition, subtraction, multiplication, or division by following chess moves and logic.

Rule: All the digits 1 to 3 must appear exactly once in every row and column. The number appears in the bottom right-hand corner is the result calculated according to the arithmetic operator(s) and chess move(s) as indicated by the darker arrow(s).

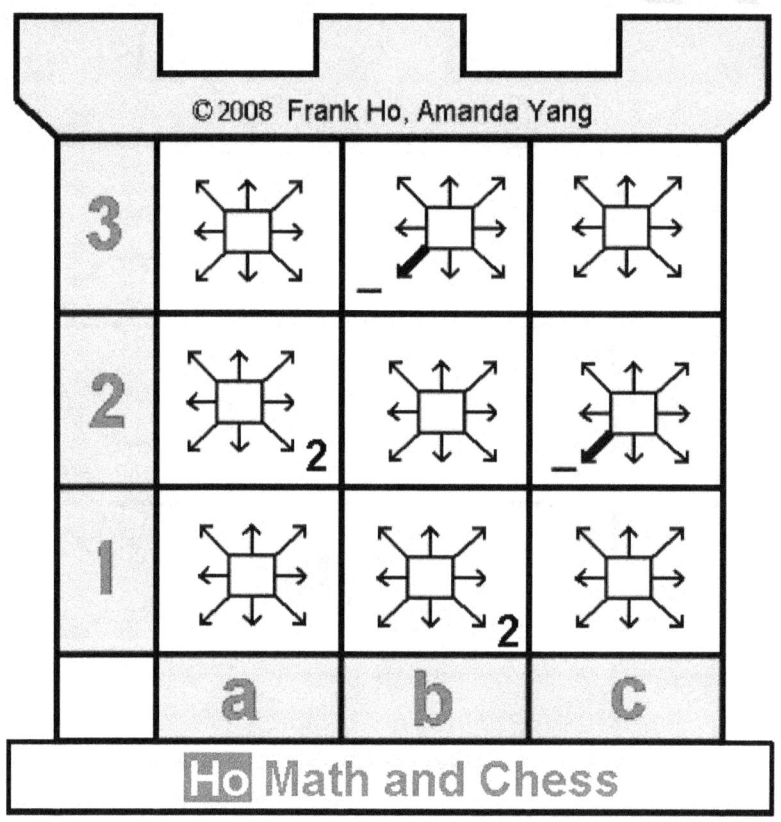

231   123   312

Math Chess Sudoku Puzzles 一青少年益智棋芸健脑

Frankho ChessDoku 一 何数棋谜算独

© 2007 — 2020 Frank Ho, Amanda Ho   All rights reserved.   www.homathchess.com

Student's name _____   Date _____

Frankho ChessDoku™ # 60

Frankho ChessDoku™ is solved by using addition, subtraction, multiplication, or division by following chess moves and logic.

Rule: All the digits 1 to 3 must appear exactly once in every row and column. The number appears in the bottom right-hand corner is the result calculated according to the arithmetic operator(s) and chess move(s) as indicated by the darker arrow(s).

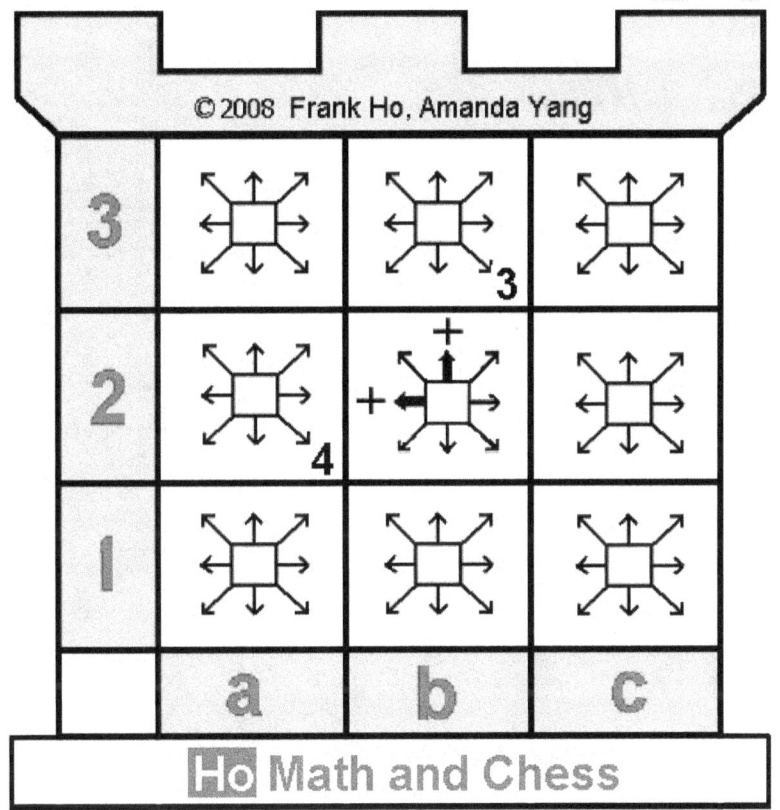

123
312
231

Frankho ChessDoku™ # 61

Frankho ChessDoku™ is solved by using addition, subtraction, multiplication, or division by following chess moves and logic.

Rule: All the digits 1 to 3 must appear exactly once in every row and column. The number appears in the bottom right-hand corner is the result calculated according to the arithmetic operator(s) and chess move(s) as indicated by the darker arrow(s).

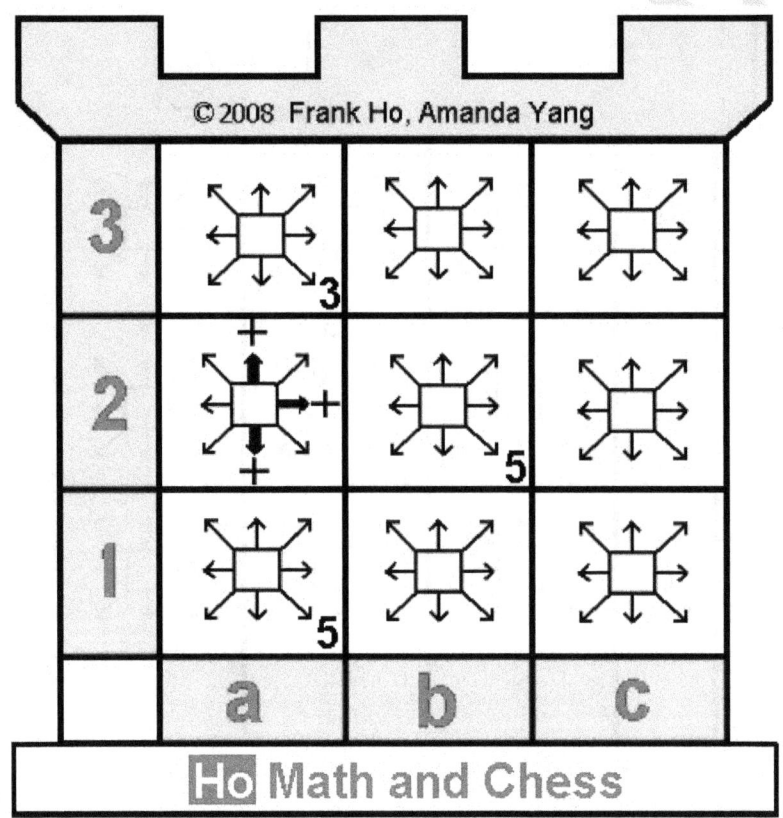

123
231
312

Frankho ChessDoku™ # 62

Frankho ChessDoku™ is solved by using addition, subtraction, multiplication, or division by following chess moves and logic.

Rule: All the digits 1 to 3 must appear exactly once in every row and column. The number appears in the bottom right-hand corner is the result calculated according to the arithmetic operator(s) and chess move(s) as indicated by the darker arrow(s).

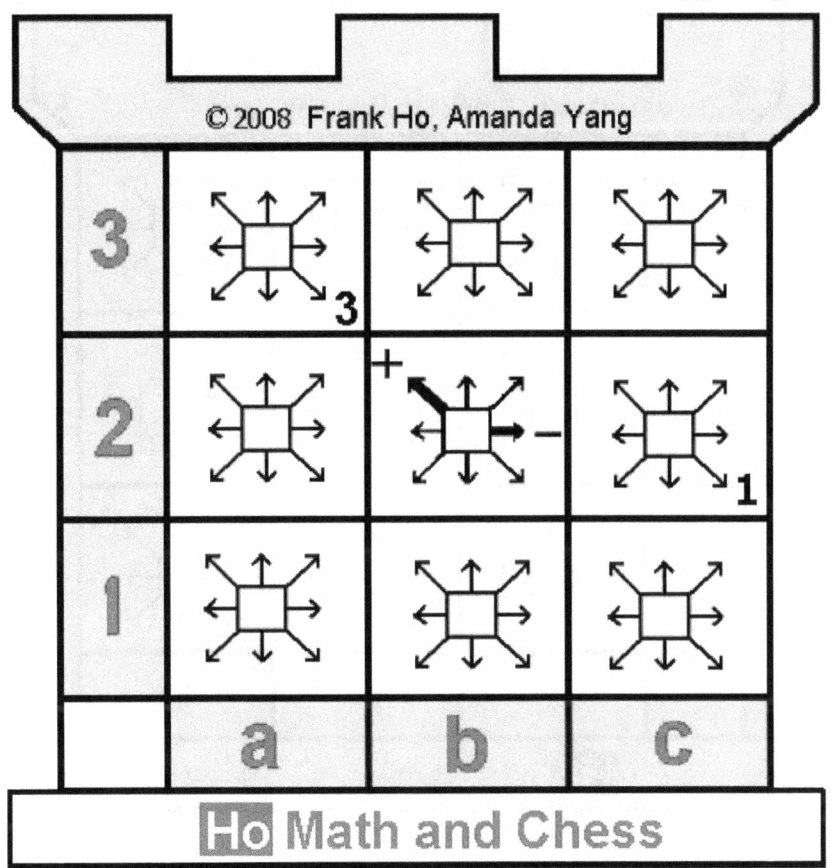

132
321
213

Frankho ChessDoku™ # 63

Frankho ChessDoku™ is solved by using addition, subtraction, multiplication, or division by following chess moves and logic.

Rule: All the digits 1 to 3 must appear exactly once in every row and column. The number appears in the bottom right-hand corner is the result calculated according to the arithmetic operator(s) and chess move(s) as indicated by the darker arrow(s).

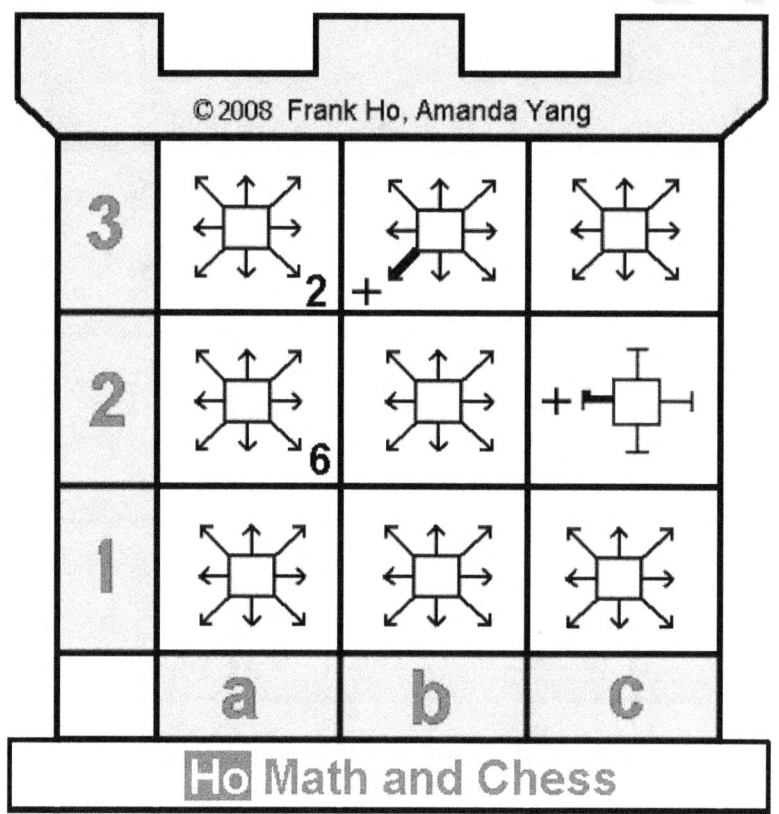

132
321
213

Frankho ChessDoku™ # 64

Frankho ChessDoku™ is solved by using addition, subtraction, multiplication, or division by following chess moves and logic.

Rule: All the digits 1 to 3 must appear exactly once in every row and column. The number appears in the bottom right-hand corner is the result calculated according to the arithmetic operator(s) and chess move(s) as indicated by the darker arrow(s).

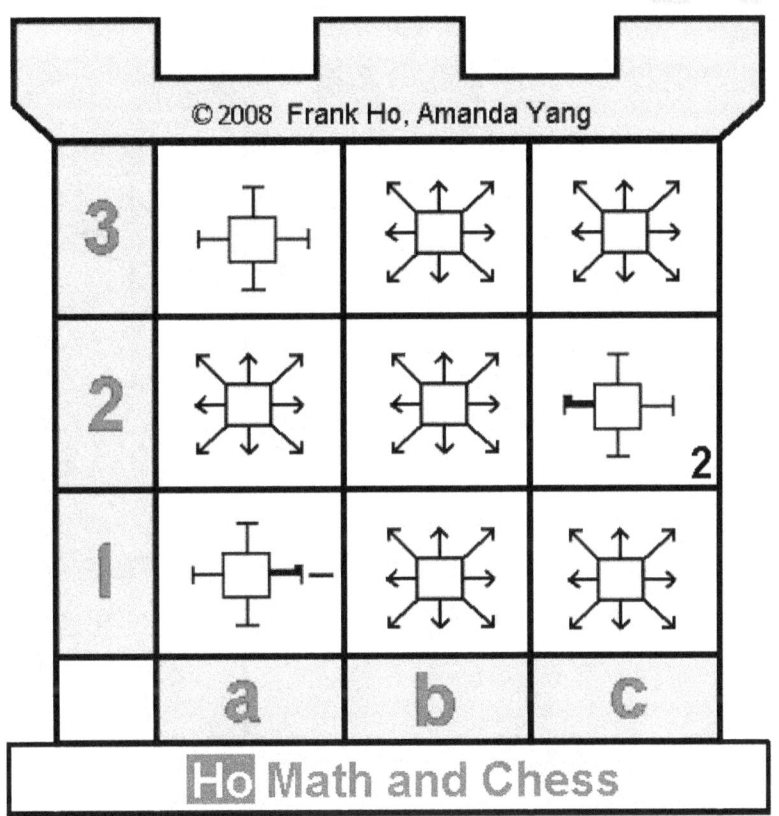

123
231
312

Frankho ChessDoku™ # 65

Frankho ChessDoku™ is solved by using addition, subtraction, multiplication, or division by following chess moves and logic.

Rule: All the digits 1 to 3 must appear exactly once in every row and column. The number appears in the bottom right-hand corner is the result calculated according to the arithmetic operator(s) and chess move(s) as indicated by the darker arrow(s).

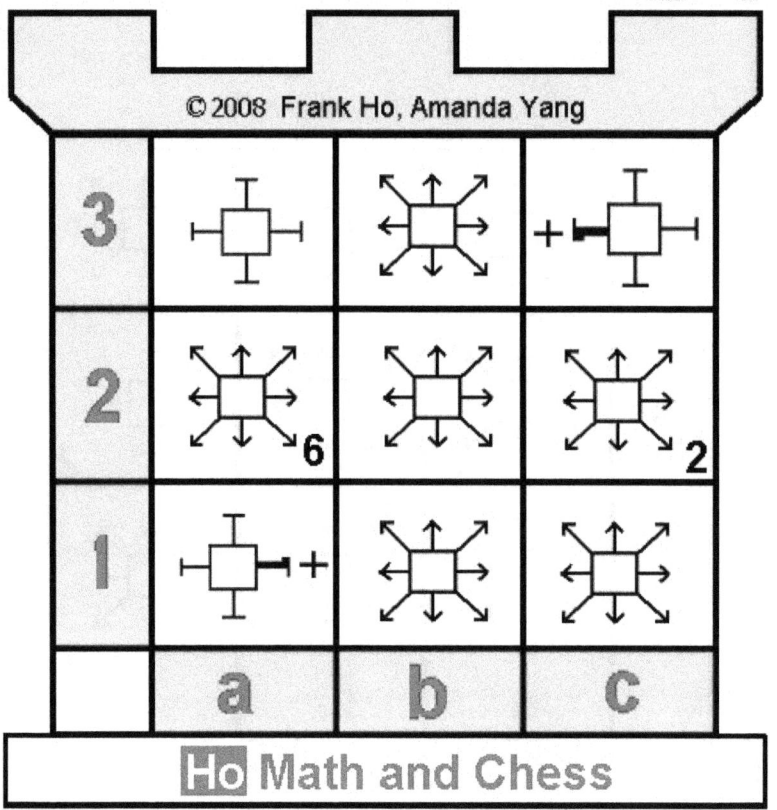

213
321
132

Frankho ChessDoku™ # 66

Rule: All the digits 1 to 3 must appear exactly once in every row and column. The number appears in the bottom right-hand corner is the result calculated according to the arithmetic operator(s) and chess move(s) as indicated by the darker arrow(s).

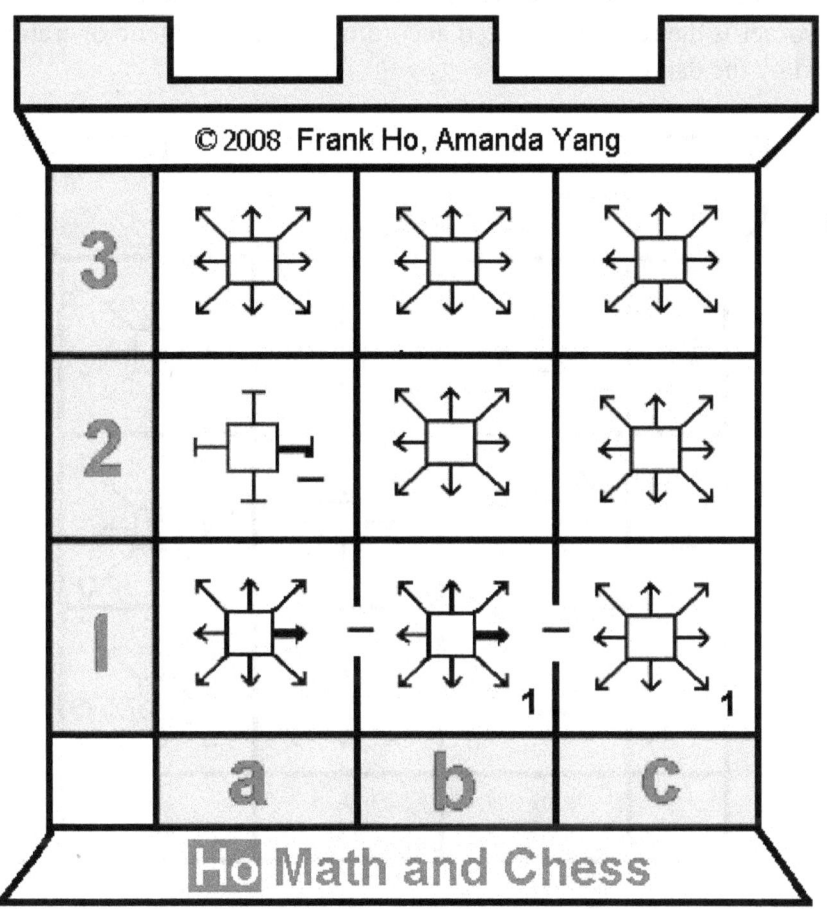

132
213
321

Frankho ChessDoku™ # 67

Frankho ChessDoku™ is solved by using addition, subtraction, multiplication, or division by following chess moves and logic.

Rule: All the digits 1 to 3 must appear exactly once in every row and column. The number appears in the bottom right-hand corner is the result calculated according to the arithmetic operator(s) and chess move(s) as indicated by the darker arrow(s).

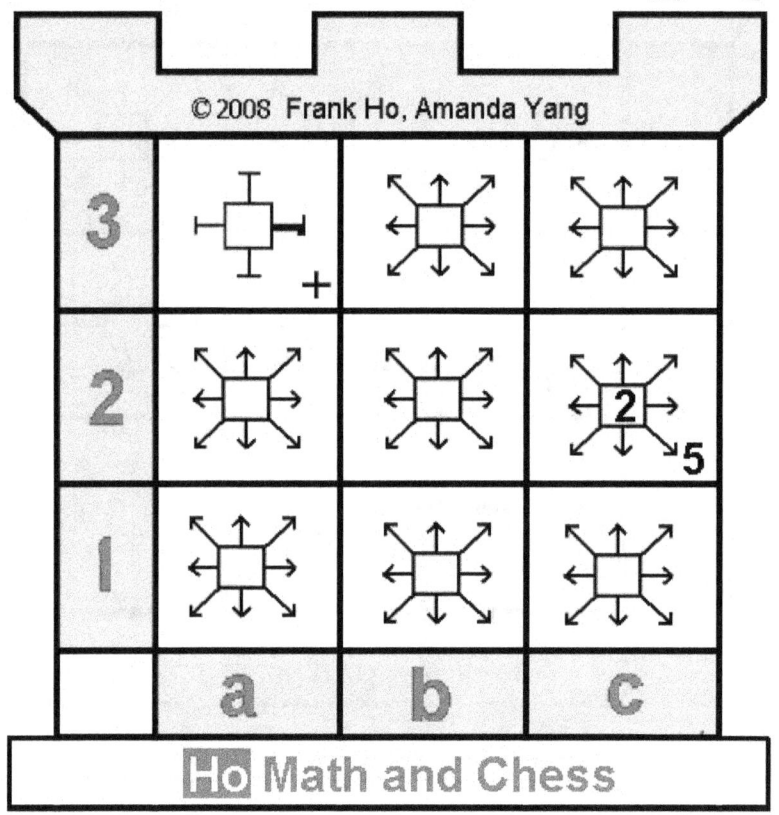

321
132
213

Frankho ChessDoku™ # 68

Frankho ChessDoku™ is solved by using addition, subtraction, multiplication, or division by following chess moves and logic.

Rule: All the digits 1 to 3 must appear exactly once in every row and column. The number appears in the bottom right-hand corner is the result calculated according to the arithmetic operator(s) and chess move(s) as indicated by the darker arrow(s).

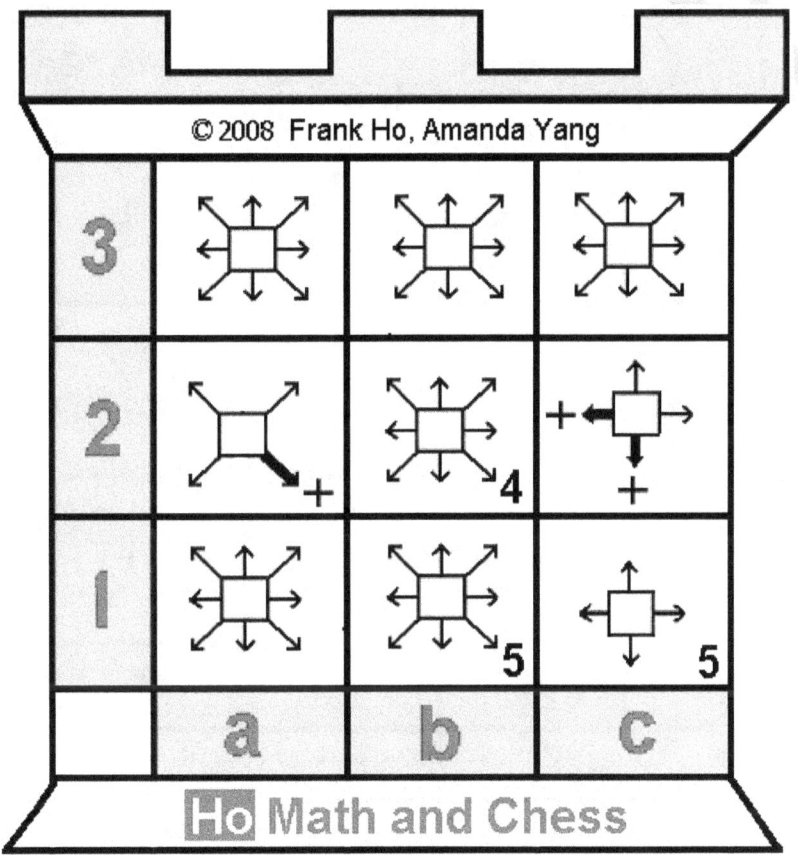

321
213
132

Frankho ChessDoku™ # 69

Frankho ChessDoku™ is solved by using addition, subtraction, multiplication, or division by following chess moves and logic.

Rule: All the digits 1 to 3 must appear exactly once in every row and column. The number appears in the bottom right-hand corner is the result calculated according to the arithmetic operator(s) and chess move(s) as indicated by the darker arrow(s).

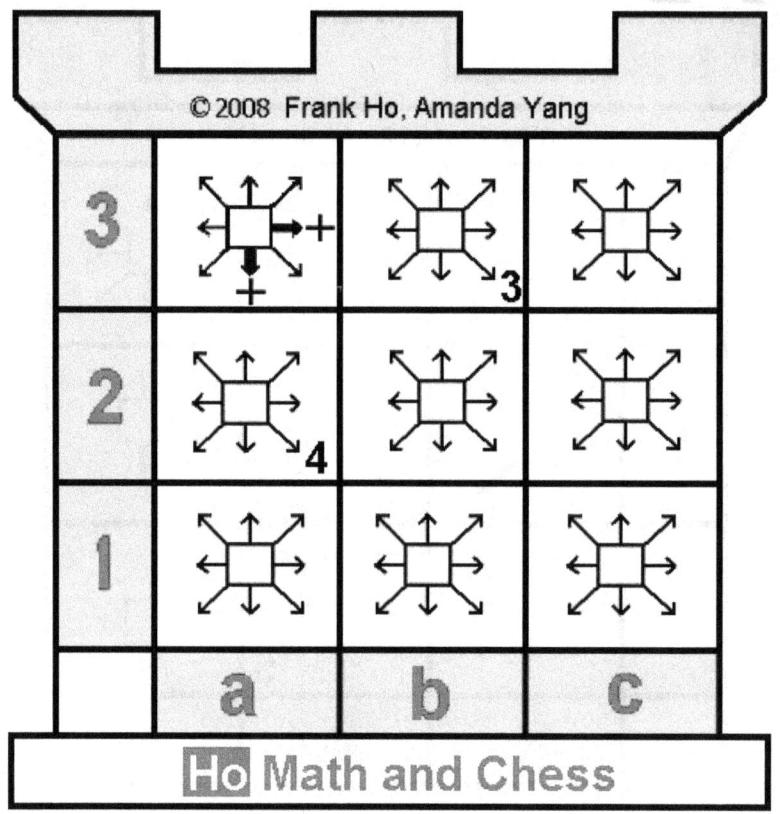

123
312
231

Frankho ChessDoku™ # 70

Frankho ChessDoku™ is solved by using addition, subtraction, multiplication, or division by following chess moves and logic.

Rule: All the digits 1 to 3 must appear exactly once in every row and column. The number appears in the bottom right-hand corner is the result calculated according to the arithmetic operator(s) and chess move(s) as indicated by the darker arrow(s).

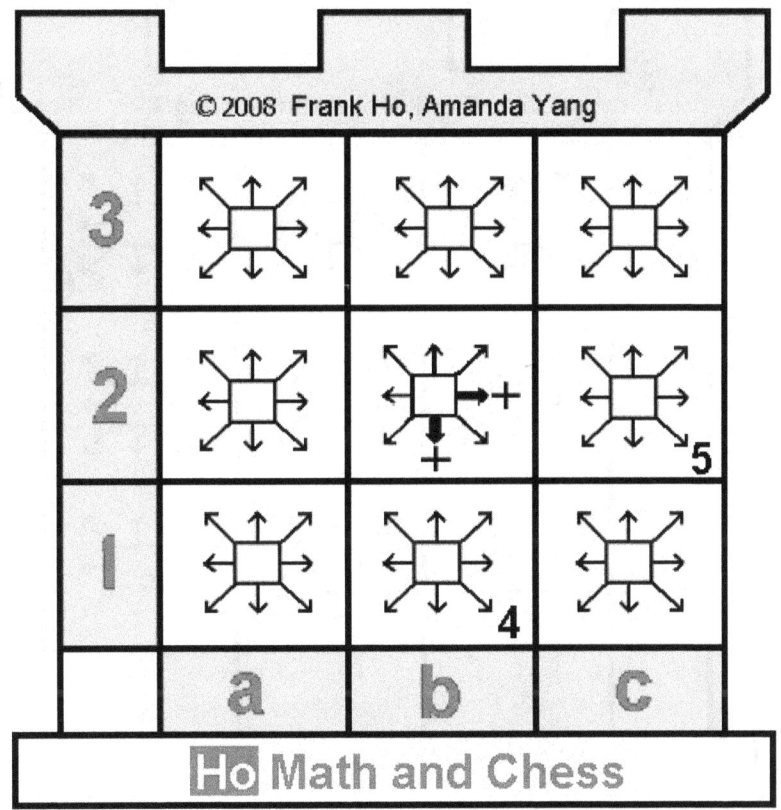

321
132
213

Frankho ChessDoku™ # 71

Frankho ChessDoku™ is solved by using addition, subtraction, multiplication, or division by following chess moves and logic.

Rule: All the digits 1 to 3 must appear exactly once in every row and column. The number appears in the bottom right-hand corner is the result calculated according to the arithmetic operator(s) and chess move(s) as indicated by the darker arrow(s).

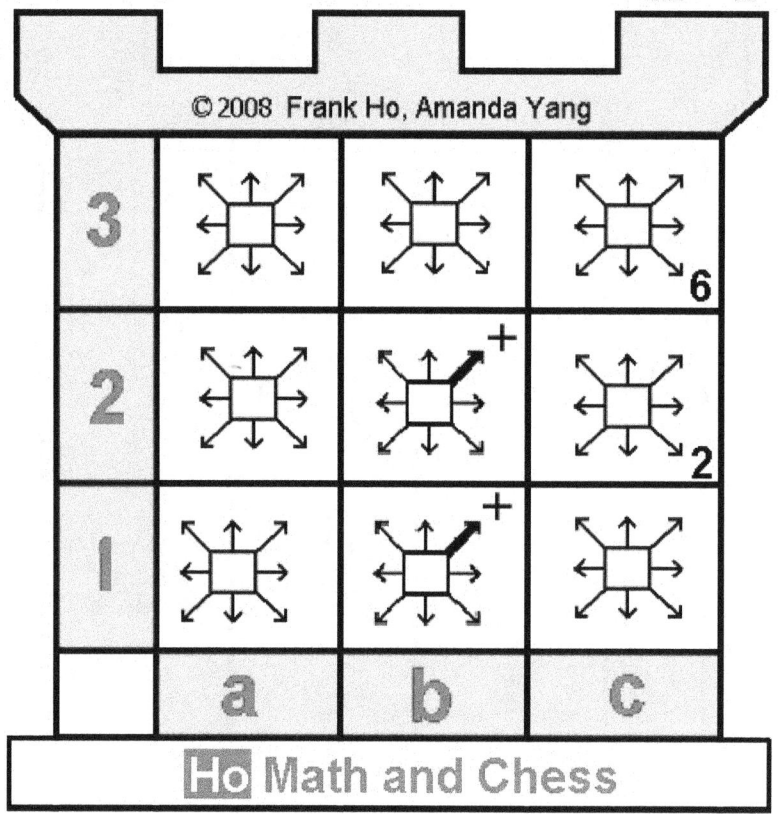

123
231
312

Frankho ChessDoku™ # 72

Frankho ChessDoku™ is solved by using addition, subtraction, multiplication, or division by following chess moves and logic.

Rule: All the digits 1 to 3 must appear exactly once in every row and column. The number appears in the bottom right-hand corner is the result calculated according to the arithmetic operator(s) and chess move(s) as indicated by the darker arrow(s).

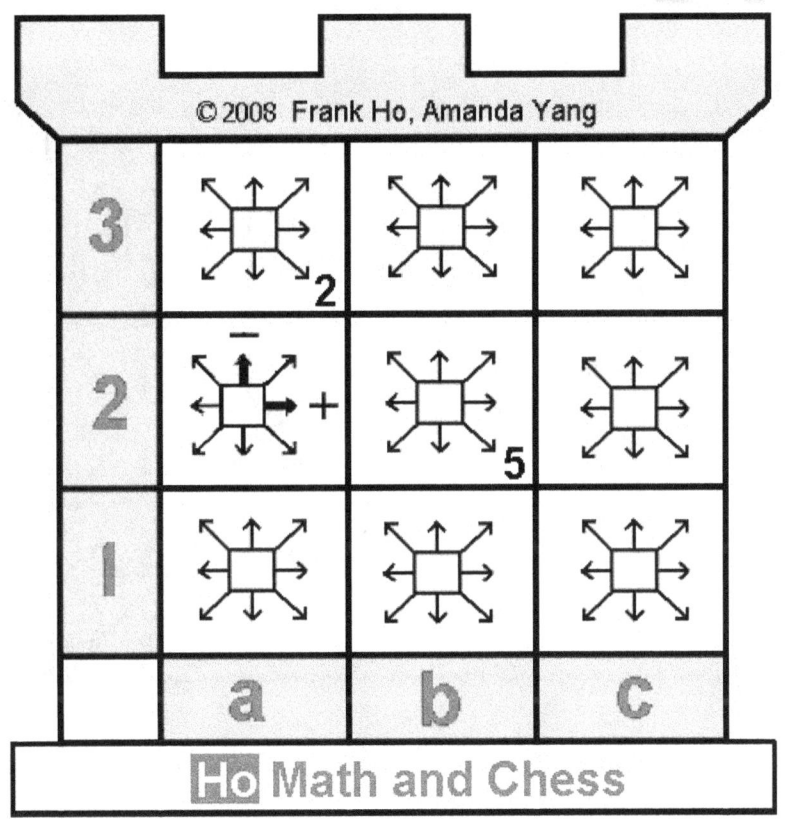

132
321
213

Frankho ChessDoku™ # 73

Frankho ChessDoku™ is solved by using addition, subtraction, multiplication, or division by following chess moves and logic.

Rule: All the digits 1 to 3 must appear exactly once in every row and column. The number appears in the bottom right-hand corner is the result calculated according to the arithmetic operator(s) and chess move(s) as indicated by the darker arrow(s).

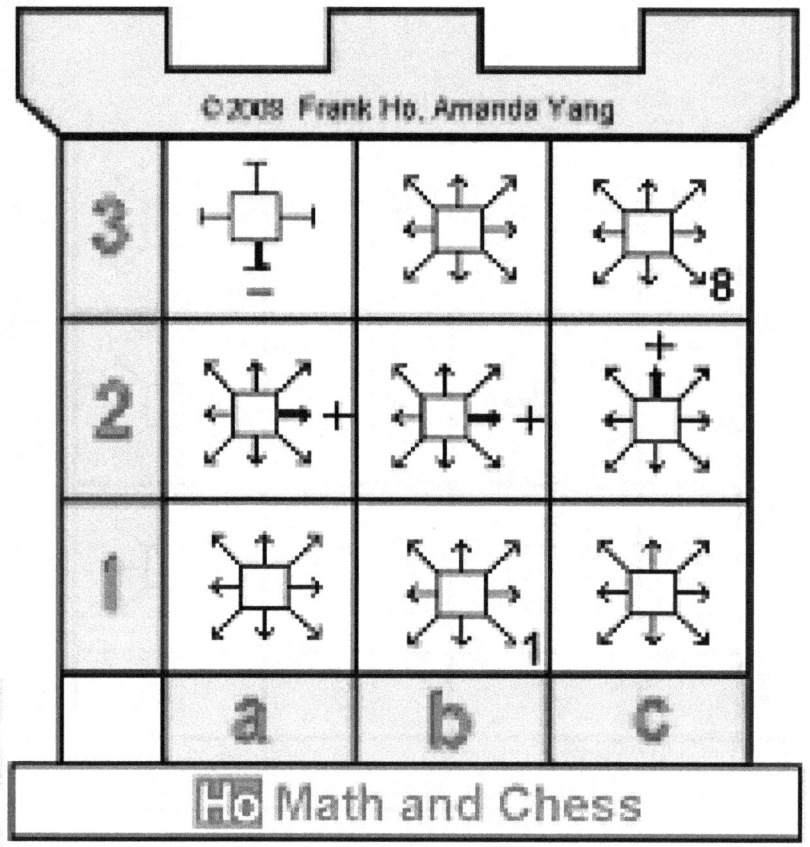

312
231
123

Frankho ChessDoku™ # 74

Frankho ChessDoku™ is solved by using addition, subtraction, multiplication, or division by following chess moves and logic.

Rule: All the digits 1 to 3 must appear exactly once in every row and column. The number appears in the bottom right-hand corner is the result calculated according to the arithmetic operator(s) and chess move(s) as indicated by the darker arrow(s).

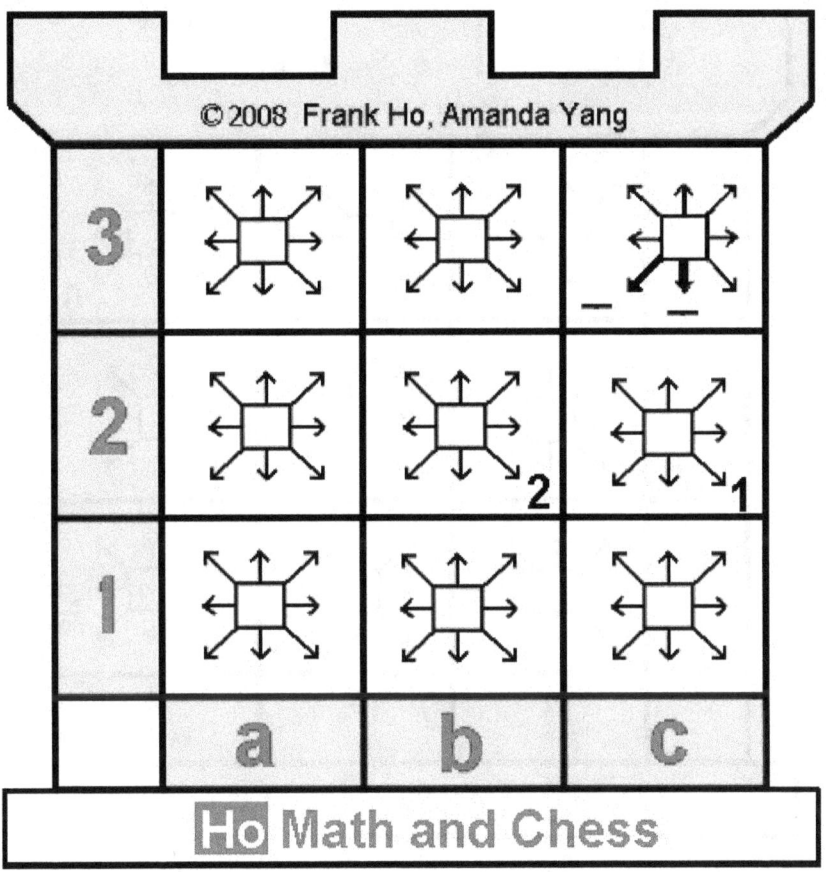

123
312
231

Frankho ChessDoku™ # 75

Frankho ChessDoku™ is solved by using addition, subtraction, multiplication, or division by following chess moves and logic.

Rule: All the digits 1 to 3 must appear exactly once in every row and column. The number appears in the bottom right-hand corner is the result calculated according to the arithmetic operator(s) and chess move(s) as indicated by the darker arrow(s).

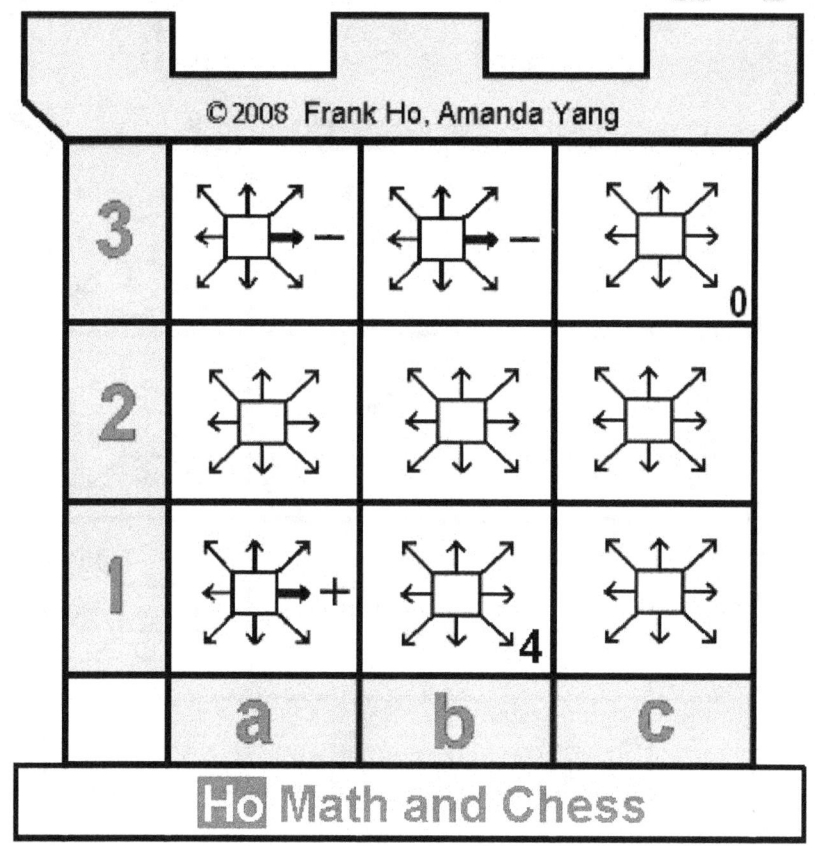

321
213
132

Frankho ChessDoku™ # 76

Frankho ChessDoku™ is solved by using addition, subtraction, multiplication, or division by following chess moves and logic.

Rule: All the digits 1 to 3 must appear exactly once in every row and column. The number appears in the bottom right-hand corner is the result calculated according to the arithmetic operator(s) and chess move(s) as indicated by the darker arrow(s).

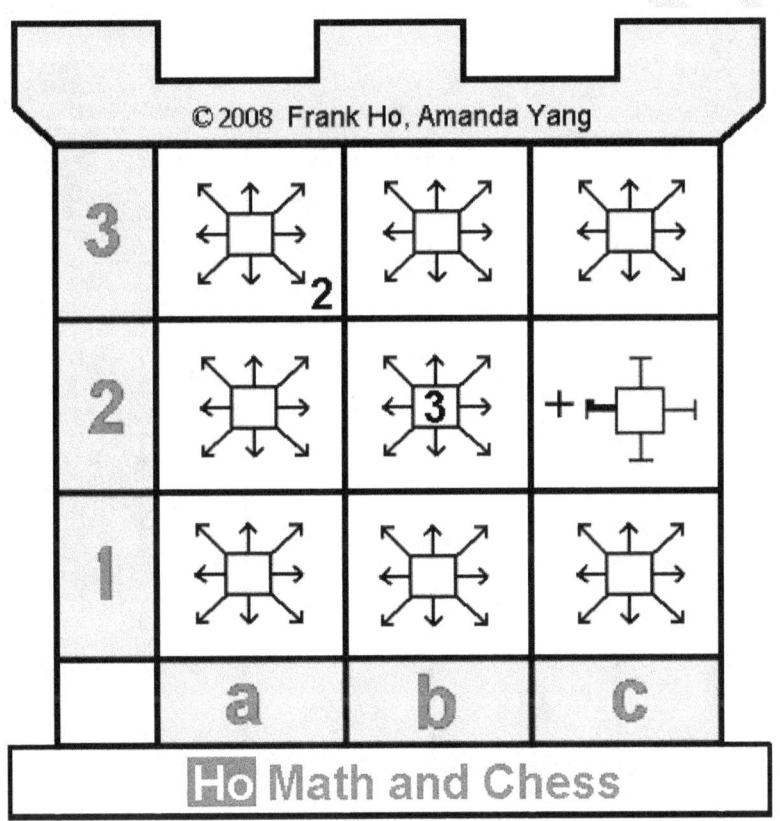

123
231
312

Frankho ChessDoku™ # 77

Frankho ChessDoku™ is solved by using addition, subtraction, multiplication, or division by following chess moves and logic.

Rule: All the digits 1 to 3 must appear exactly once in every row and column. The number appears in the bottom right-hand corner is the result calculated according to the arithmetic operator(s) and chess move(s) as indicated by the darker arrow(s).

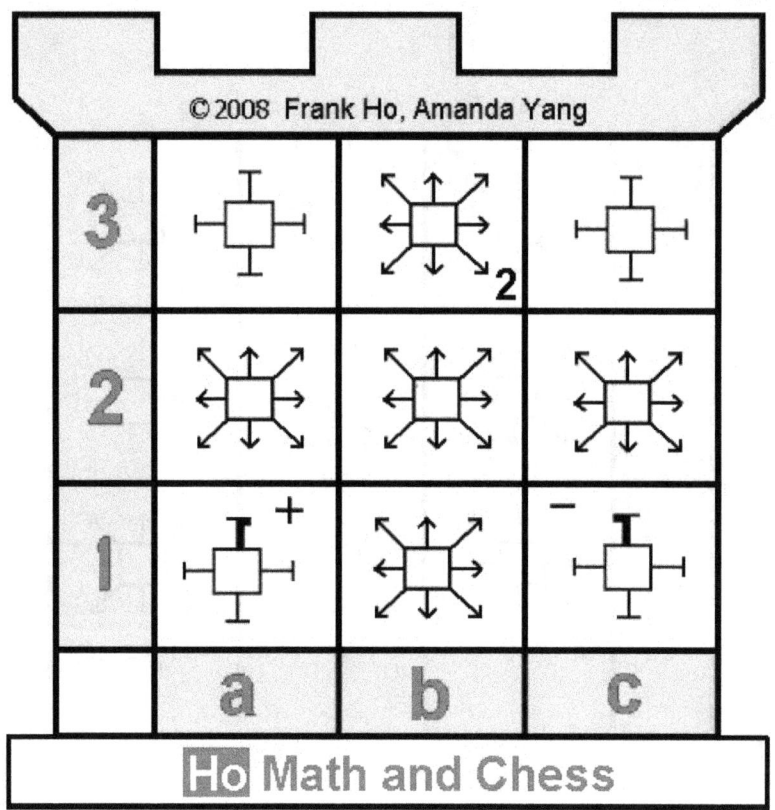

312
231
123

Frankho ChessDoku™ # 78

Frankho ChessDoku™ is solved by using addition, subtraction, multiplication, or division by following chess moves and logic.

Rule: All the digits 1 to 3 must appear exactly once in every row and column. The number appears in the bottom right-hand corner is the result calculated according to the arithmetic operator(s) and chess move(s) as indicated by the darker arrow(s).

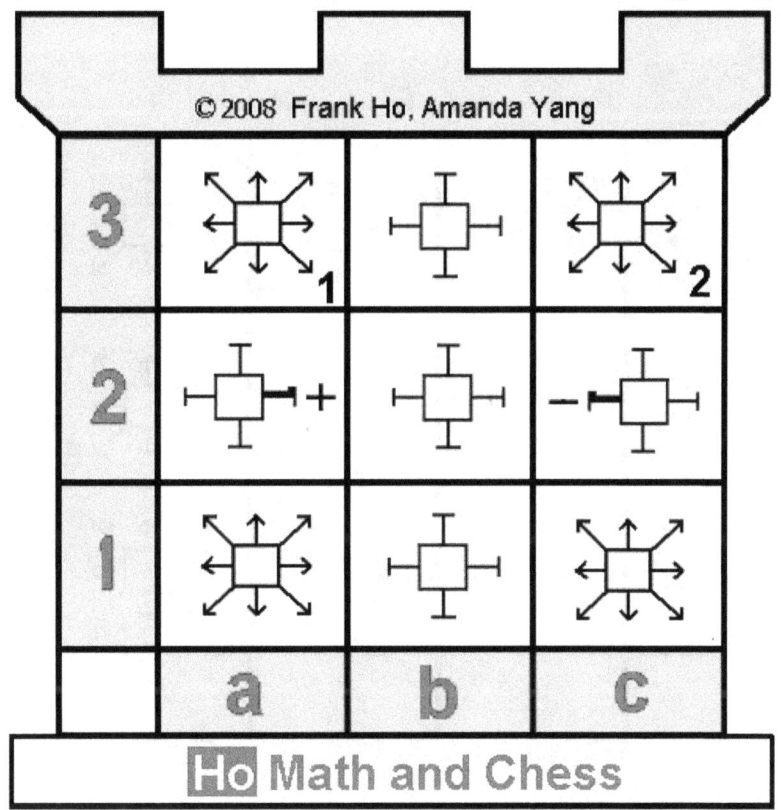

231
123
312

Frankho ChessDoku™ # 79

Frankho ChessDoku™ is solved by using addition, subtraction, multiplication, or division by following chess moves and logic.

Rule: All the digits 1 to 3 must appear exactly once in every row and column. The number appears in the bottom right-hand corner is the result calculated according to the arithmetic operator(s) and chess move(s) as indicated by the darker arrow(s).

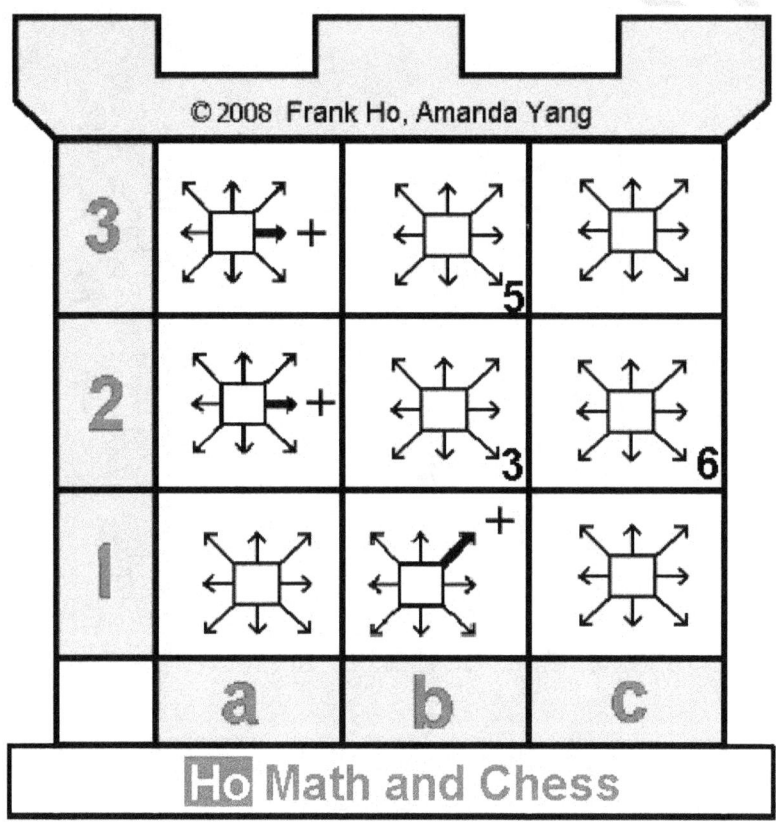

321
213
132

# Frankho ChessDoku™ # 80

Frankho ChessDoku™ is solved by using addition, subtraction, multiplication, or division by following chess moves and logic.

Rule: All the digits 1 to 3 must appear exactly once in every row and column. The number appears in the bottom right-hand corner is the result calculated according to the arithmetic operator(s) and chess move(s) as indicated by the darker arrow(s).

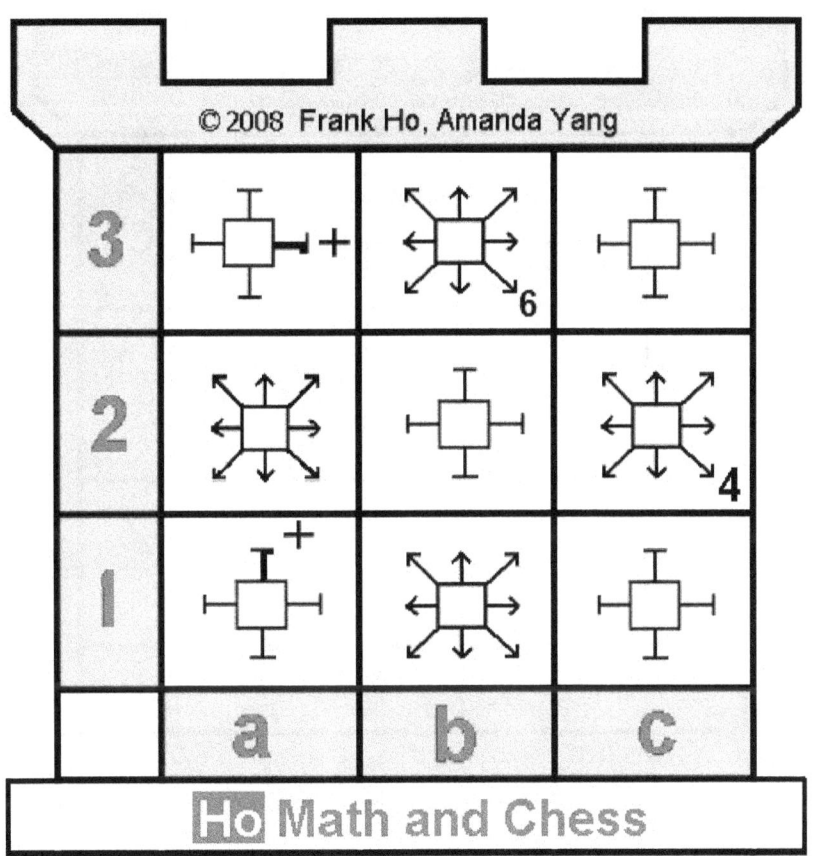

132
213
321

Frankho ChessDoku™ # 81

Frankho ChessDoku™ is solved by using addition, subtraction, multiplication, or division by following chess moves and logic.

Rule: All the digits 1 to 3 must appear exactly once in every row and column. The number appears in the bottom right-hand corner is the result calculated according to the arithmetic operator(s) and chess move(s) as indicated by the darker arrow(s).

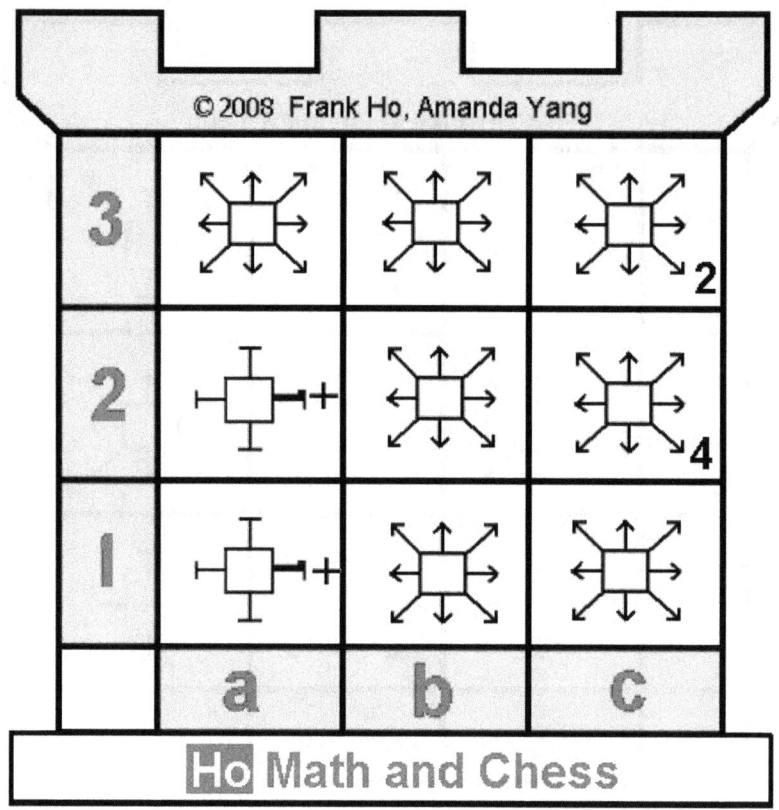

321
132
213

Frankho ChessDoku™ # 82

Frankho ChessDoku™ is solved by using addition, subtraction, multiplication, or division by following chess moves and logic.

Rule: All the digits 1 to 3 must appear exactly once in every row and column. The number appears in the bottom right-hand corner is the result calculated according to the arithmetic operator(s) and chess move(s) as indicated by the darker arrow(s).

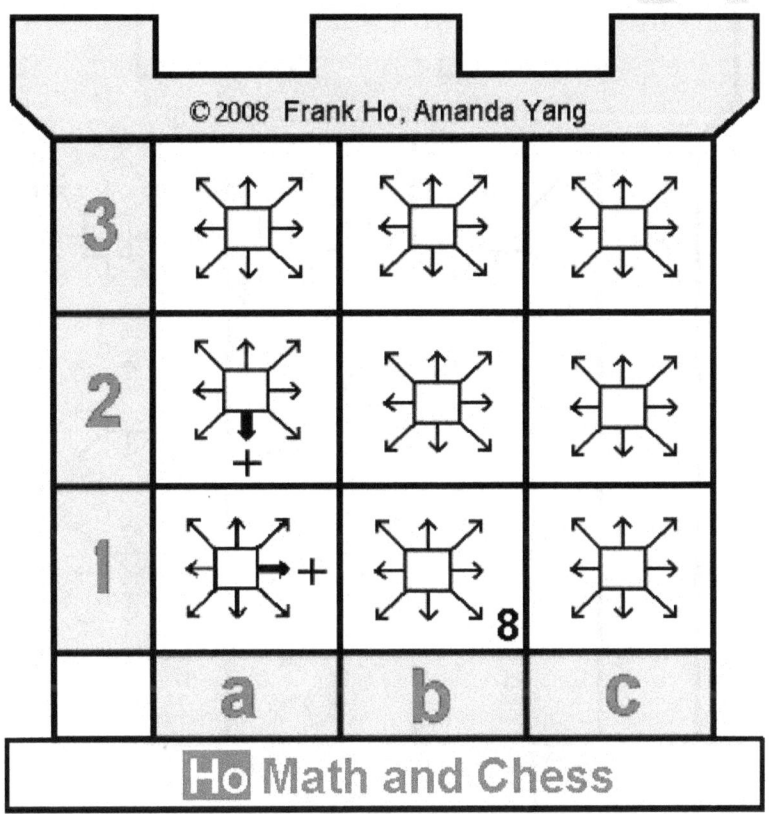

123
312
231

Frankho ChessDoku™ # 83

Frankho ChessDoku™ is solved by using addition, subtraction, multiplication, or division by following chess moves and logic.

Rule: All the digits 1 to 3 must appear exactly once in every row and column. The number appears in the bottom right-hand corner is the result calculated according to the arithmetic operator(s) and chess move(s) as indicated by the darker arrow(s).

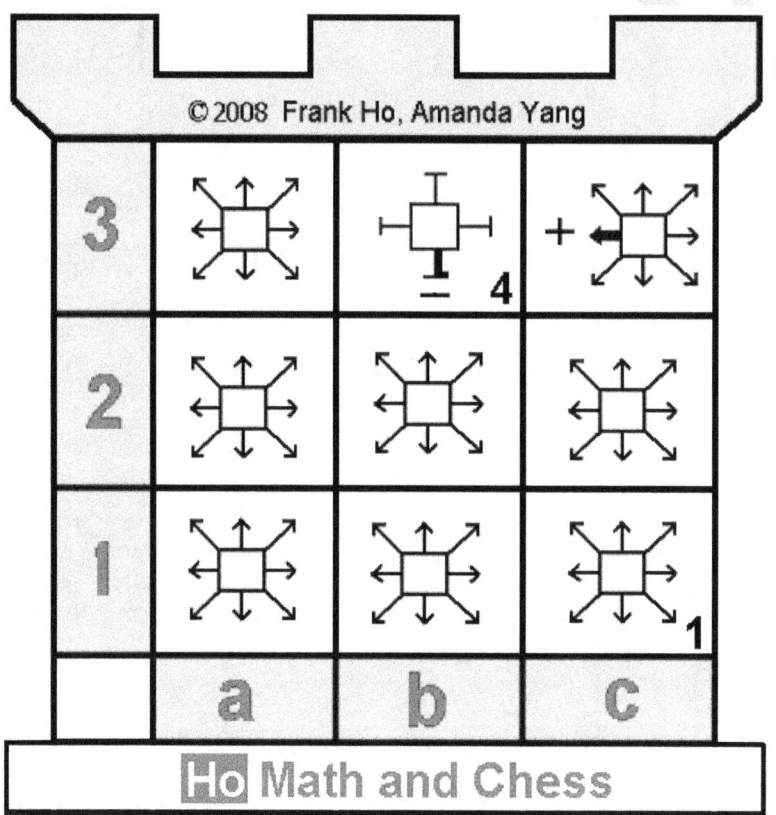

231
123
312

Math Chess Sudoku Puzzles －青少年益智棋芸健脑

Frankho ChessDoku － 何数棋谜算独

© 2007 － 2020   Frank Ho, Amanda Ho   All rights reserved.   www.homathchess.com

Student's name _____ Date _____

Frankho ChessDoku™ # 84

Frankho ChessDoku™ is solved by using addition, subtraction, multiplication, or division by following chess moves and logic.

Rule: All the digits 1 to 3 must appear exactly once in every row and column. The number appears in the bottom right-hand corner is the result calculated according to the arithmetic operator(s) and chess move(s) as indicated by the darker arrow(s).

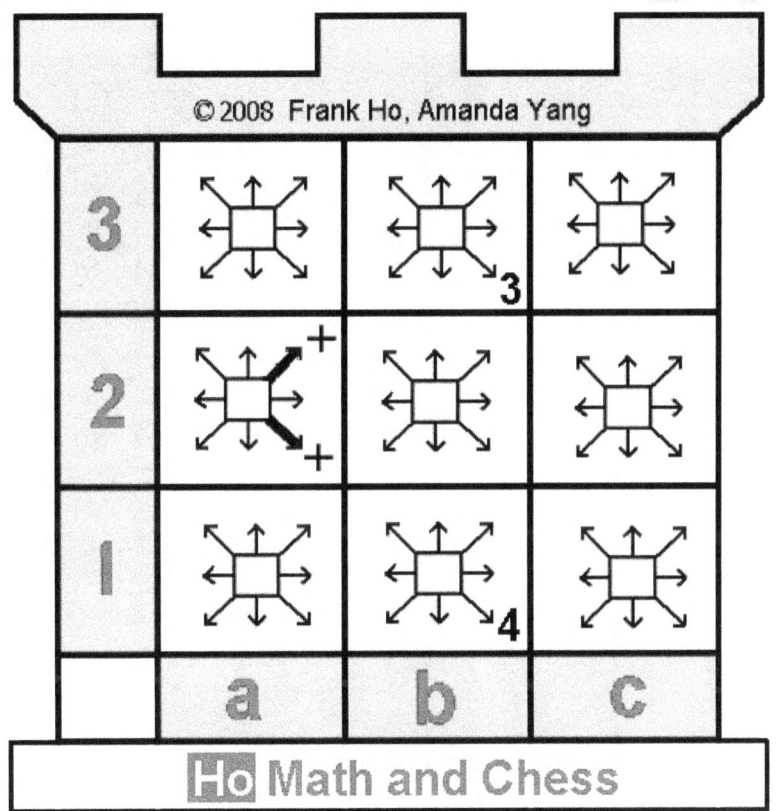

312
231
123

Frankho ChessDoku™ # 85

Frankho ChessDoku™ is solved by using addition, subtraction, multiplication, or division by following chess moves and logic.

Rule: All the digits 1 to 3 must appear exactly once in every row and column. The number appears in the bottom right-hand corner is the result calculated according to the arithmetic operator(s) and chess move(s) as indicated by the darker arrow(s).

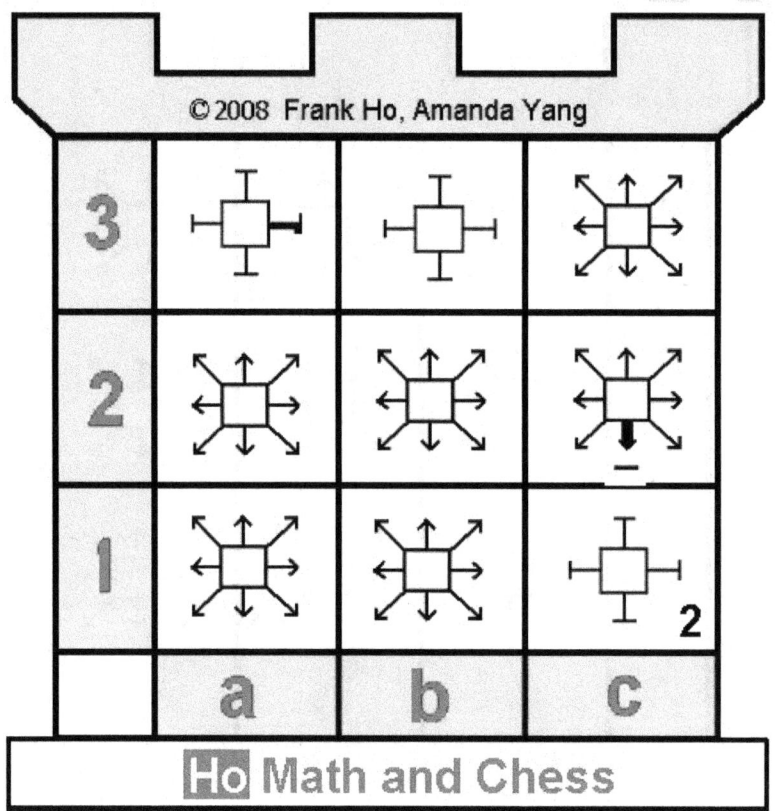

312
123
231

Frankho ChessDoku™ # 86

Frankho ChessDoku™ is solved by using addition, subtraction, multiplication, or division by following chess moves and logic.

Rule: All the digits 1 to 3 must appear exactly once in every row and column. The number appears in the bottom right-hand corner is the result calculated according to the arithmetic operator(s) and chess move(s) as indicated by the darker arrow(s).

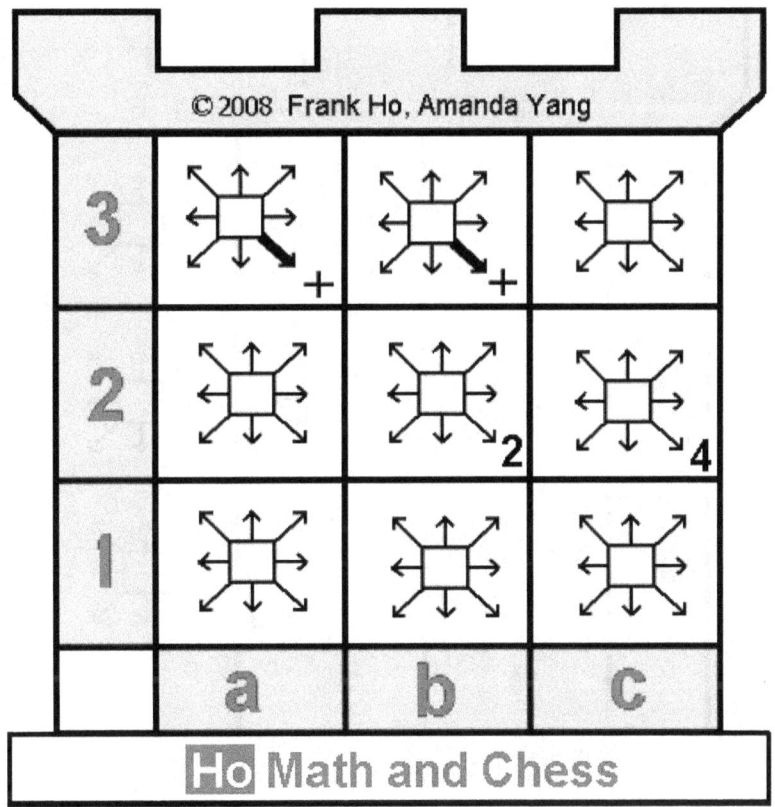

123
312
231

Frankho ChessDoku™ # 87

Frankho ChessDoku™ is solved by using addition, subtraction, multiplication, or division by following chess moves and logic.

Rule: All the digits 1 to 3 must appear exactly once in every row and column. The number appears in the bottom right-hand corner is the result calculated according to the arithmetic operator(s) and chess move(s) as indicated by the darker arrow(s).

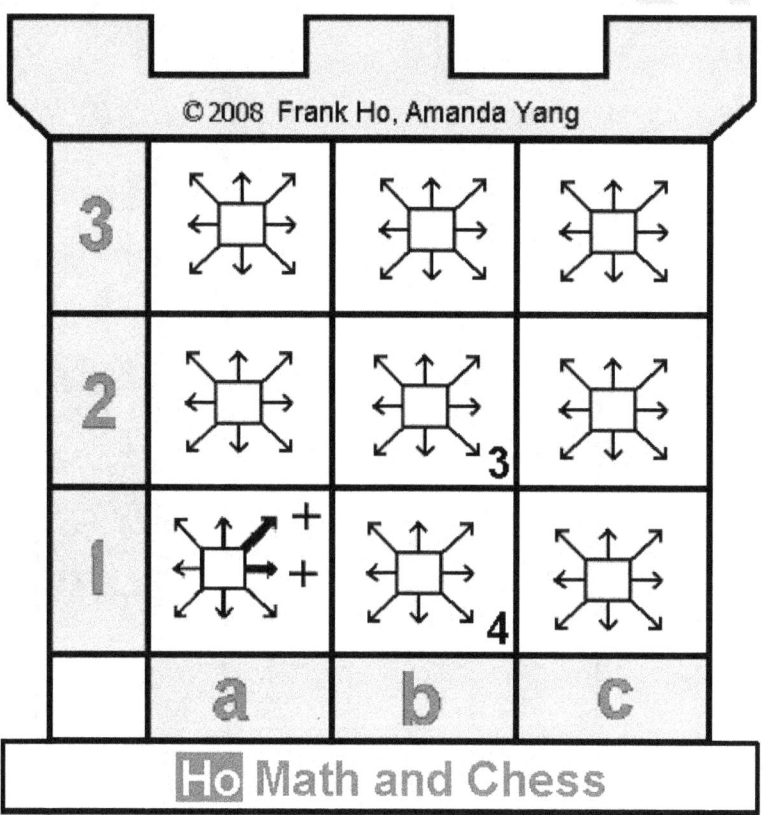

213
321
132

Frankho ChessDoku™ # 88

Frankho ChessDoku™ is solved by using addition, subtraction, multiplication, or division by following chess moves and logic.

Rule: All the digits 1 to 3 must appear exactly once in every row and column. The number appears in the bottom right-hand corner is the result calculated according to the arithmetic operator(s) and chess move(s) as indicated by the darker arrow(s).

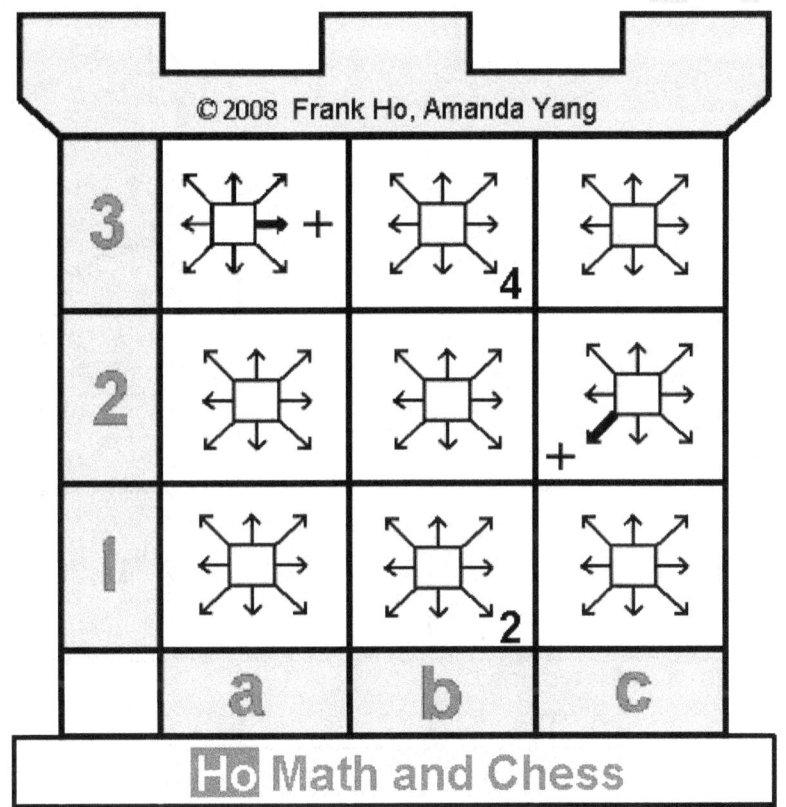

132
321
213

Frankho ChessDoku™ # 89

Frankho ChessDoku™ is solved by using addition, subtraction, multiplication, or division by following chess moves and logic.

Rule: All the digits 1 to 3 must appear exactly once in every row and column. The number appears in the bottom right-hand corner is the result calculated according to the arithmetic operator(s) and chess move(s) as indicated by the darker arrow(s).

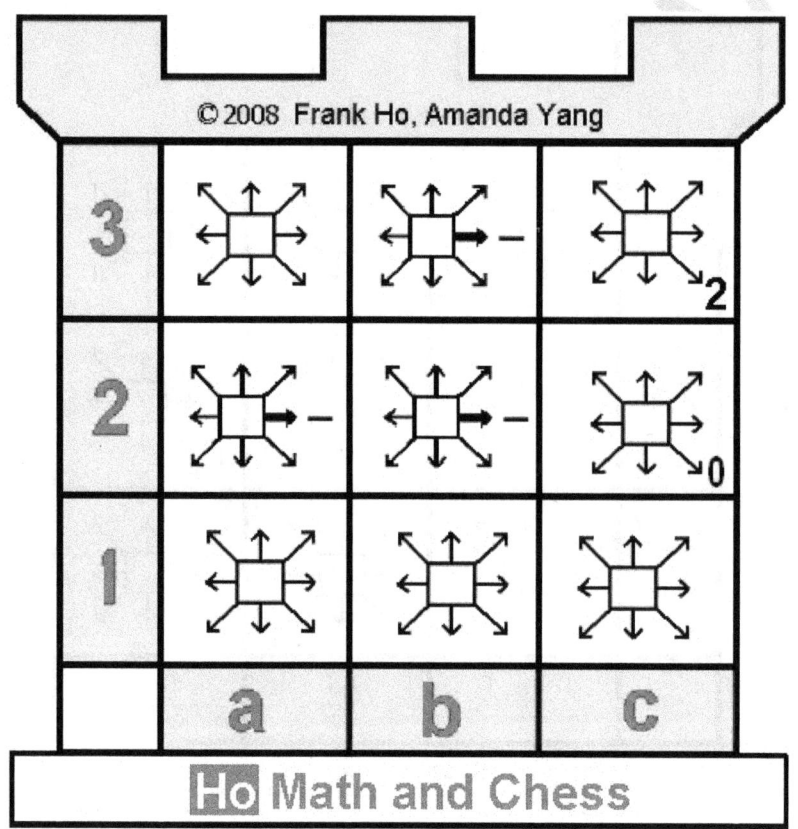

231
312
123

Frankho ChessDoku™ # 90

Frankho ChessDoku™ is solved by using addition, subtraction, multiplication, or division by following chess moves and logic.

Rule: All the digits 1 to 3 must appear exactly once in every row and column. The number appears in the bottom right-hand corner is the result calculated according to the arithmetic operator(s) and chess move(s) as indicated by the darker arrow(s).

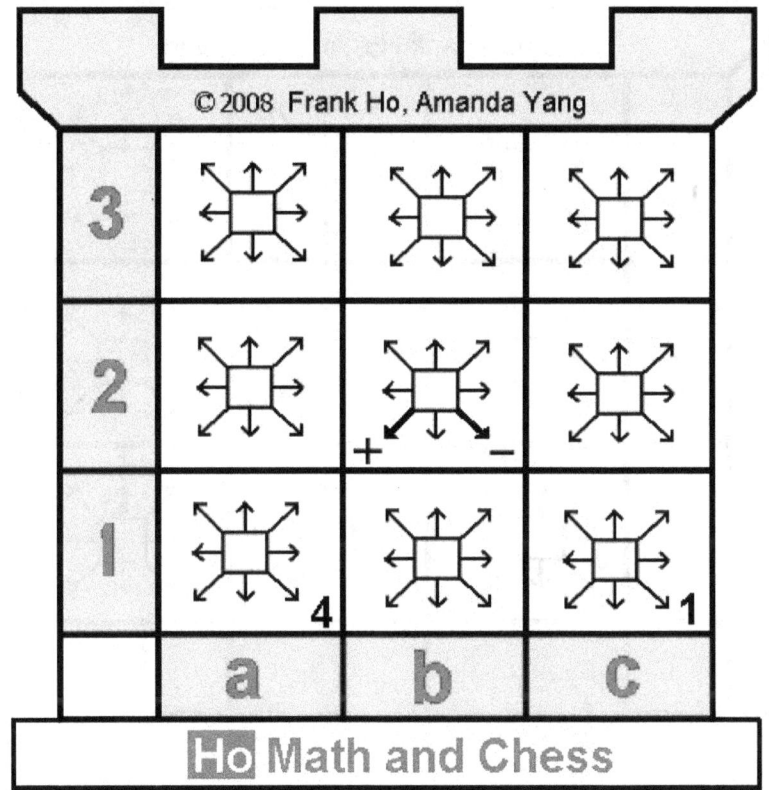

312
123
231

Frankho ChessDoku™ # 91

RULES:

All the digits 1 to 3 must appear in every row and column. The number appears in the bottom right-hand corner is the result calculated according to operator(s) and chess move(s).

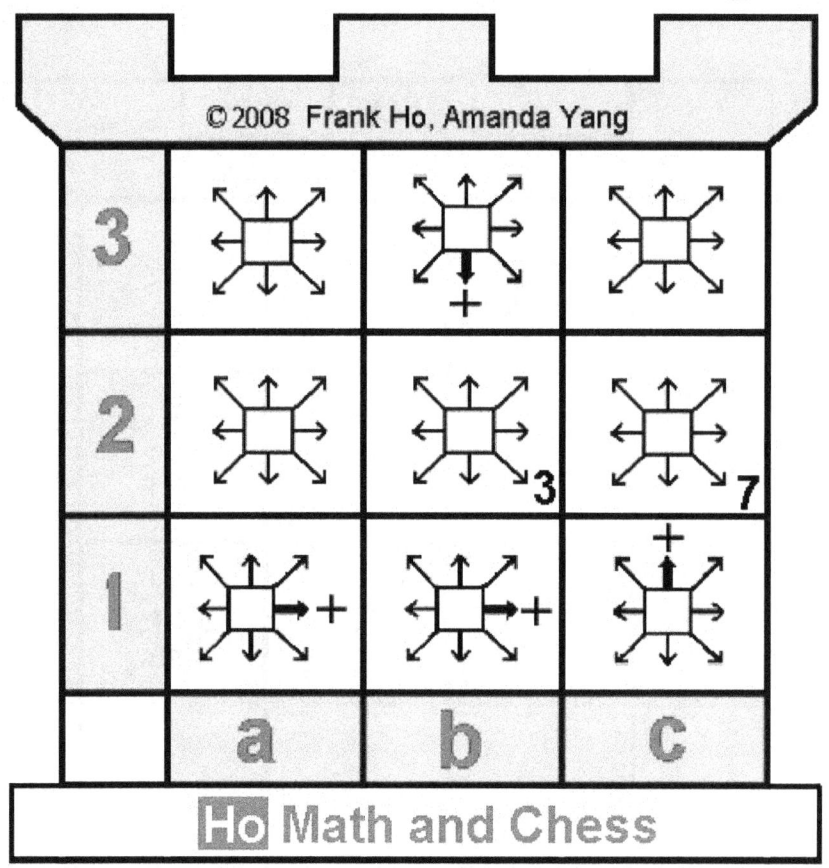

213
321
132

Math Chess Sudoku Puzzles －青少年益智棋芸健脑

Frankho ChessDoku － 何数棋谜算独

© 2007 － 2020 Frank Ho, Amanda Ho   All rights reserved.   www.homathchess.com

Student's name_____Date_____

Frankho ChessDoku™ # 92

Frankho ChessDoku™ is solved by using addition, subtraction, multiplication, or division by following chess moves and logic.

Rule: All the digits 1 to 3 must appear exactly once in every row and column. The number appears in the bottom right-hand corner is the result calculated according to the arithmetic operator(s) and chess move(s) as indicated by the darker arrow(s).

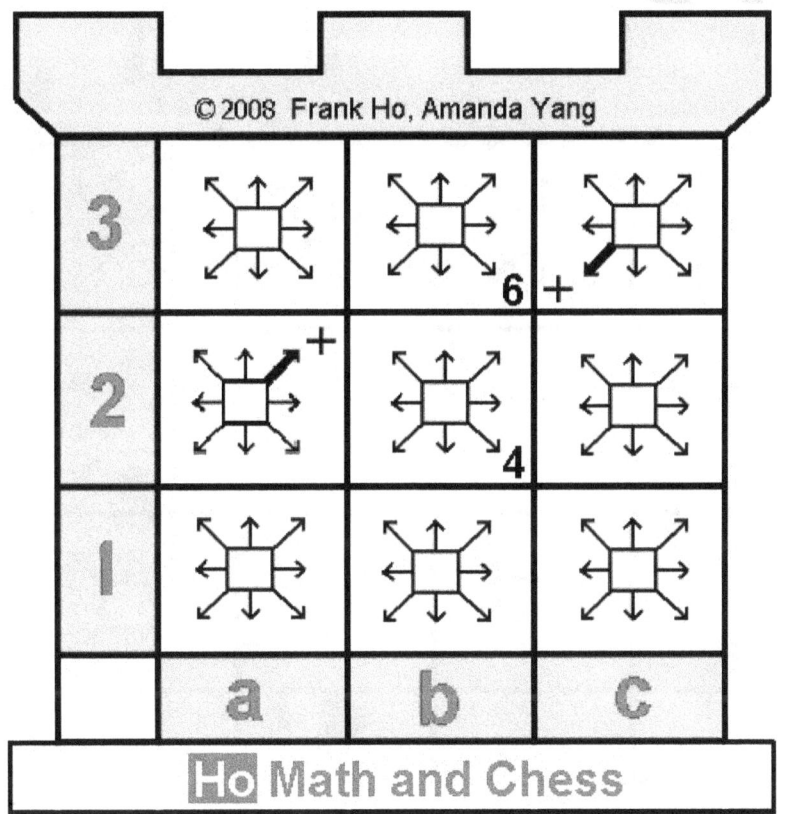

132
321
213

Frankho ChessDoku™ # 93

Frankho ChessDoku™ is solved by using addition, subtraction, multiplication, or division by following chess moves and logic.

Rule: All the digits 1 to 3 must appear exactly once in every row and column. The number appears in the bottom right-hand corner is the result calculated according to the arithmetic operator(s) and chess move(s) as indicated by the darker arrow(s).

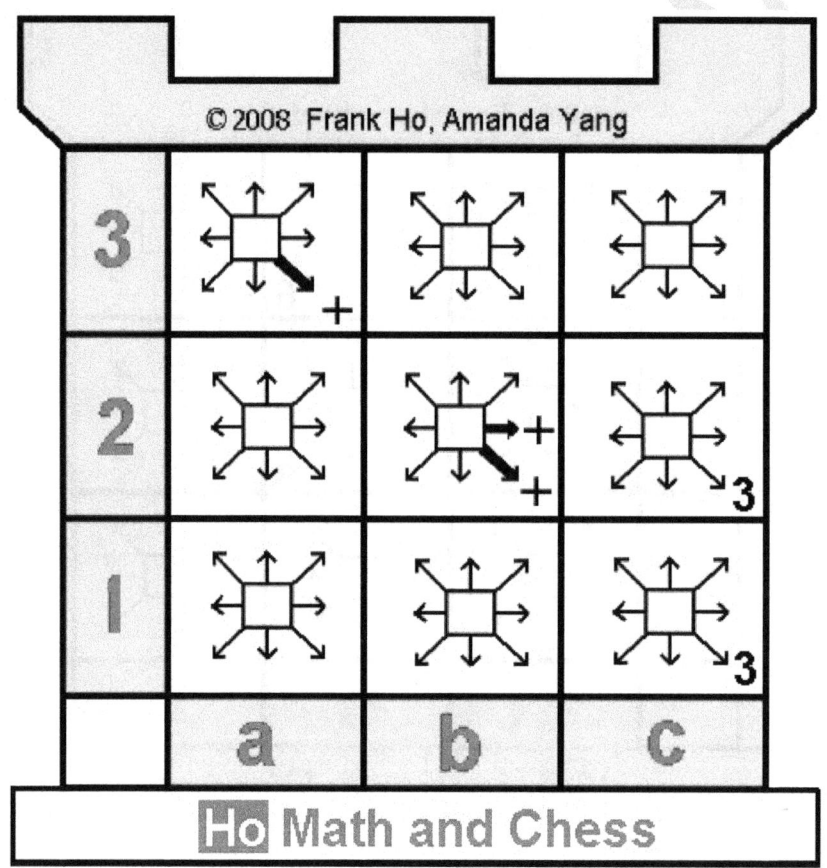

123
312
231

Frankho ChessDoku™ # 94

Frankho ChessDoku™ is solved by using addition, subtraction, multiplication, or division by following chess moves and logic.

Rule: All the digits 1 to 3 must appear exactly once in every row and column. The number appears in the bottom right-hand corner is the result calculated according to the arithmetic operator(s) and chess move(s) as indicated by the darker arrow(s).

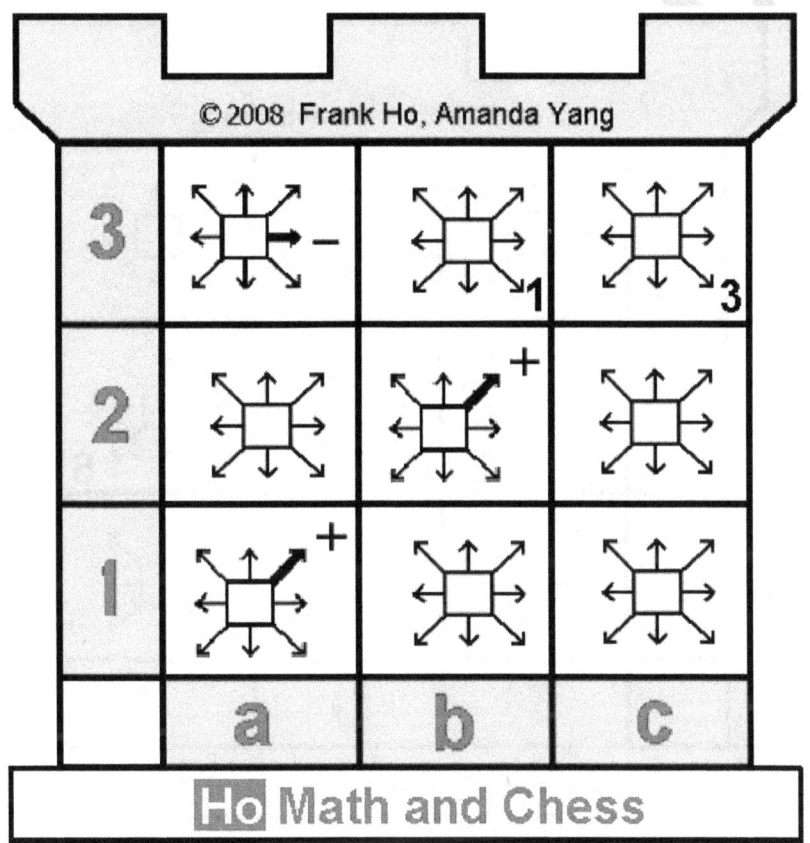

321
213
132

Frankho ChessDoku™ # 95

Frankho ChessDoku™ is solved by using addition, subtraction, multiplication, or division by following chess moves and logic.

Rule: All the digits 1 to 3 must appear exactly once in every row and column. The number appears in the bottom right-hand corner is the result calculated according to the arithmetic operator(s) and chess move(s) as indicated by the darker arrow(s).

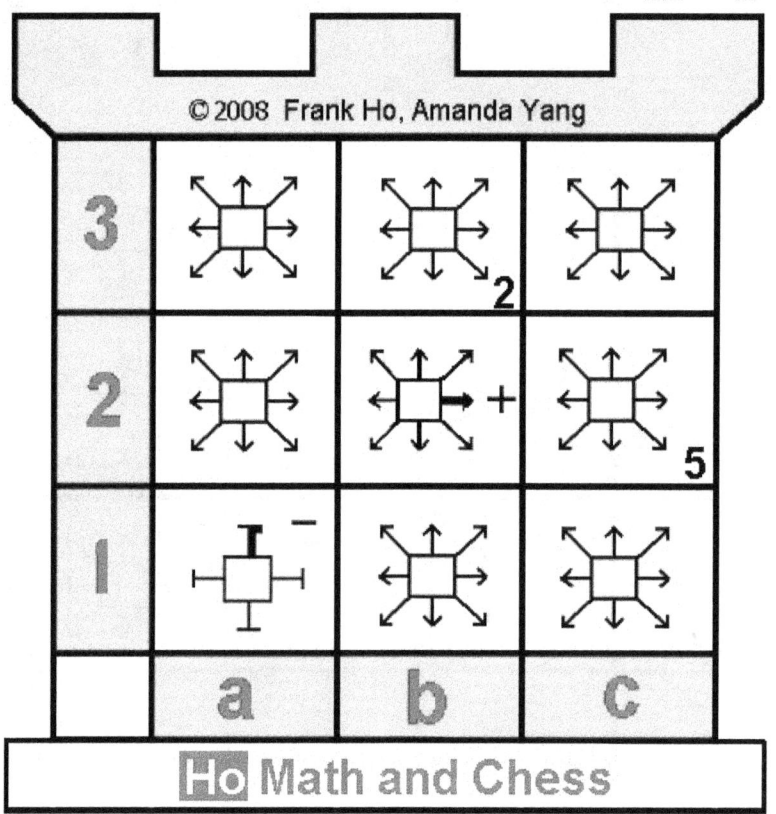

213
132
321

Frankho ChessDoku™ # 96

Frankho ChessDoku™ is solved by using addition, subtraction, multiplication, or division by following chess moves and logic.

Rule: All the digits 1 to 3 must appear exactly once in every row and column. The number appears in the bottom right-hand corner is the result calculated according to the arithmetic operator(s) and chess move(s) as indicated by the darker arrow(s).

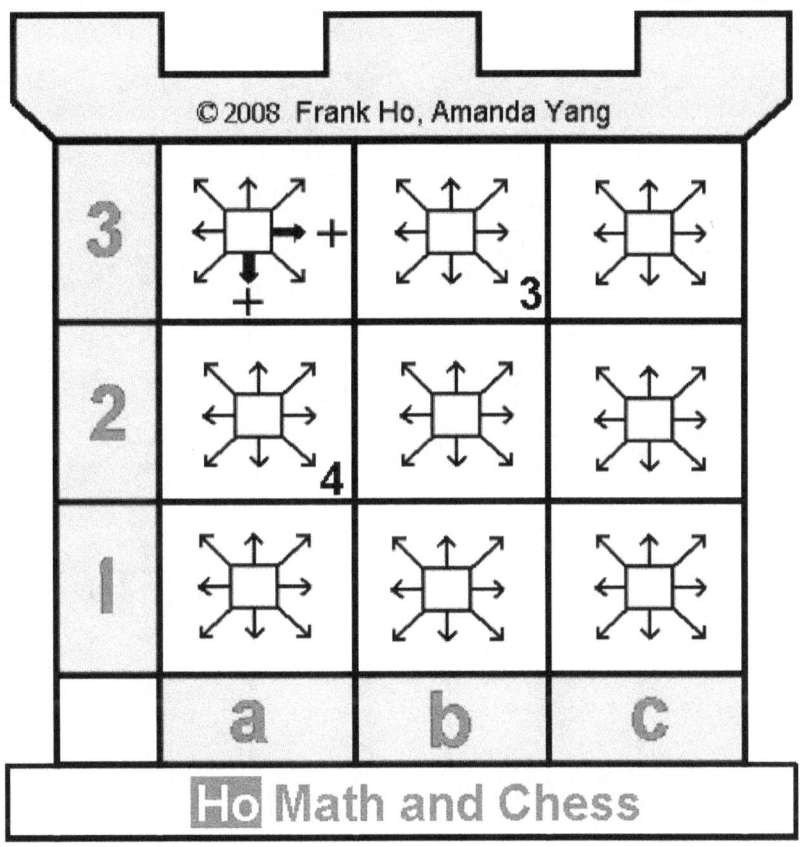

123
312
231

Frankho ChessDoku™ # 97

Frankho ChessDoku™ is solved by using addition, subtraction, multiplication, or division by following chess moves and logic.

Rule: All the digits 1 to 3 must appear exactly once in every row and column. The number appears in the bottom right-hand corner is the result calculated according to the arithmetic operator(s) and chess move(s) as indicated by the darker arrow(s).

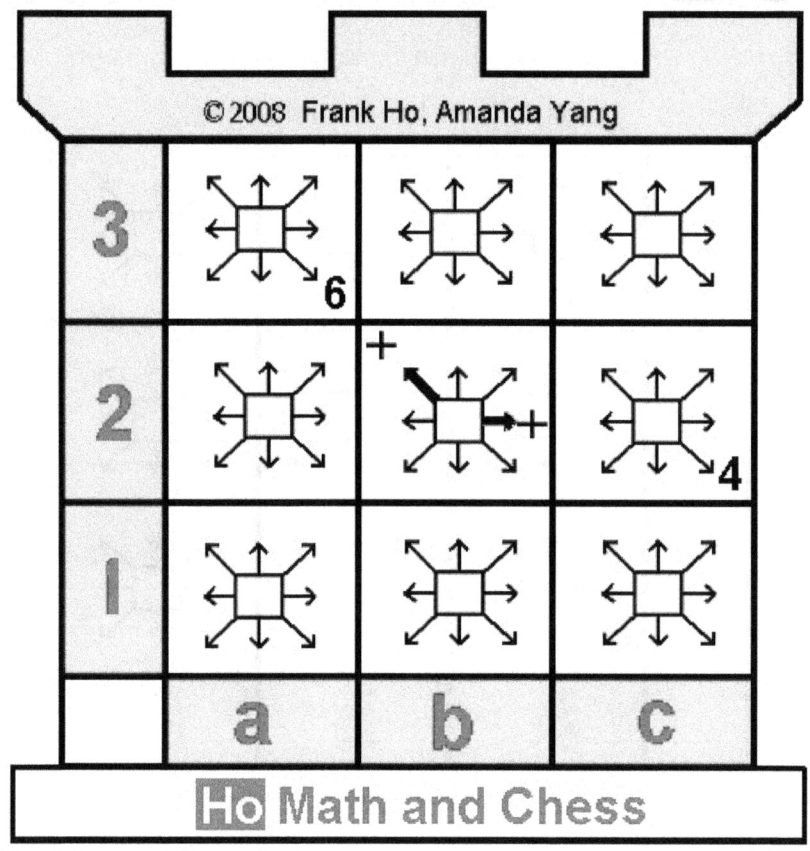

312
231
123

Frankho ChessDoku™ # 98

Frankho ChessDoku™ is solved by using addition, subtraction, multiplication, or division by following chess moves and logic.

Rule: All the digits 1 to 3 must appear exactly once in every row and column. The number appears in the bottom right-hand corner is the result calculated according to the arithmetic operator(s) and chess move(s) as indicated by the darker arrow(s).

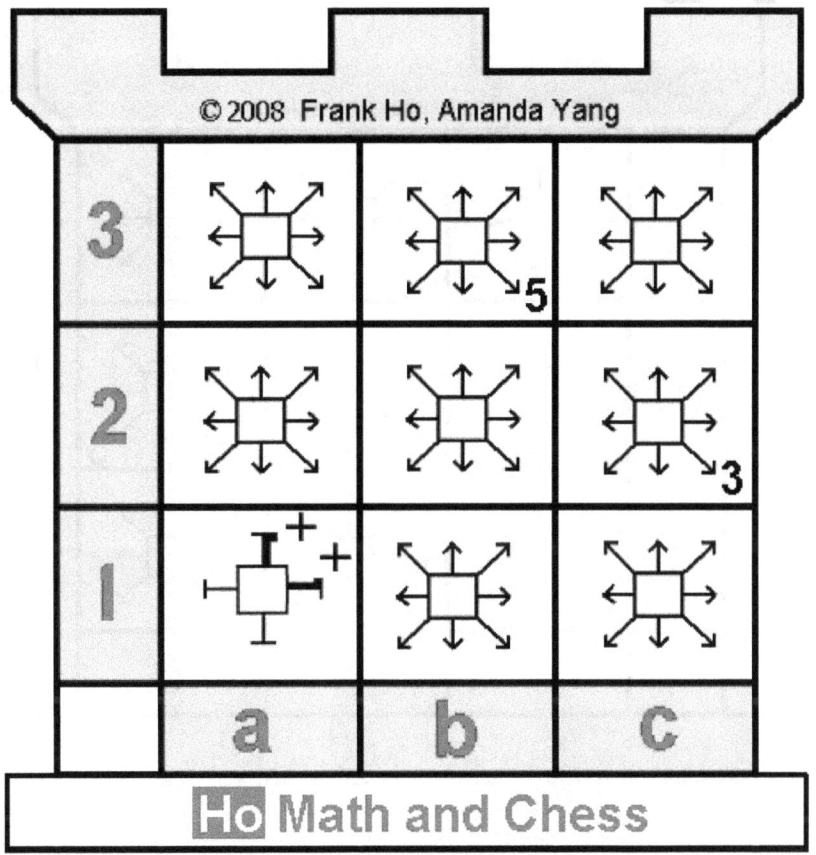

132
321
213

Frankho ChessDoku™ # 99

Frankho ChessDoku™ is solved by using addition, subtraction, multiplication, or division by following chess moves and logic.

Rule: All the digits 1 to 3 must appear exactly once in every row and column. The number appears in the bottom right-hand corner is the result calculated according to the arithmetic operator(s) and chess move(s) as indicated by the darker arrow(s).

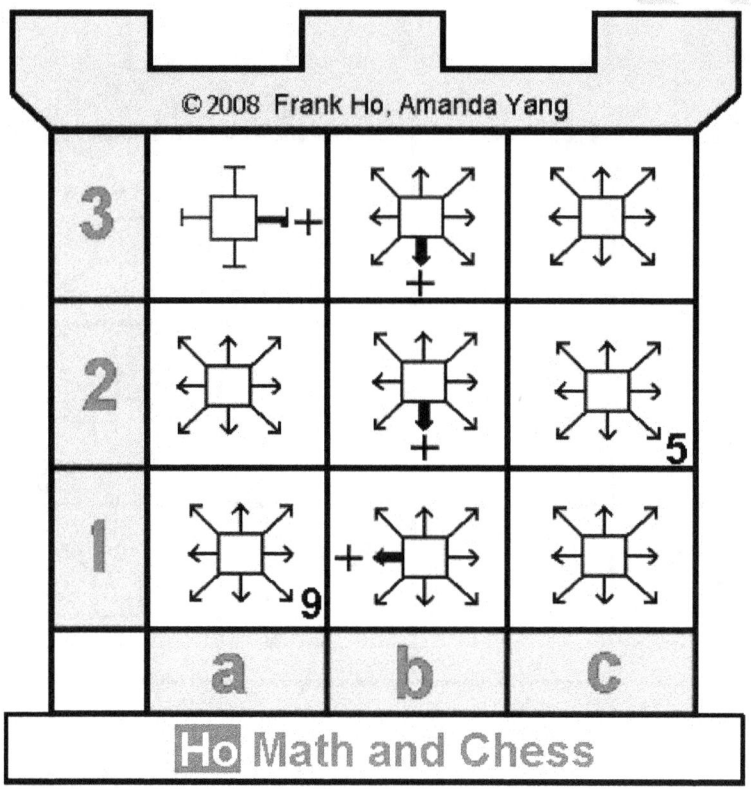

231
123
312

Frankho ChessDoku™ # 100

Frankho ChessDoku™ is solved by using addition, subtraction, multiplication, or division by following chess moves and logic.

Rule: All the digits 1 to 3 must appear exactly once in every row and column. The number appears in the bottom right-hand corner is the result calculated according to the arithmetic operator(s) and chess move(s) as indicated by the darker arrow(s).

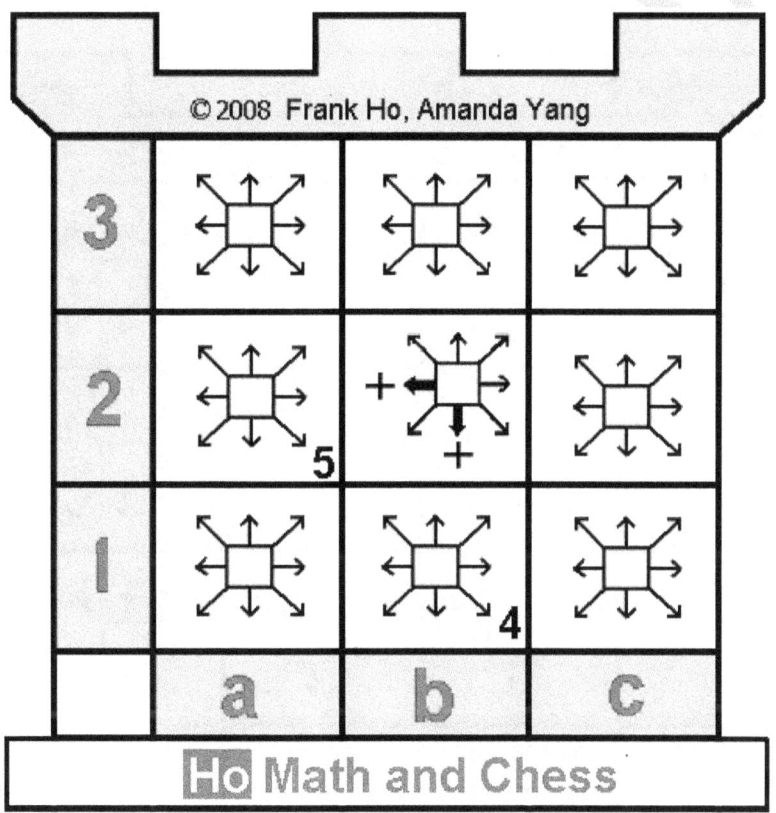

123
231
312

Frankho ChessDoku™ # 101

Frankho ChessDoku™ is solved by using addition, subtraction, multiplication, or division by following chess moves and logic.

Rule: All the digits 1 to 3 must appear exactly once in every row and column. The number appears in the bottom right-hand corner is the result calculated according to the arithmetic operator(s) and chess move(s) as indicated by the darker arrow(s).

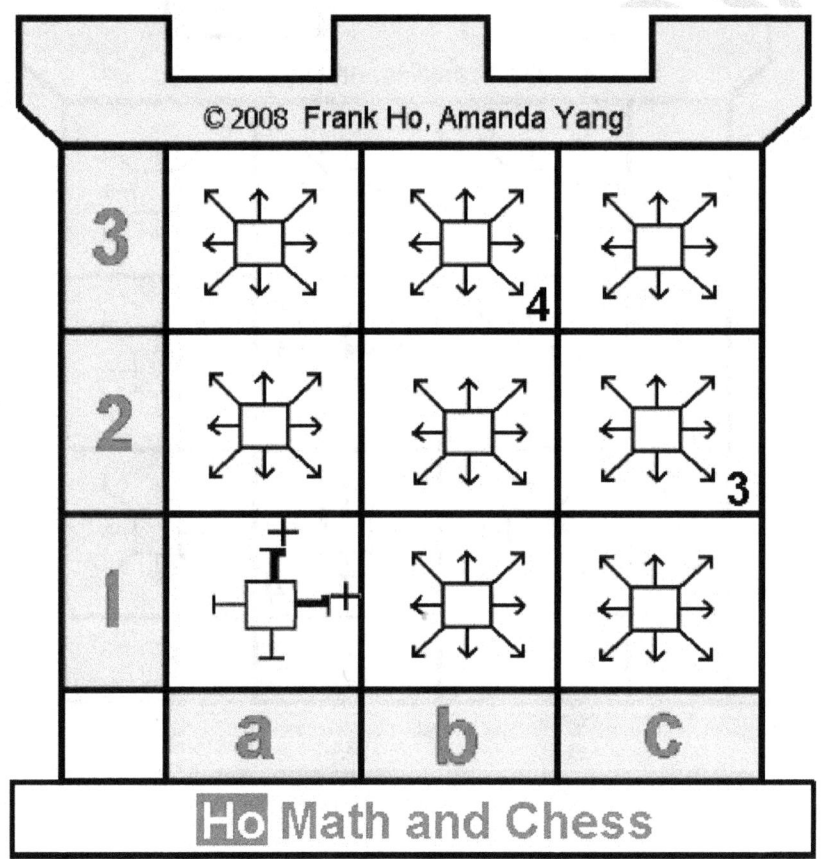

231
312
123

Math Chess Sudoku Puzzles 一青少年益智棋芸健脑

Frankho ChessDoku 一 何数棋谜算独

© 2007 — 2020 Frank Ho, Amanda Ho   All rights reserved.   www.homathchess.com

Student's name _____   Date _____

Frankho ChessDoku™ # 102

Frankho ChessDoku™ is solved by using addition, subtraction, multiplication, or division by following chess moves and logic.

Rule: All the digits 1 to 3 must appear exactly once in every row and column. The number appears in the bottom right-hand corner is the result calculated according to the arithmetic operator(s) and chess move(s) as indicated by the darker arrow(s).

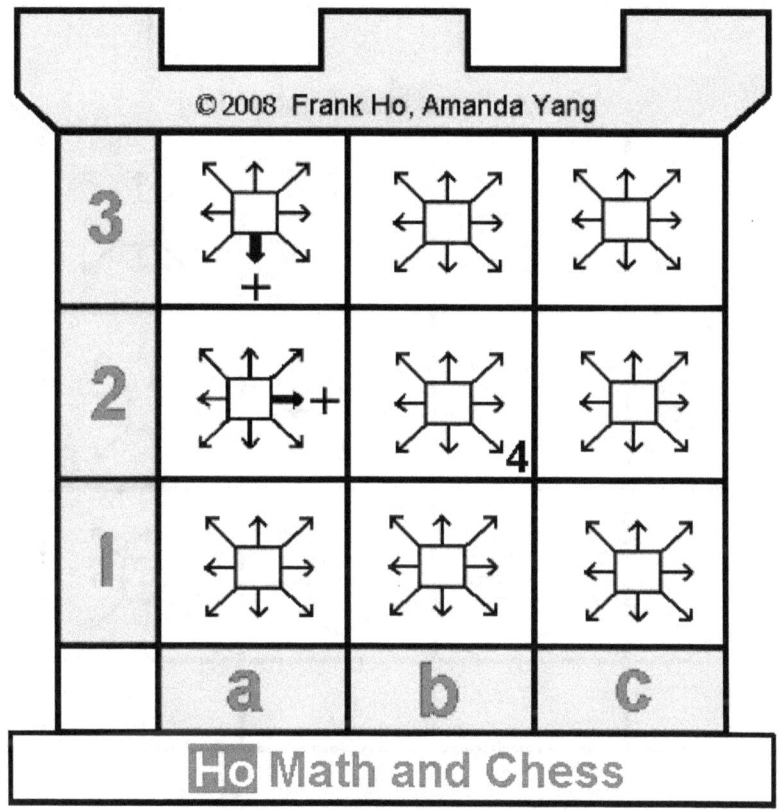

132
213
321

Frankho ChessDoku™ # 103

Frankho ChessDoku™ is solved by using addition, subtraction, multiplication, or division by following chess moves and logic.

Rule: All the digits 1 to 3 must appear exactly once in every row and column. The number appears in the bottom right-hand corner is the result calculated according to the arithmetic operator(s) and chess move(s) as indicated by the darker arrow(s).

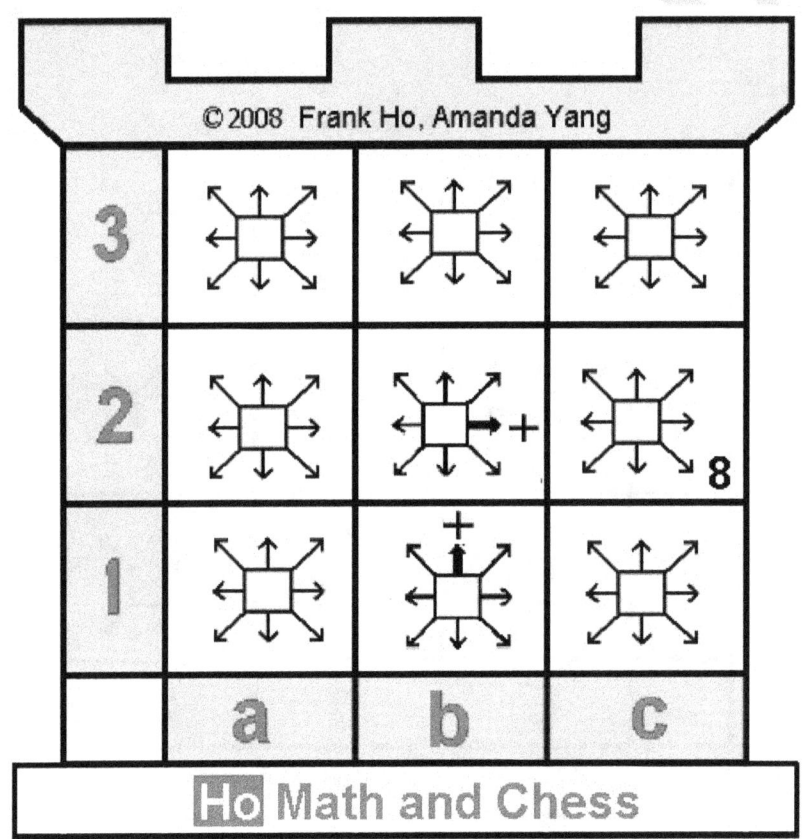

312
123
213

Frankho ChessDoku™ # 104

Frankho ChessDoku™ is solved by using addition, subtraction, multiplication, or division by following chess moves and logic.

Rule: All the digits 1 to 3 must appear exactly once in every row and column. The number appears in the bottom right-hand corner is the result calculated according to the arithmetic operator(s) and chess move(s) as indicated by the darker arrow(s).

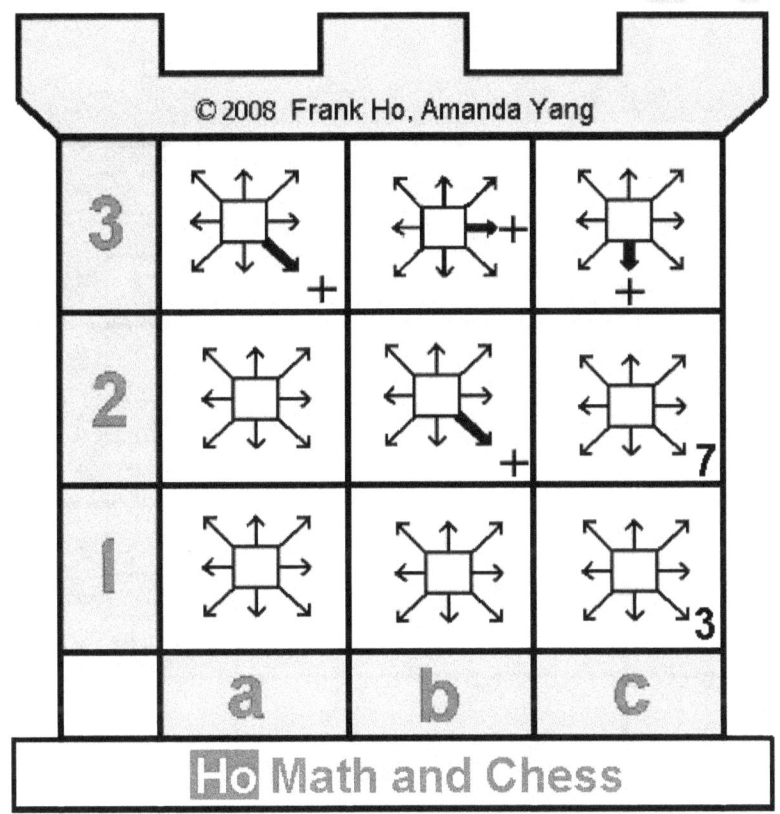

123
312
231

Frankho ChessDoku™ # 105

Frankho ChessDoku™ is solved by using addition, subtraction, multiplication, or division by following chess moves and logic.

Rule: All the digits 1 to 3 must appear exactly once in every row and column. The number appears in the bottom right-hand corner is the result calculated according to the arithmetic operator(s) and chess move(s) as indicated by the darker arrow(s).

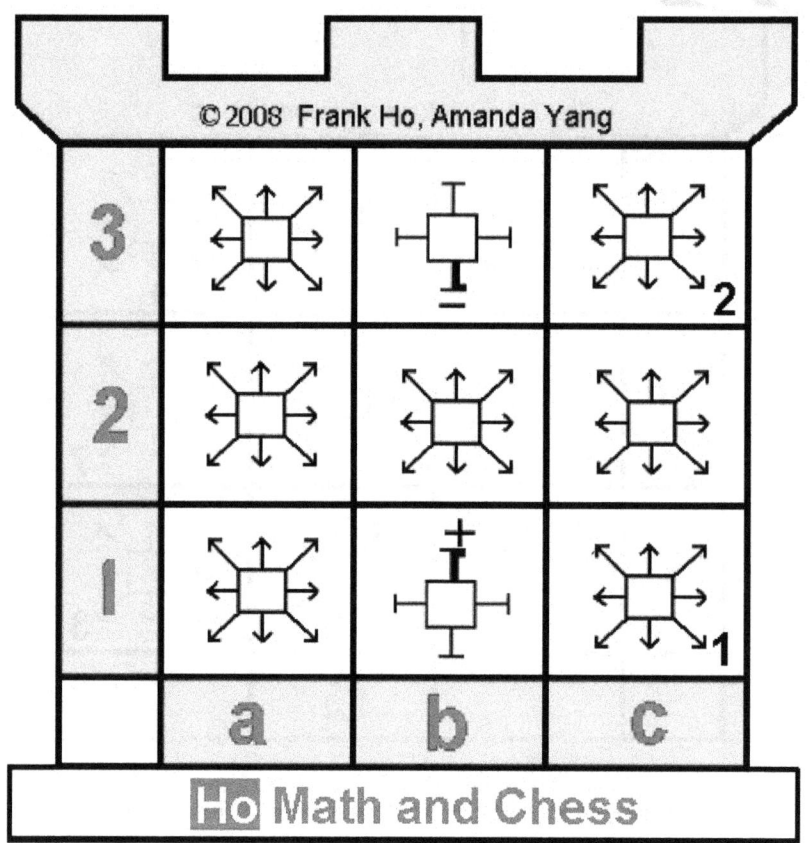

231
123
312

Frankho ChessDoku™ # 106

Frankho ChessDoku™ is solved by using addition, subtraction, multiplication, or division by following chess moves and logic.

Rule: All the digits 1 to 3 must appear exactly once in every row and column. The number appears in the bottom right-hand corner is the result calculated according to the arithmetic operator(s) and chess move(s) as indicated by the darker arrow(s).

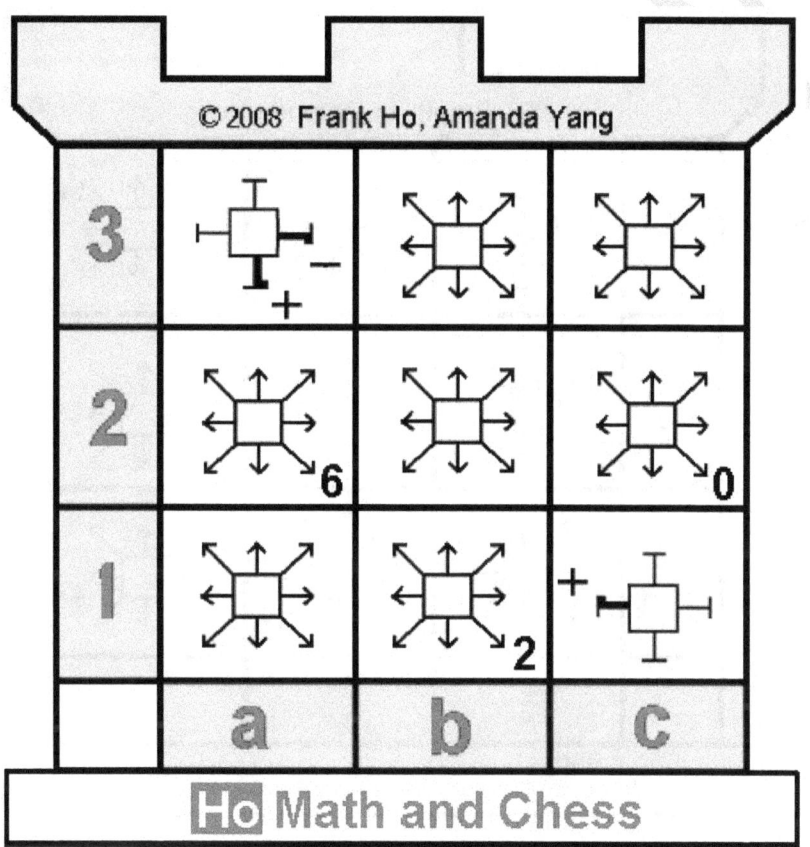

132
321
213

Frankho ChessDoku™ # 107

Frankho ChessDoku™ is solved by using addition, subtraction, multiplication, or division by following chess moves and logic.

Rule: All the digits 1 to 3 must appear exactly once in every row and column. The number appears in the bottom right-hand corner is the result calculated according to the arithmetic operator(s) and chess move(s) as indicated by the darker arrow(s).

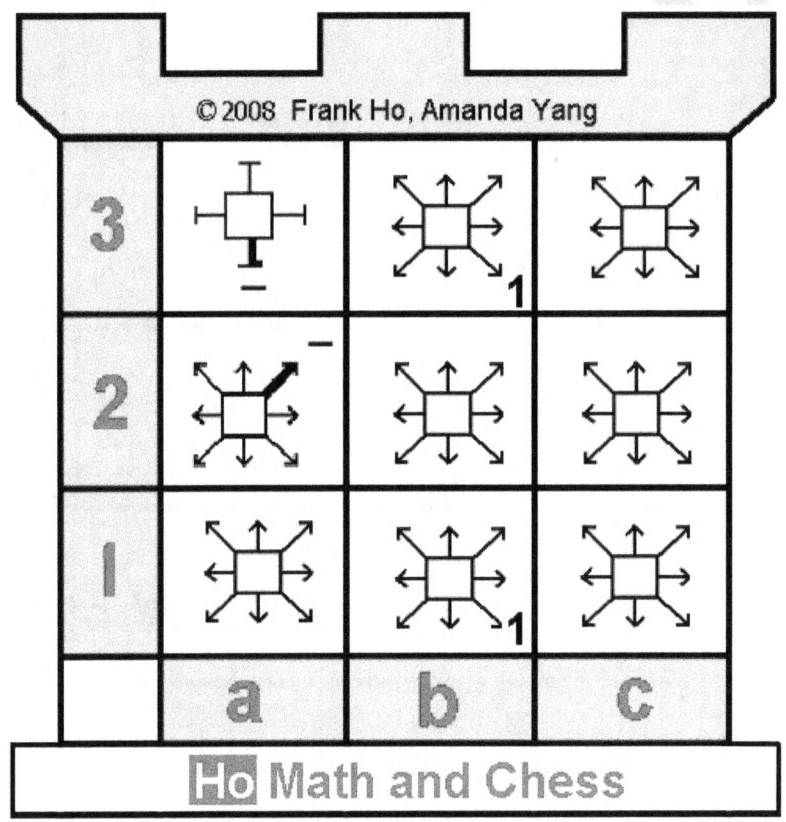

312
231
123

Frankho ChessDoku™ # 108

Frankho ChessDoku™ is solved by using addition, subtraction, multiplication, or division by following chess moves and logic.

Rule: All the digits 1 to 3 must appear exactly once in every row and column. The number appears in the bottom right-hand corner is the result calculated according to the arithmetic operator(s) and chess move(s) as indicated by the darker arrow(s).

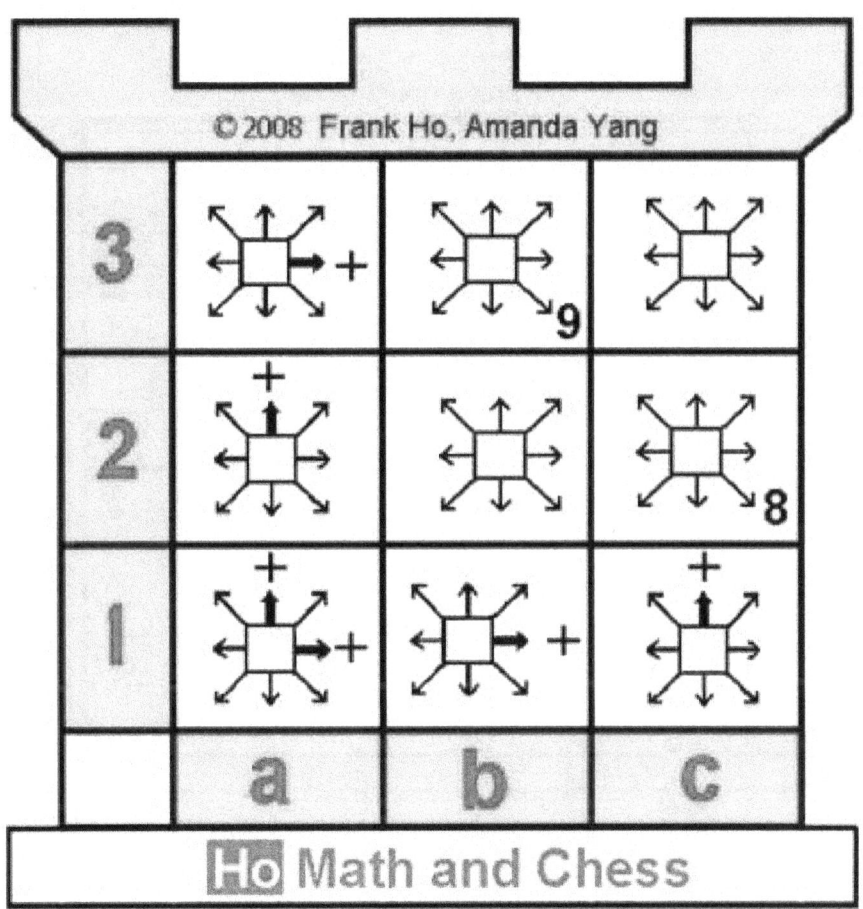

231
312
123

Frankho ChessDoku™ # 109

Frankho ChessDoku™ is solved by using addition, subtraction, multiplication, or division by following chess moves and logic.

Rule: All the digits 1 to 3 must appear exactly once in every row and column. The number appears in the bottom right-hand corner is the result calculated according to the arithmetic operator(s) and chess move(s) as indicated by the darker arrow(s).

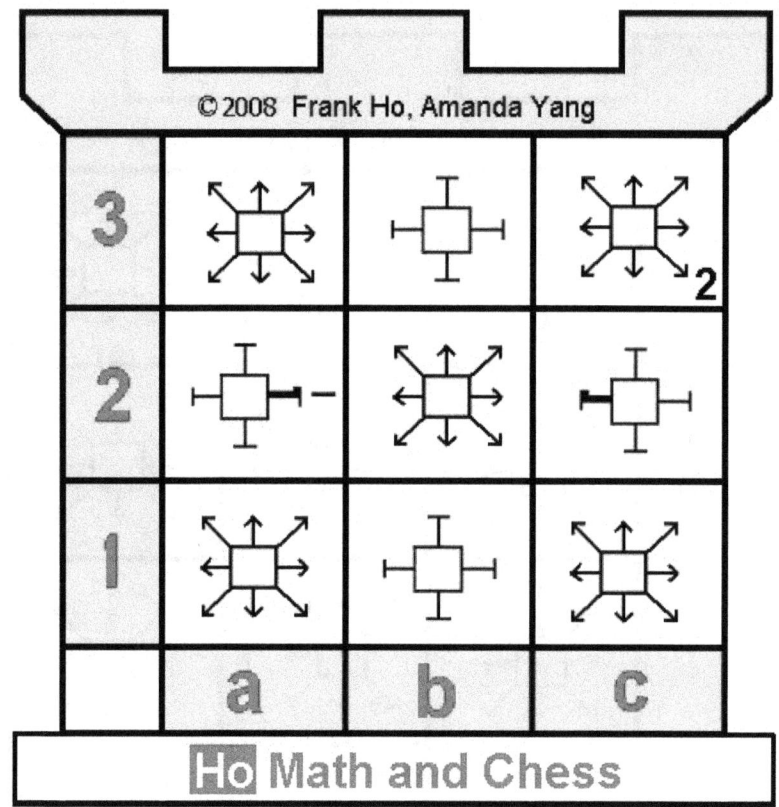

231
312
123

Math Chess Sudoku Puzzles 一青少年益智棋芸健脑

Frankho ChessDoku 一 何数棋谜算独

© 2007 — 2020   Frank Ho, Amanda Ho   All rights reserved.   www.homathchess.com

Student's name _____ Date _____

Frankho ChessDoku™ # 110

Frankho ChessDoku™ is solved by using addition, subtraction, multiplication, or division by following chess moves and logic.

Rule: All the digits 1 to 3 must appear exactly once in every row and column. The number appears in the bottom right-hand corner is the result calculated according to the arithmetic operator(s) and chess move(s) as indicated by the darker arrow(s).

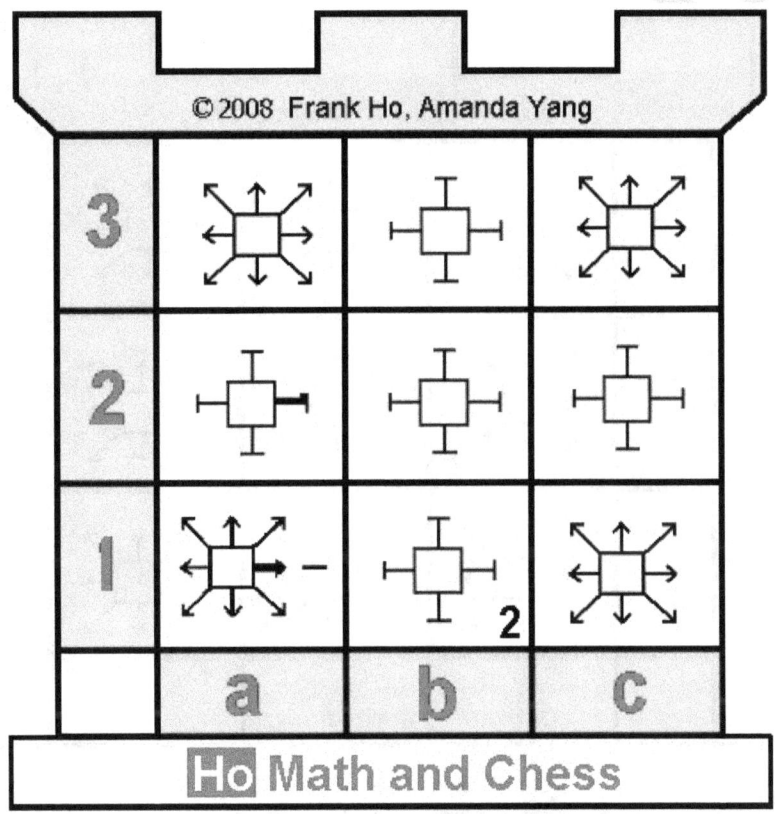

231
123
312

Frankho ChessDoku™ # 111

Frankho ChessDoku™ is solved by using addition, subtraction, multiplication, or division by following chess moves and logic.

Rule: All the digits 1 to 3 must appear exactly once in every row and column. The number appears in the bottom right-hand corner is the result calculated according to the arithmetic operator(s) and chess move(s) as indicated by the darker arrow(s).

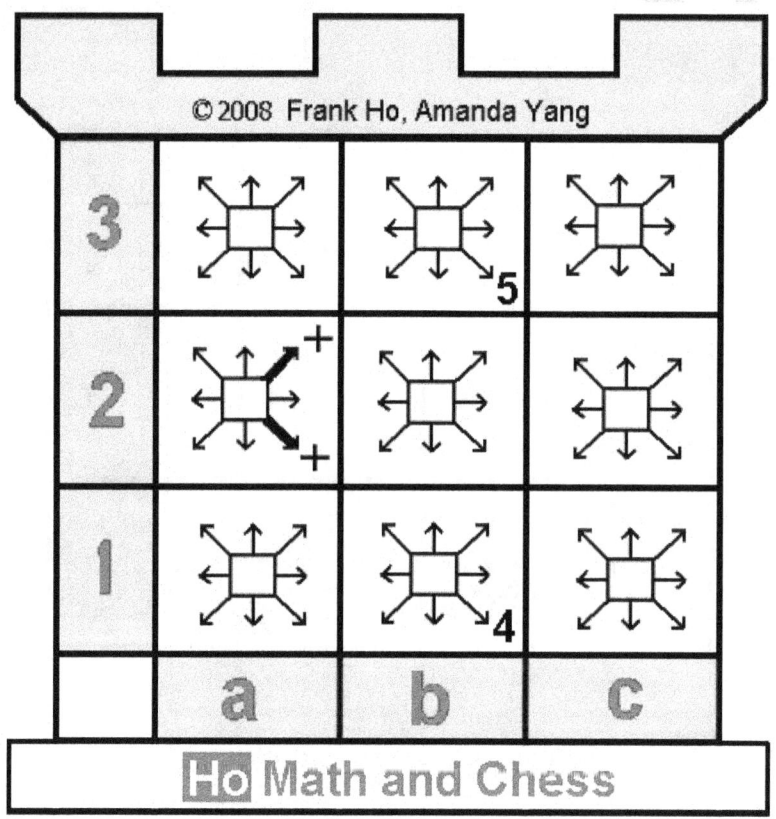

132
213
321

Frankho ChessDoku™ # 112

Frankho ChessDoku™ is solved by using addition, subtraction, multiplication, or division by following chess moves and logic.

Rule: All the digits 1 to 3 must appear exactly once in every row and column. The number appears in the bottom right-hand corner is the result calculated according to the arithmetic operator(s) and chess move(s) as indicated by the darker arrow(s).

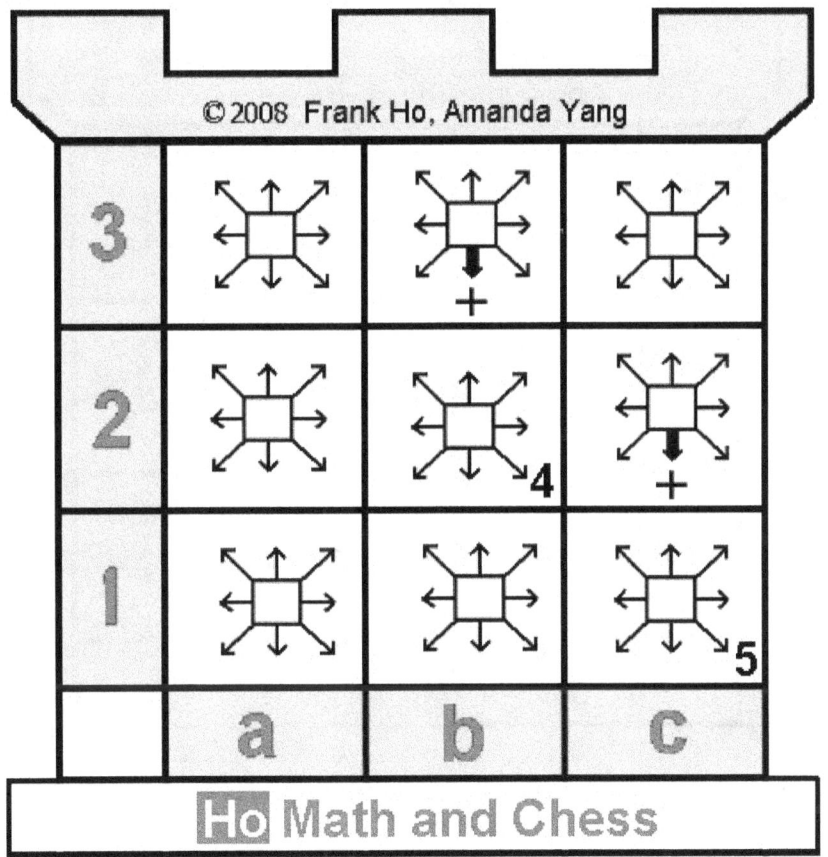

231
312
123

Frankho ChessDoku™ # 113

Frankho ChessDoku™ is solved by using addition, subtraction, multiplication, or division by following chess moves and logic.

Rule: All the digits 1 to 3 must appear exactly once in every row and column. The number appears in the bottom right-hand corner is the result calculated according to the arithmetic operator(s) and chess move(s) as indicated by the darker arrow(s).

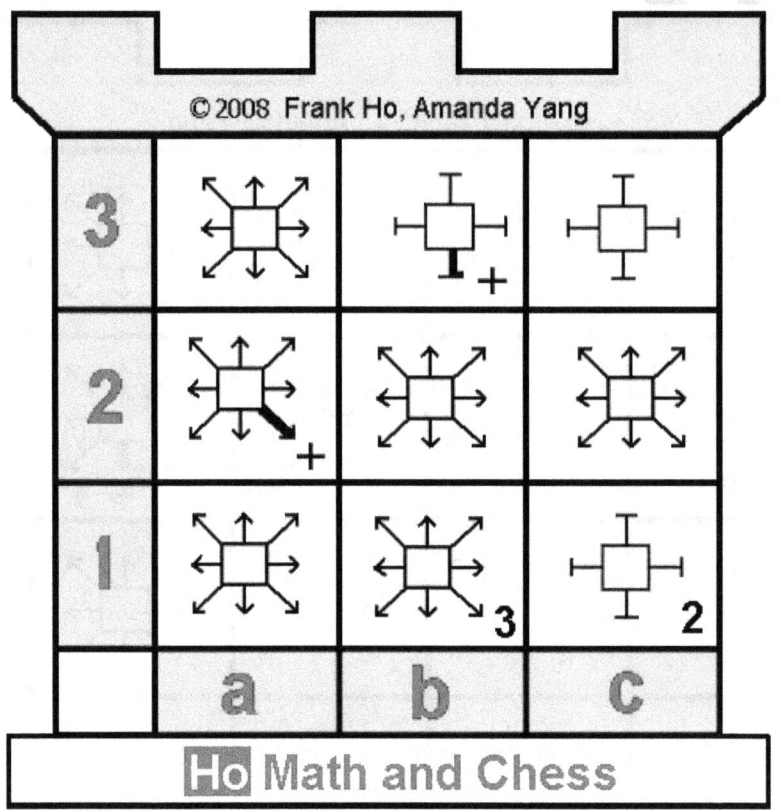

213
132
321

Frankho ChessDoku™ # 114

Frankho ChessDoku™ is solved by using addition, subtraction, multiplication, or division by following chess moves and logic.

Rule: All the digits 1 to 3 must appear exactly once in every row and column. The number appears in the bottom right-hand corner is the result calculated according to the arithmetic operator(s) and chess move(s) as indicated by the darker arrow(s).

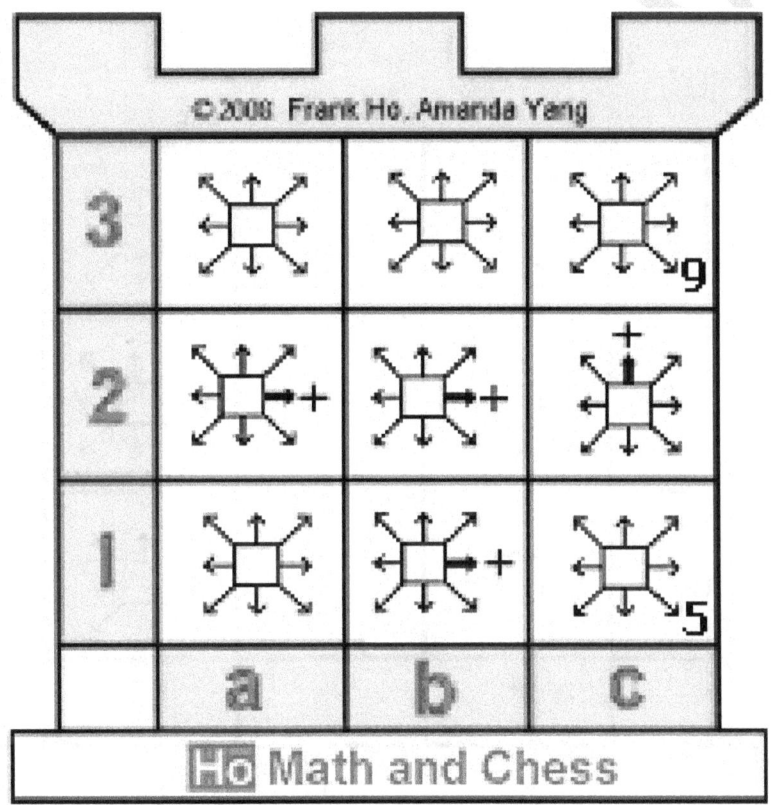

213
321
132

Frankho ChessDoku™ # 115

Frankho ChessDoku™ is solved by using addition, subtraction, multiplication, or division by following chess moves and logic.

Rule: All the digits 1 to 3 must appear exactly once in every row and column. The number appears in the bottom right-hand corner is the result calculated according to the arithmetic operator(s) and chess move(s) as indicated by the darker arrow(s).

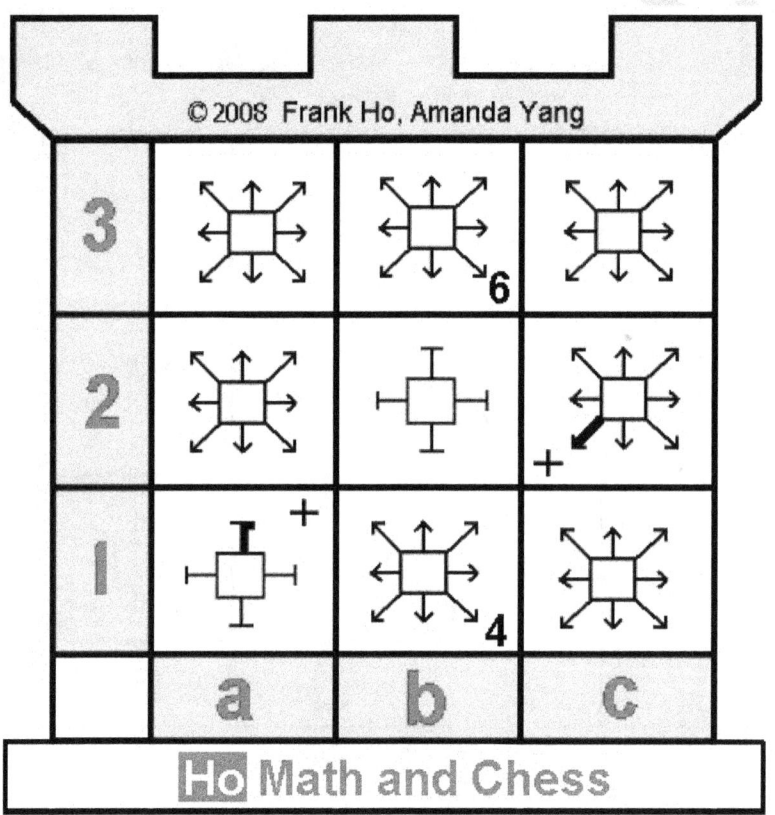

231
123
312

Frankho ChessDoku™ # 116

Frankho ChessDoku™ is solved by using addition, subtraction, multiplication, or division by following chess moves and logic.

Rule: All the digits 1 to 3 must appear exactly once in every row and column. The number appears in the bottom right-hand corner is the result calculated according to the arithmetic operator(s) and chess move(s) as indicated by the darker arrow(s).

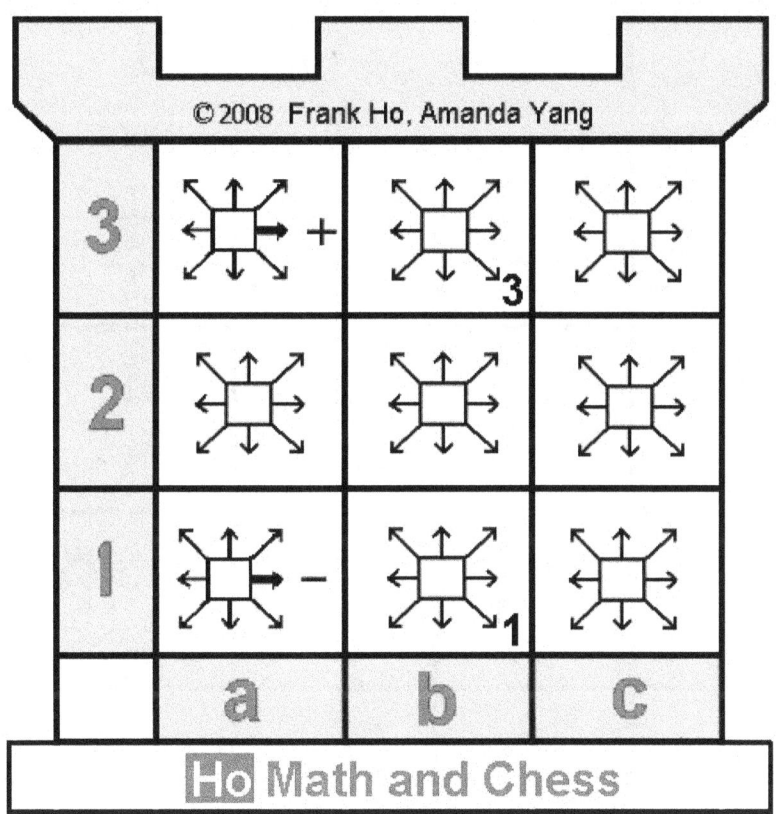

213
132
321

Frankho ChessDoku™ # 117

Frankho ChessDoku™ is solved by using addition, subtraction, multiplication, or division by following chess moves and logic.

Rule: All the digits 1 to 3 must appear exactly once in every row and column. The number appears in the bottom right-hand corner is the result calculated according to the arithmetic operator(s) and chess move(s) as indicated by the darker arrow(s).

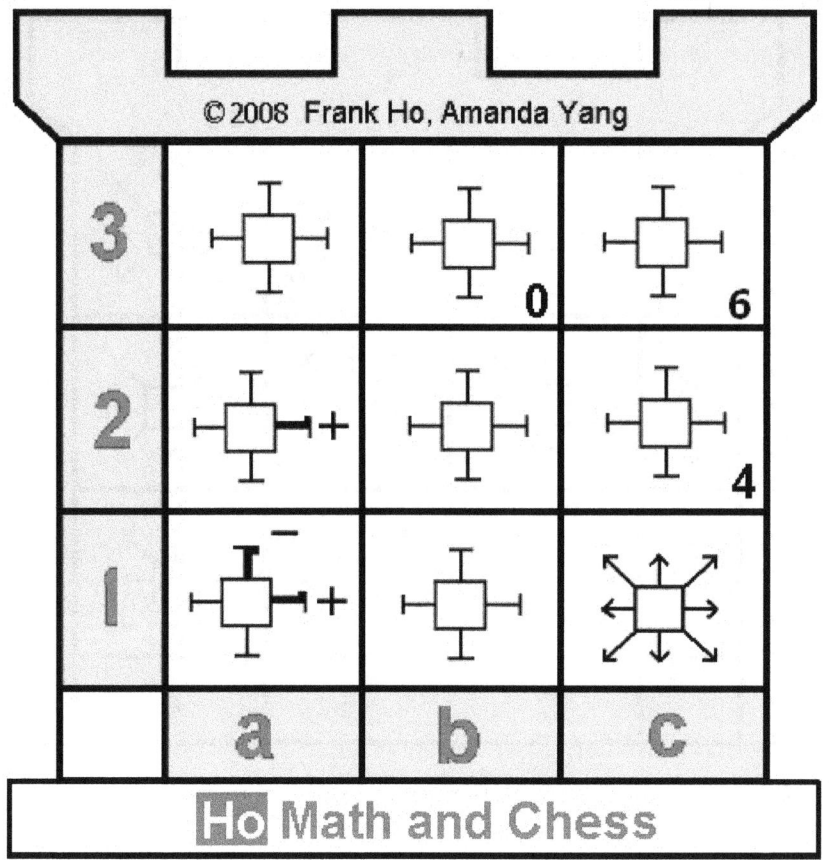

123
312
231

# Frankho ChessDoku™ # 118

RULES:

All the digits 1 to 3 must appear in every row and column. The number appears in the bottom right-hand corner is the result calculated according to operator(s) and chess move(s).

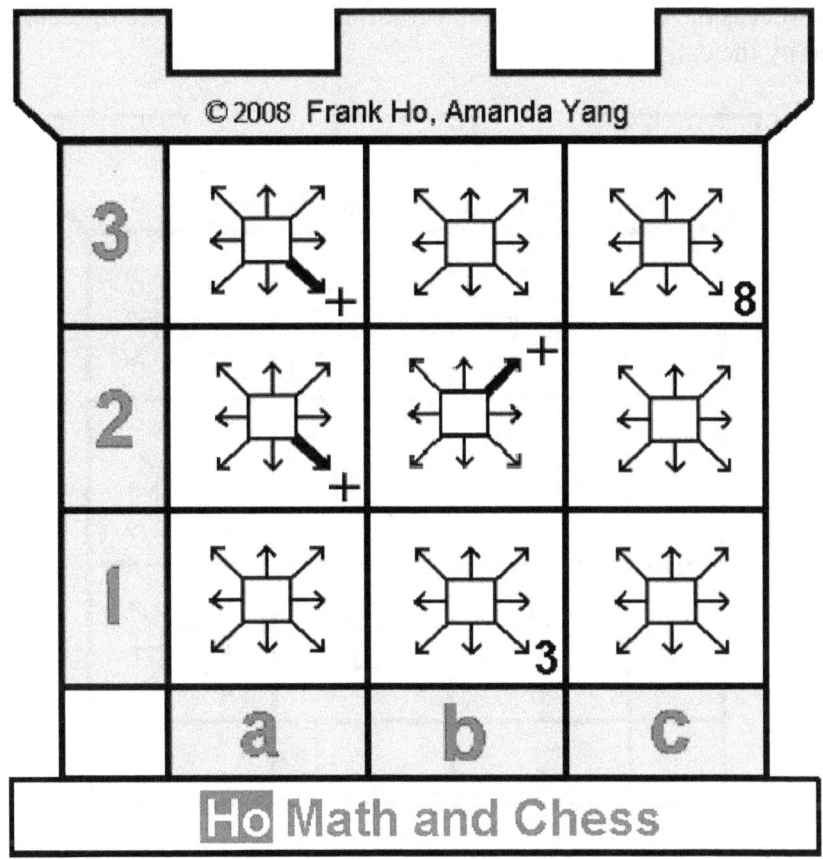

213
132
321

Frankho ChessDoku™ # 119

Frankho ChessDoku™ is solved by using addition, subtraction, multiplication, or division by following chess moves and logic.

Rule: All the digits 1 to 3 must appear exactly once in every row and column. The number appears in the bottom right-hand corner is the result calculated according to the arithmetic operator(s) and chess move(s) as indicated by the darker arrow(s).

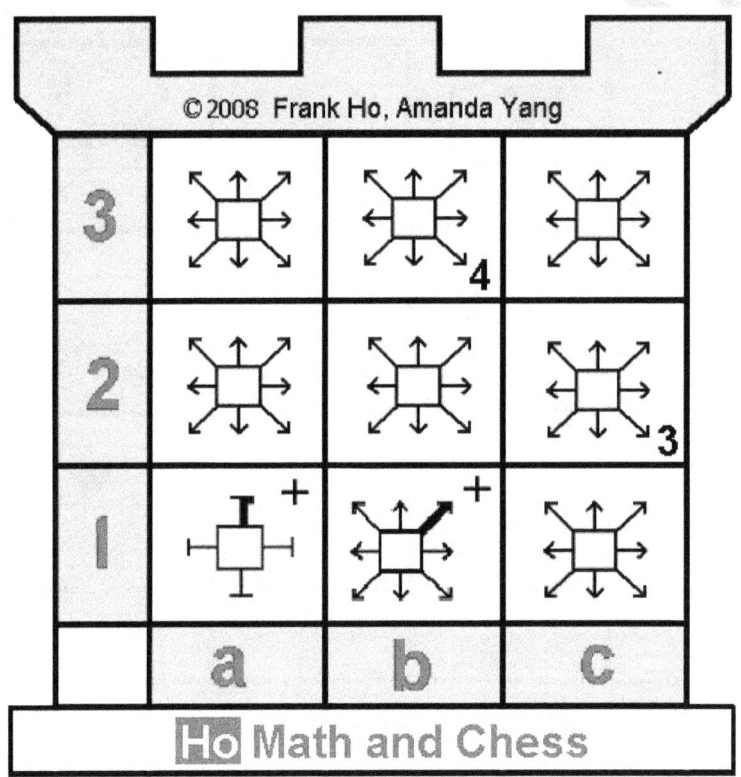

321
132
213

Frankho ChessDoku™ # 120

Frankho ChessDoku™ is solved by using addition, subtraction, multiplication, or division by following chess moves and logic.

Rule: All the digits 1 to 3 must appear exactly once in every row and column. The number appears in the bottom right-hand corner is the result calculated according to the arithmetic operator(s) and chess move(s) as indicated by the darker arrow(s).

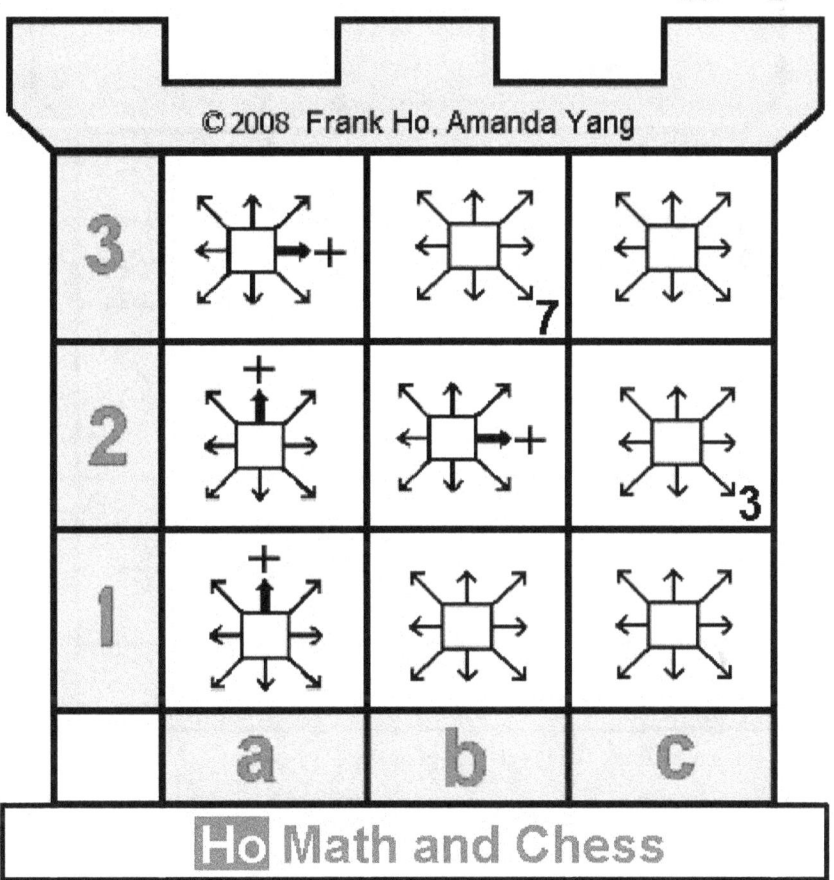

213
321
132

Frankho ChessDoku™ # 121

Frankho ChessDoku™ is solved by using addition, subtraction, multiplication, or division by following chess moves and logic.

Rule: All the digits 1 to 3 must appear exactly once in every row and column. The number appears in the bottom right-hand corner is the result calculated according to the arithmetic operator(s) and chess move(s) as indicated by the darker arrow(s).

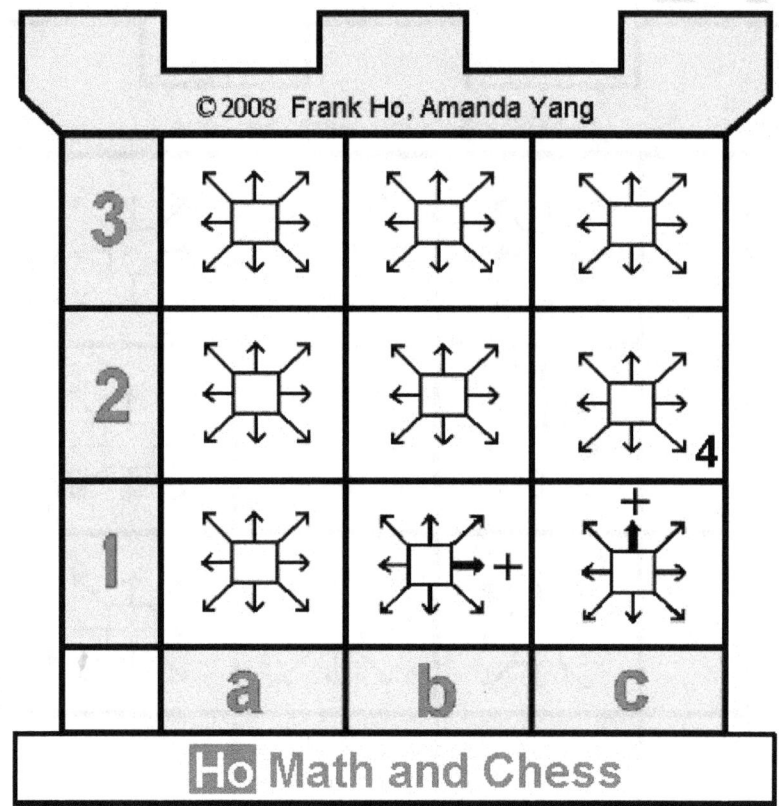

123
231
312

Frankho ChessDoku™ # 122

Frankho ChessDoku™ is solved by using addition, subtraction, multiplication, or division by following chess moves and logic.

Rule: All the digits 1 to 3 must appear exactly once in every row and column. The number appears in the bottom right-hand corner is the result calculated according to the arithmetic operator(s) and chess move(s) as indicated by the darker arrow(s).

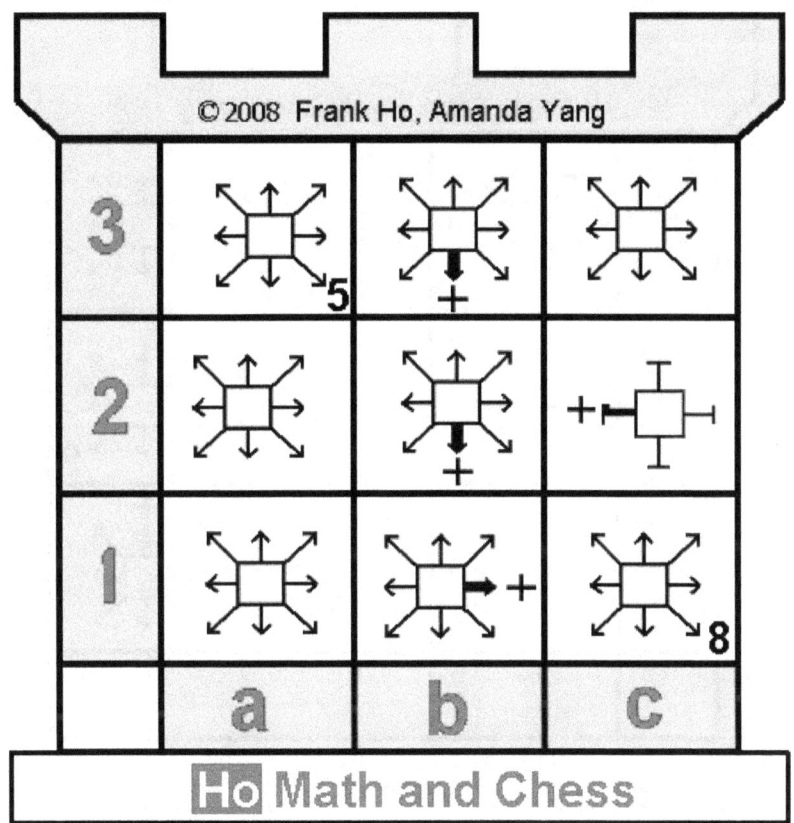

231
123
312

Frankho ChessDoku™ # 123

Frankho ChessDoku™ is solved by using addition, subtraction, multiplication, or division by following chess moves and logic.

Rule: All the digits 1 to 3 must appear exactly once in every row and column. The number appears in the bottom right-hand corner is the result calculated according to the arithmetic operator(s) and chess move(s) as indicated by the darker arrow(s).

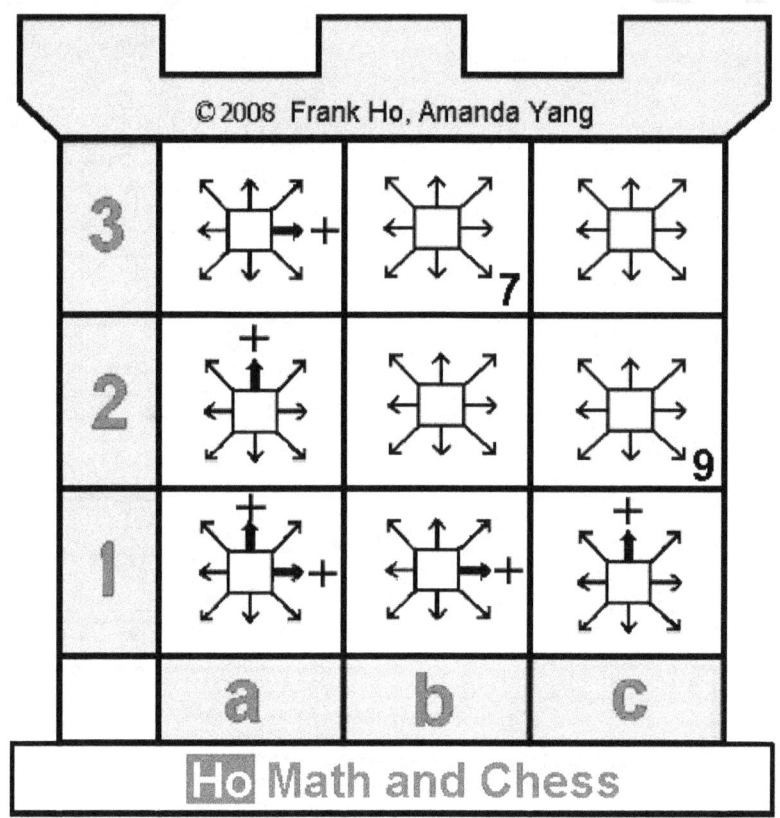

312
123
213

Frankho ChessDoku™ # 124

Frankho ChessDoku™ is solved by using addition, subtraction, multiplication, or division by following chess moves and logic.

Rule: All the digits 1 to 3 must appear exactly once in every row and column. The number appears in the bottom right-hand corner is the result calculated according to the arithmetic operator(s) and chess move(s) as indicated by the darker arrow(s).

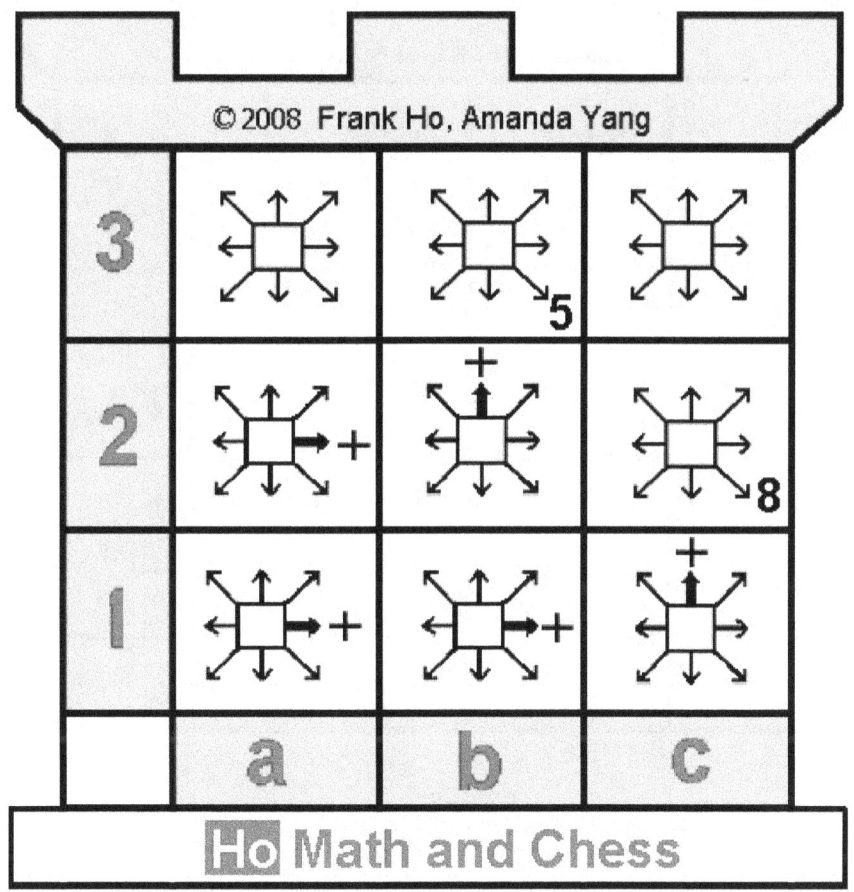

213
132
321

Math Chess Sudoku Puzzles 一青少年益智棋芸健脑

Frankho ChessDoku 一 何数棋谜算独

© 2007 一 2020 Frank Ho, Amanda Ho   All rights reserved.   www.homathchess.com

Student's name_____ Date_____

Frankho ChessDoku™ # 125

RULES:

All the digits 1 to 3 must appear in every row and column. The number appears in the bottom right-hand corner is the result calculated according to operator(s) and chess move(s).

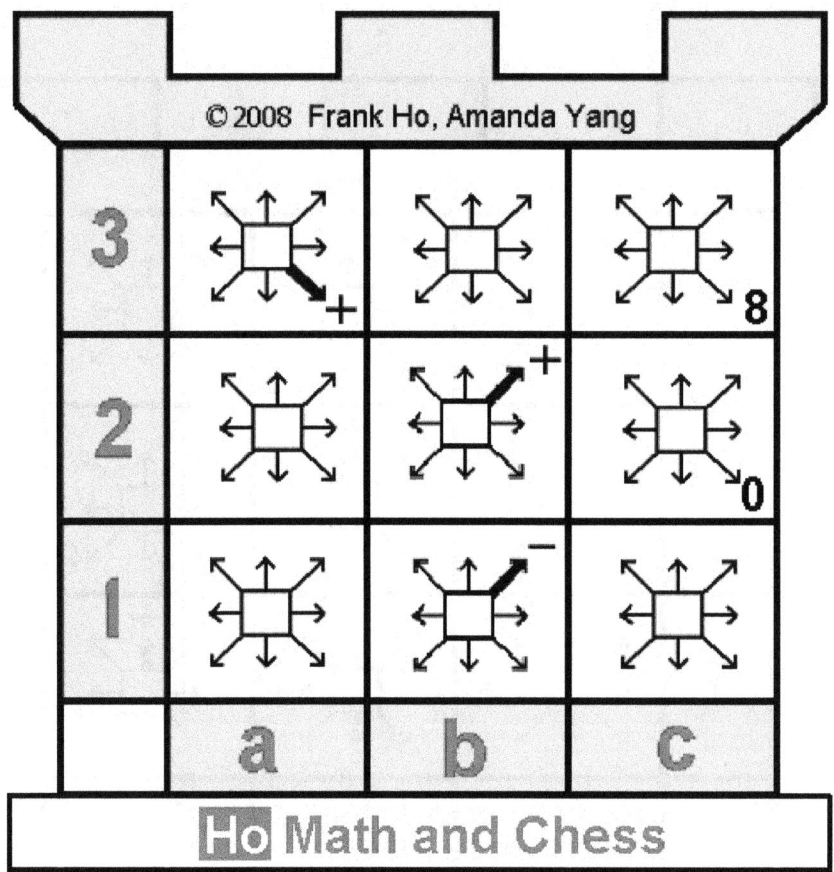

213
132
321

Frankho ChessDoku™ # 126

Frankho ChessDoku™ is solved by using addition, subtraction, multiplication, or division by following chess moves and logic.

Rule: All the digits 1 to 3 must appear exactly once in every row and column. The number appears in the bottom right-hand corner is the result calculated according to the arithmetic operator(s) and chess move(s) as indicated by the darker arrow(s).

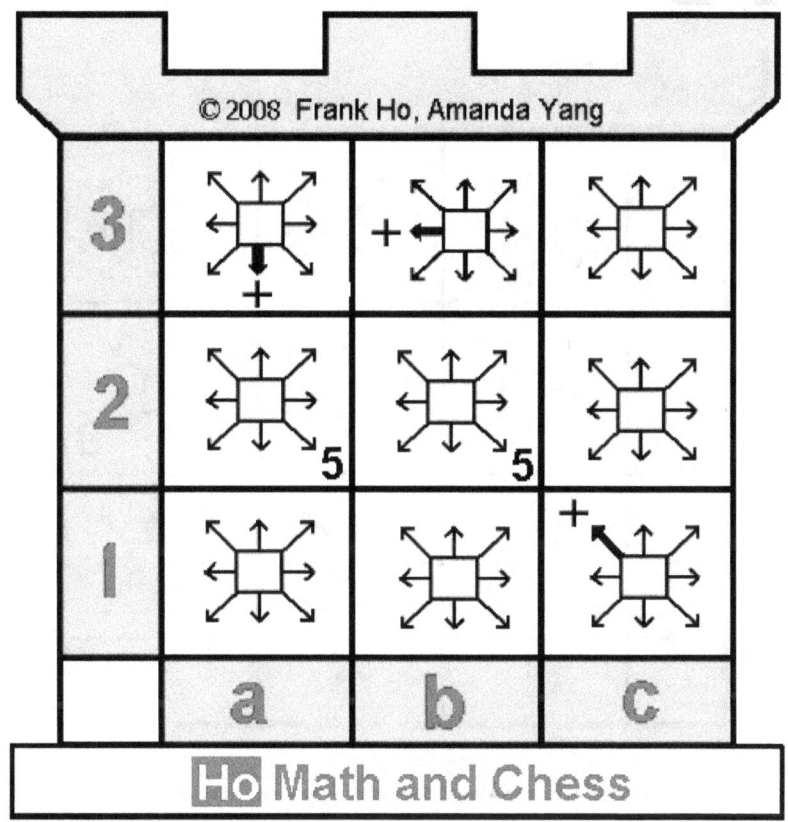

123
231
312

Frankho ChessDoku™ # 127

Frankho ChessDoku™ is solved by using addition, subtraction, multiplication, or division by following chess moves and logic.

Rule: All the digits 1 to 3 must appear exactly once in every row and column. The number appears in the bottom right-hand corner is the result calculated according to the arithmetic operator(s) and chess move(s) as indicated by the darker arrow(s).

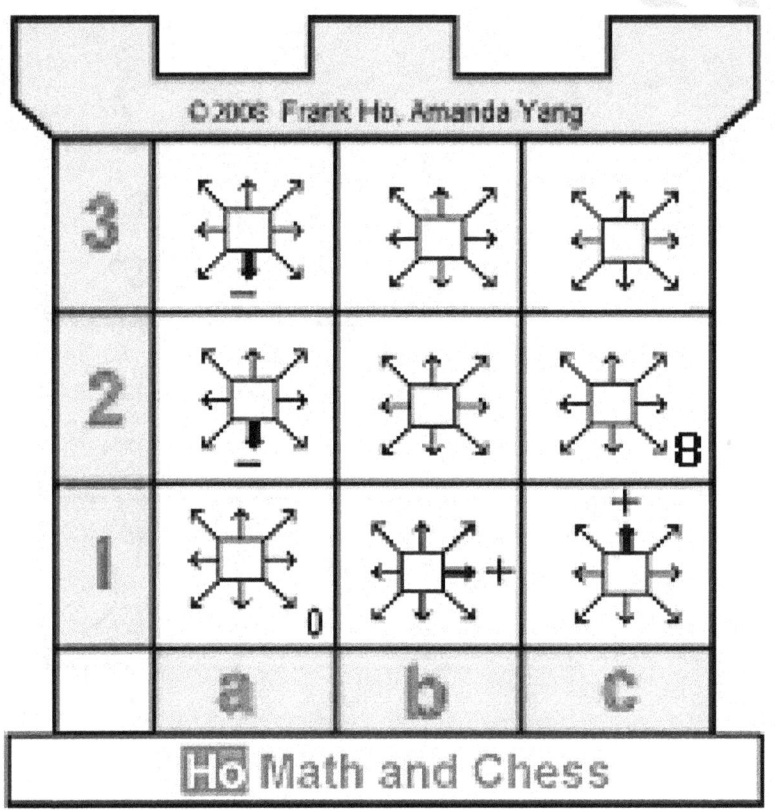

321
213
132

Frankho ChessDoku™ # 128

Frankho ChessDoku™ is solved by using addition, subtraction, multiplication, or division by following chess moves and logic.

Rule: All the digits 1 to 3 must appear exactly once in every row and column. The number appears in the bottom right-hand corner is the result calculated according to the arithmetic operator(s) and chess move(s) as indicated by the darker arrow(s).

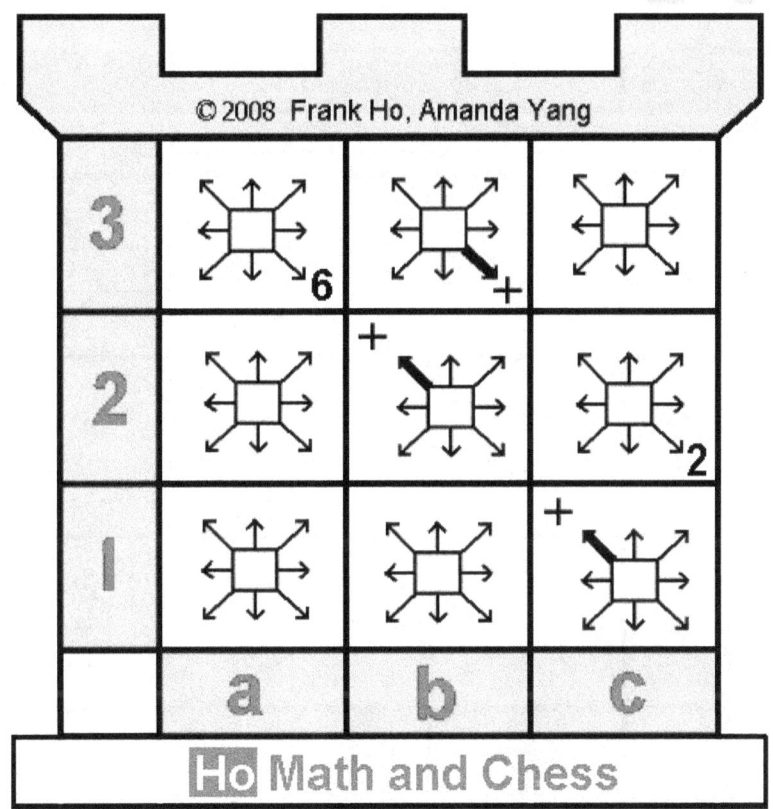

213
321
132

Frankho ChessDoku™ # 129

Frankho ChessDoku™ is solved by using addition, subtraction, multiplication, or division by following chess moves and logic.

Rule: All the digits 1 to 3 must appear exactly once in every row and column. The number appears in the bottom right-hand corner is the result calculated according to the arithmetic operator(s) and chess move(s) as indicated by the darker arrow(s).

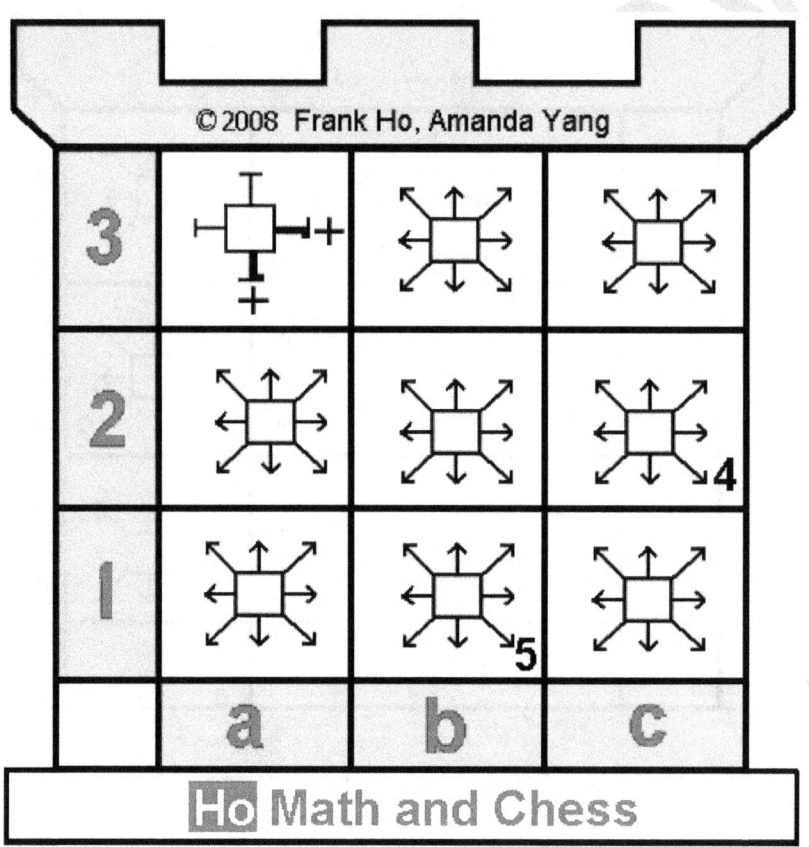

312
231
123

Math Chess Sudoku Puzzles 一青少年益智棋芸健脑

Frankho ChessDoku 一 何数棋谜算独

© 2007 — 2020 Frank Ho, Amanda Ho   All rights reserved.   www.homathchess.com

Student's name _____ Date _____

Frankho ChessDoku™ # 130

RULES:

All the digits 1 to 3 must appear in every row and column. The number appears in the bottom right-hand corner is the result calculated according to operator(s) and chess move(s).

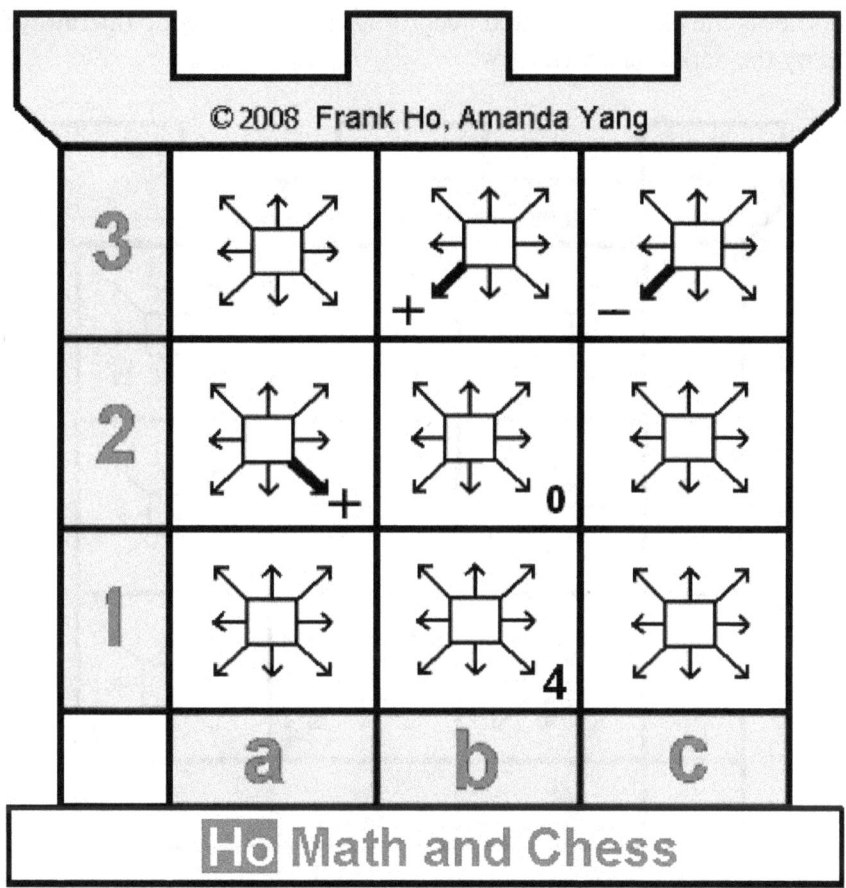

213
321
132

Frankho ChessDoku™ # 131

Frankho ChessDoku™ is solved by using addition, subtraction, multiplication, or division by following chess moves and logic.

Rule: All the digits 1 to 3 must appear exactly once in every row and column. The number appears in the bottom right-hand corner is the result calculated according to the arithmetic operator(s) and chess move(s) as indicated by the darker arrow(s).

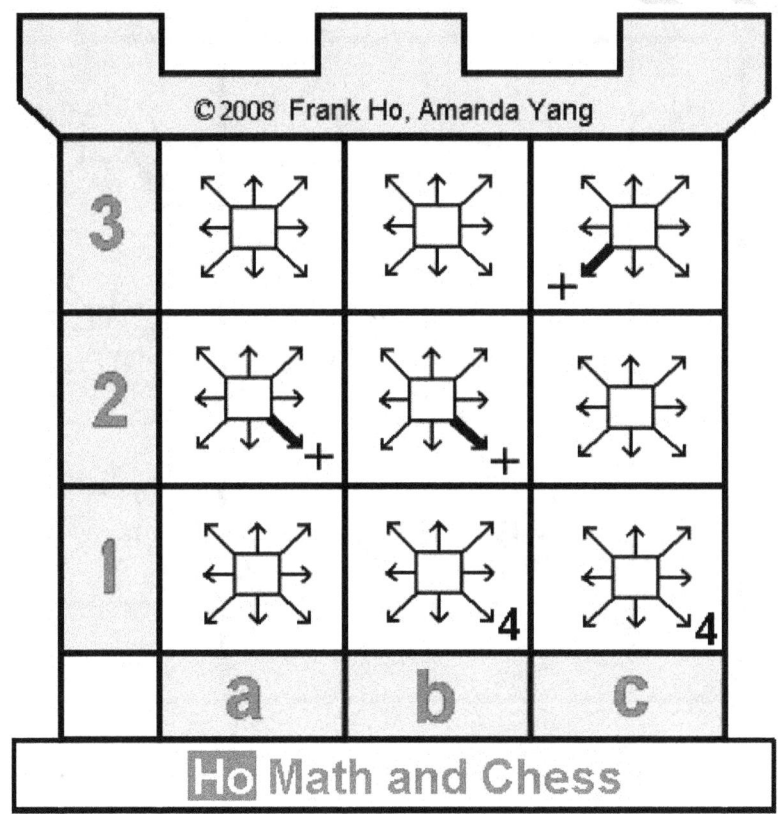

132
213
321

Frankho ChessDoku™ # 132

Frankho ChessDoku™ is solved by using addition, subtraction, multiplication, or division by following chess moves and logic.

Rule: All the digits 1 to 3 must appear exactly once in every row and column. The number appears in the bottom right-hand corner is the result calculated according to the arithmetic operator(s) and chess move(s) as indicated by the darker arrow(s).

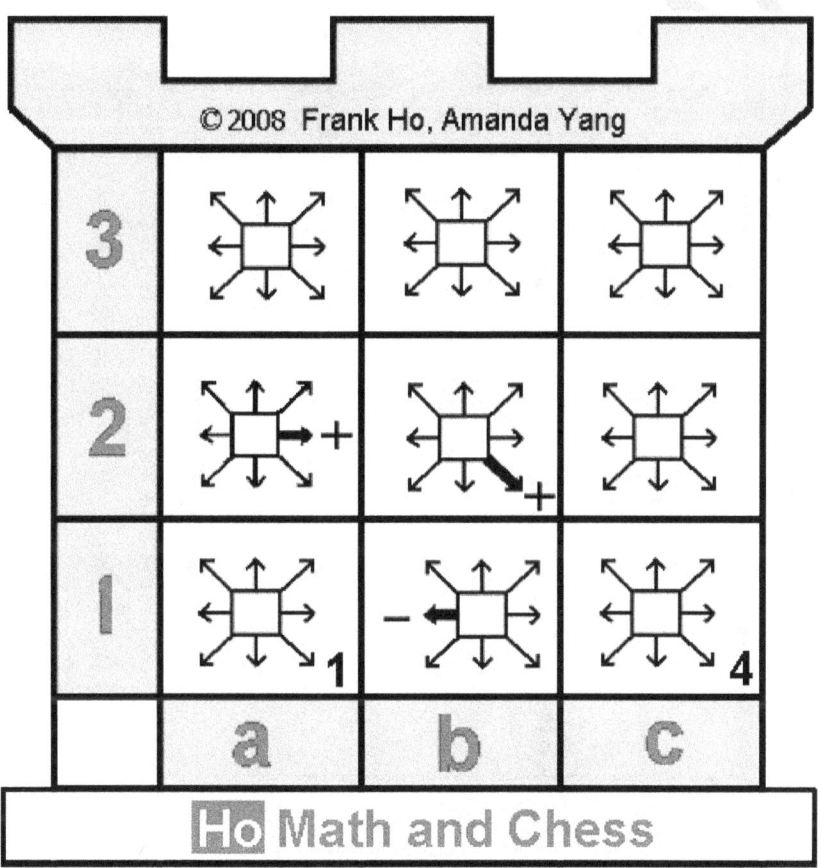

312
123
231

Frankho ChessDoku™ # 133

Frankho ChessDoku™ is solved by using addition, subtraction, multiplication, or division by following chess moves and logic.

Rule: All the digits 1 to 3 must appear exactly once in every row and column. The number appears in the bottom right-hand corner is the result calculated according to the arithmetic operator(s) and chess move(s) as indicated by the darker arrow(s).

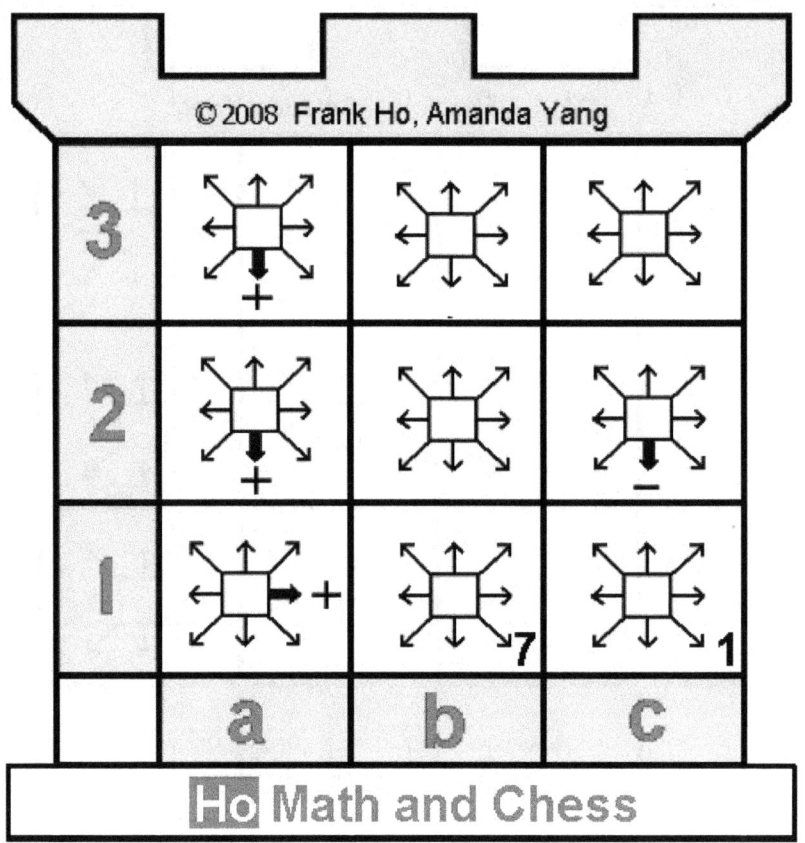

231
123
312

Frankho ChessDoku™ # 134

Frankho ChessDoku™ is solved by using addition, subtraction, multiplication, or division by following chess moves and logic.

Rule: All the digits 1 to 3 must appear exactly once in every row and column. The number appears in the bottom right-hand corner is the result calculated according to the arithmetic operator(s) and chess move(s) as indicated by the darker arrow(s).

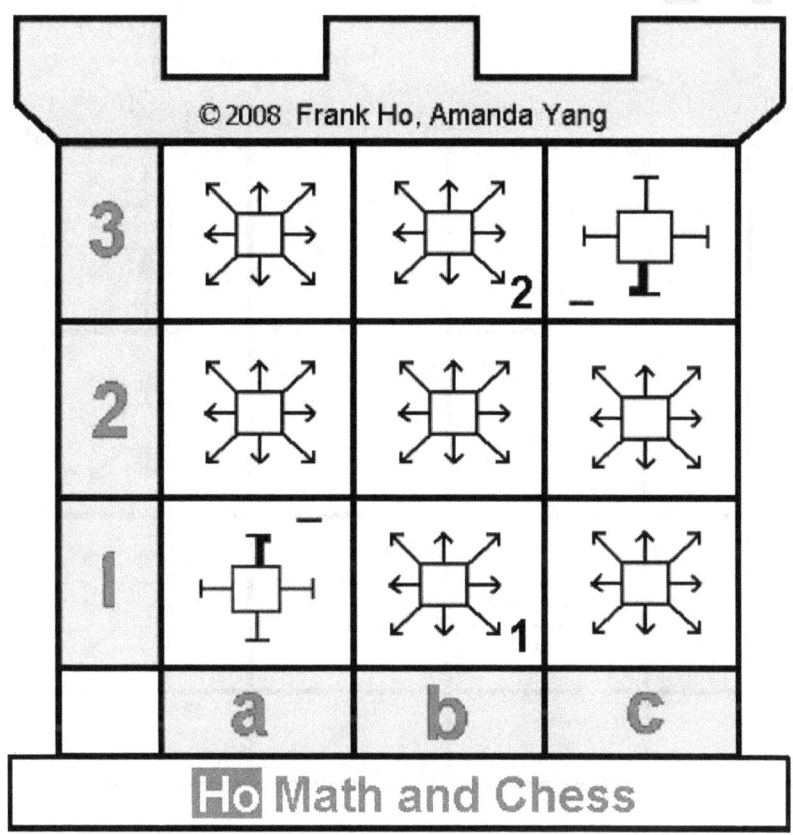

213
132
321

Frankho ChessDoku™ # 135

Frankho ChessDoku™ is solved by using addition, subtraction, multiplication, or division by following chess moves and logic.

Rule: All the digits 1 to 3 must appear exactly once in every row and column. The number appears in the bottom right-hand corner is the result calculated according to the arithmetic operator(s) and chess move(s) as indicated by the darker arrow(s).

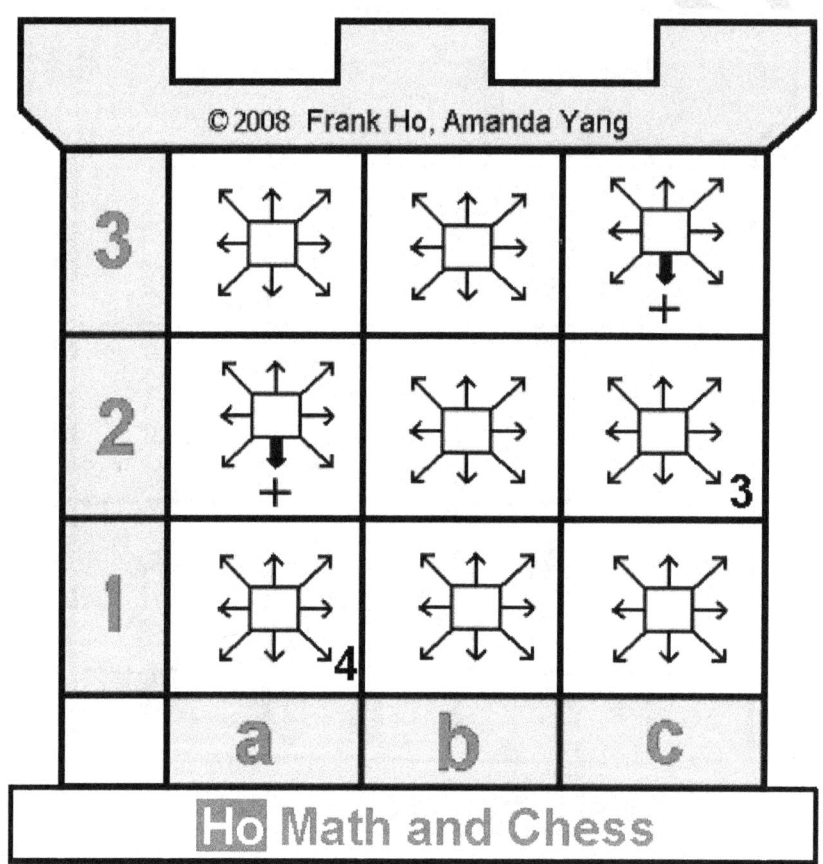

231
312
123

Frankho ChessDoku™ # 136

Rule: All the digits 1 to 3 must appear exactly once in every row and column. The number appears in the bottom right-hand corner is the result calculated according to the arithmetic operator(s) and chess move(s) as indicated by the darker arrow(s).

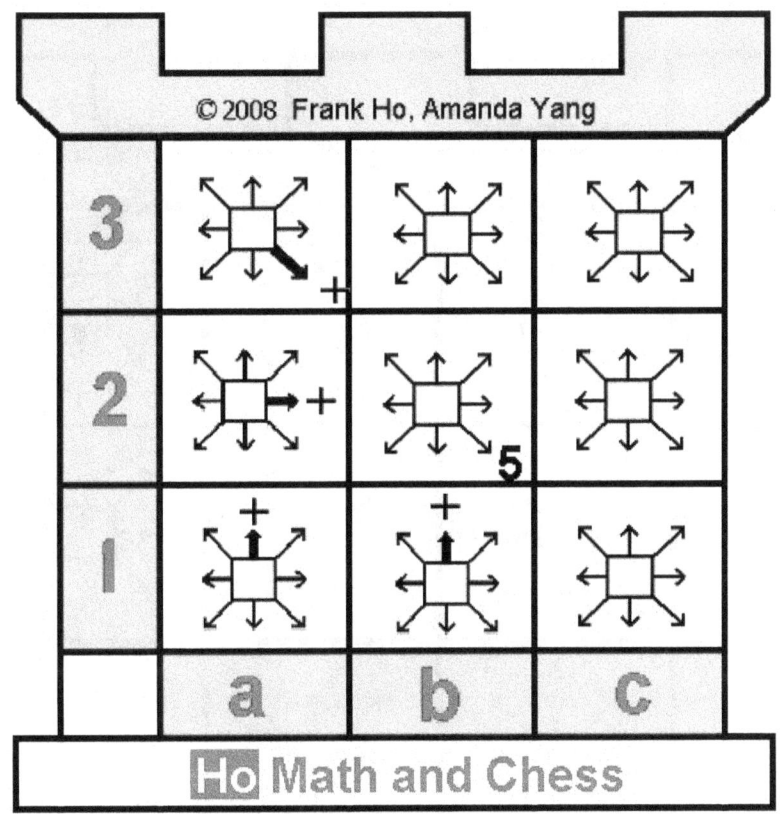

312
123
231

Frankho ChessDoku™ # 137

Rule: All the digits 1 to 3 must appear exactly once in every row and column. The number appears in the bottom right-hand corner is the result calculated according to the arithmetic operator(s) and chess move(s) as indicated by the darker arrow(s).

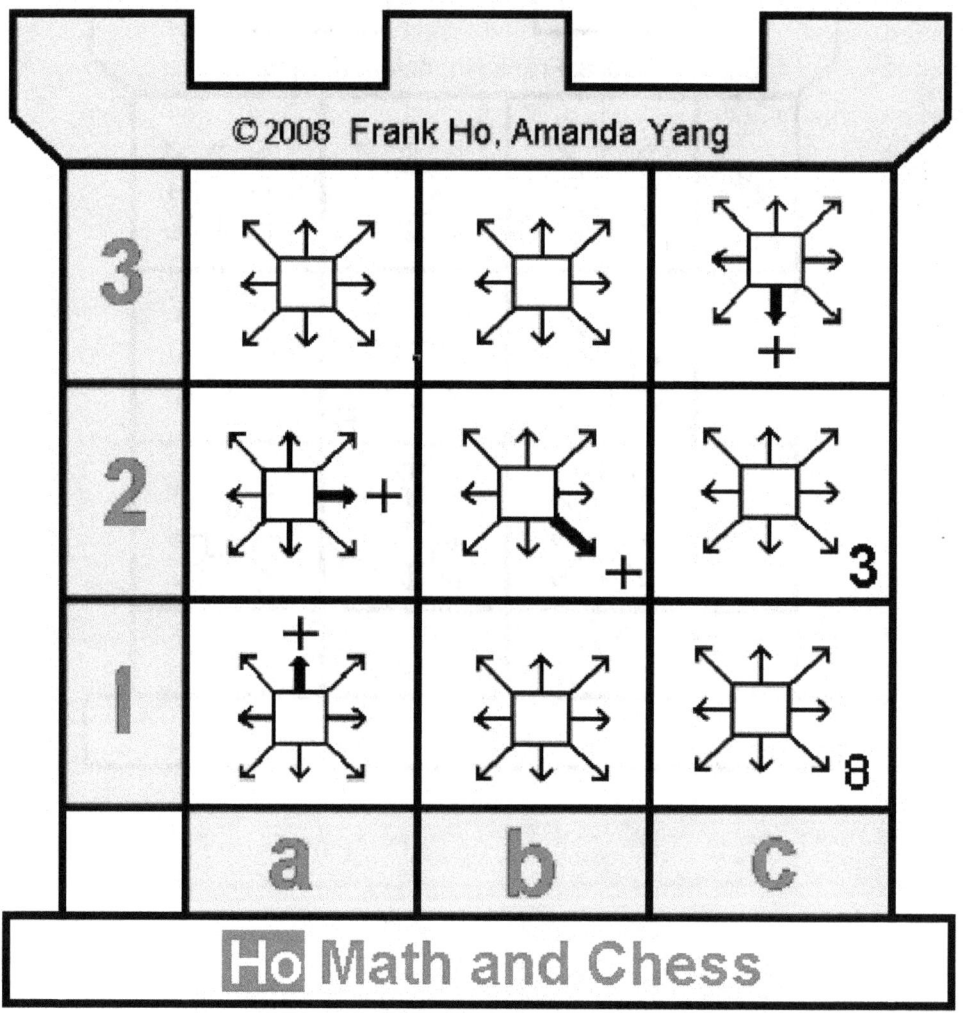

231
312
123

Frankho ChessDoku™ # 138

Frankho ChessDoku™ is solved by using addition, subtraction, multiplication, or division by following chess moves and logic.

Rule: All the digits 1 to 3 must appear exactly once in every row and column. The number appears in the bottom right-hand corner is the result calculated according to the arithmetic operator(s) and chess move(s) as indicated by the darker arrow(s).

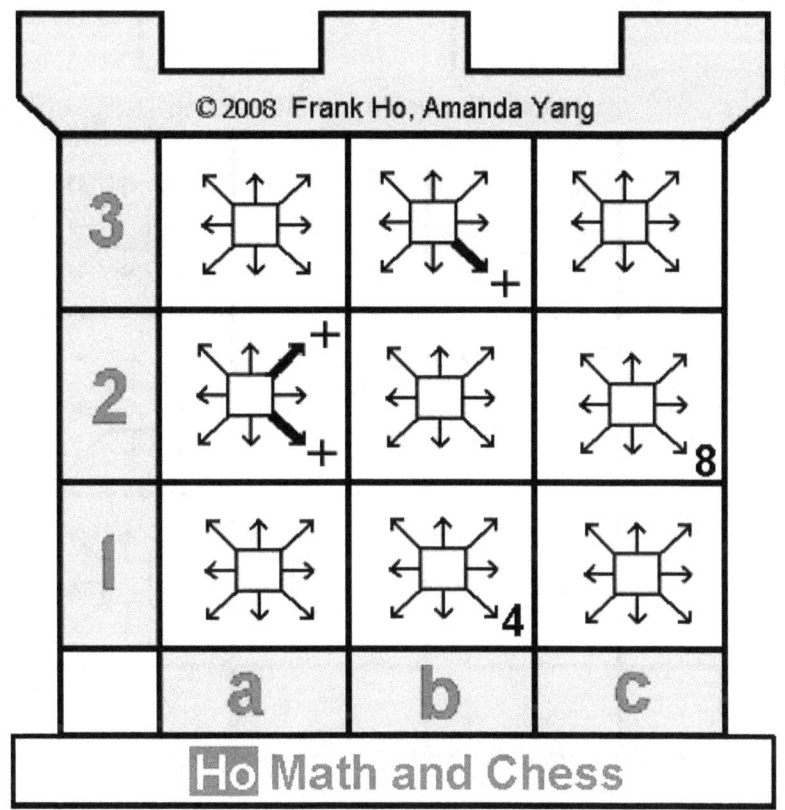

132
213
321

Frankho ChessDoku™ # 139

Frankho ChessDoku™ is solved by using addition, subtraction, multiplication, or division by following chess moves and logic.

Rule: All the digits 1 to 3 must appear exactly once in every row and column. The number appears in the bottom right-hand corner is the result calculated according to the arithmetic operator(s) and chess move(s) as indicated by the darker arrow(s).

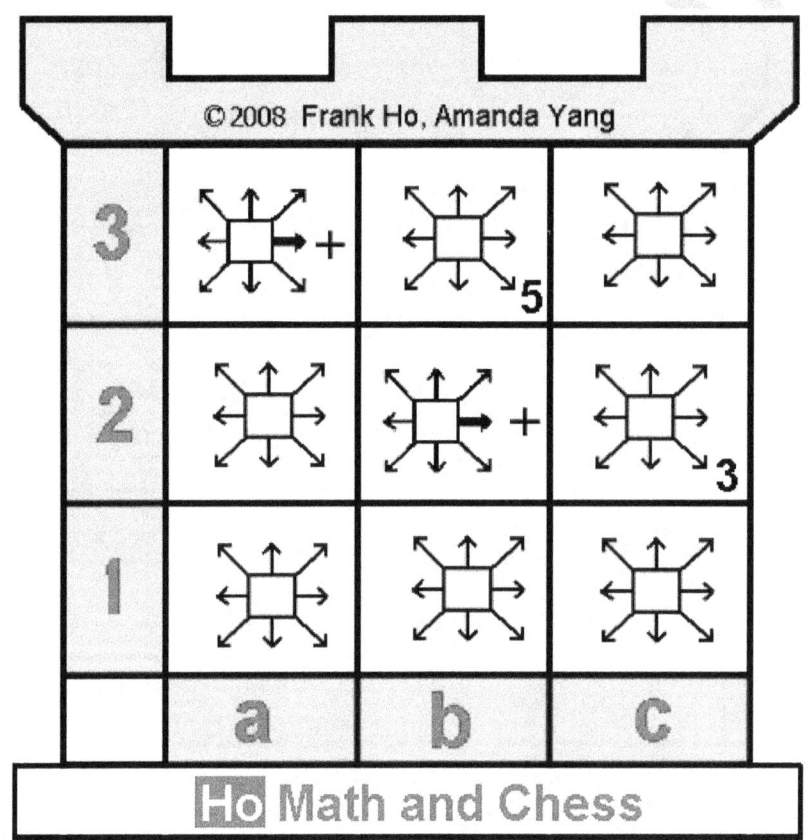

231
312
123

Frankho ChessDoku™ # 140

Frankho ChessDoku™ is solved by using addition, subtraction, multiplication, or division by following chess moves and logic.

Rule: All the digits 1 to 3 must appear exactly once in every row and column. The number appears in the bottom right-hand corner is the result calculated according to the arithmetic operator(s) and chess move(s) as indicated by the darker arrow(s).

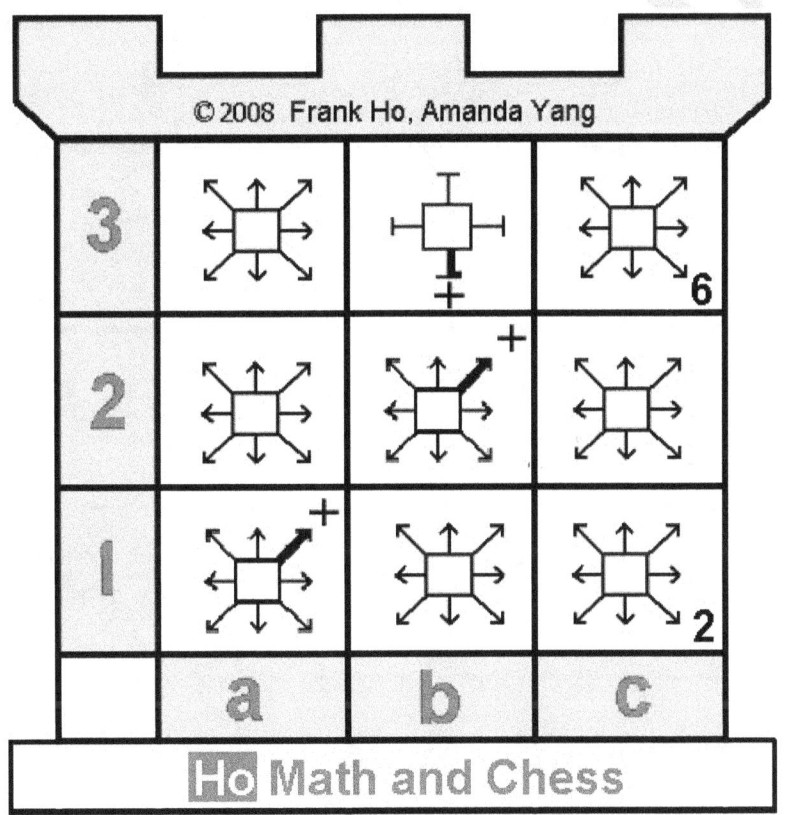

312
123
231

Frankho ChessDoku™ # 141

Frankho ChessDoku™ is solved by using addition, subtraction, multiplication, or division by following chess moves and logic.

Rule: All the digits 1 to 3 must appear exactly once in every row and column. The number appears in the bottom right-hand corner is the result calculated according to the arithmetic operator(s) and chess move(s) as indicated by the darker arrow(s).

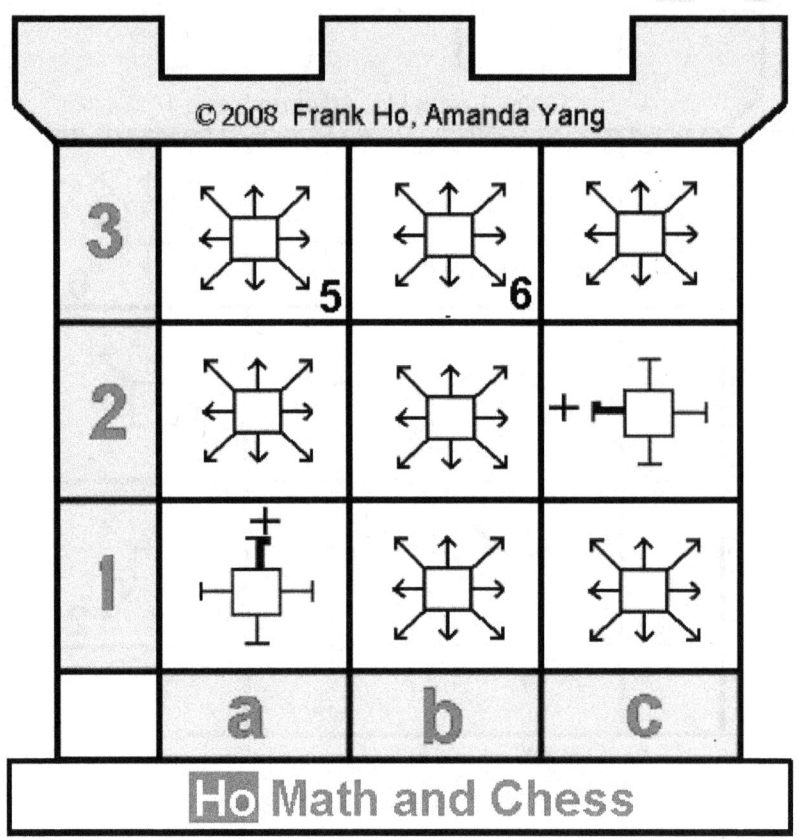

231
123
312

Math Chess Sudoku Puzzles 一 青少年益智棋芸健脑

Frankho ChessDoku 一 何数棋谜算独

© 2007 — 2020 Frank Ho, Amanda Ho   All rights reserved.   www.homathchess.com

Student's name _____   Date _____

Frankho ChessDoku™ # 142

Frankho ChessDoku™ is solved by using addition, subtraction, multiplication, or division by following chess moves and logic.

Rule: All the digits 1 to 3 must appear exactly once in every row and column. The number appears in the bottom right-hand corner is the result calculated according to the arithmetic operator(s) and chess move(s) as indicated by the darker arrow(s).

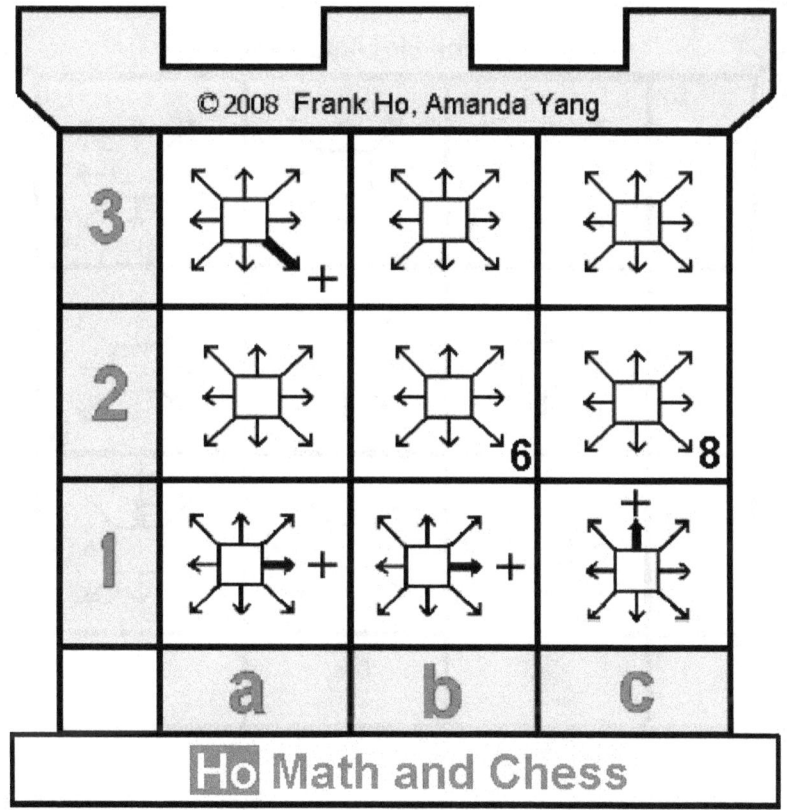

321
132
213

Frankho ChessDoku™ # 143

RULES:

All the digits 1 to 3 must appear in every row and column. The number appears in the bottom right-hand corner is the result calculated according to operator(s) and chess move(s).

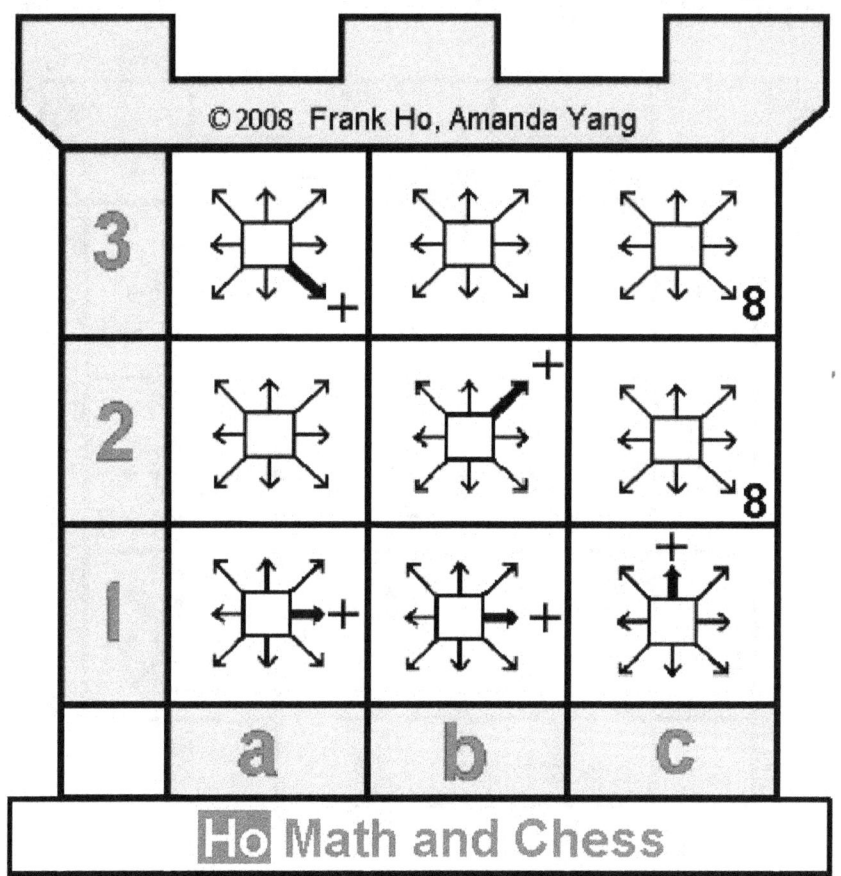

213
132
321

# Frankho ChessDoku™ # 144

Frankho ChessDoku™ is solved by using addition, subtraction, multiplication, or division by following chess moves and logic.

Rule: All the digits 1 to 3 must appear exactly once in every row and column. The number appears in the bottom right-hand corner is the result calculated according to the arithmetic operator(s) and chess move(s) as indicated by the darker arrow(s).

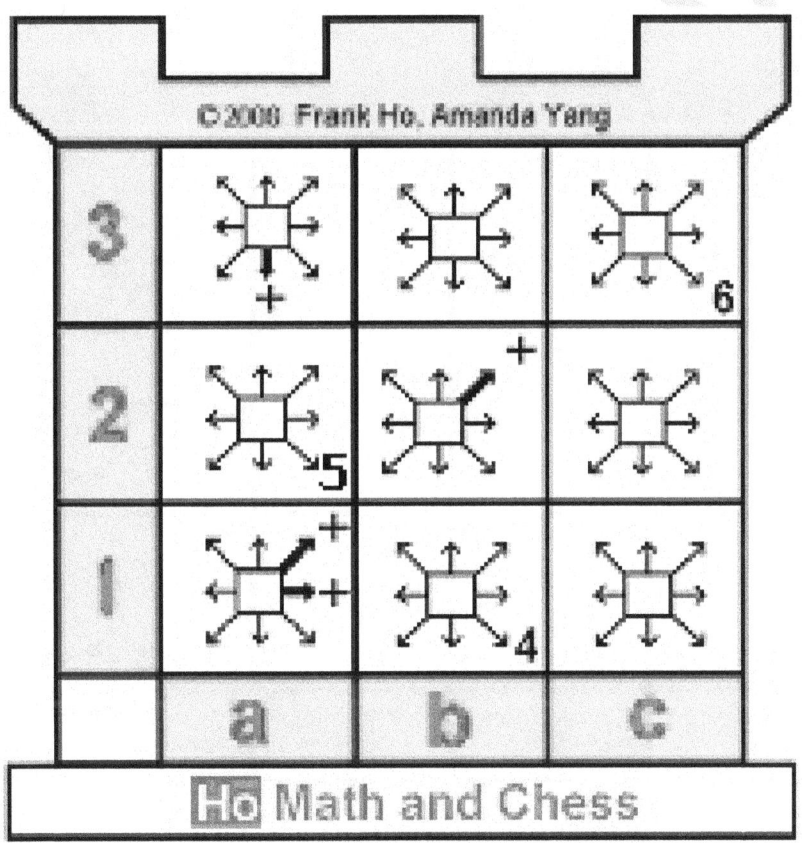

213
321
132

Frankho ChessDoku™ # 145

Frankho ChessDoku™ is solved by using addition, subtraction, multiplication, or division by following chess moves and logic.

Rule: All the digits 1 to 3 must appear exactly once in every row and column. The number appears in the bottom right-hand corner is the result calculated according to the arithmetic operator(s) and chess move(s) as indicated by the darker arrow(s).

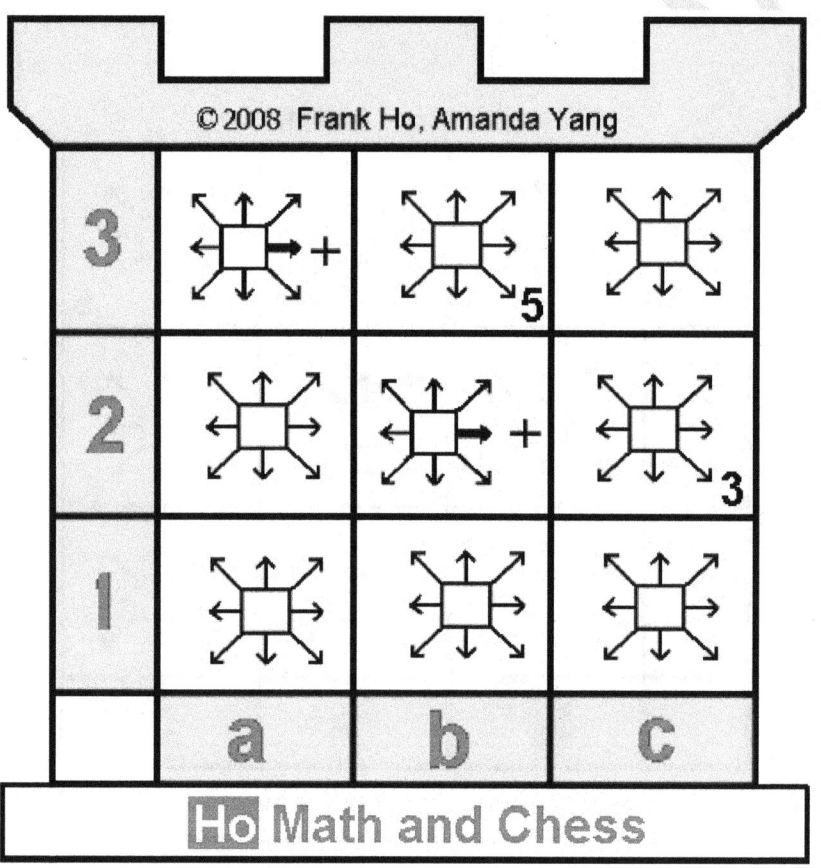

231
312
123

Frankho ChessDoku™ # 146

Frankho ChessDoku™ is solved by using addition, subtraction, multiplication, or division by following chess moves and logic.

Rule: All the digits 1 to 3 must appear exactly once in every row and column. The number appears in the bottom right-hand corner is the result calculated according to the arithmetic operator(s) and chess move(s) as indicated by the darker arrow(s).

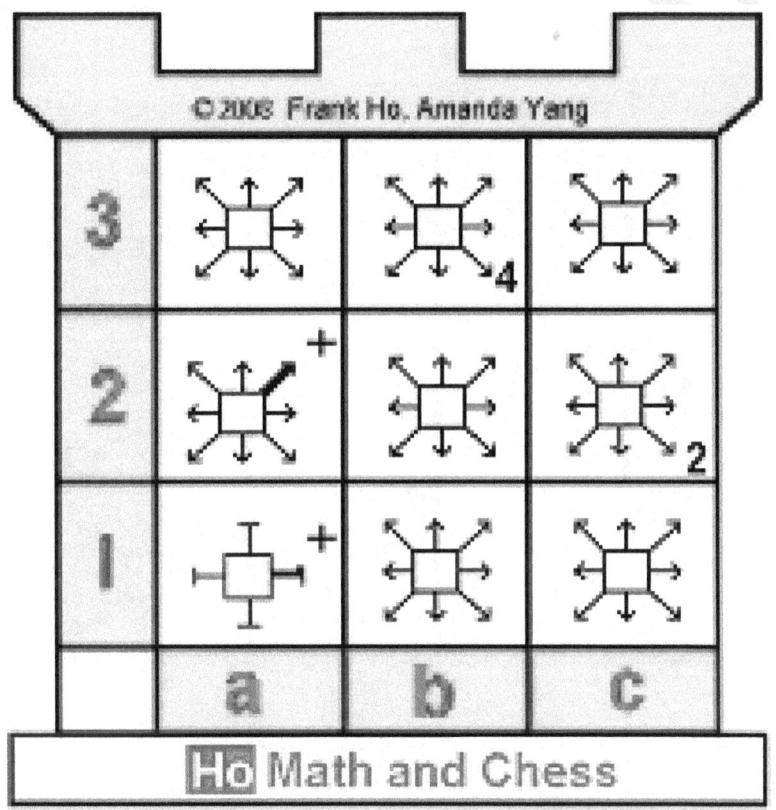

213
321
132

Frankho ChessDoku™ # 147

Frankho ChessDoku™ is solved by using addition, subtraction, multiplication, or division by following chess moves and logic.

Rule: All the digits 1 to 3 must appear exactly once in every row and column. The number appears in the bottom right-hand corner is the result calculated according to the arithmetic operator(s) and chess move(s) as indicated by the darker arrow(s).

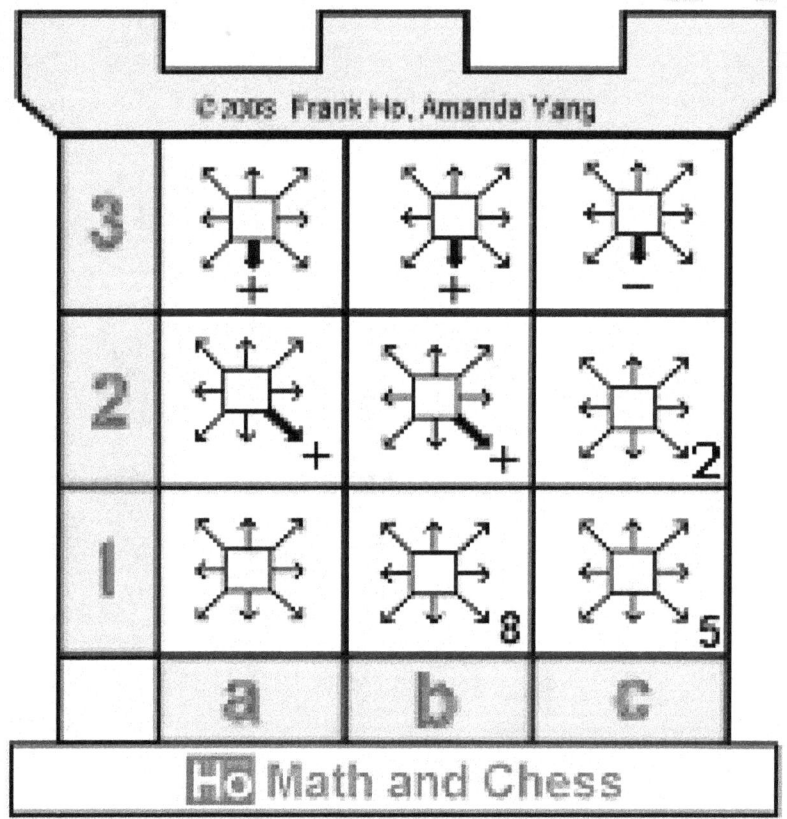

321
213
132

| Math Chess Sudoku Puzzles 一青少年益智棋芸健脑 |
| Frankho ChessDoku 一 何数棋谜算独 |
| © 2007 — 2020 Frank Ho, Amanda Ho   All rights reserved.   www.homathchess.com |
| Student's name _____ Date _____ |

Frankho ChessDoku™ # 148

Frankho ChessDoku™ is solved by using addition, subtraction, multiplication, or division by following chess moves and logic.

Rule: All the digits 1 to 3 must appear exactly once in every row and column. The number appears in the bottom right-hand corner is the result calculated according to the arithmetic operator(s) and chess move(s) as indicated by the darker arrow(s).

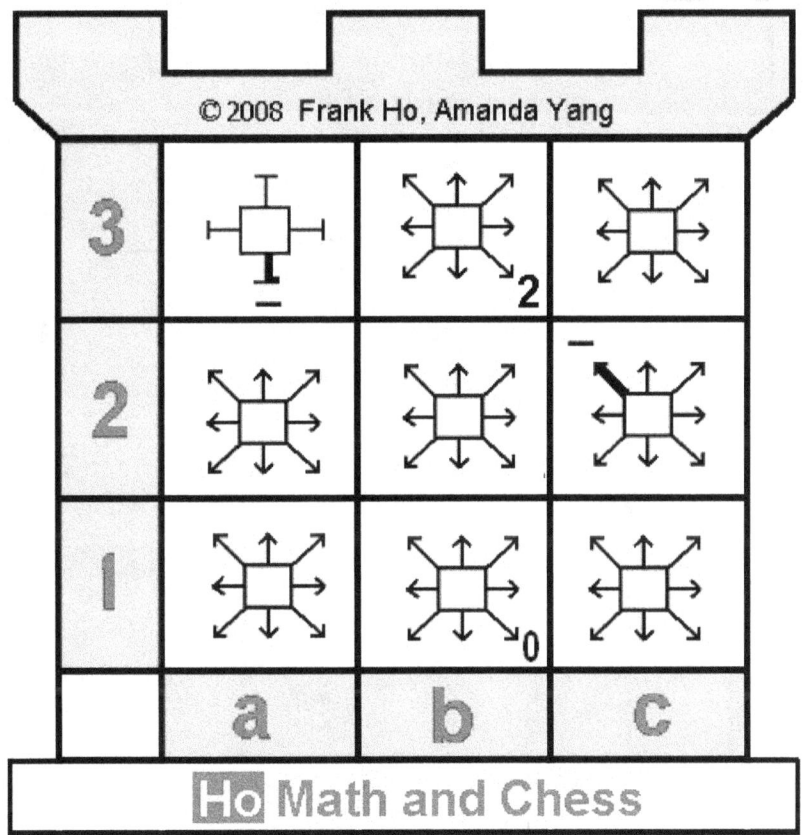

312
123
213

Frankho ChessDoku™ # 149

Frankho ChessDoku™ is solved by using addition, subtraction, multiplication, or division by following chess moves and logic.

Rule: All the digits 1 to 3 must appear exactly once in every row and column. The number appears in the bottom right-hand corner is the result calculated according to the arithmetic operator(s) and chess move(s) as indicated by the darker arrow(s).

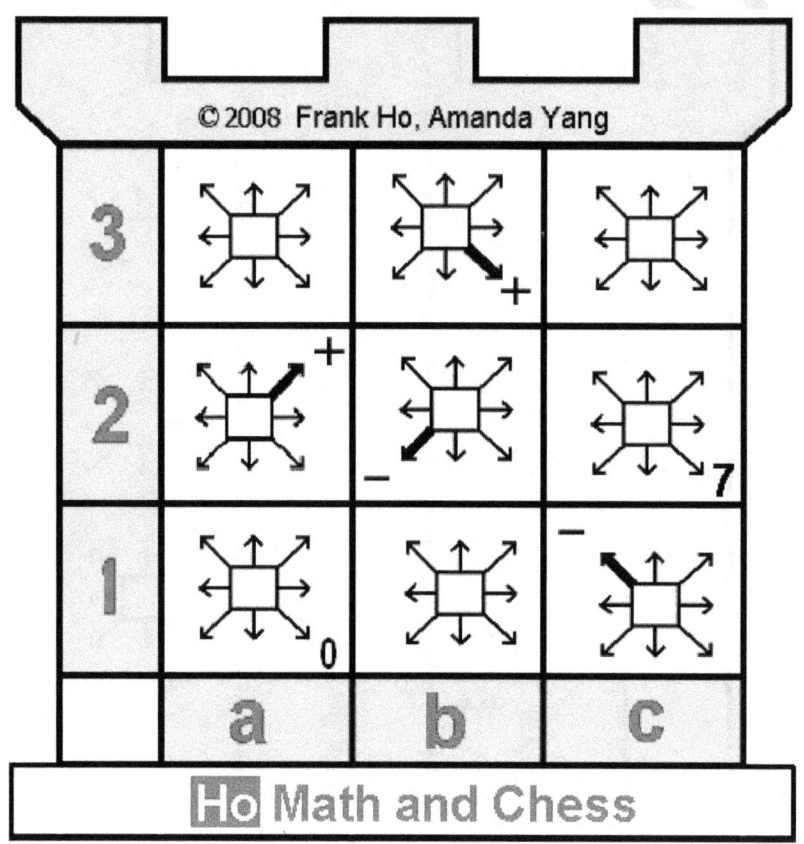

321
213
132

Frankho ChessDoku™ # 150

RULES:

Rule: All the digits 1 to 3 must appear exactly once in every row and column. The number appears in the bottom right-hand corner is the result calculated according to the arithmetic operator(s) and chess move(s) as indicated by the darker arrow(s).

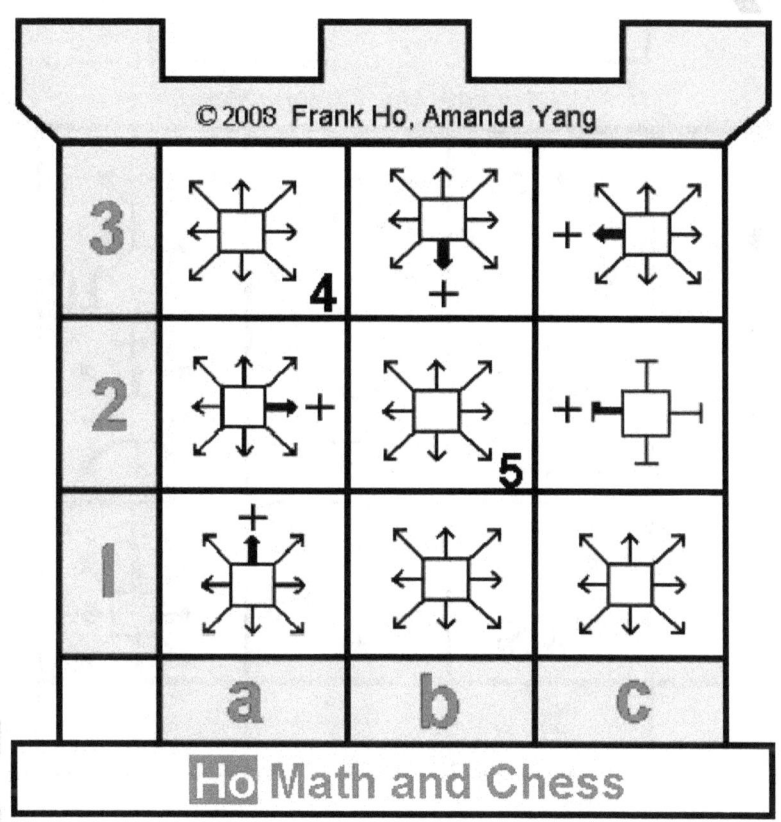

231
312
123

Frankho ChessDoku™ # 151

RULES:

All the digits 1 to 3 must appear in every row and column. The number appears in the bottom right-hand corner is the result calculated according to operator(s) and chess move(s).

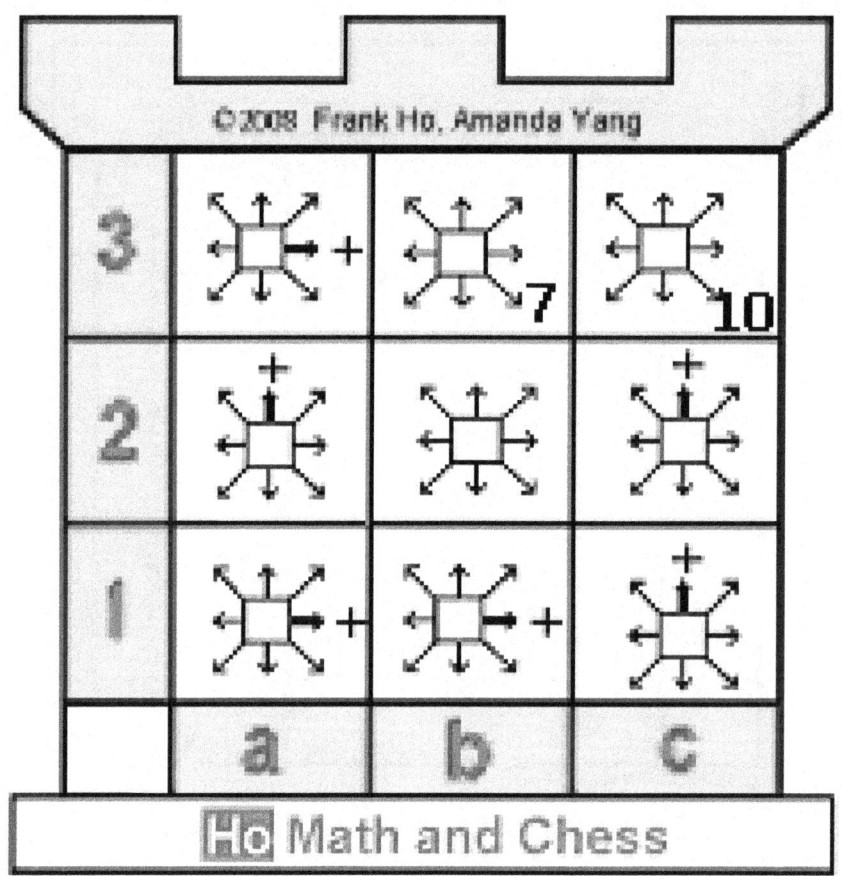

321
213
132

Math Chess Sudoku Puzzles－青少年益智棋芸健脑

Frankho ChessDoku－何数棋谜算独

© 2007－2020 Frank Ho, Amanda Ho   All rights reserved.   www.homathchess.com

Student's name_____   Date_____

Frankho ChessDoku™ # 152

RULES:

All the digits 1 to 3 must appear in every row and column. The number appears in the bottom right-hand corner is the result calculated according to operator(s) and chess move(s).

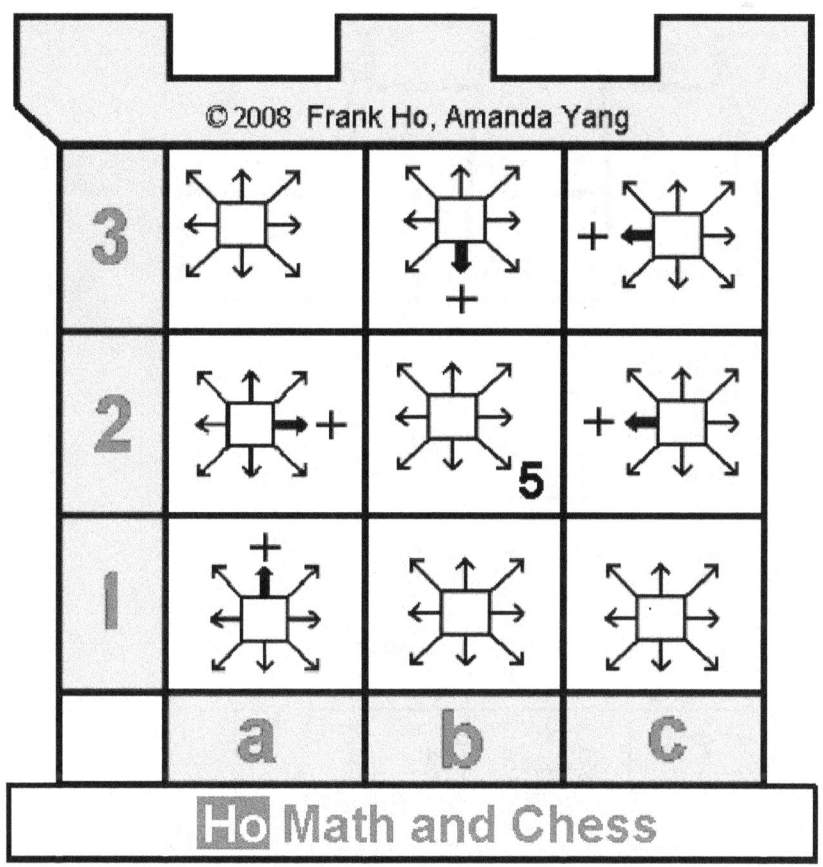

312
123
231

***** Part 2 – 3 Dimensional Frankho ChessDoku *****
3 Dimensional Frankho ChessDoku™ # 1

Rule: All the digits 1 to 3 must appear in every row and column but cannot repeat on the same row of the same column of each layer. The number appears in the bottom right-hand corner is the result calculated according to operator(s) and chess move(s).

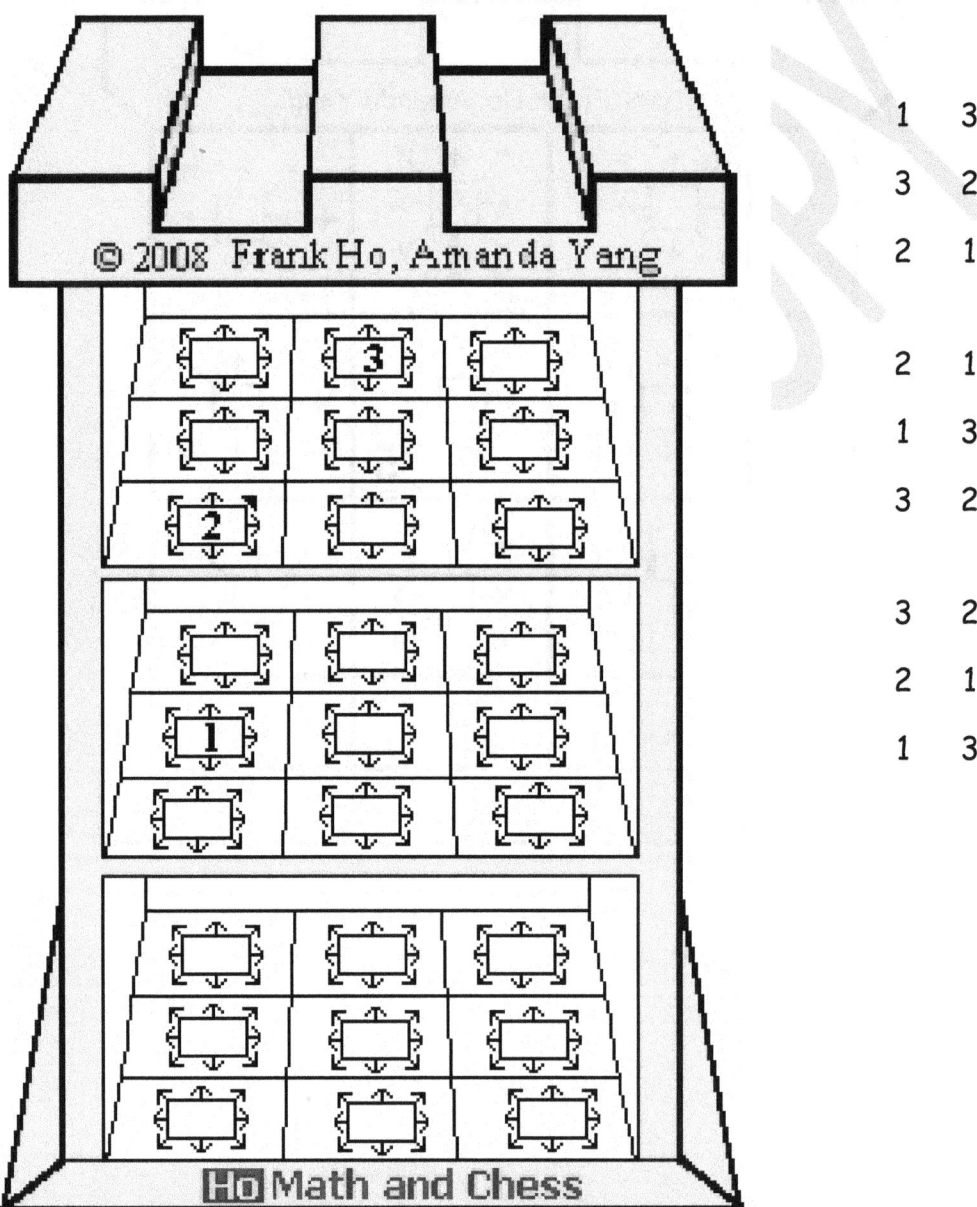

1	3	2
3	2	1
2	1	3

2	1	3
1	3	2
3	2	1

3	2	1
2	1	3
1	3	2

3 Dimensional Frankho ChessDoku™ # 2

Rule: All the digits 1 to 3 must appear in every row and column but cannot repeat on the same row of the same column of each layer. The number appears in the bottom right-hand corner is the result calculated according to operator(s) and chess move(s).

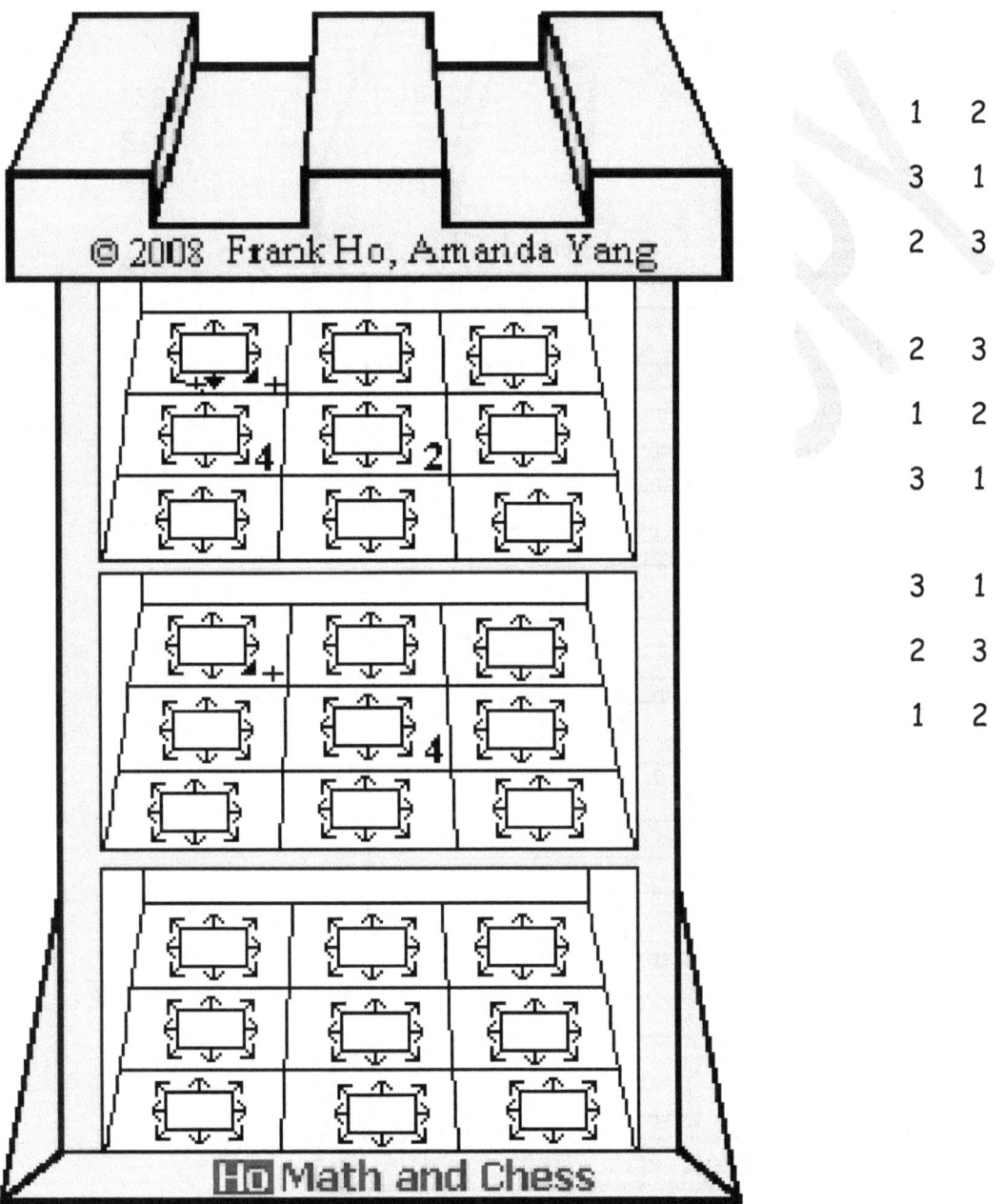

3 Dimensional Frankho ChessDoku™ # 3

Rule: All the digits 1 to 3 must appear in every row and column but cannot repeat on the same row of the same column of each layer. The number appears in the bottom right-hand corner is the result calculated according to operator(s) and chess move(s).

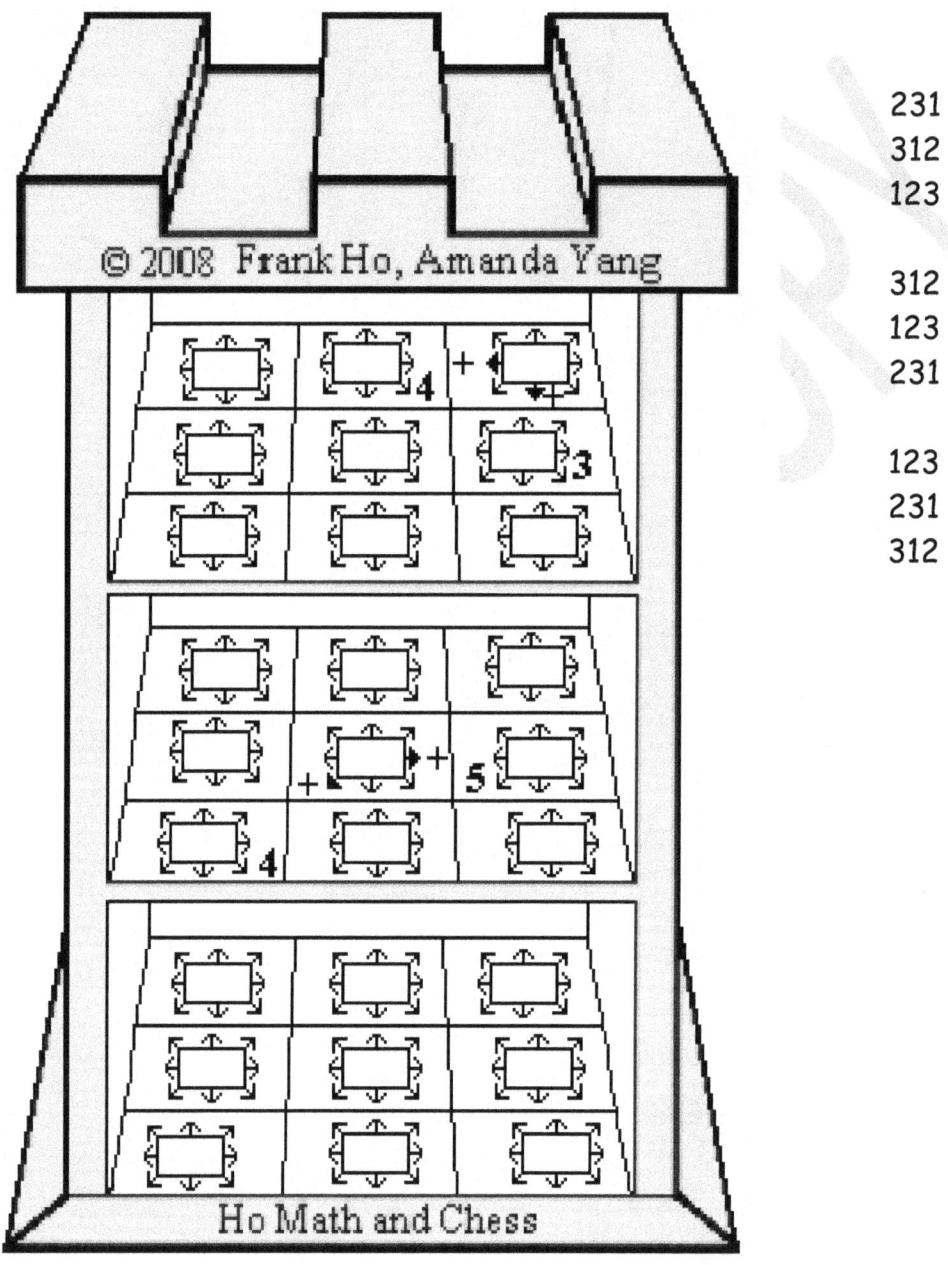

231
312
123

312
123
231

123
231
312

3 Dimensional Frankho ChessDoku™ # 4

Rule: All the digits 1 to 3 must appear in every row and column but cannot repeat on the same row of the same column of each layer. The number appears in the bottom right-hand corner is the result calculated according to operator(s) and chess move(s).

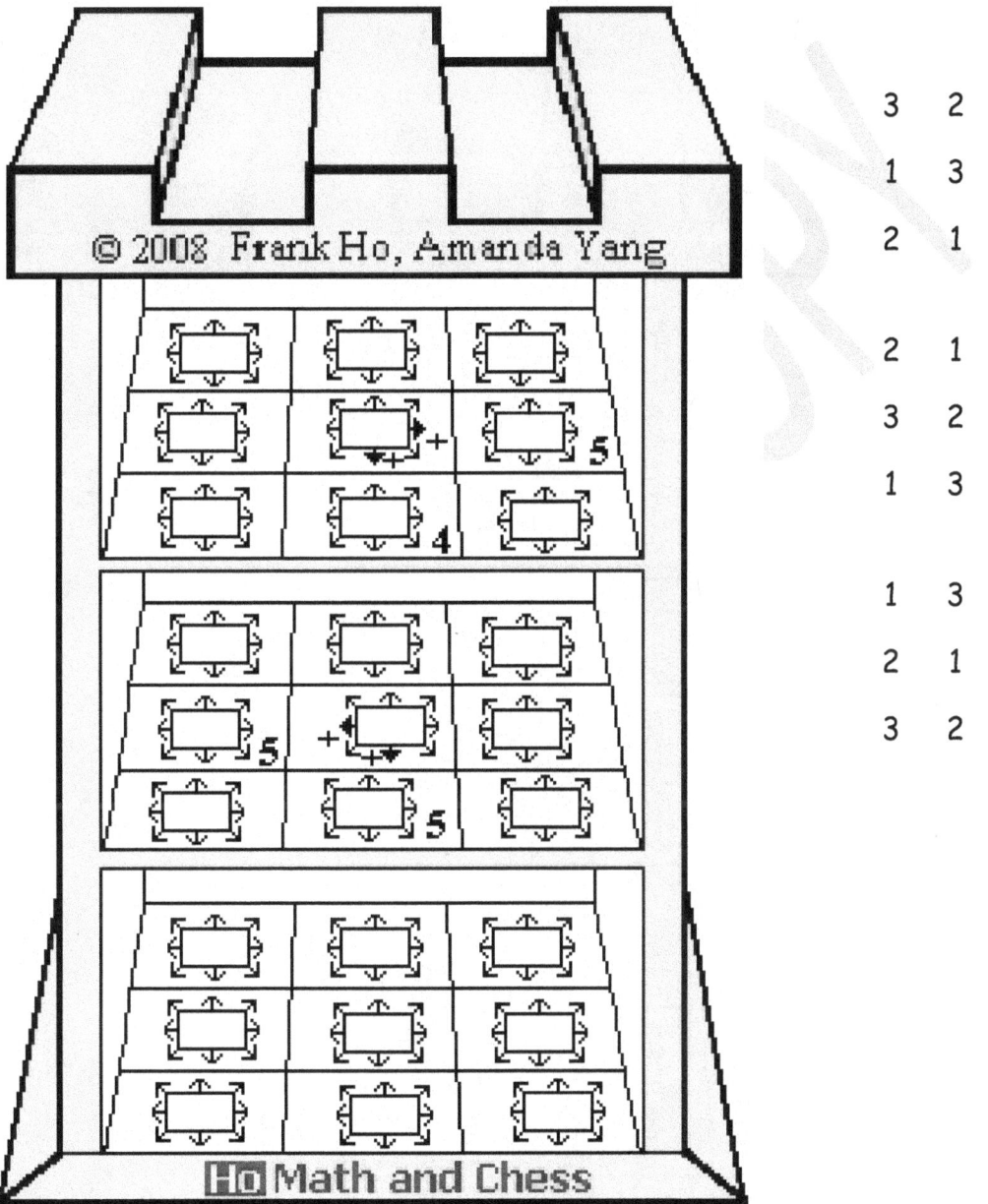

3 Dimensional Frankho ChessDoku™ # 5

Rule: All the digits 1 to 3 must appear in every row and column but cannot repeat on the same row of the same column of each layer. The number appears in the bottom right-hand corner is the result calculated according to operator(s) and chess move(s).

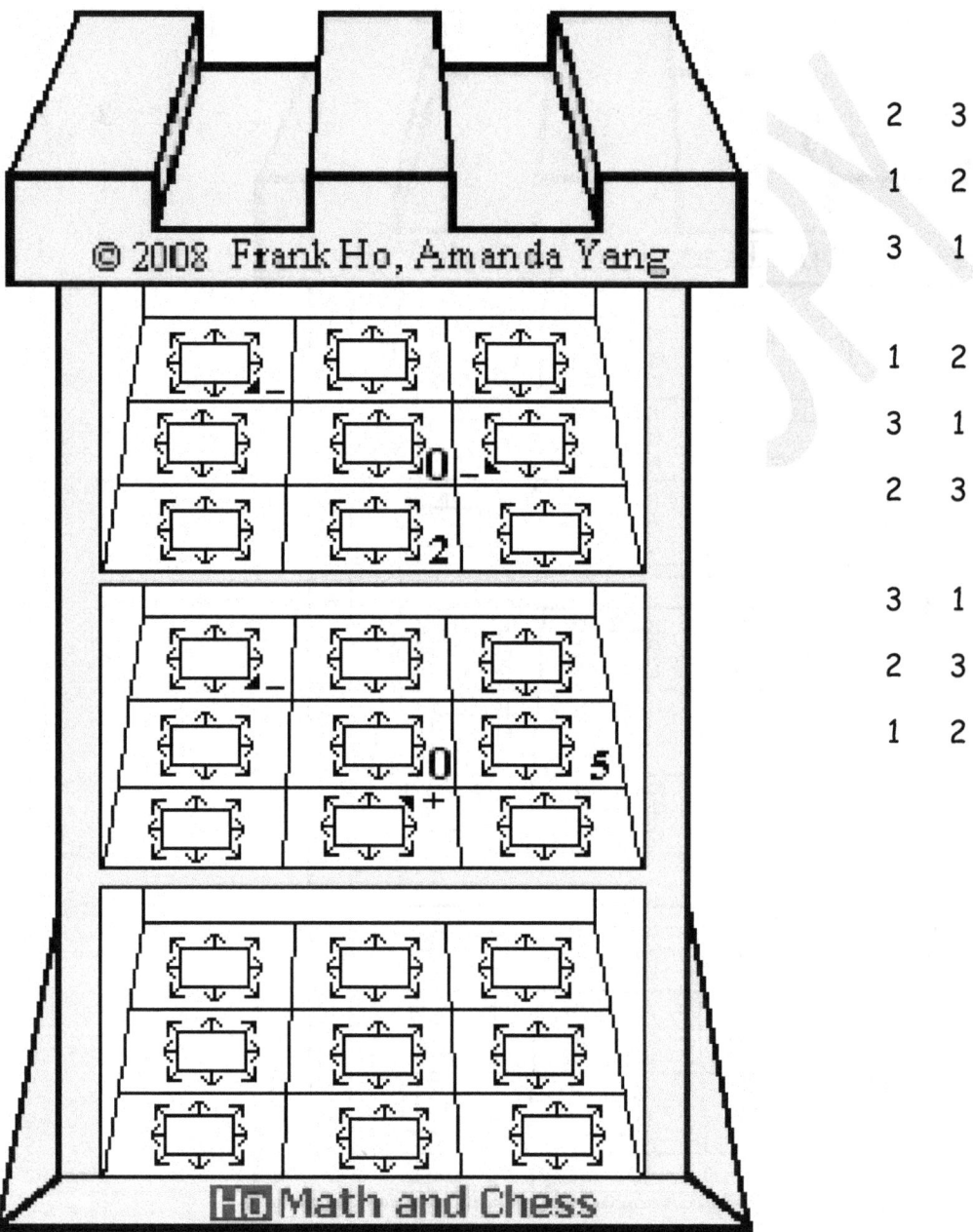

3 Dimensional Frankho ChessDoku™ # 6

Rule: All the digits 1 to 3 must appear in every row and column but cannot repeat on the same row of the same column of each layer. The number appears in the bottom right-hand corner is the result calculated according to operator(s) and chess move(s).

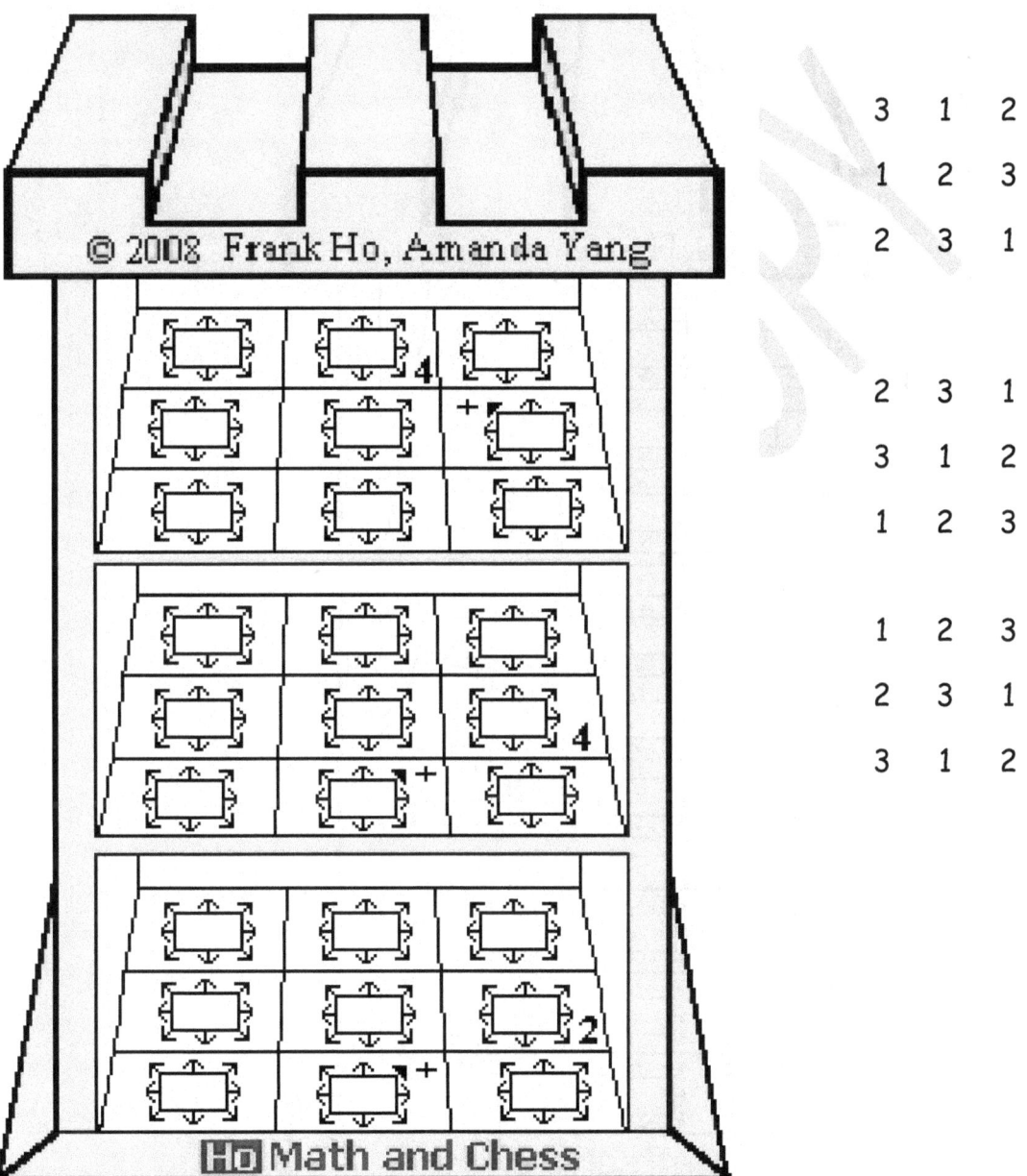

3 Dimensional Frankho ChessDoku™ # 7

Rule: All the digits 1 to 3 must appear in every row and column but cannot repeat on the same row of the same column of each layer. The number appears in the bottom right-hand corner is the result calculated according to operator(s) and chess move(s).

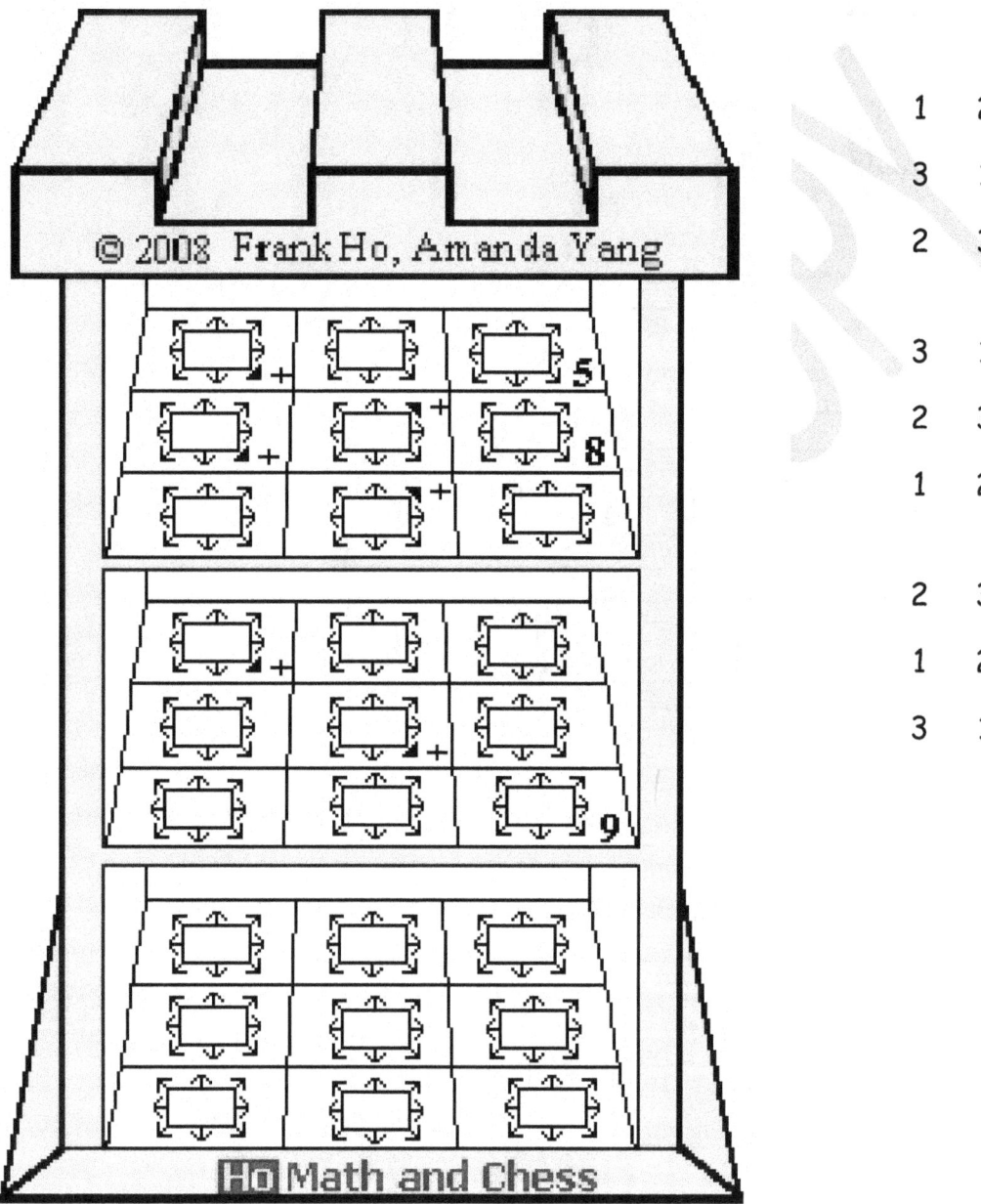

3 Dimensional Frankho ChessDoku™ # 8

Rule: All the digits 1 to 3 must appear in every row and column but cannot repeat on the same row of the same column of each layer. The number appears in the bottom right-hand corner is the result calculated according to operator(s) and chess move(s).

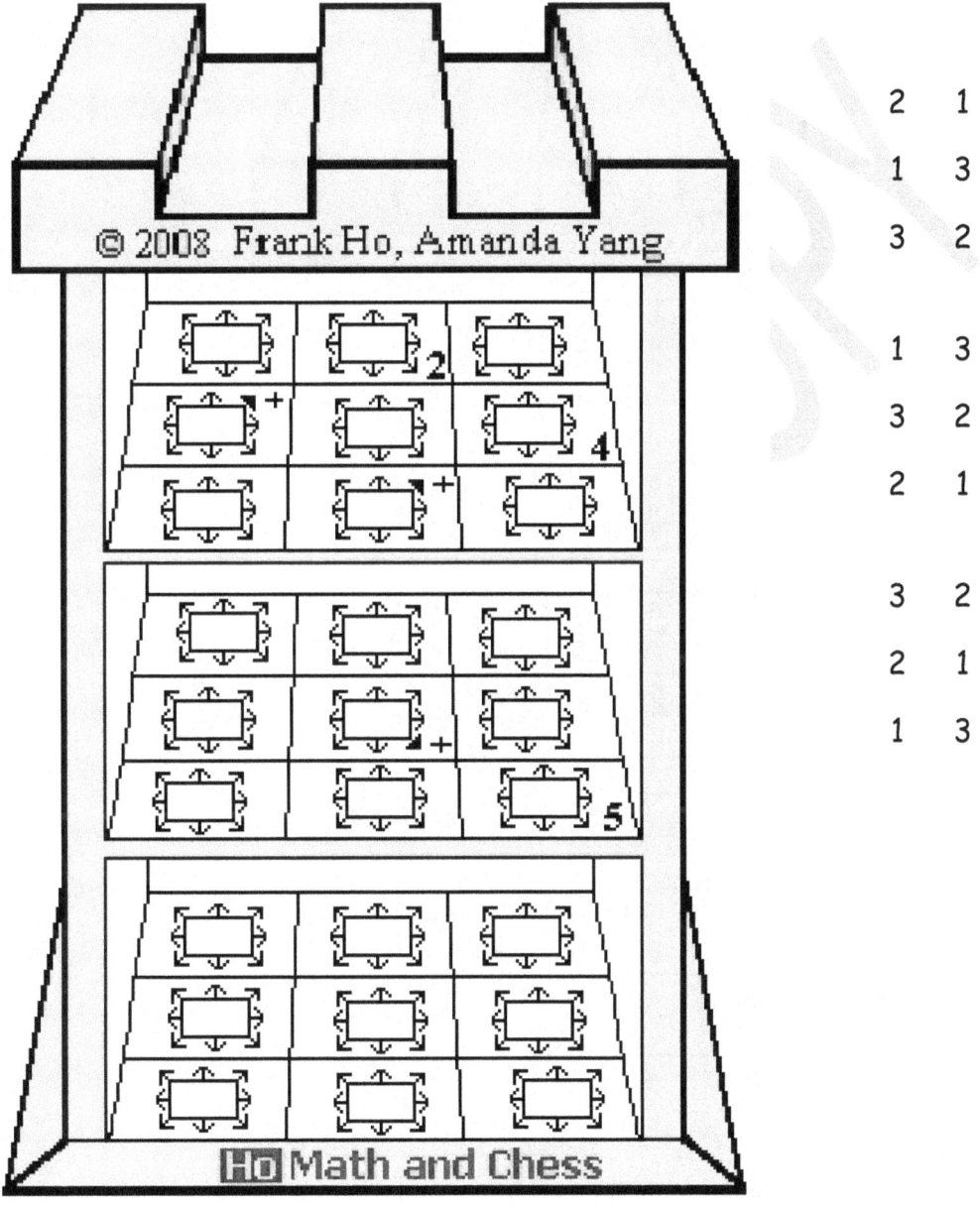

3 Dimensional Frankho ChessDoku™ # 9

Rule: All the digits 1 to 3 must appear in every row and column but cannot repeat on the same row of the same column of each layer. The number appears in the bottom right-hand corner is the result calculated according to operator(s) and chess move(s).

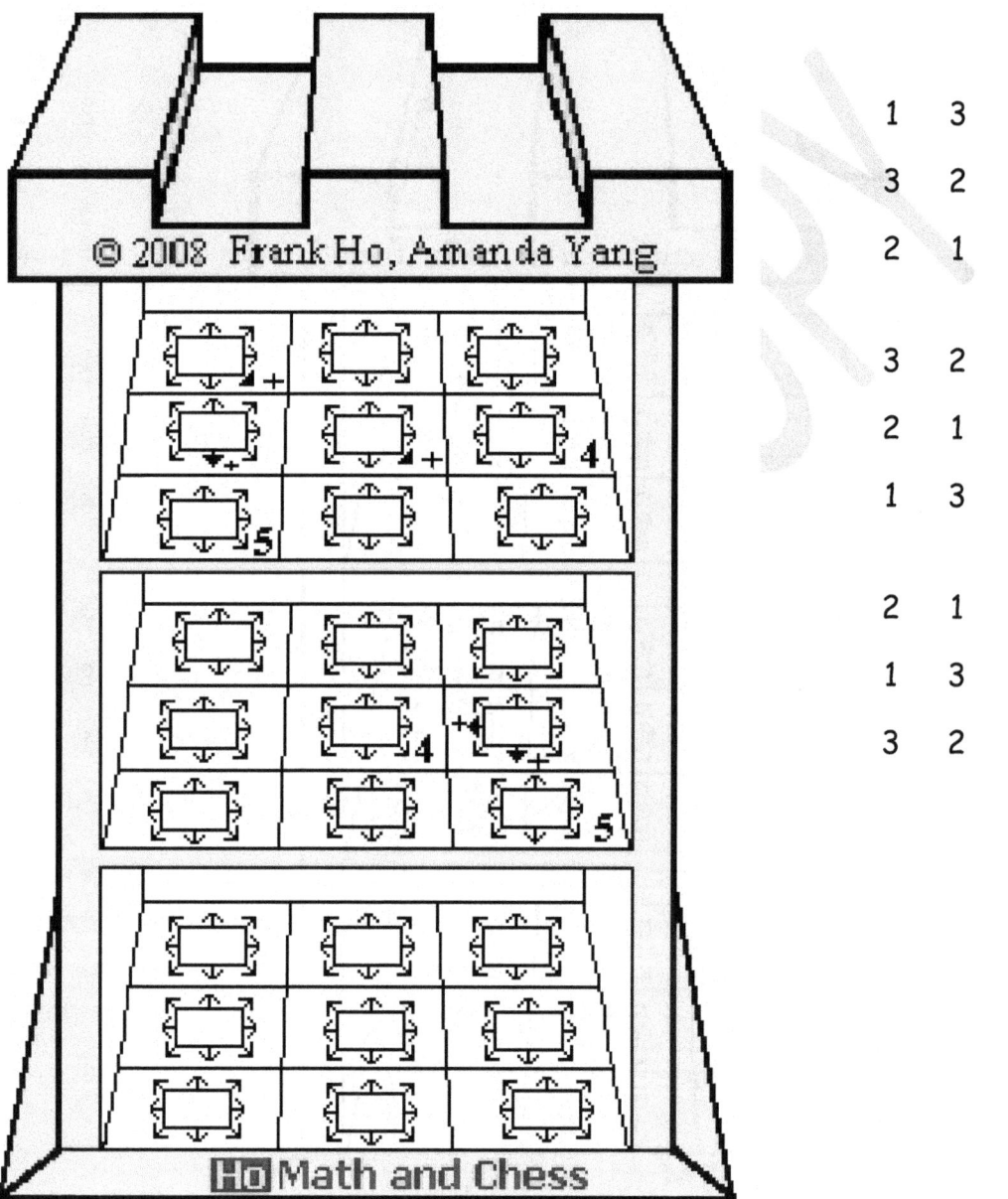

3 Dimensional Frankho ChessDoku™ # 10

Rule: All the digits 1 to 3 must appear in every row and column but cannot repeat on the same row of the same column of each layer. The number appears in the bottom right-hand corner is the result calculated according to operator(s) and chess move(s).

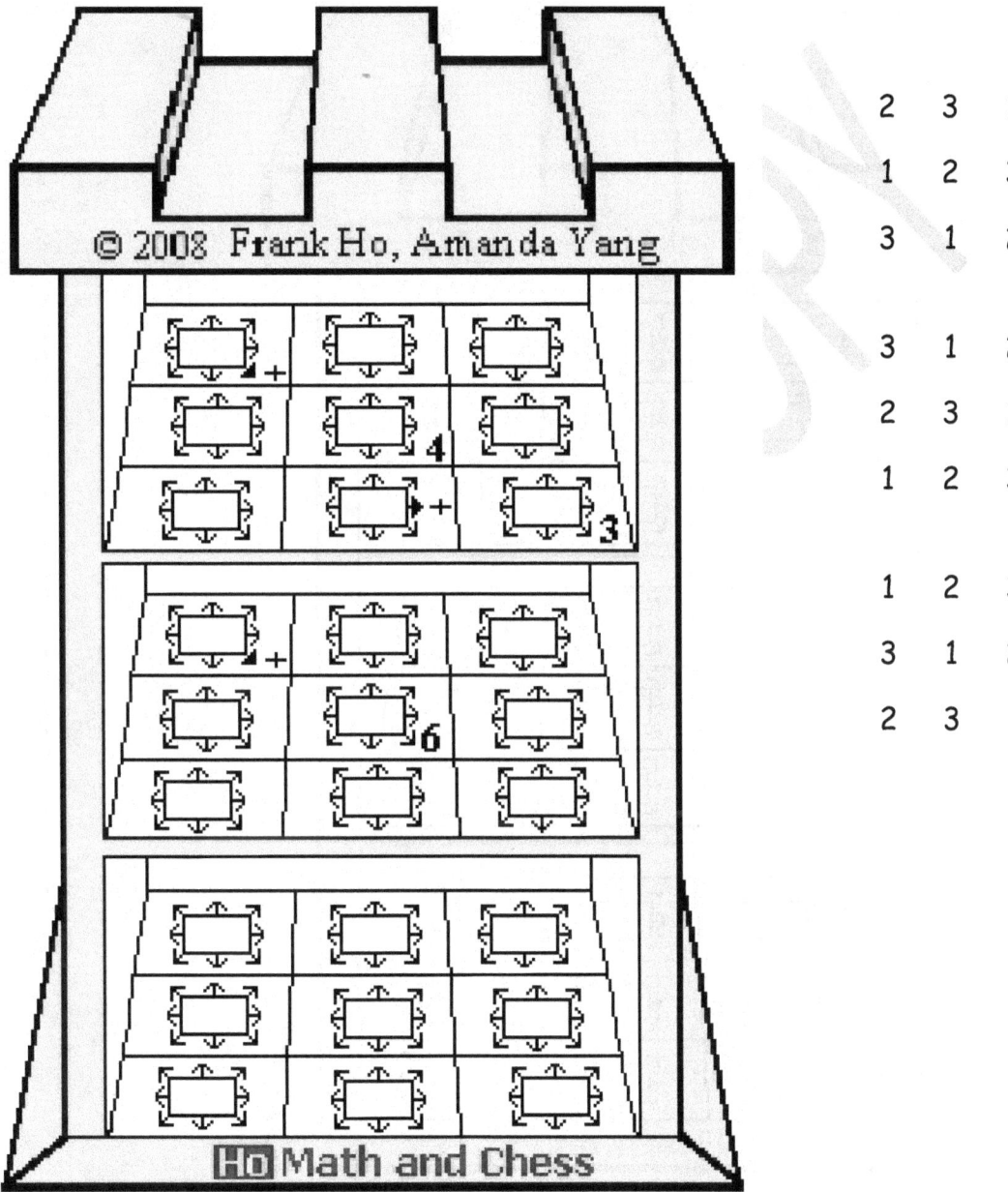

3 Dimensional Frankho ChessDoku™ # 11

Rule: All the digits 1 to 3 must appear in every row and column but cannot repeat on the same row of the same column of each layer. The number appears in the bottom right-hand corner is the result calculated according to operator(s) and chess move(s).

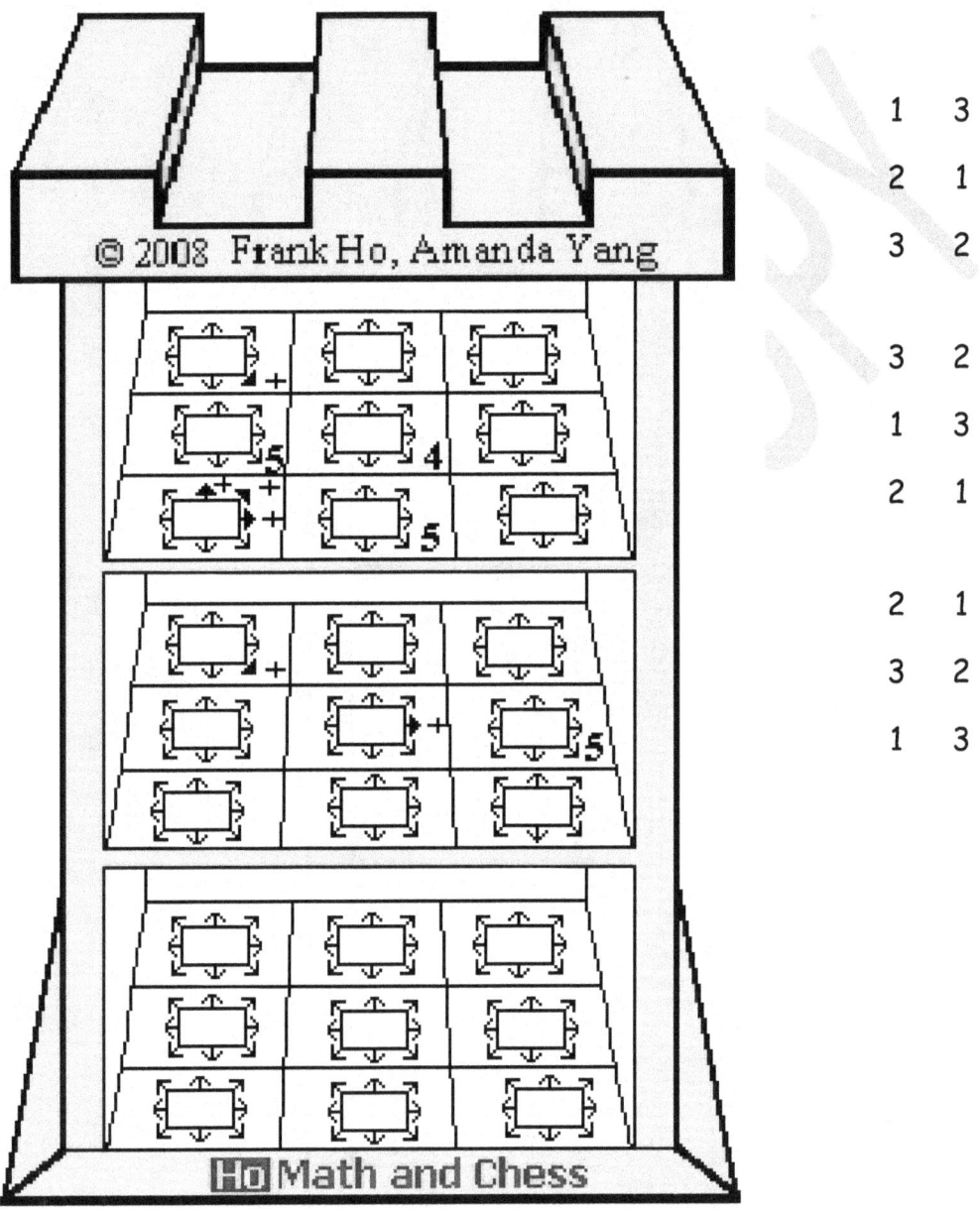

3 Dimensional Frankho ChessDoku™ # 12

Rule: All the digits 1 to 3 must appear in every row and column but cannot repeat on the same row of the same column of each layer. The number appears in the bottom right-hand corner is the result calculated according to operator(s) and chess move(s).

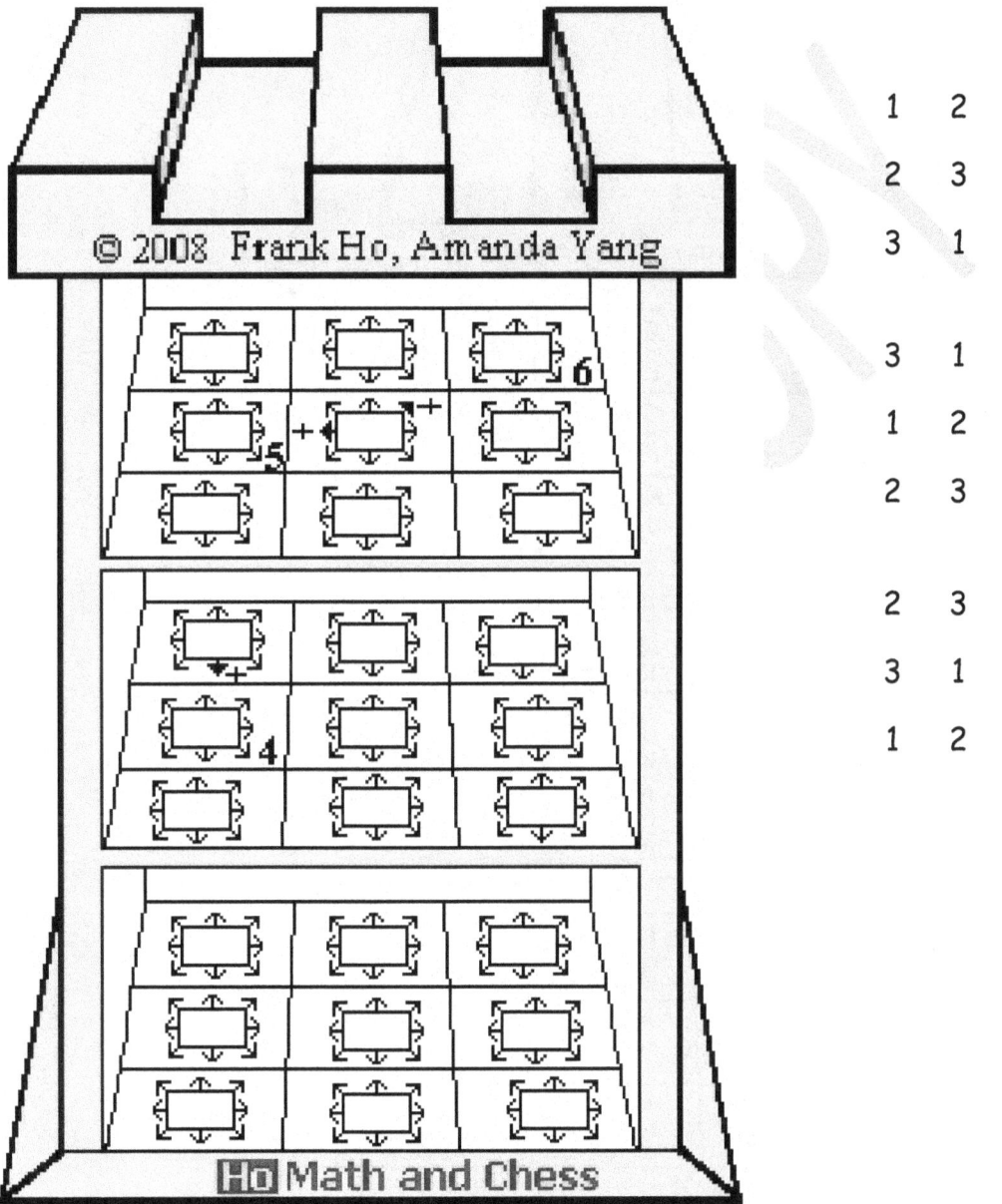

1	2	3
2	3	1
3	1	2

3	1	2
1	2	3
2	3	1

2	3	1
3	1	2
1	2	3

3 Dimensional Frankho ChessDoku™ # 13

Rule: All the digits 1 to 3 must appear in every row and column but cannot repeat on the same row of the same column of each layer. The number appears in the bottom right-hand corner is the result calculated according to operator(s) and chess move(s).

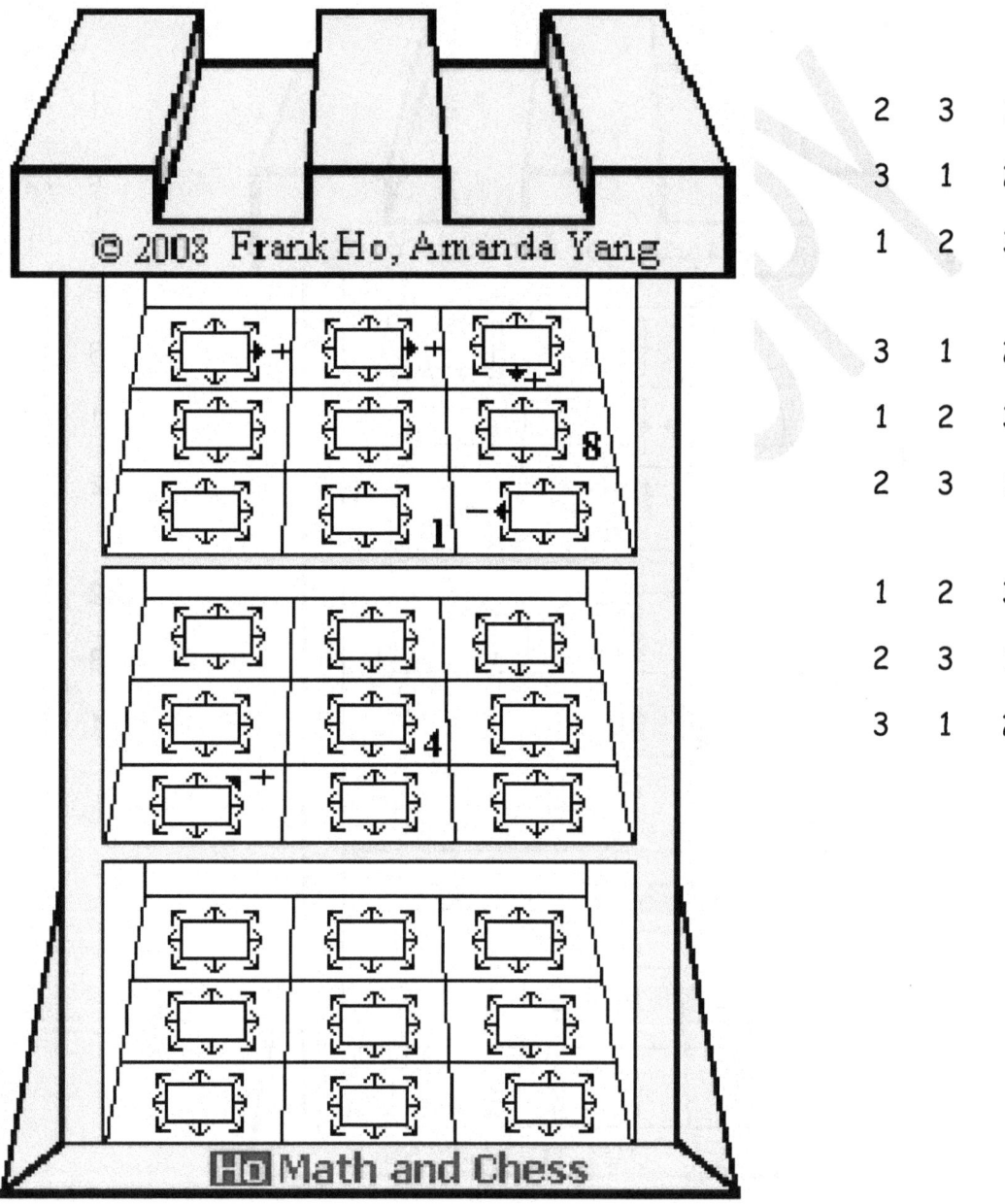

3 Dimensional Frankho ChessDoku™ # 14

Rule: All the digits 1 to 3 must appear in every row and column but cannot repeat on the same row of the same column of each layer. The number appears in the bottom right-hand corner is the result calculated according to operator(s) and chess move(s).

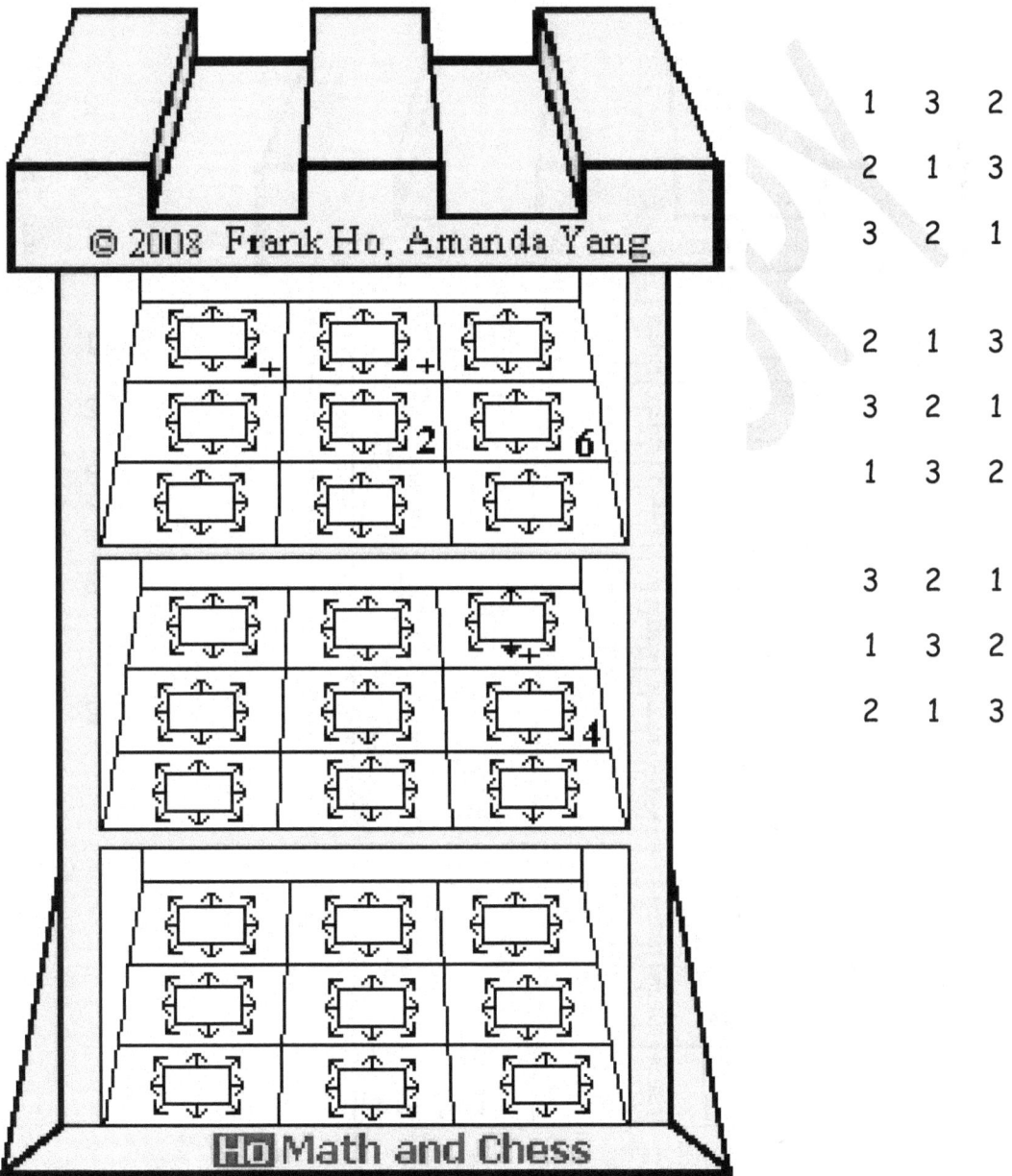

1	3	2
2	1	3
3	2	1

2	1	3
3	2	1
1	3	2

3	2	1
1	3	2
2	1	3

3 Dimensional Frankho ChessDoku™ # 15

Rule: All the digits 1 to 3 must appear in every row and column but cannot repeat on the same row of the same column of each layer. The number appears in the bottom right-hand corner is the result calculated according to operator(s) and chess move(s).

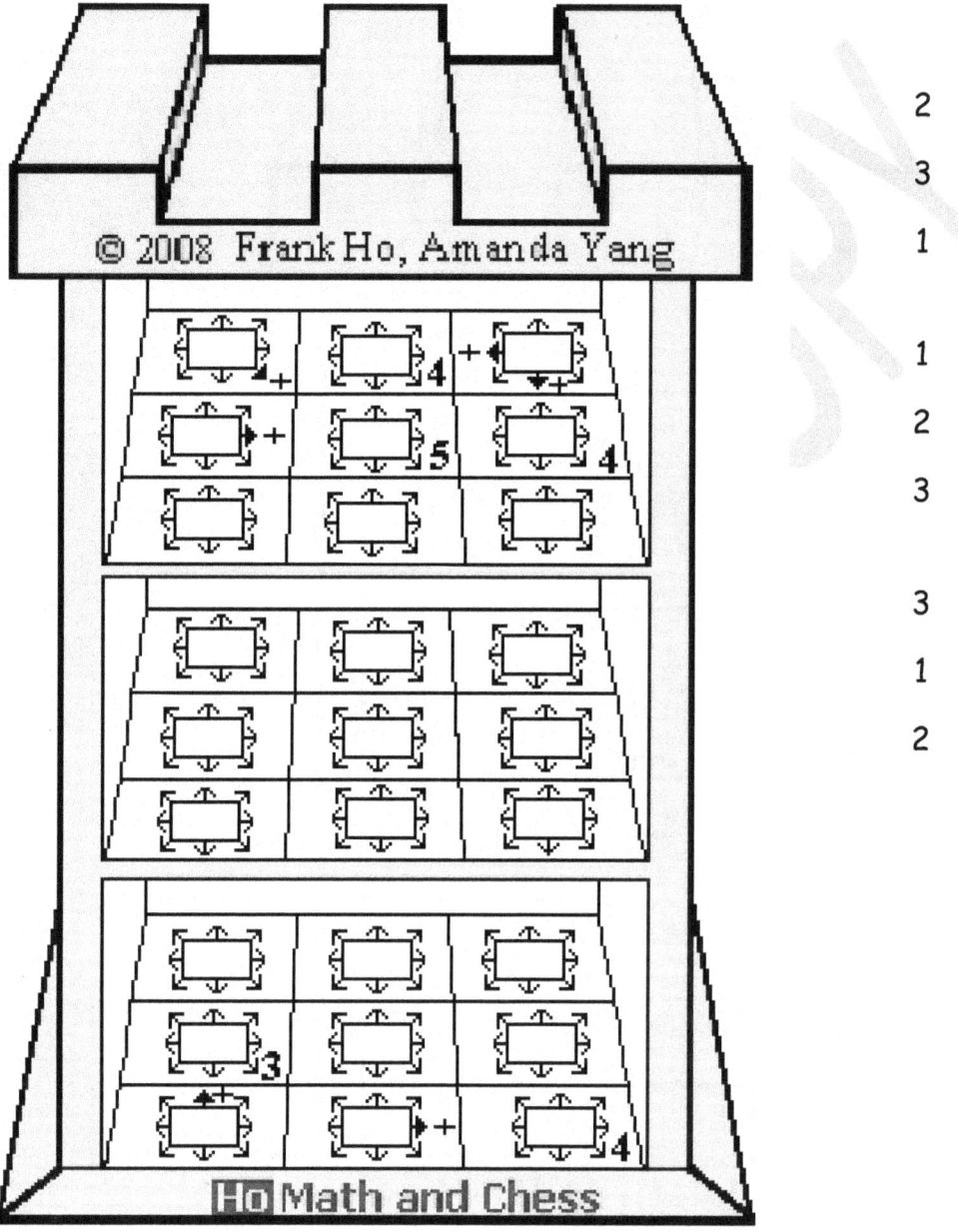

3 Dimensional Frankho ChessDoku™ # 16

Rule: All the digits 1 to 3 must appear in every row and column but cannot repeat on the same row of the same column of each layer. The number appears in the bottom right-hand corner is the result calculated according to operator(s) and chess move(s).

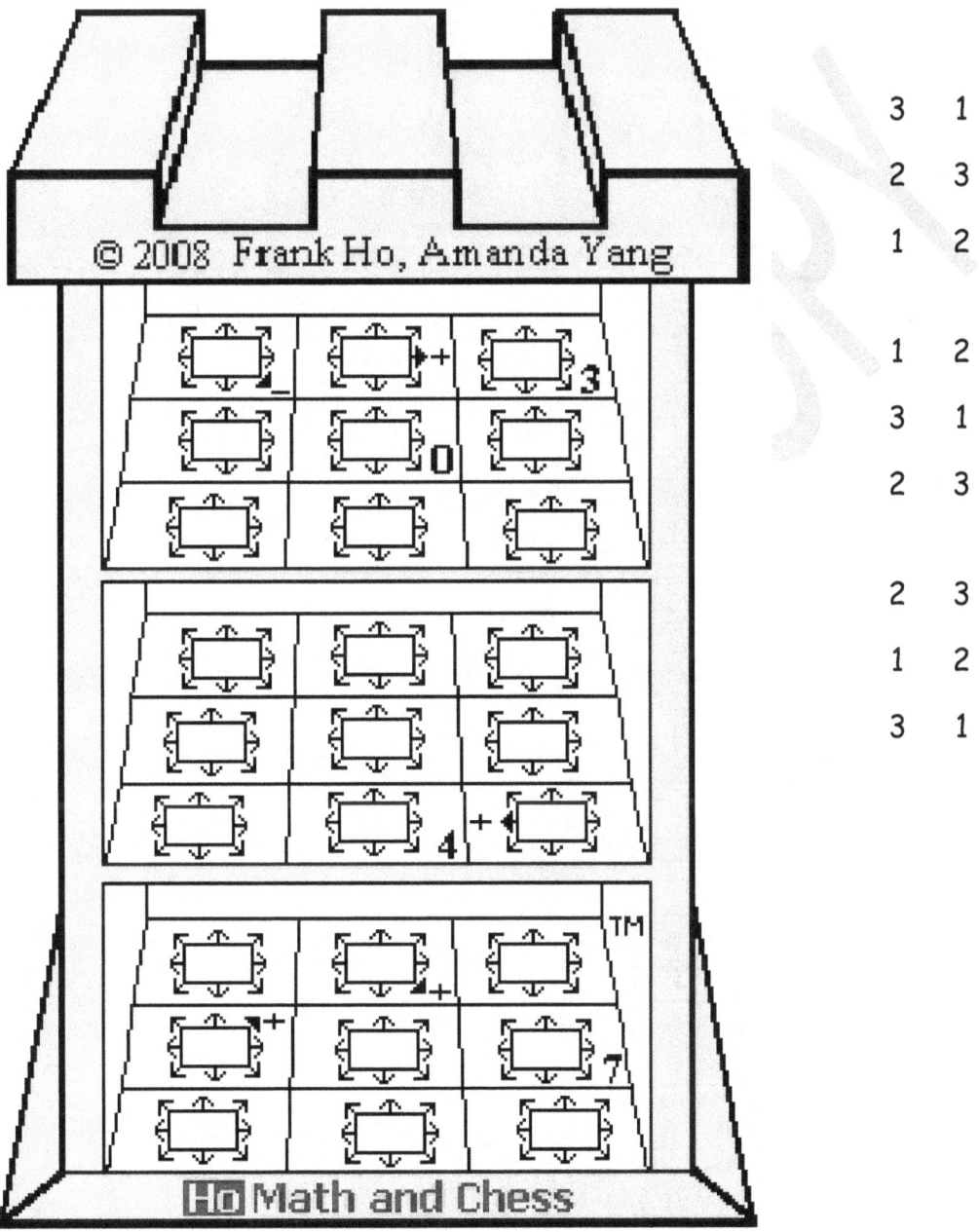

3 Dimensional Frankho ChessDoku™ # 17

Rule: All the digits 1 to 3 must appear in every row and column but cannot repeat on the same row of the same column of each layer. The number appears in the bottom right-hand corner is the result calculated according to operator(s) and chess move(s).

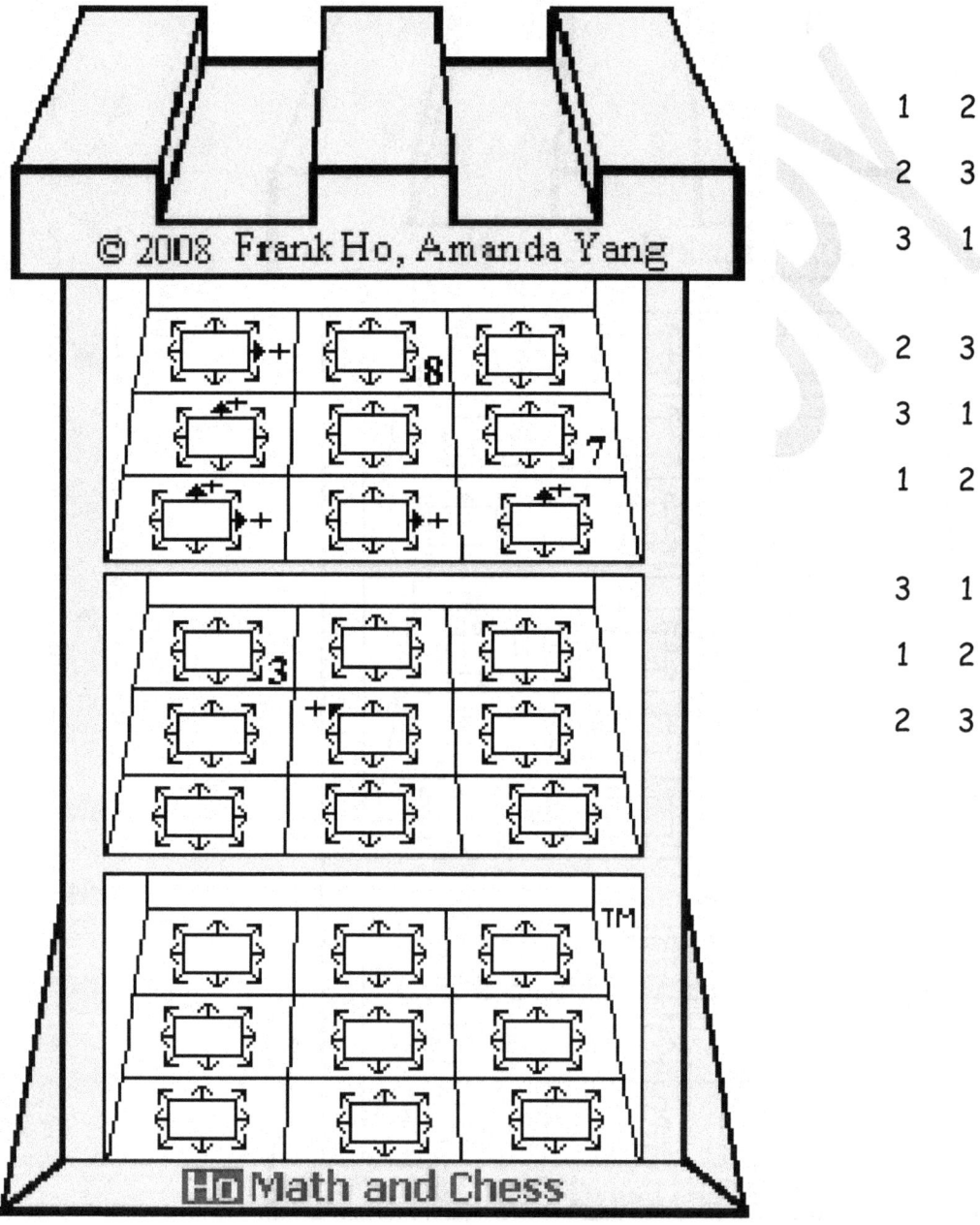

3 Dimensional Frankho ChessDoku™ # 18

Rule: All the digits 1 to 3 must appear in every row and column but cannot repeat on the same row of the same column of each layer. The number appears in the bottom right-hand corner is the result calculated according to operator(s) and chess move(s).

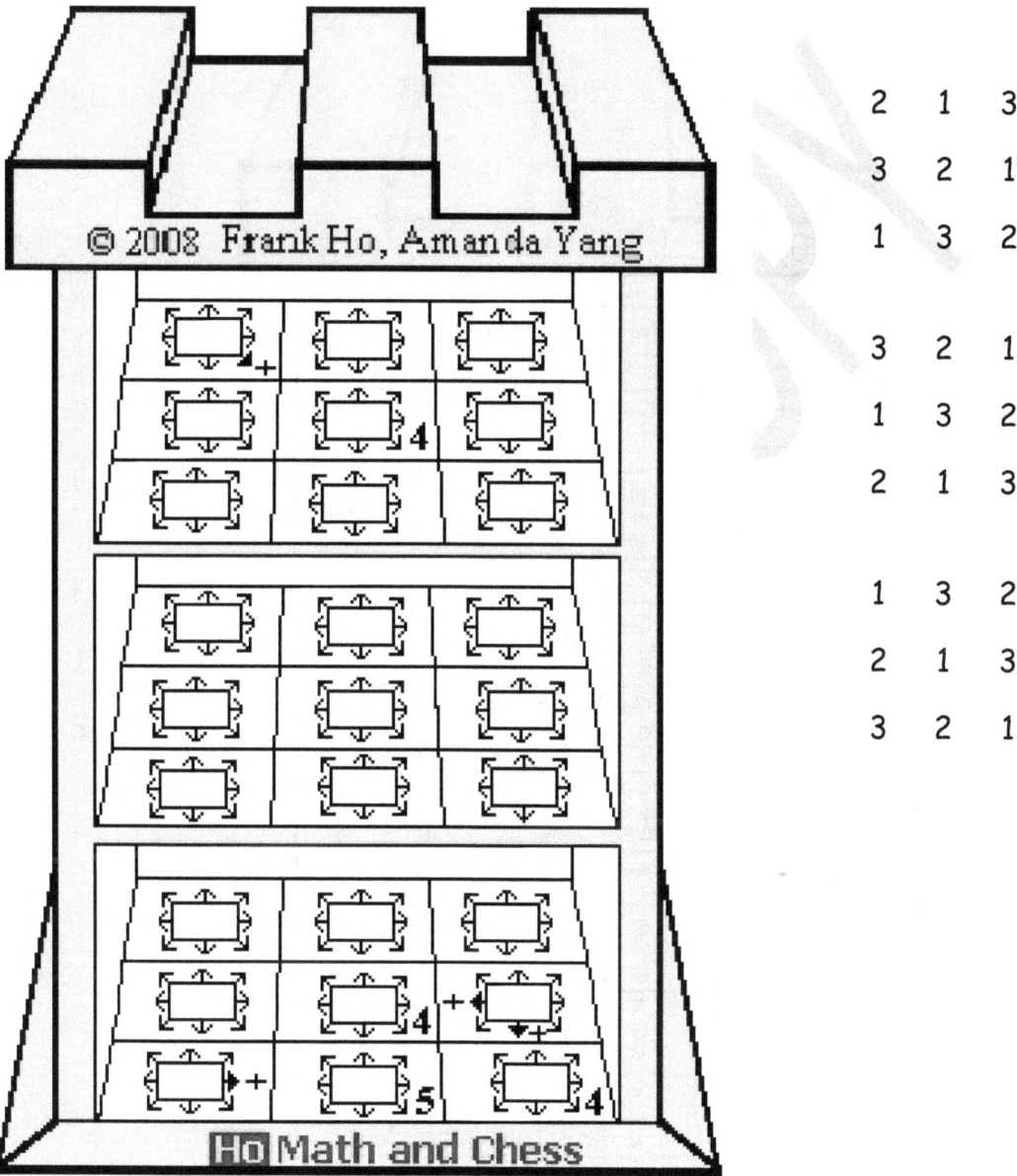

3 Dimensional Frankho ChessDoku™ # 19

Rule: All the digits 1 to 3 must appear in every row and column but cannot repeat on the same row of the same column of each layer. The number appears in the bottom right-hand corner is the result calculated according to operator(s) and chess move(s).

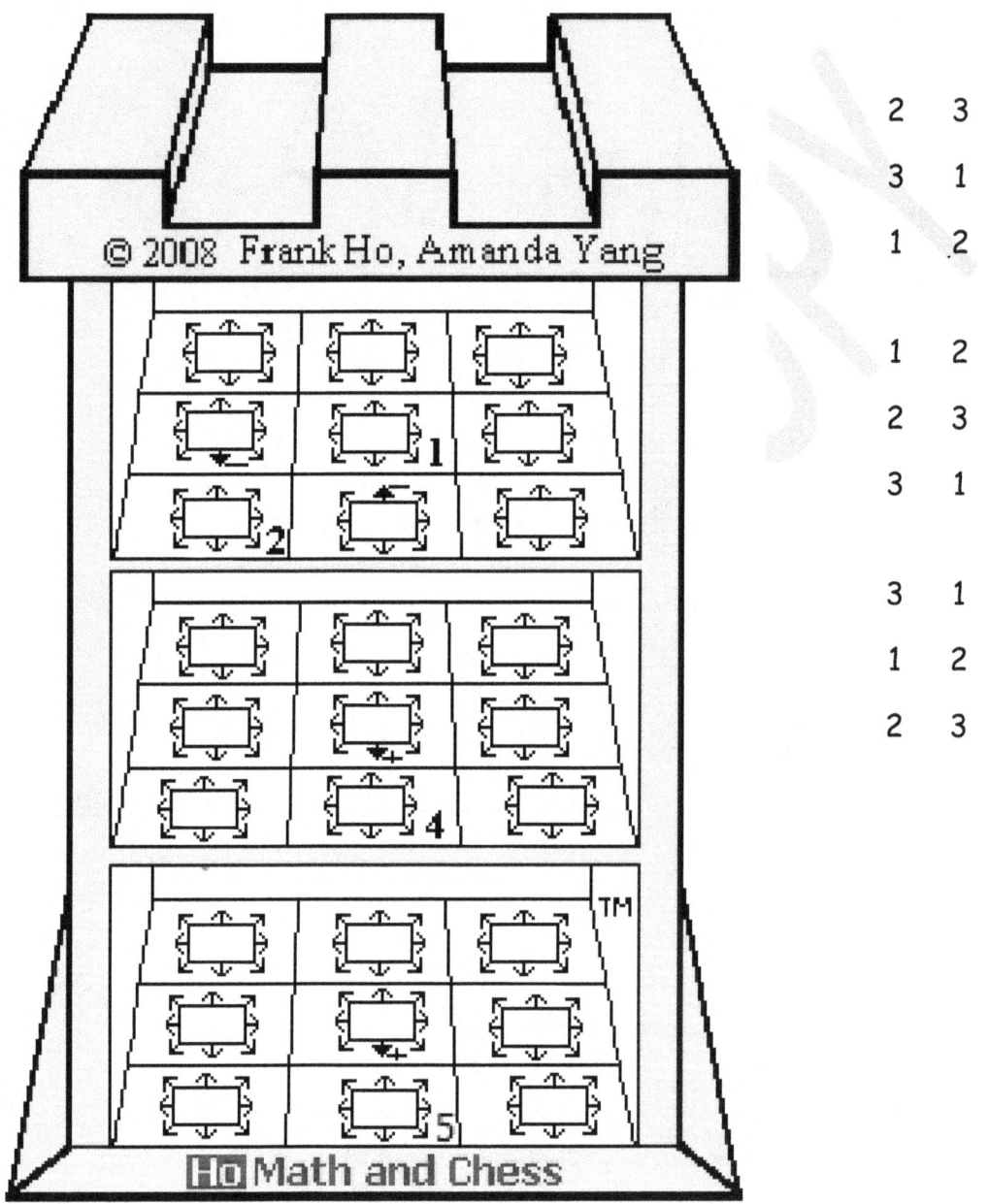

3 Dimensional Frankho ChessDoku™ # 20

Rule: All the digits 1 to 3 must appear in every row and column but cannot repeat on the same row of the same column of each layer. The number appears in the bottom right-hand corner is the result calculated according to operator(s) and chess move(s).

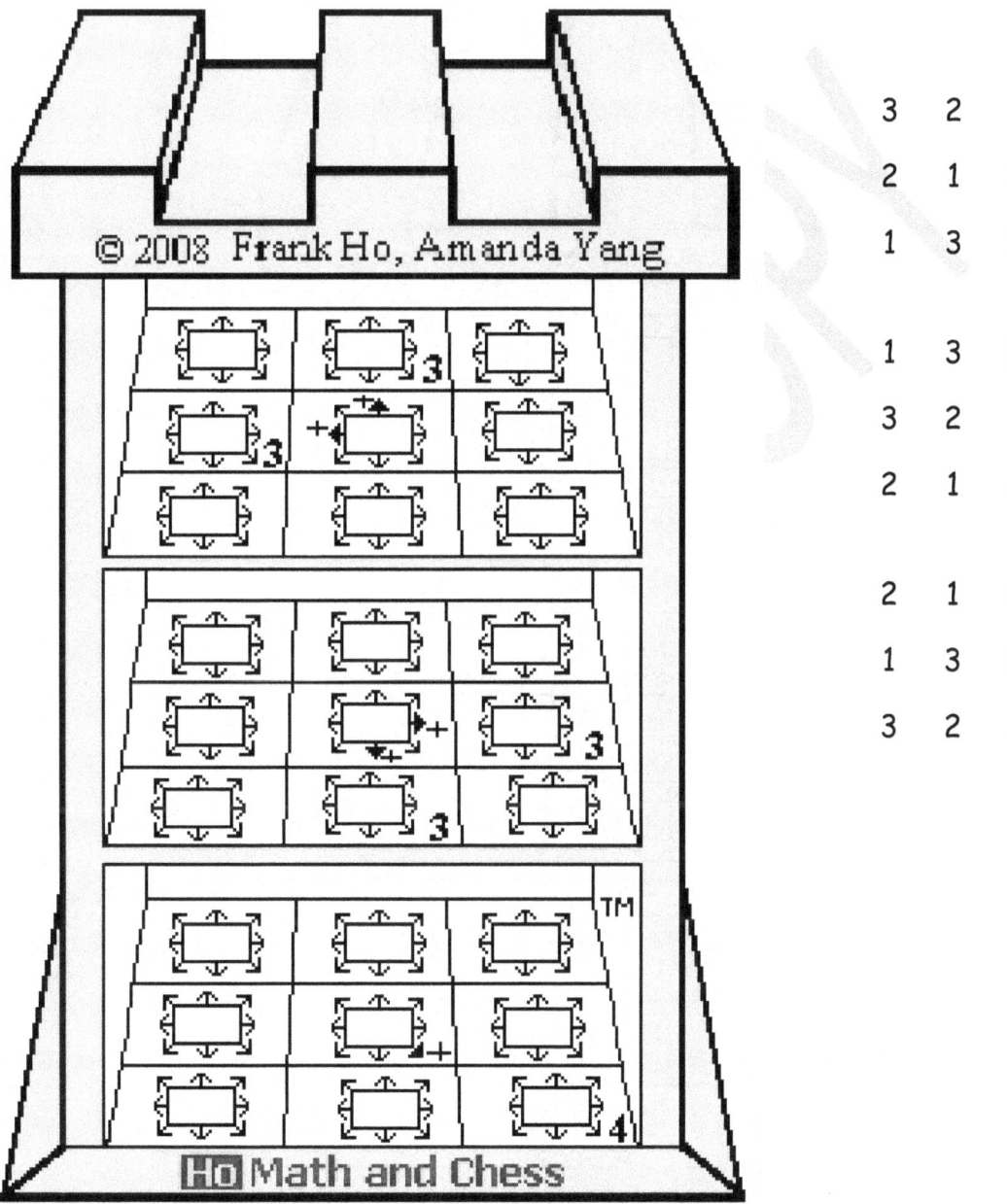

3 Dimensional Frankho ChessDoku™ # 21

Rule: All the digits 1 to 3 must appear in every row and column but cannot repeat on the same row of the same column of each layer. The number appears in the bottom right-hand corner is the result calculated according to operator(s) and chess move(s).

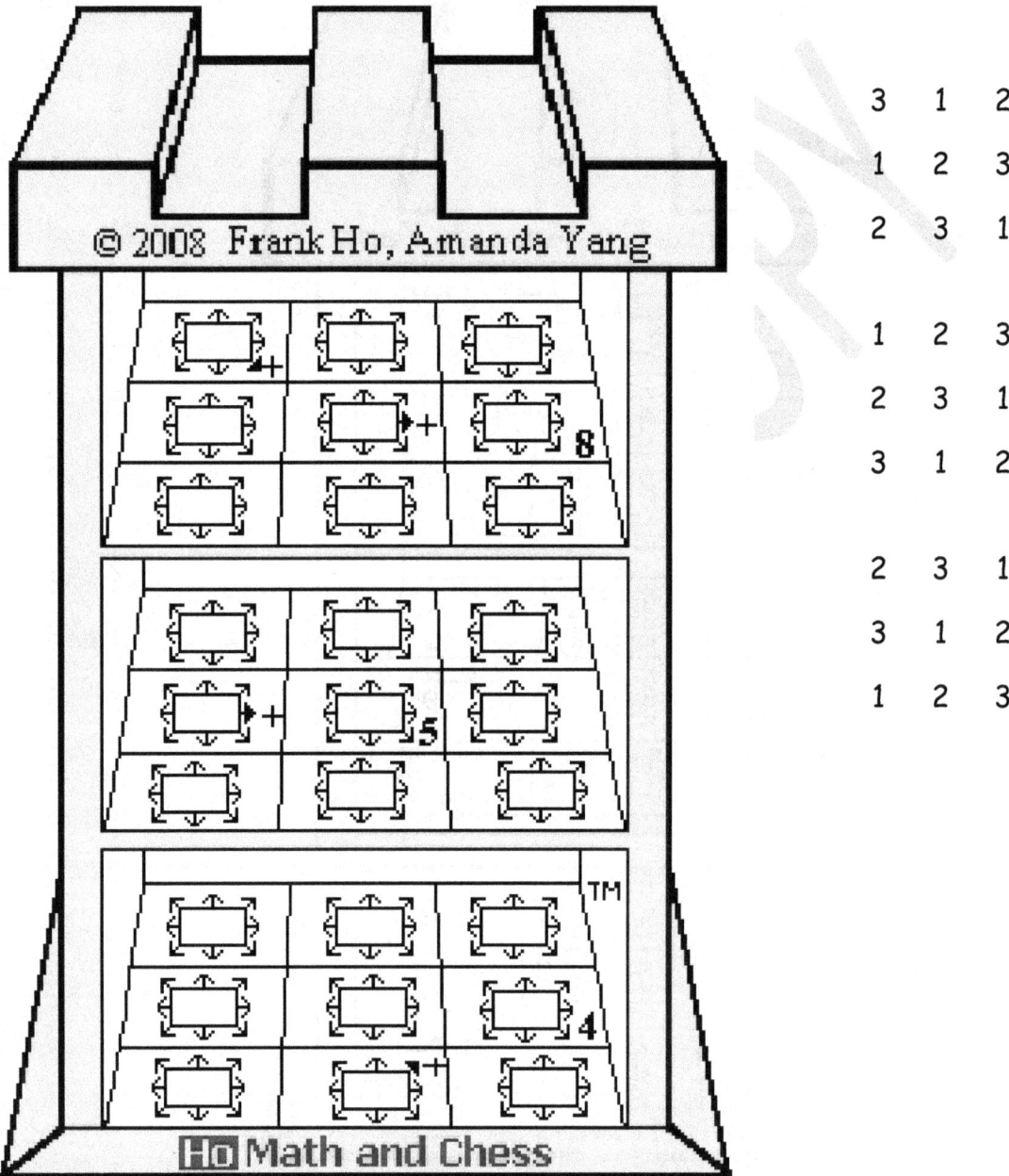

3 Dimensional Frankho ChessDoku™ # 22

Rule: All the digits 1 to 3 must appear in every row and column but cannot repeat on the same row of the same column of each layer. The number appears in the bottom right-hand corner is the result calculated according to operator(s) and chess move(s).

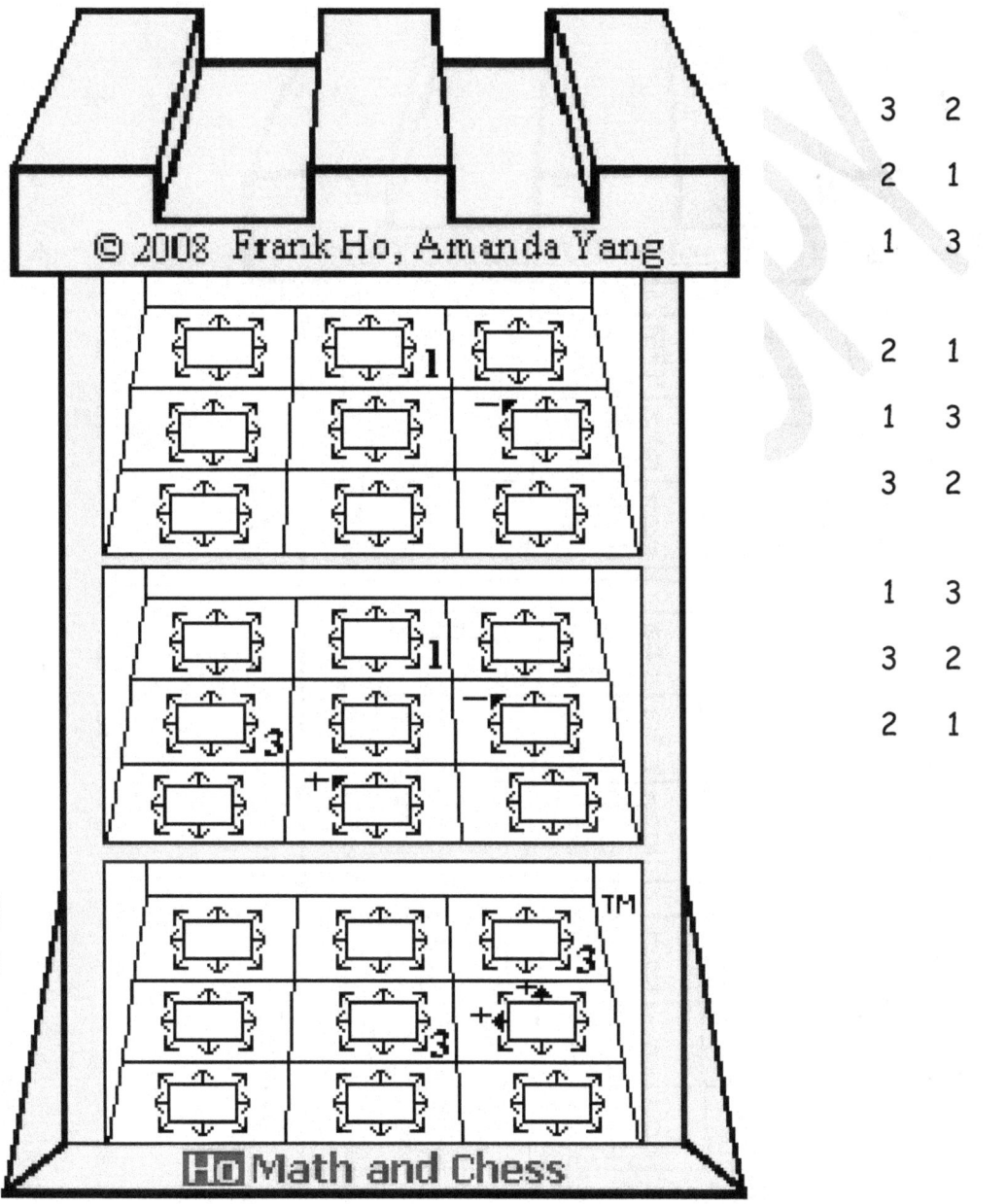

3 Dimensional Frankho ChessDoku™ # 23

Rule: All the digits 1 to 3 must appear in every row and column but cannot repeat on the same row of the same column of each layer. The number appears in the bottom right-hand corner is the result calculated according to operator(s) and chess move(s).

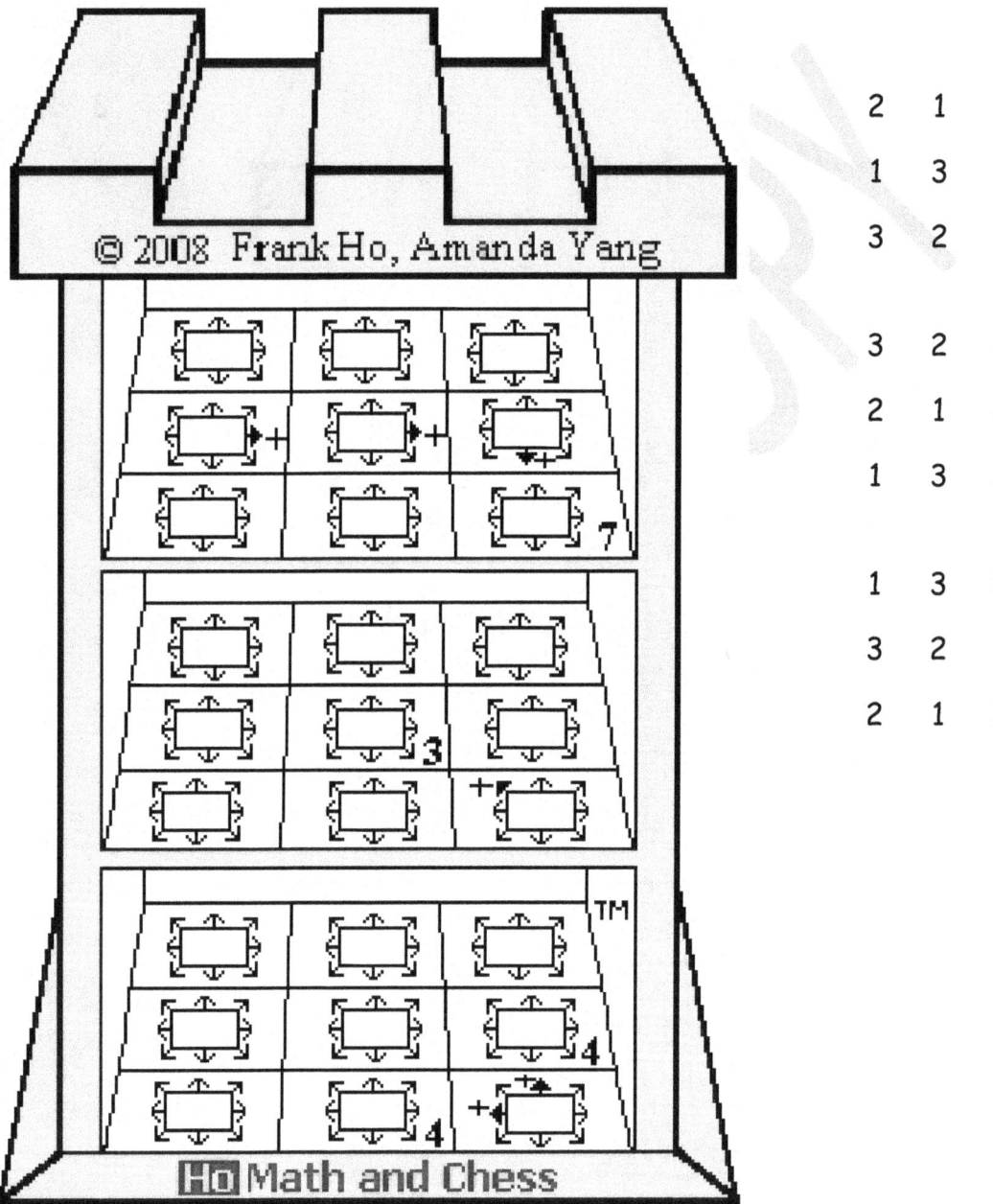

3 Dimensional Frankho ChessDoku™ # 24

Rule: All the digits 1 to 3 must appear in every row and column but cannot repeat on the same row of the same column of each layer. The number appears in the bottom right-hand corner is the result calculated according to operator(s) and chess move(s).

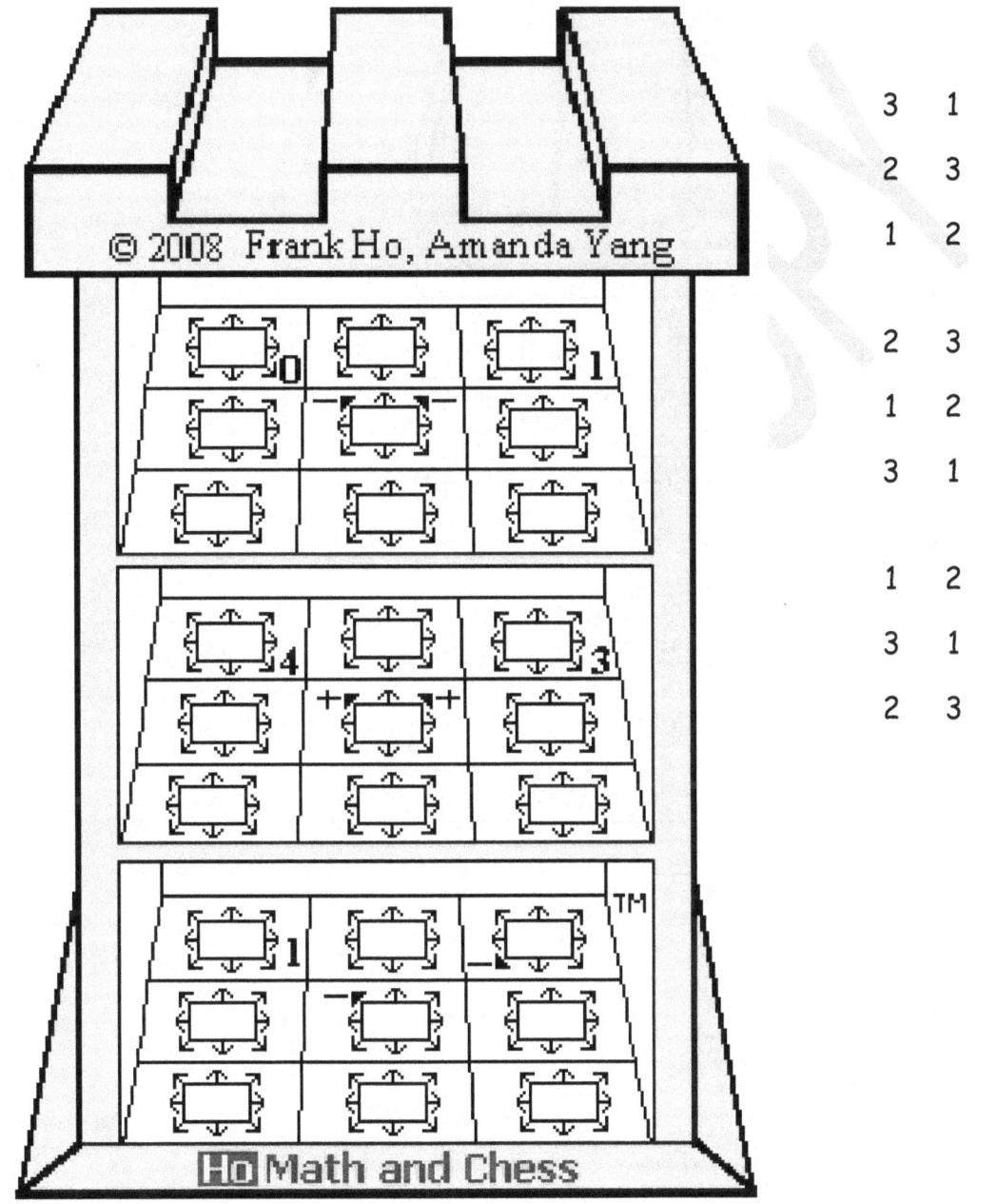

3 Dimensional Frankho ChessDoku™ # 25

Rule: All the digits 1 to 3 must appear in every row and column but cannot repeat on the same row of the same column of each layer. The number appears in the bottom right-hand corner is the result calculated according to operator(s) and chess move(s).

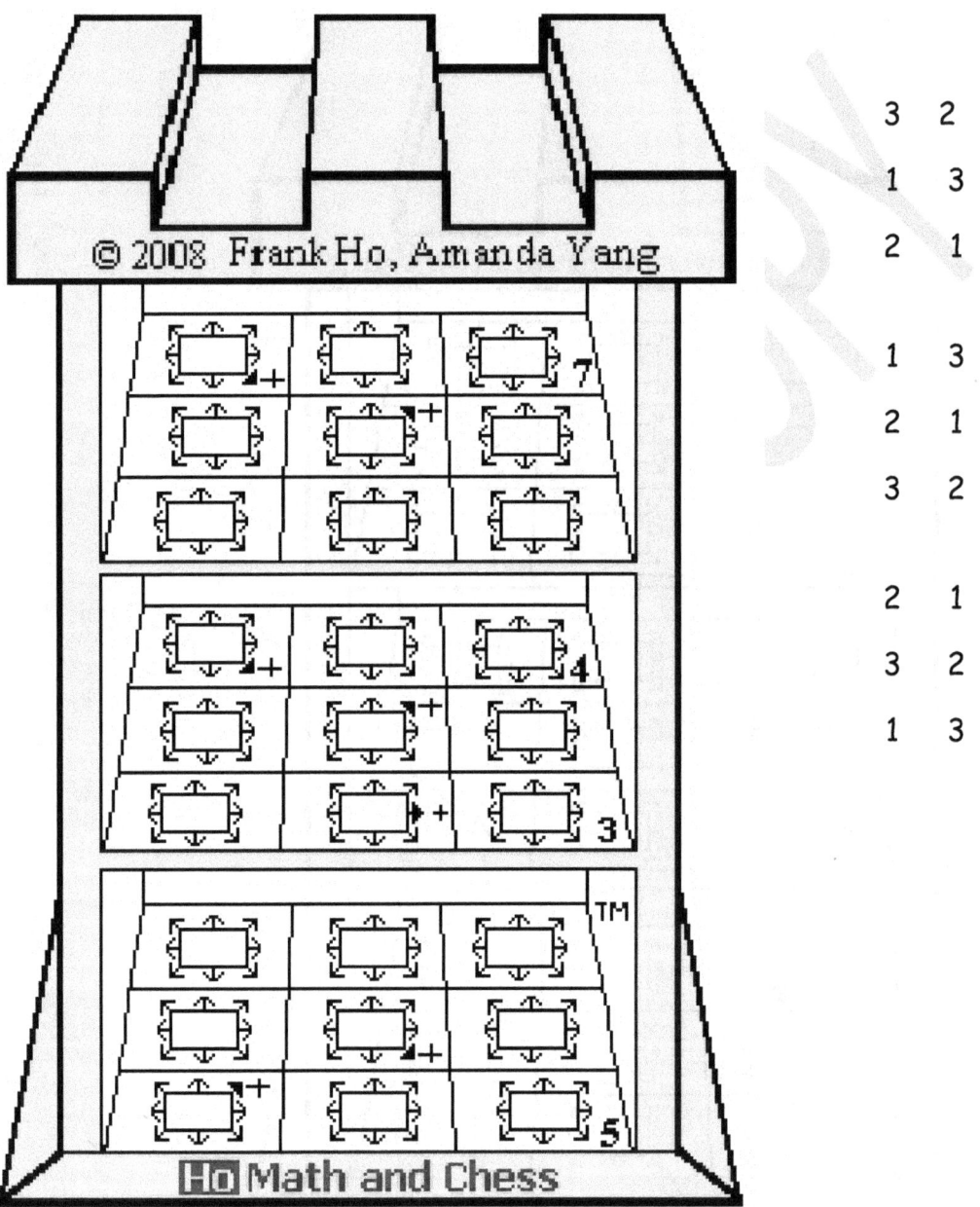

3 Dimensional Frankho ChessDoku™ # 26

Rule: All the digits 1 to 3 must appear in every row and column but cannot repeat on the same row of the same column of each layer. The number appears in the bottom right-hand corner is the result calculated according to operator(s) and chess move(s).

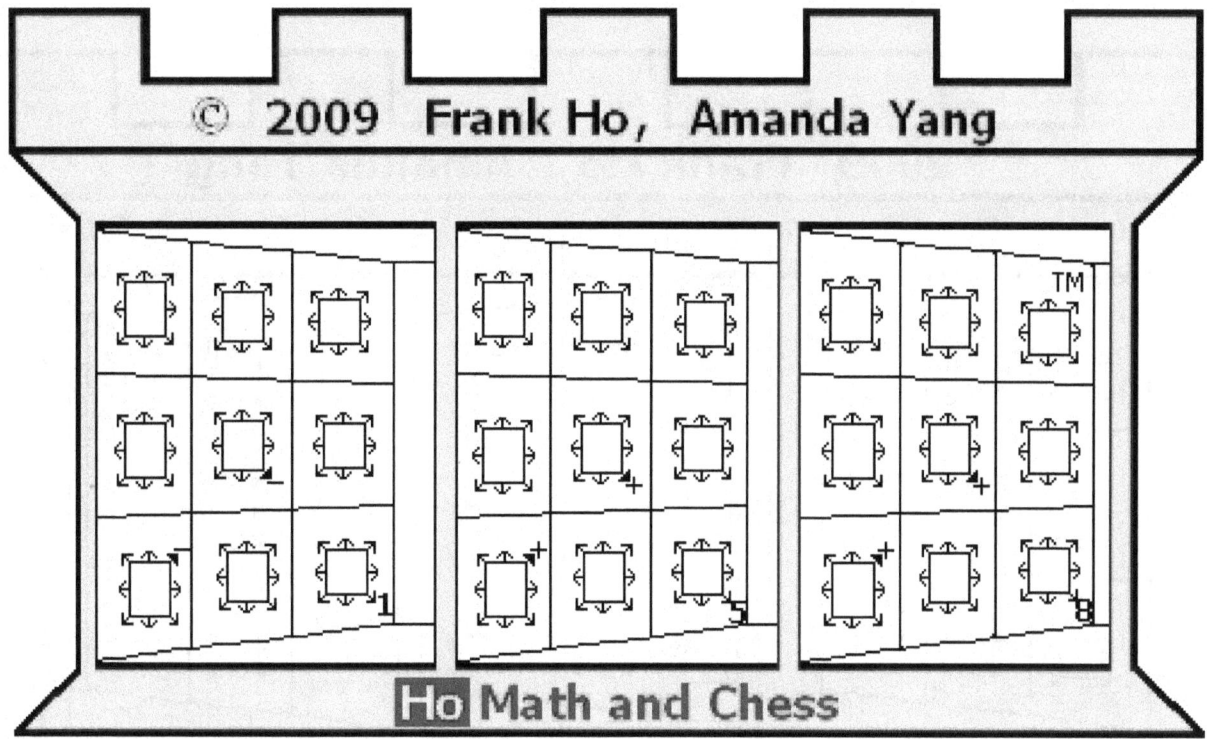

```
1 3 2       2 1 3       3 2 1
2 1 3       3 2 1       1 3 2
3 2 1       1 3 2       2 1 3
```

3 Dimensional Frankho ChessDoku™ # 27

Rule: All the digits 1 to 3 must appear in every row and column but cannot repeat on the same row of the same column of each layer. The number appears in the bottom right-hand corner is the result calculated according to operator(s) and chess move(s).

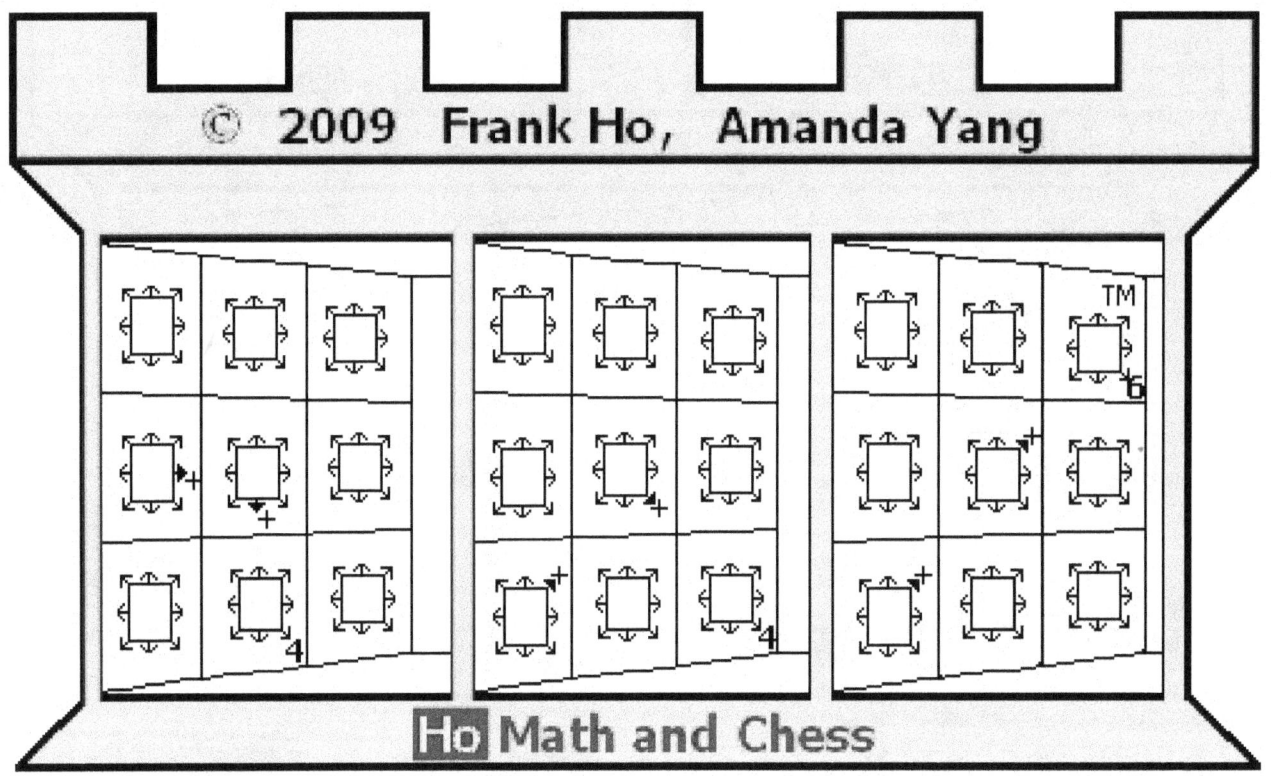

```
  2  3  1         1  2  3         3  1  2
  1  2  3         3  1  2         2  3  1
  3  1  2         2  3  1         1  2  3
```

3 Dimensional Frankho ChessDoku™ # 28

Rule: All the digits 1 to 3 must appear in every row and column but cannot repeat on the same row of the same column of each layer. The number appears in the bottom right-hand corner is the result calculated according to operator(s) and chess move(s).

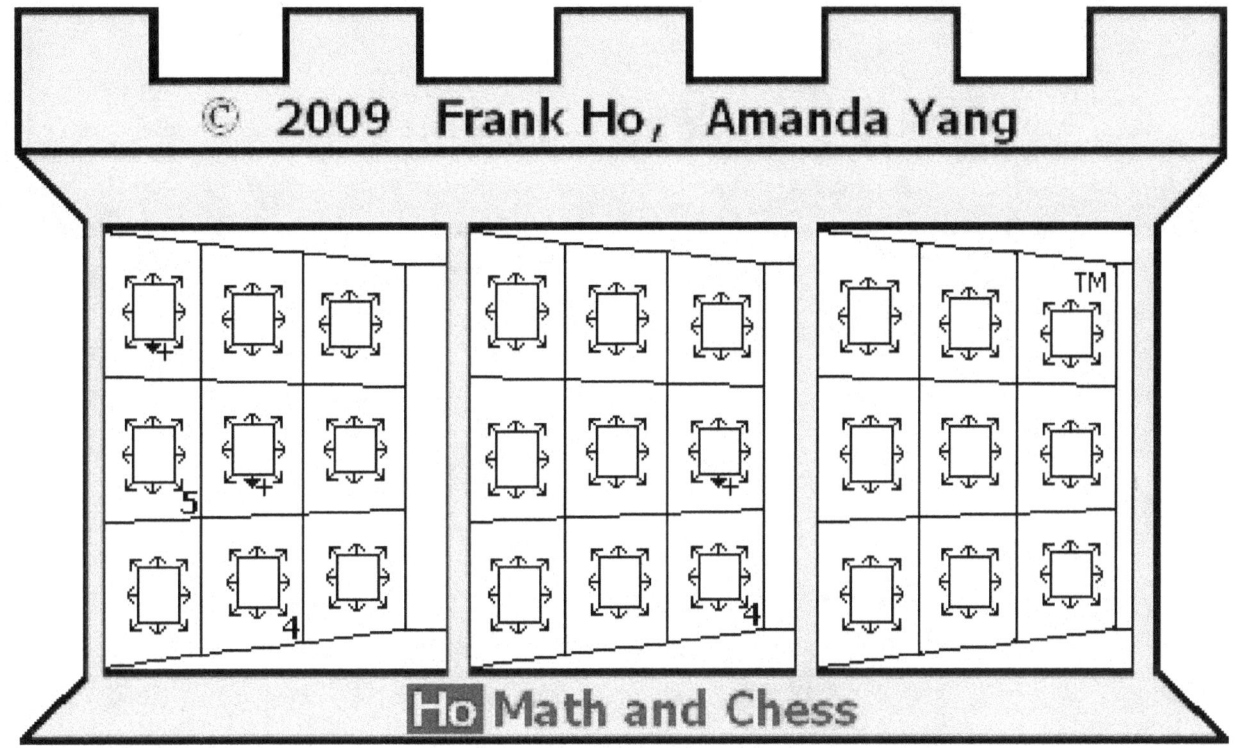

3 2 1	1 3 2	2 1 3
2 1 3	3 2 1	1 3 2
1 3 2	2 1 3	3 2 1

3 Dimensional Frankho ChessDoku™ # 29

Rule: All the digits 1 to 3 must appear in every row and column but cannot repeat on the same row of the same column of each layer. The number appears in the bottom right-hand corner is the result calculated according to operator(s) and chess move(s).

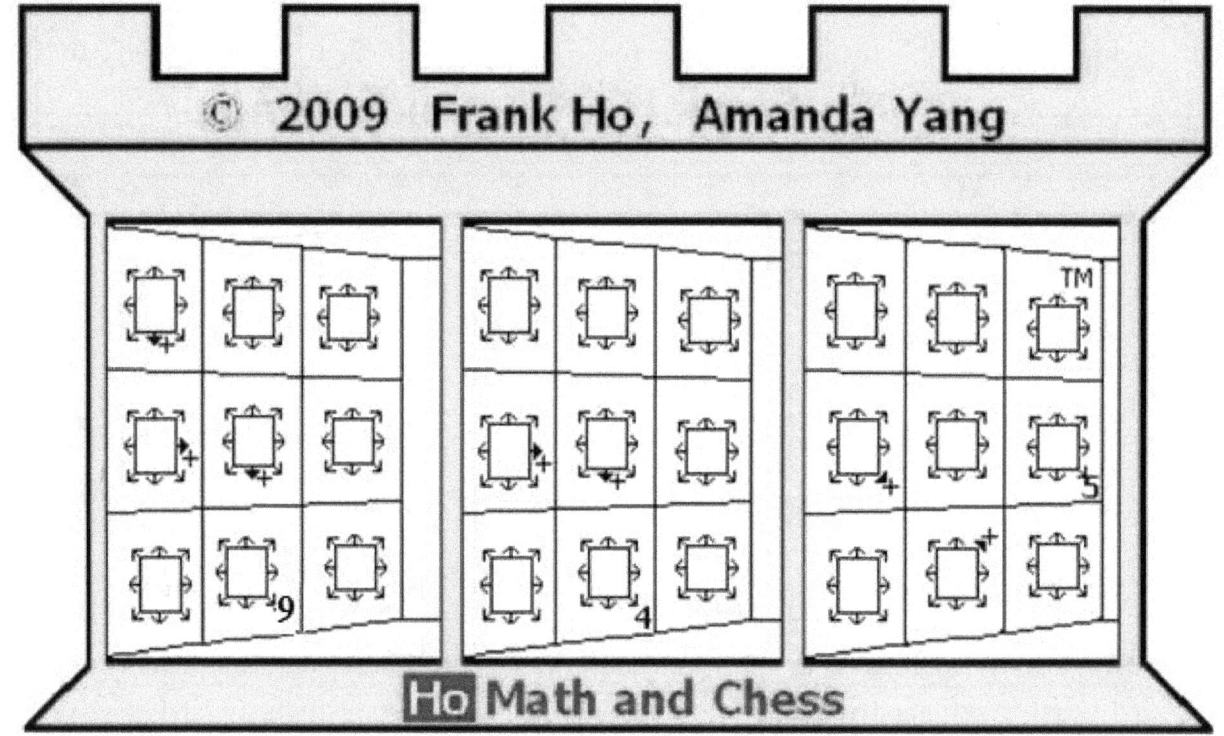

```
1 2 3      2 3 1      3 1 2
3 1 2      1 2 3      2 3 1
2 3 1      3 1 2      1 2 3
```

3 Dimensional Frankho ChessDoku™ # 30

Rule: All the digits 1 to 3 must appear in every row and column but cannot repeat on the same row of the same column of each layer. The number appears in the bottom right-hand corner is the result calculated according to operator(s) and chess move(s).

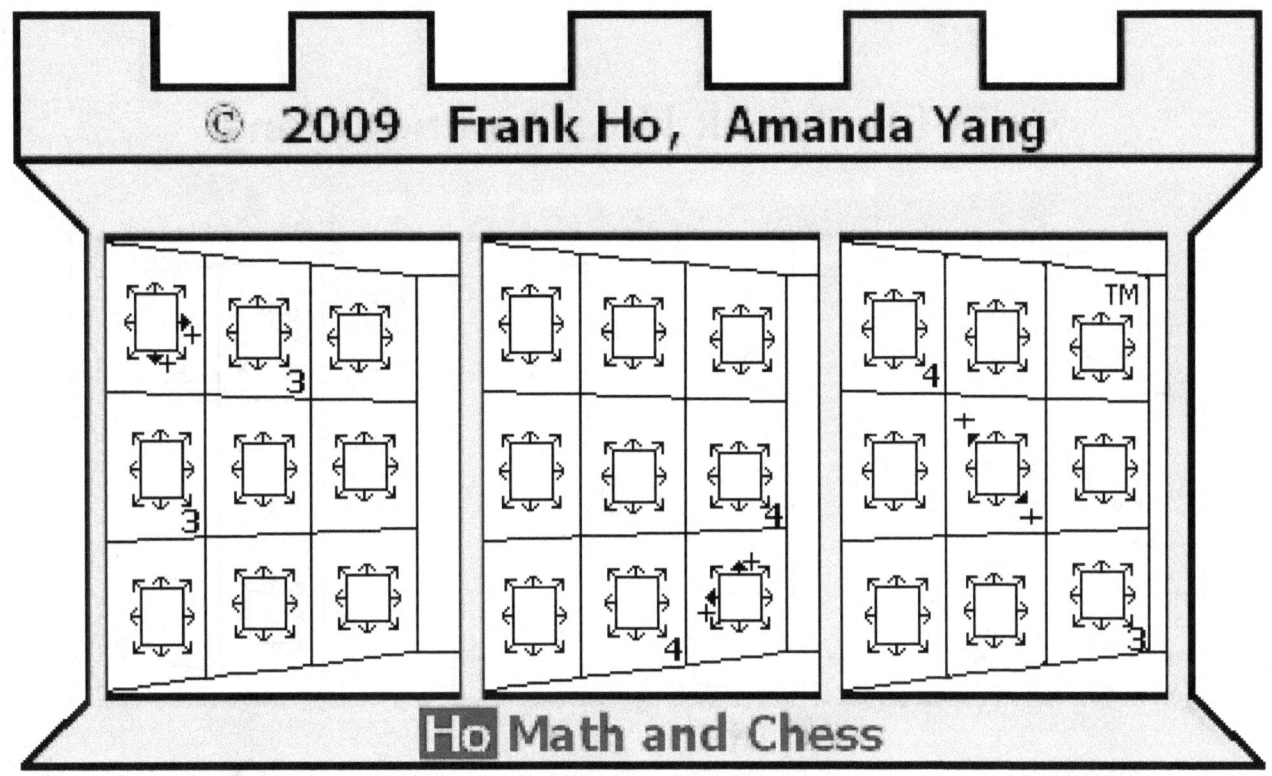

```
2  1  3        1  3  2        3  2  1
1  3  2        3  2  1        2  1  3
3  2  1        2  1  3        1  3  2
```

3 Dimensional Frankho ChessDoku™ # 31

Rule: All the digits 1 to 3 must appear in every row and column but cannot repeat on the same row of the same column of each layer. The number appears in the bottom right-hand corner is the result calculated according to operator(s) and chess move(s).

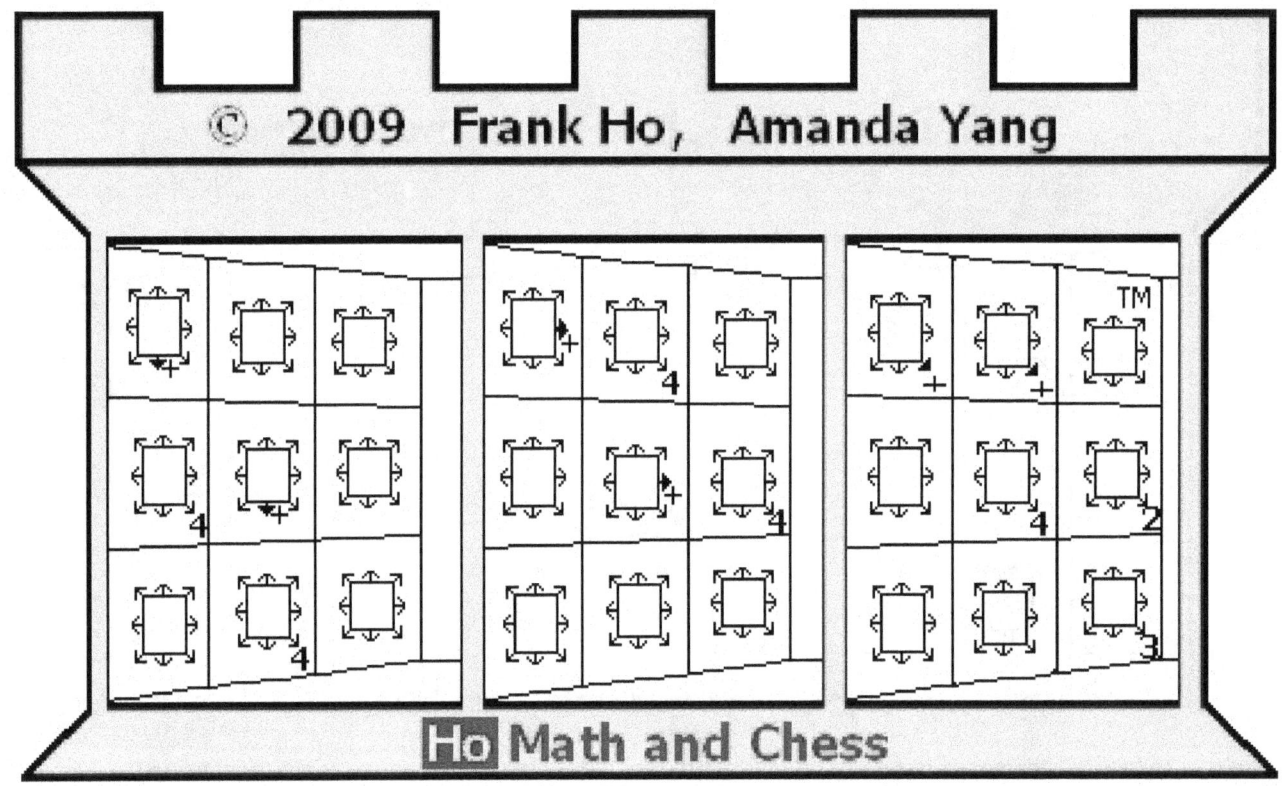

```
3 2 1     1 3 2     2 1 3
1 3 2     2 1 3     3 2 1
2 1 3     3 2 1     1 3 2
```

3 Dimensional Frankho ChessDoku™ # 32

Rule: All the digits 1 to 3 must appear in every row and column but cannot repeat on the same row of the same column of each layer. The number appears in the bottom right-hand corner is the result calculated according to operator(s) and chess move(s).

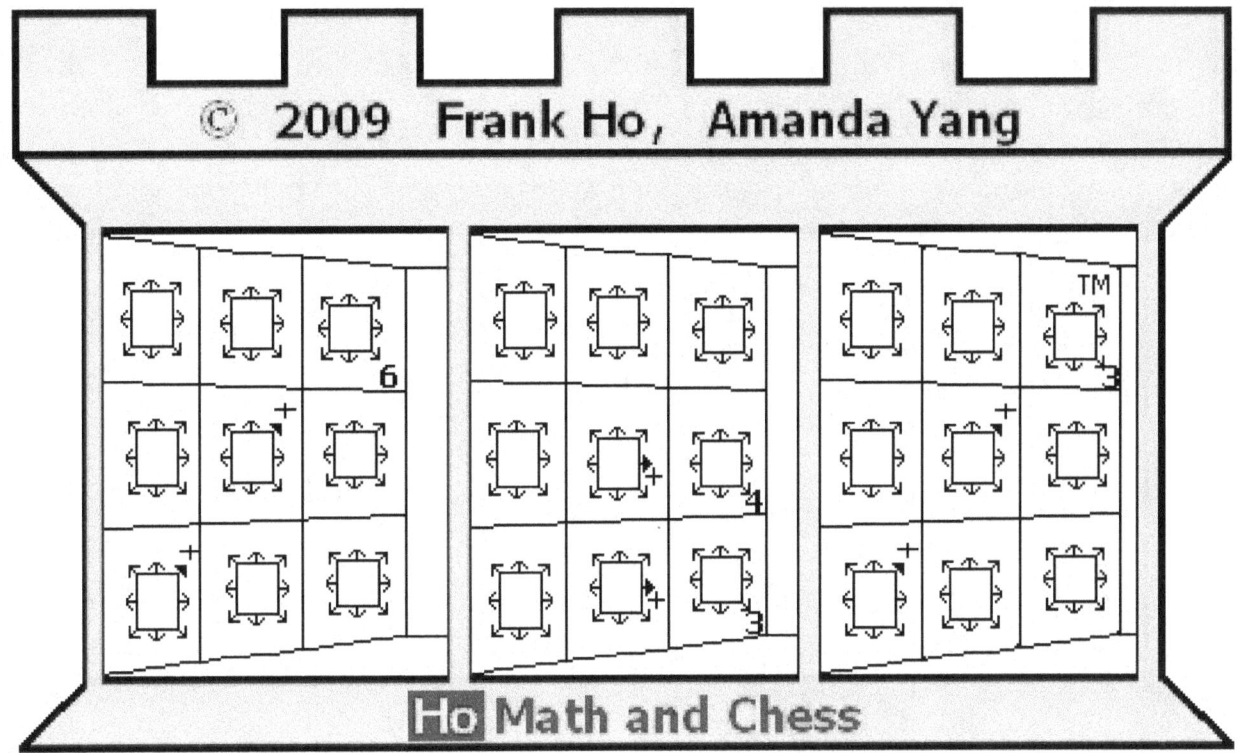

```
3 1 2        1 2 3        2 3 1
1 2 3        2 3 1        3 1 2
2 3 1        3 1 2        1 2 3
```

3 Dimensional Frankho ChessDoku™ # 33

Rule: All the digits 1 to 3 must appear in every row and column but cannot repeat on the same row of the same column of each layer. The number appears in the bottom right-hand corner is the result calculated according to operator(s) and chess move(s).

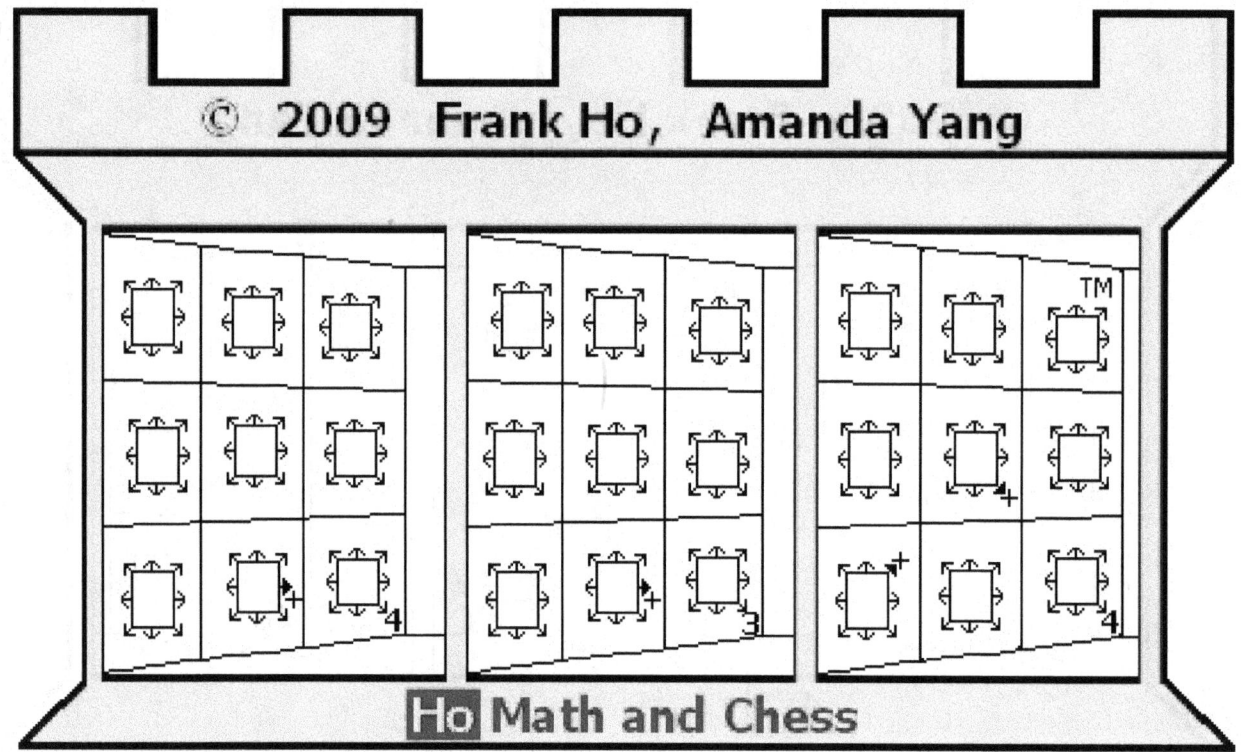

3 Dimensional Frankho ChessDoku™ # 34

Rule: All the digits 1 to 3 must appear in every row and column but cannot repeat on the same row of the same column of each layer. The number appears in the bottom right-hand corner is the result calculated according to operator(s) and chess move(s).

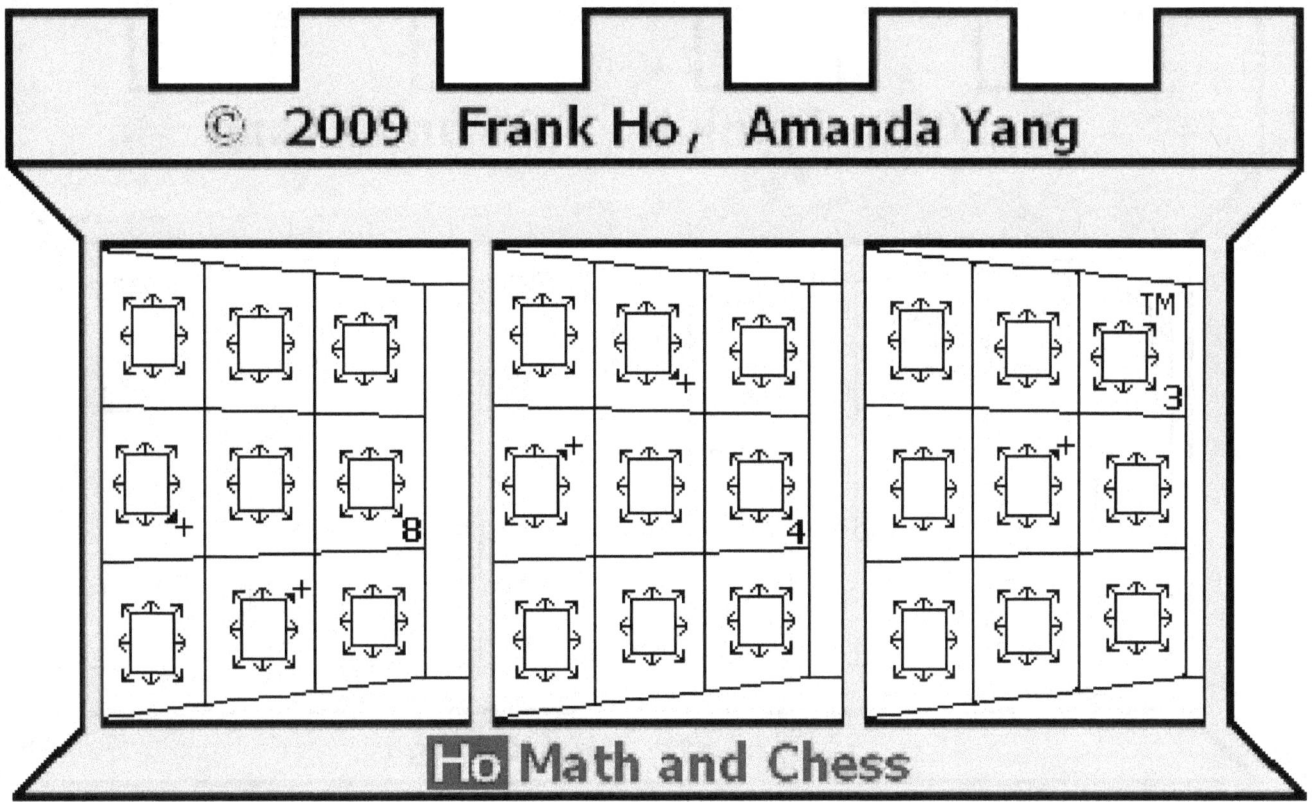

```
1  2  3        3  1  2        2  3  1
3  1  2        2  3  1        1  2  3
2  3  1        1  2  3        3  1  2
```

3 Dimensional Frankho ChessDoku™ # 35

Rule: All the digits 1 to 3 must appear in every row and column but cannot repeat on the same row of the same column of each layer. The number appears in the bottom right-hand corner is the result calculated according to operator(s) and chess move(s).

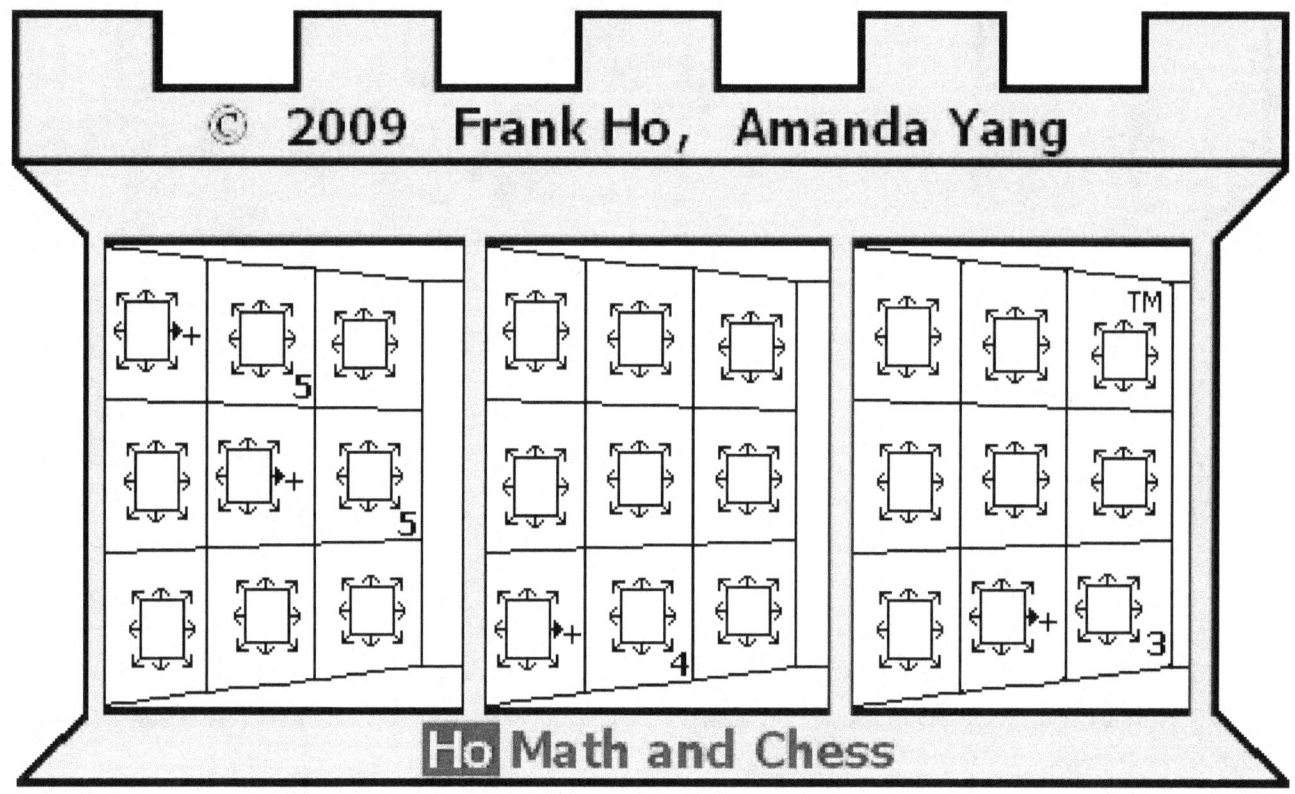

3 Dimensional Frankho ChessDoku™ # 36

Rule: All the digits 1 to 3 must appear in every row and column but cannot repeat on the same row of the same column of each layer. The number appears in the bottom right-hand corner is the result calculated according to operator(s) and chess move(s).

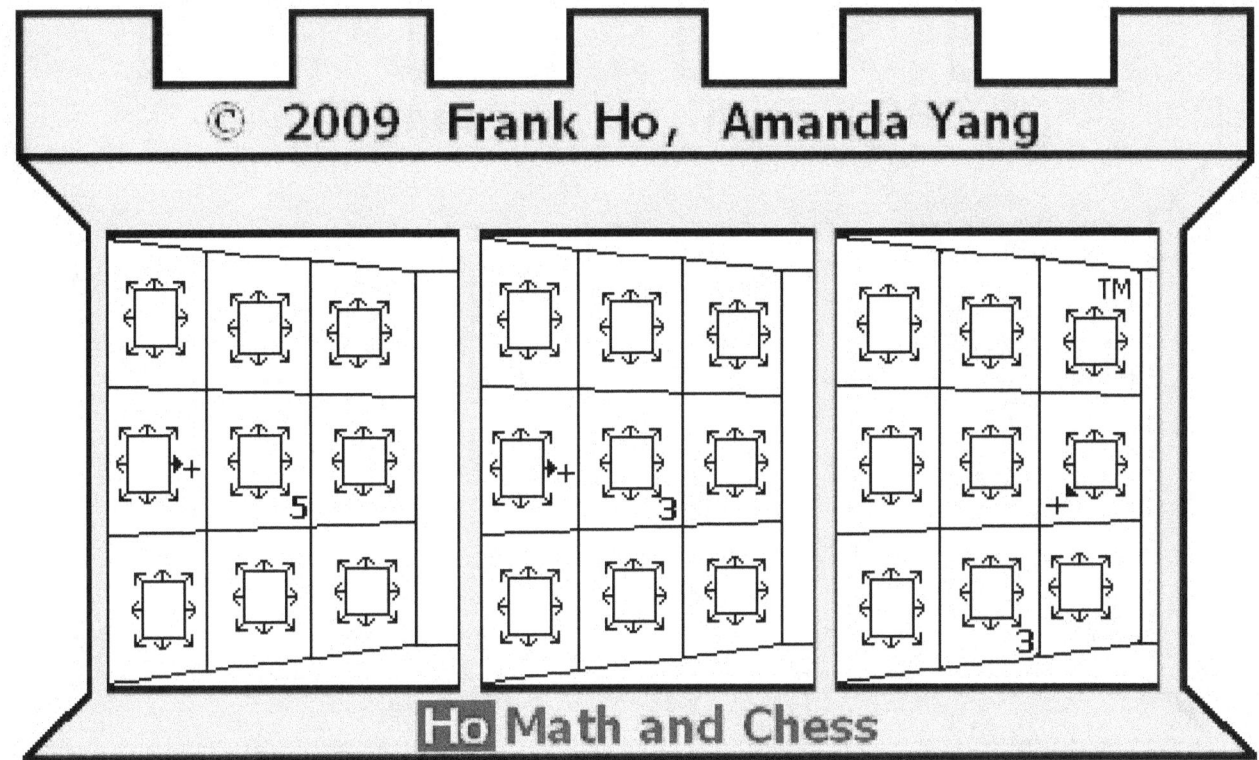

```
2  1  3        1  3  2        3  2  1
3  2  1        2  1  3        1  3  2
1  3  2        3  2  1        2  1  3
```

3 Dimensional Frankho ChessDoku™ # 37

Rule: All the digits 1 to 3 must appear in every row and column but cannot repeat on the same row of the same column of each layer. The number appears in the bottom right-hand corner is the result calculated according to operator(s) and chess move(s).

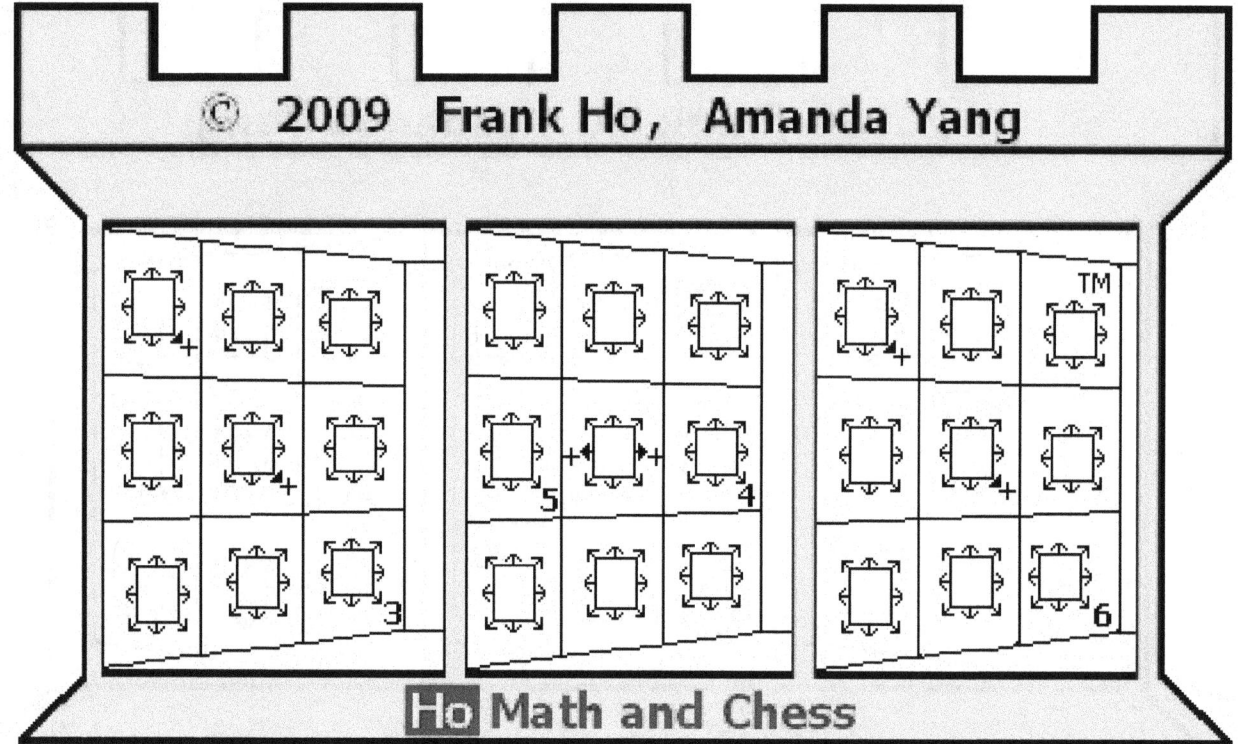

```
    1  2  3         3  1  2         2  3  1
    3  1  2         2  3  1         1  2  3
    2  3  1         1  2  3         3  1  2
```

3 Dimensional Frankho ChessDoku™ # 38

Rule: All the digits 1 to 3 must appear in every row and column but cannot repeat on the same row of the same column of each layer. The number appears in the bottom right-hand corner is the result calculated according to operator(s) and chess move(s).

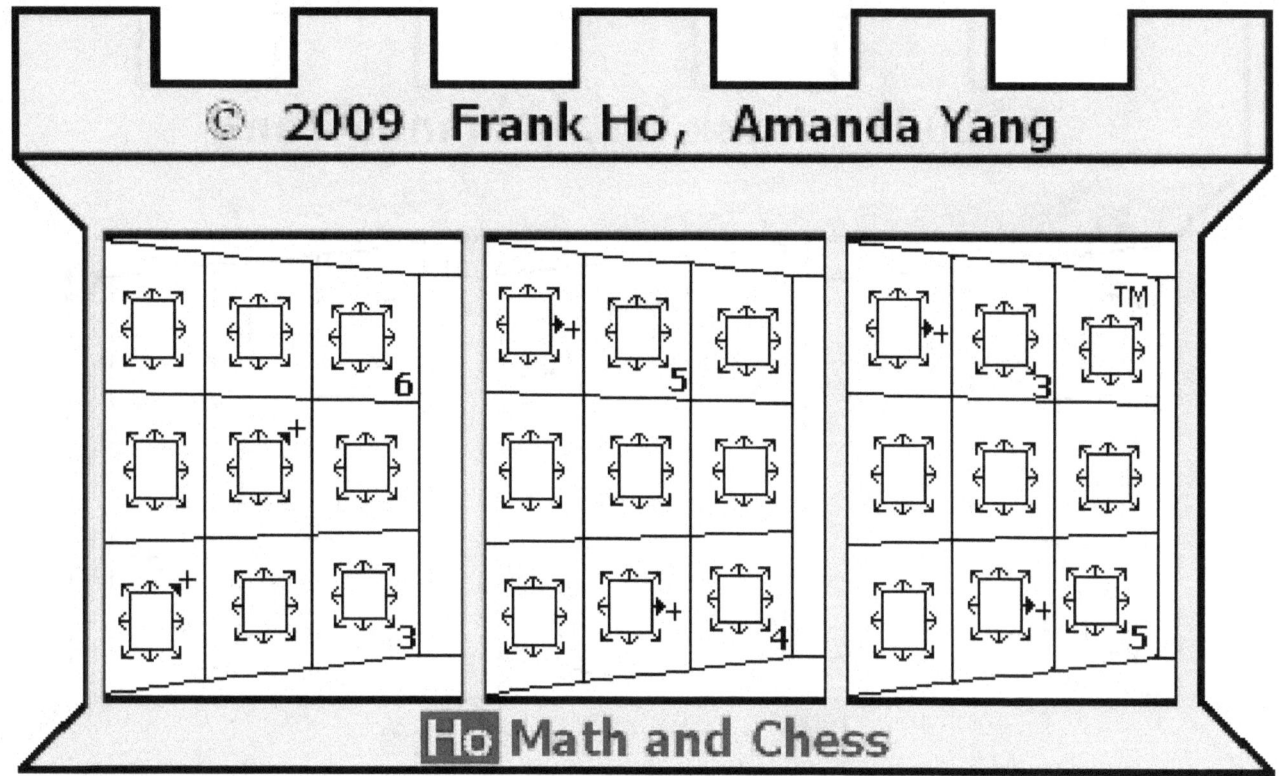

```
1  3  2        3  2  1        2  1  3
2  1  3        1  3  2        3  2  1
3  2  1        2  1  3        1  3  2
```

3 Dimensional Frankho ChessDoku™ # 39

Rule: All the digits 1 to 3 must appear in every row and column but cannot repeat on the same row of the same column of each layer. The number appears in the bottom right-hand corner is the result calculated according to operator(s) and chess move(s).

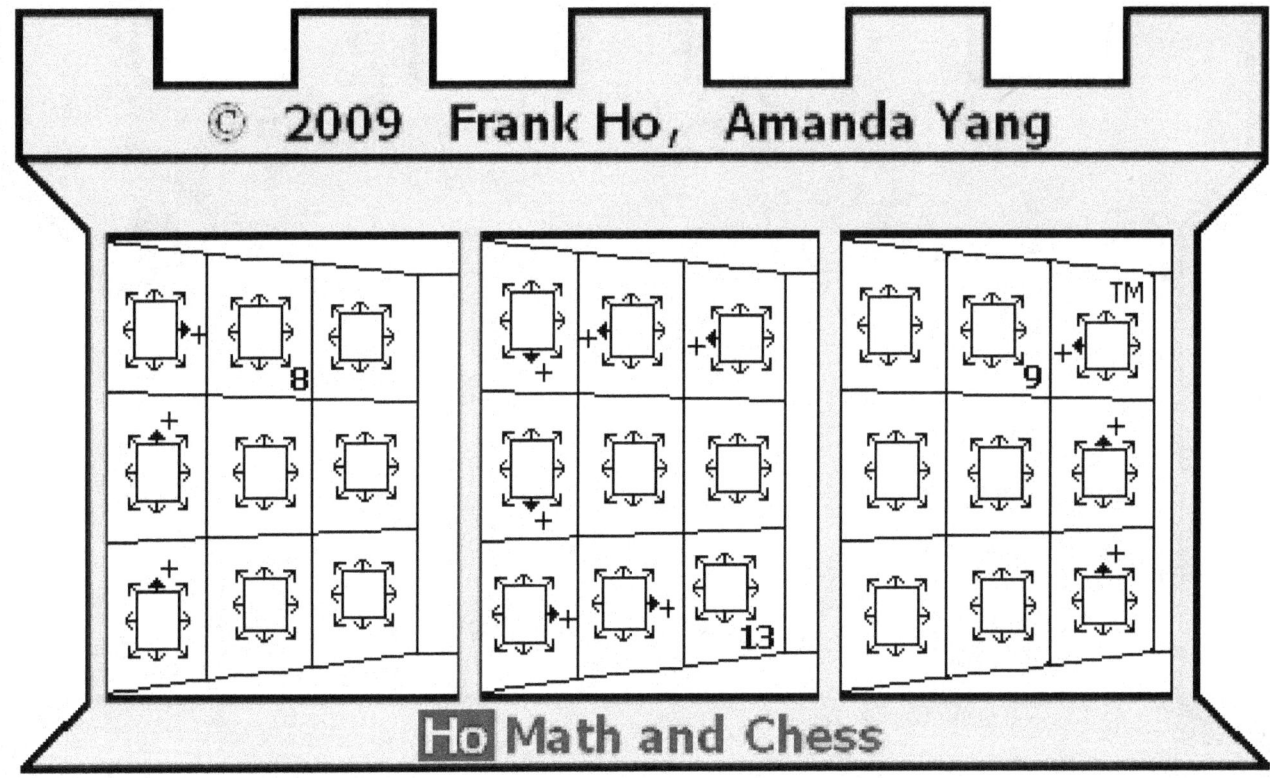

```
3 2 1        2 1 3        1 3 2
2 1 3        1 3 2        3 2 1
1 3 2        3 2 1        2 1 3
```

3 Dimensional Frankho ChessDoku™ # 40

Rule: All the digits 1 to 3 must appear in every row and column but cannot repeat on the same row of the same column of each layer. The number appears in the bottom right-hand corner is the result calculated according to operator(s) and chess move(s).

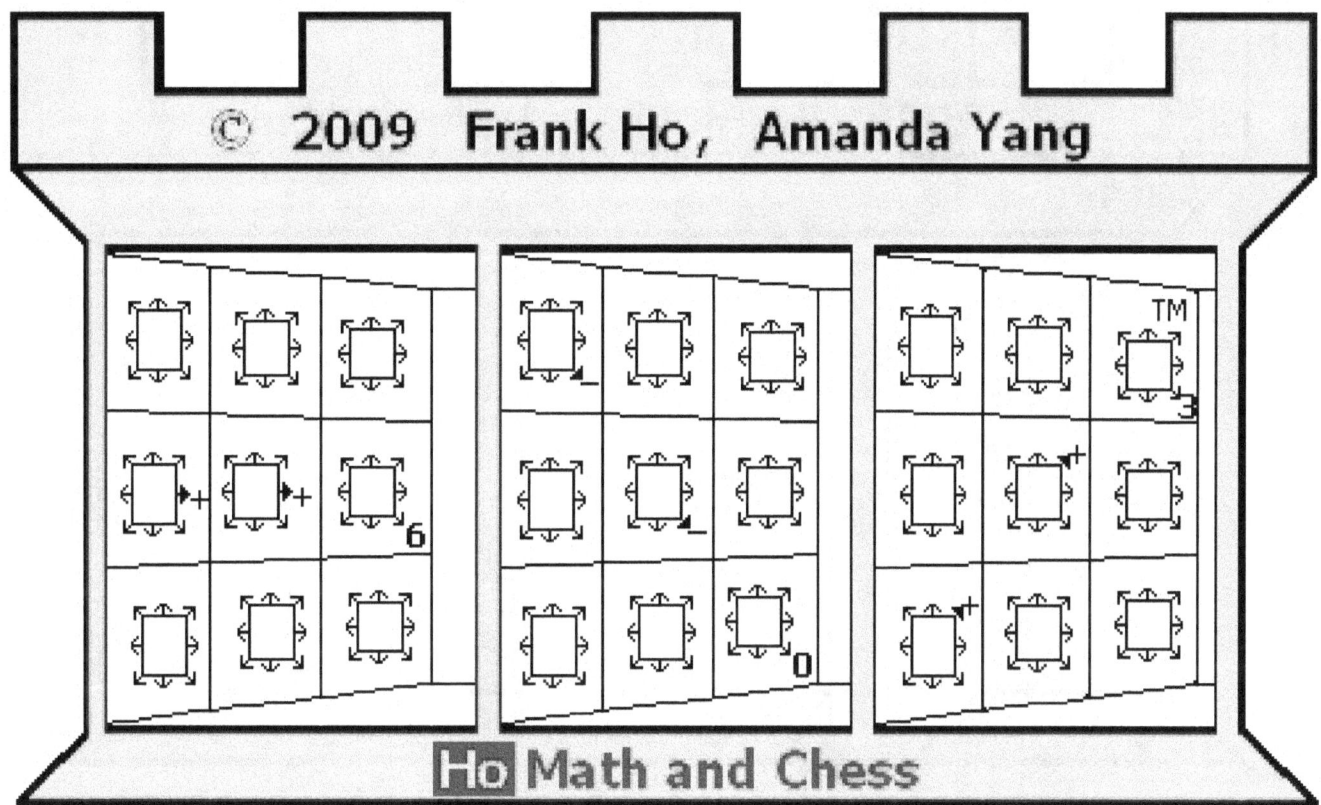

```
   1  2  3        3  1  2        2  3  1
   2  3  1        1  2  3        3  1  2
   3  1  2        2  3  1        1  2  3
```

3 Dimensional Frankho ChessDoku™ # 41

Rule: All the digits 1 to 3 must appear in every row and column but cannot repeat on the same row of the same column of each layer. The number appears in the bottom right-hand corner is the result calculated according to operator(s) and chess move(s).

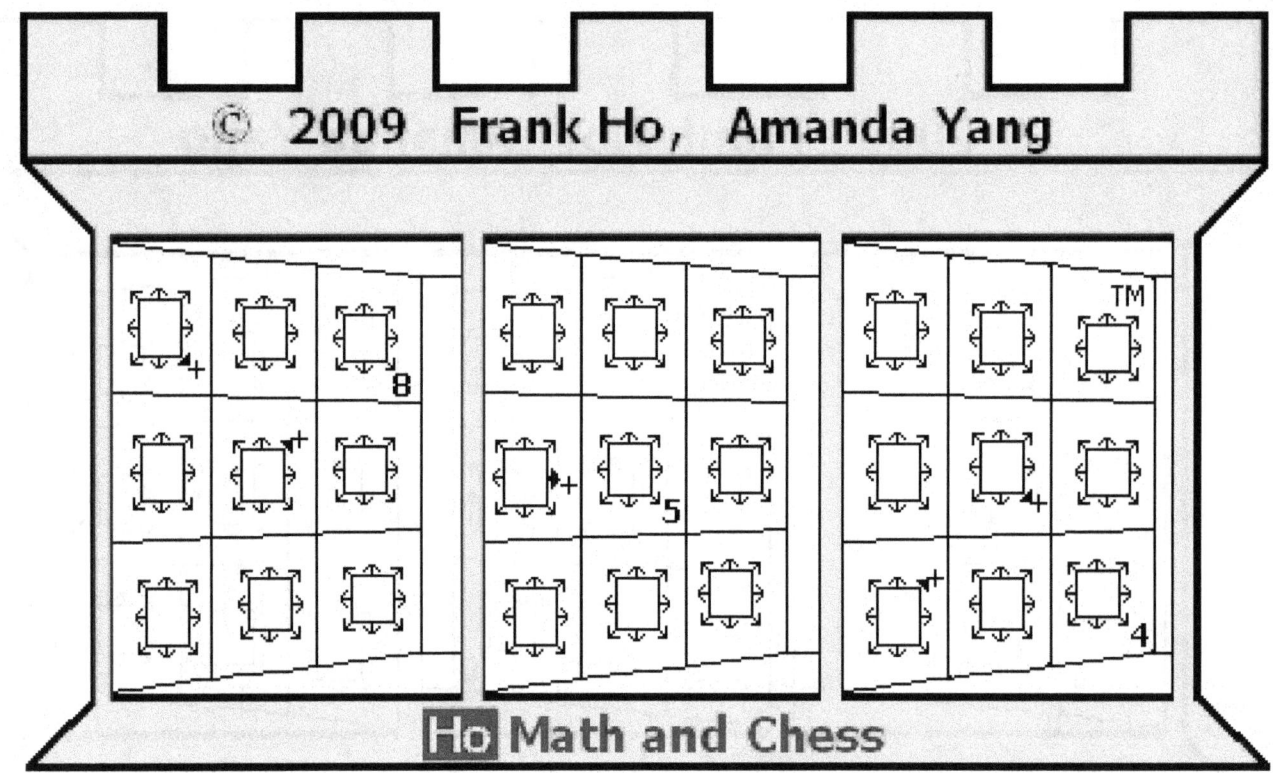

```
2 1 3      1 3 2      3 2 1
1 3 2      3 2 1      2 1 3
3 2 1      2 1 3      1 3 2
```

3 Dimensional Frankho ChessDoku™ # 42

Rule: All the digits 1 to 3 must appear in every row and column but cannot repeat on the same row of the same column of each layer. The number appears in the bottom right-hand corner is the result calculated according to operator(s) and chess move(s).

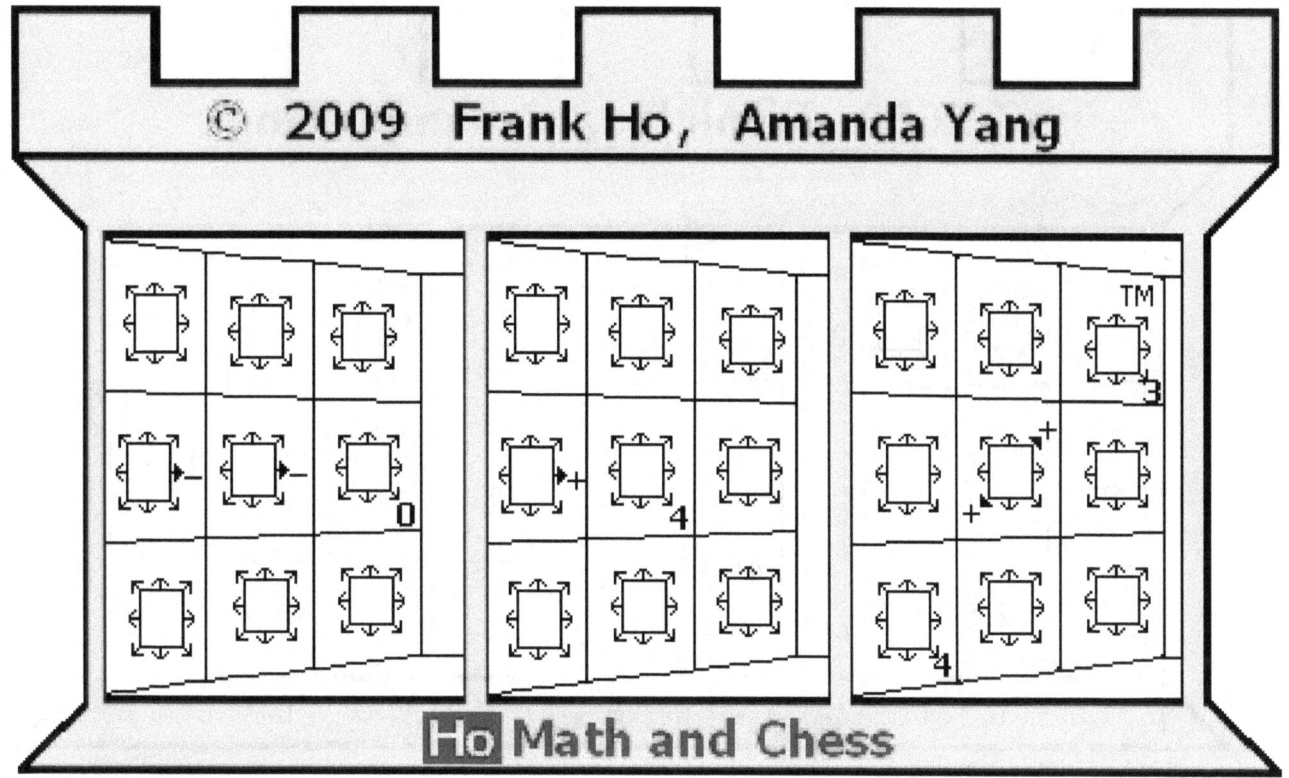

```
2 1 3        3 2 1        1 3 2
3 2 1        1 3 2        2 1 3
1 3 2        2 1 3        3 2 1
```

3 Dimensional Frankho ChessDoku™ # 43

Rule: All the digits 1 to 3 must appear in every row and column but cannot repeat on the same row of the same column of each layer. The number appears in the bottom right-hand corner is the result calculated according to operator(s) and chess move(s).

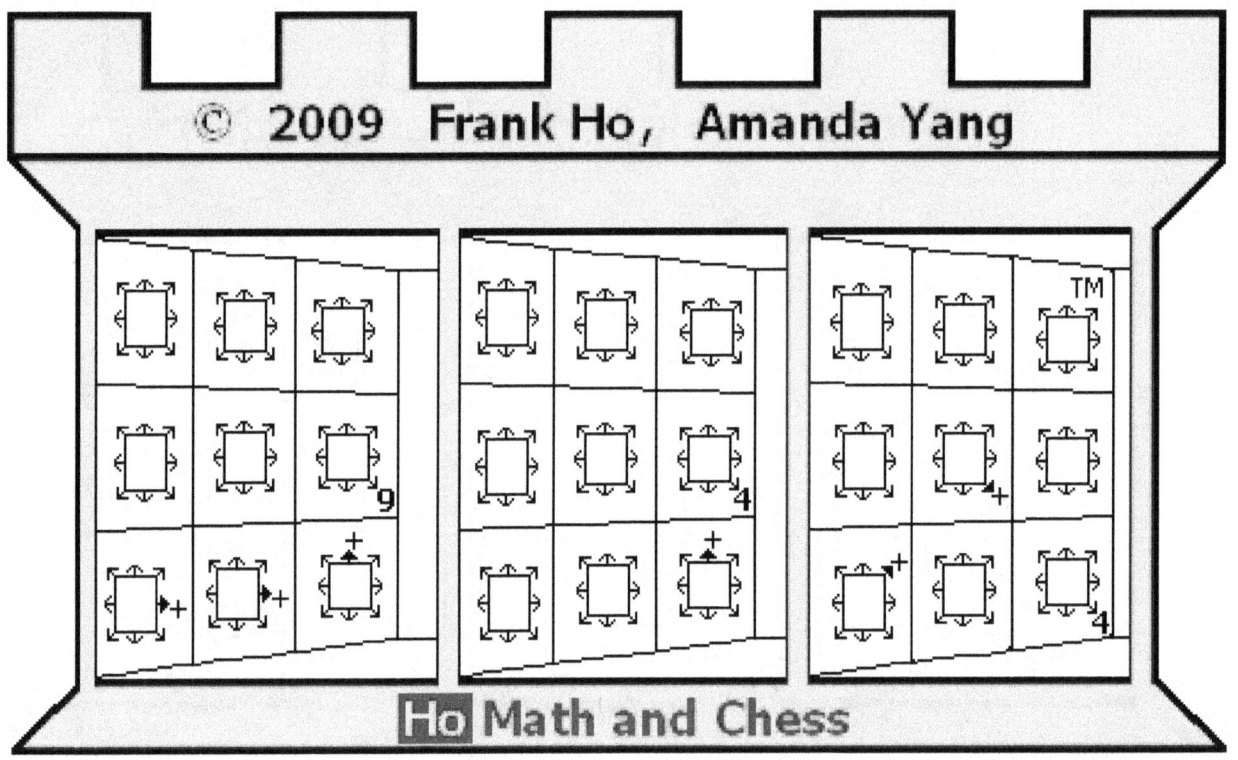

```
2 3 1        3 1 2        1 2 3
1 2 3        2 3 1        3 1 2
3 1 2        1 2 3        2 3 1
```

3 Dimensional Frankho ChessDoku™ # 44

Rule: All the digits 1 to 3 must appear in every row and column but cannot repeat on the same row of the same column of each layer. The number appears in the bottom right-hand corner is the result calculated according to operator(s) and chess move(s).

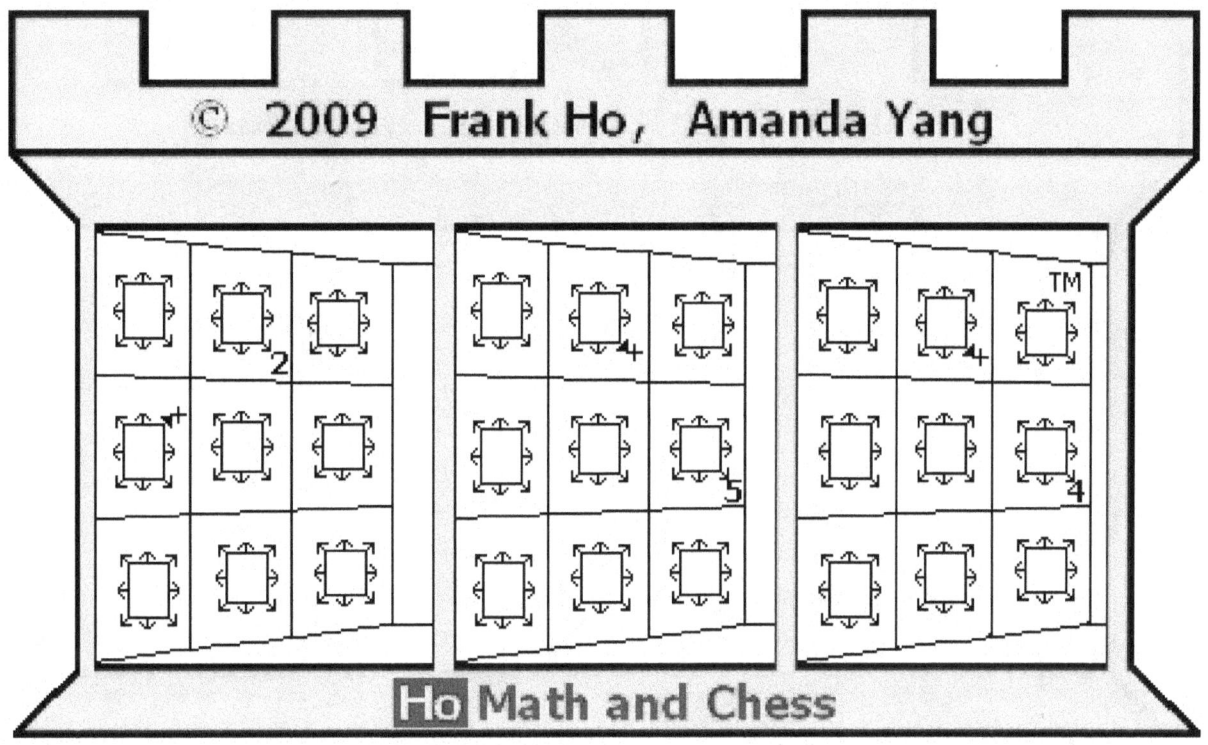

```
2 1 3      3 2 1      1 3 2
1 3 2      2 1 3      3 2 1
3 2 1      1 3 2      2 1 3
```

3 Dimensional Frankho ChessDoku™ # 45

Rule: All the digits 1 to 3 must appear in every row and column but cannot repeat on the same row of the same column of each layer. The number appears in the bottom right-hand corner is the result calculated according to operator(s) and chess move(s).

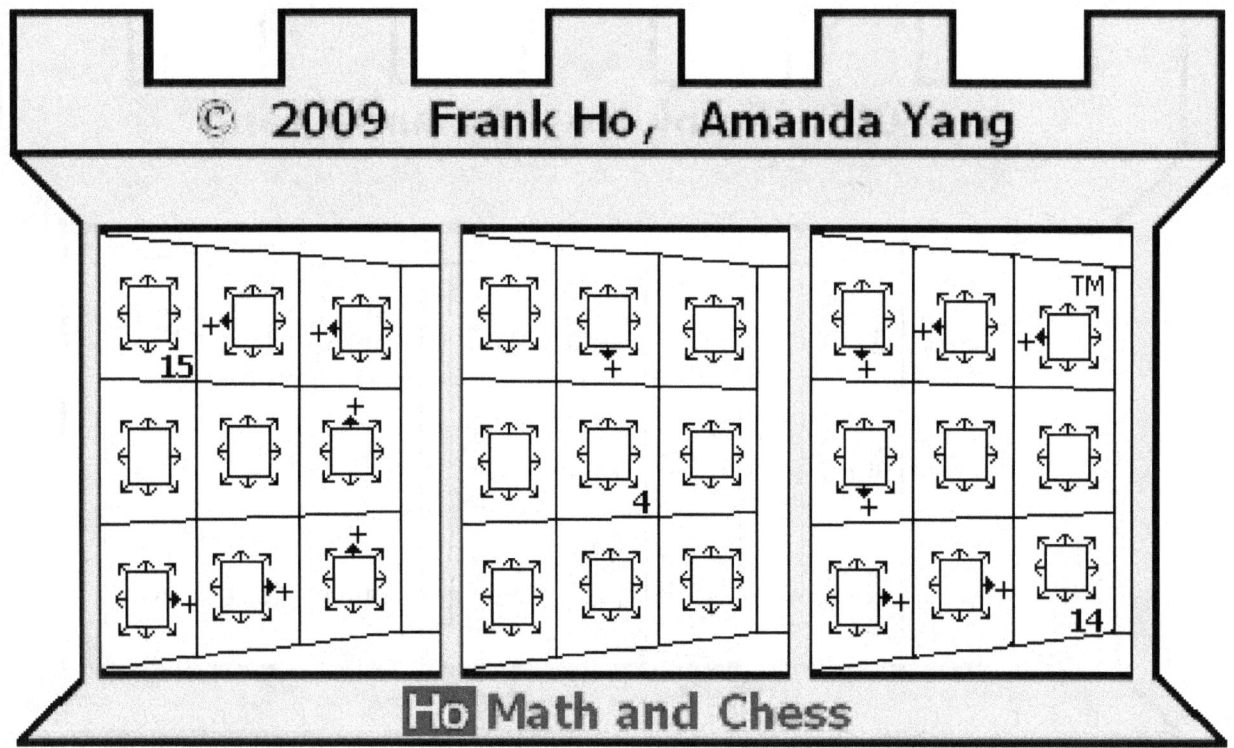

```
3  1  2        1  2  3        2  3  1
2  3  1        3  1  2        1  2  3
1  2  3        2  3  1        3  1  2
```

3 Dimensional Frankho ChessDoku™ # 46

Rule: All the digits 1 to 3 must appear in every row and column but cannot repeat on the same row of the same column of each layer. The number appears in the bottom right-hand corner is the result calculated according to operator(s) and chess move(s).

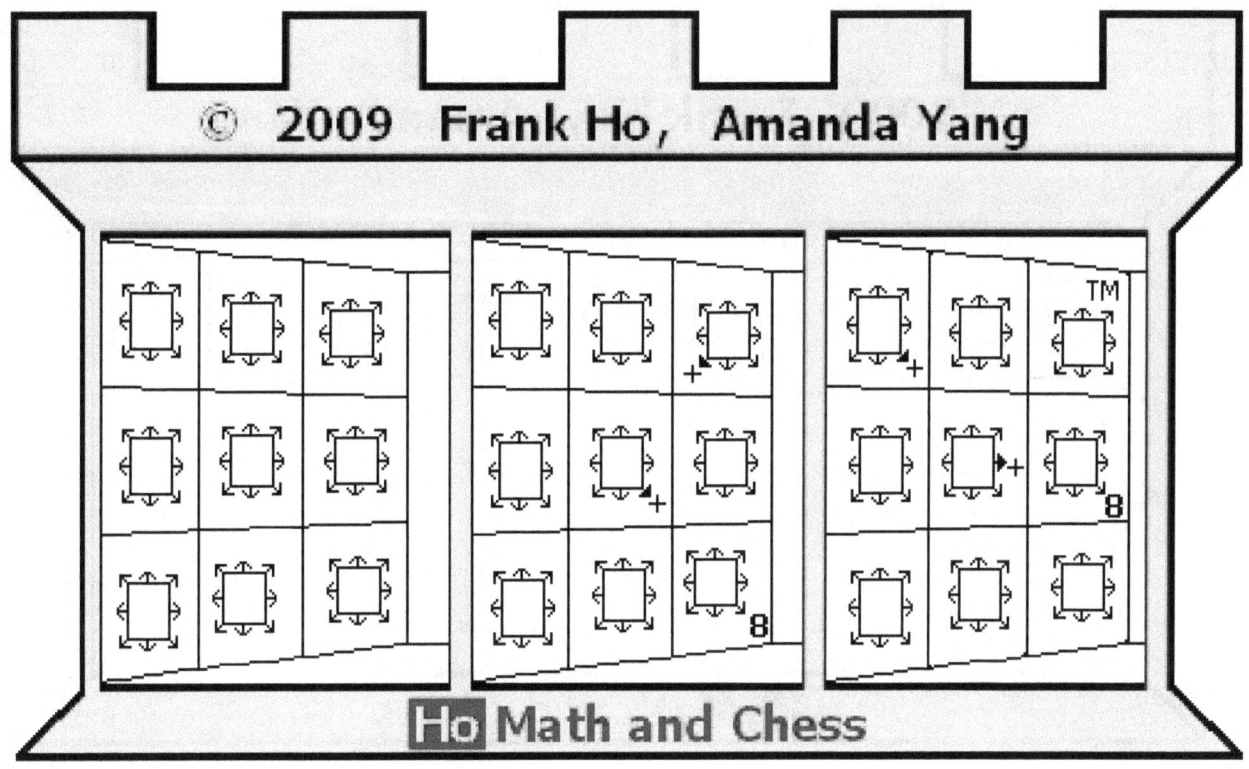

```
2 3 1        1 2 3        3 1 2
3 1 2        2 3 1        1 2 3
1 2 3        3 1 2        2 3 1
```

3 Dimensional Frankho ChessDoku™ # 47

Rule: All the digits 1 to 3 must appear in every row and column but cannot repeat on the same row of the same column of each layer. The number appears in the bottom right-hand corner is the result calculated according to operator(s) and chess move(s).

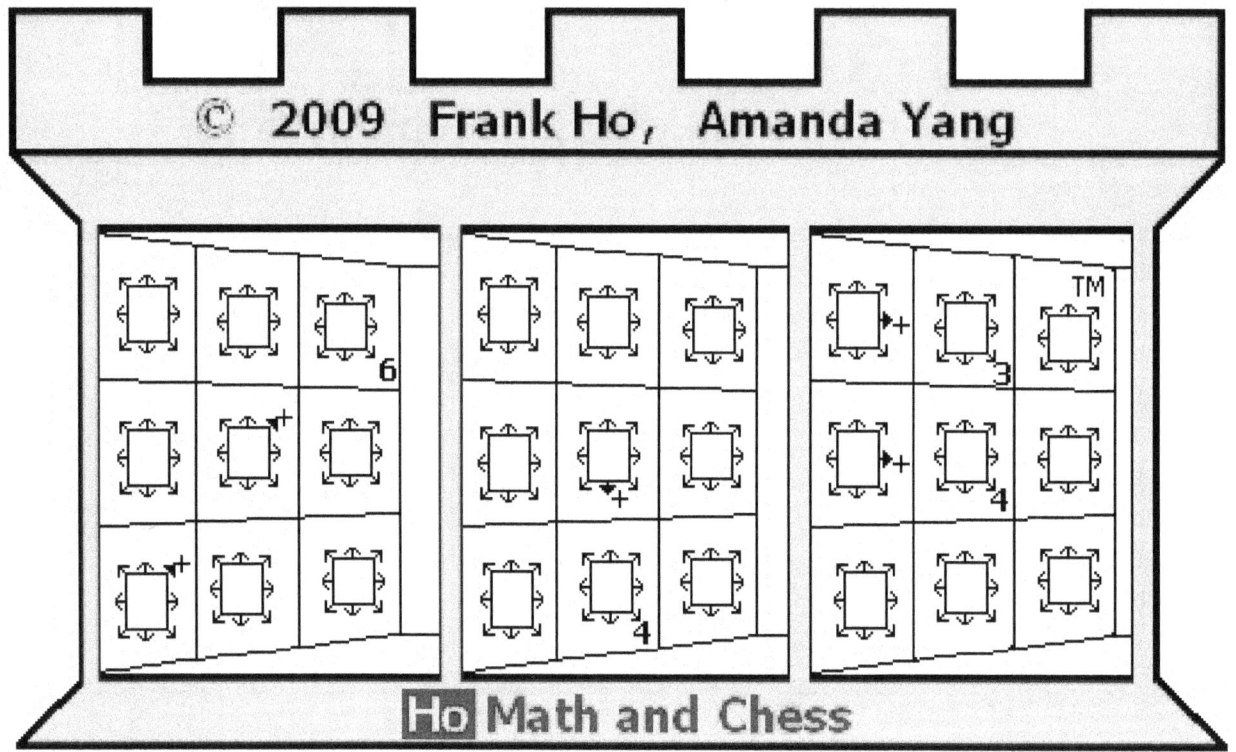

```
1 3 2        3 2 1        2 1 3
3 2 1        2 1 3        1 3 2
2 1 3        1 3 2        3 2 1
```

3 Dimensional Frankho ChessDoku™ # 48

Rule: All the digits 1 to 3 must appear in every row and column but cannot repeat on the same row of the same column of each layer. The number appears in the bottom right-hand corner is the result calculated according to operator(s) and chess move(s).

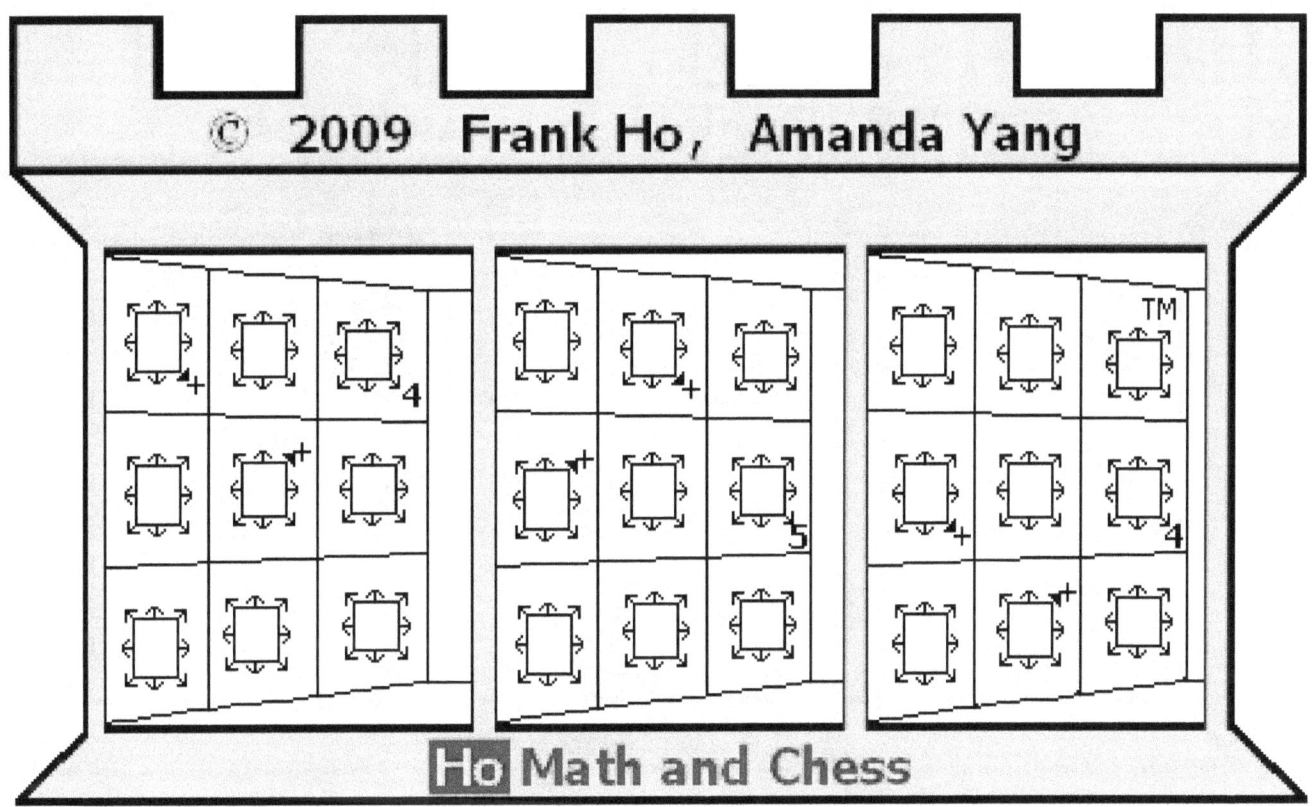

```
  2 3 1         3 1 2         1 2 3
  3 1 2         1 2 3         2 3 1
  1 2 3         2 3 1         3 1 2
```

3 Dimensional Frankho ChessDoku™ # 49

Rule: All the digits 1 to 3 must appear in every row and column but cannot repeat on the same row of the same column of each layer. The number appears in the bottom right-hand corner is the result calculated according to operator(s) and chess move(s).

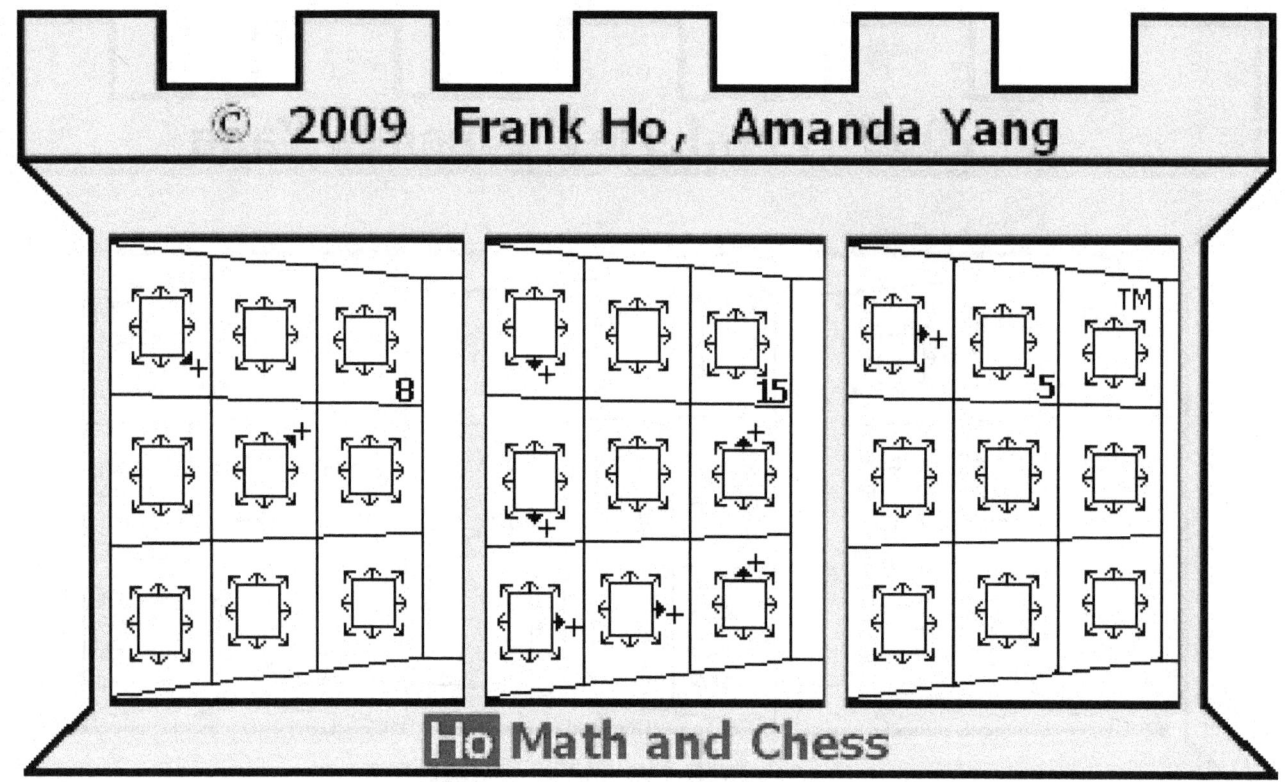

3	1	2		1	2	3		2	3	1
2	3	1		3	1	2		1	2	3
1	2	3		2	3	1		3	1	2

3 Dimensional Frankho ChessDoku™ # 50

Rule: All the digits 1 to 3 must appear exactly once in every row and column but cannot repeat on the same row or the same column of each layer. The number appears in the bottom right-hand corner is the result calculated according to operator(s) and chess move(s) as indicated by the darker arrow(s).

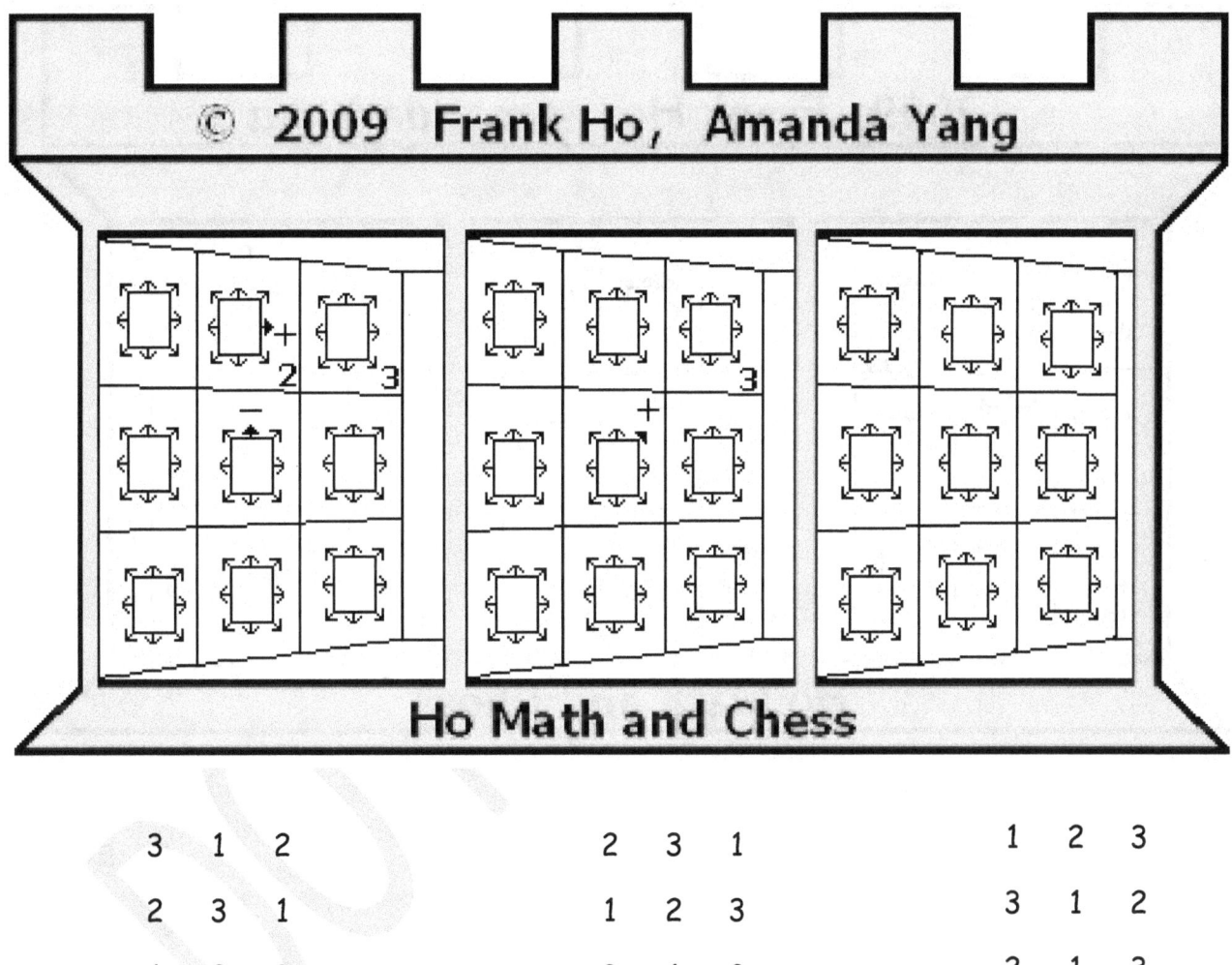

```
3  1  2      2  3  1      1  2  3
2  3  1      1  2  3      3  1  2
1  2  3      3  1  2      2  1  3
```

3 Dimensional Frankho ChessDoku™ # 51

Rule: All the digits 4 to 6 must appear exactly once in every row and column but cannot repeat on the same row or the same column of each layer. The number appears in the bottom right-hand corner is the result calculated according to operator(s) and chess move(s) as indicated by the darker arrow(s).

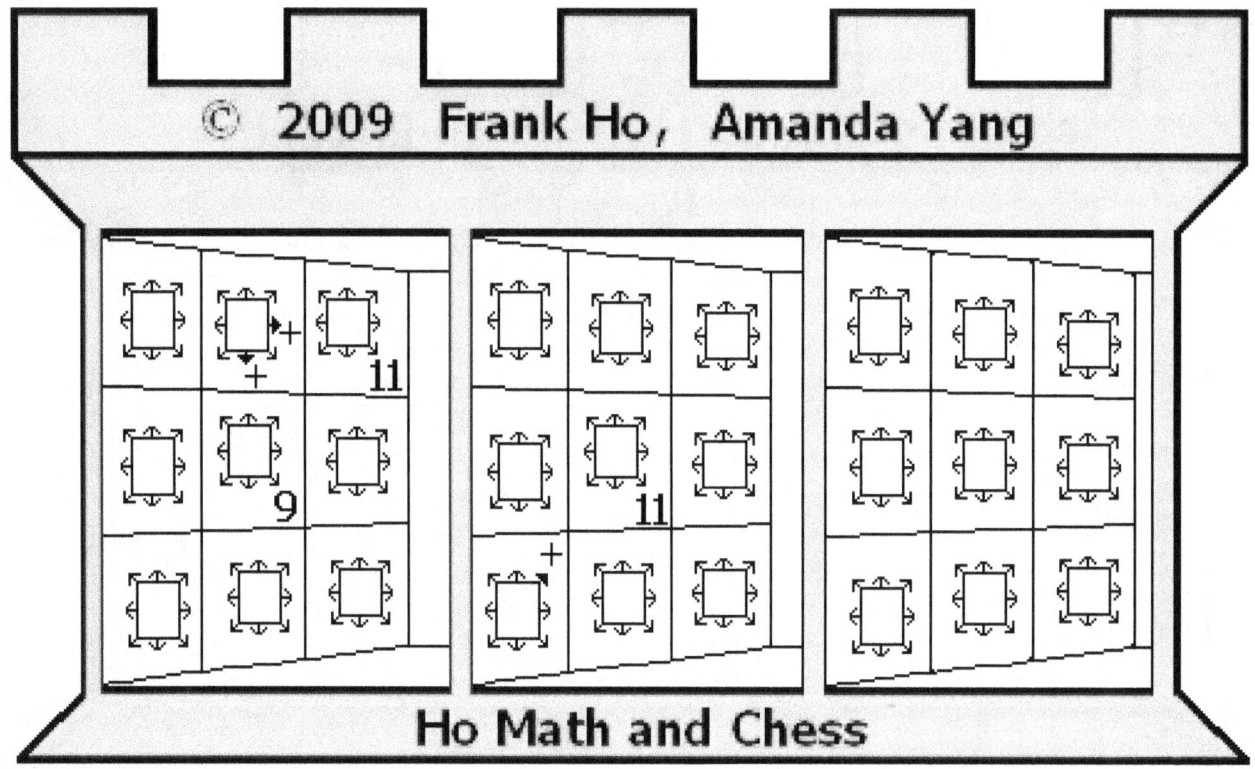

4	5	6
6	4	5
5	6	4

5	6	4
4	5	6
6	4	5

6	4	5
5	6	4
4	5	6

Math Chess Sudoku Puzzles 一青少年益智棋芸健脑

Frankho ChessDoku 一 何数棋谜算独

© 2007 一 2020   Frank Ho, Amanda Ho   All rights reserved.   www.homathchess.com

Student's name _____ Date_____

Comparing Frankho ChessDoku and CalcuDoku

何数棋算独与普通算独的比较
何数棋算独是由加拿大何老师发明以数独游戏与数学运算及国际象棋的巧妙结合

Frank Ho, Amanda Ho

April 2013

Introduction of Frankho ChessDoku ©

Frankho ChessDoku was invented by a Canadian math teacher Frank Ho (1, 2). Seeing the popularity of Sudoku but with no computation capability, Frank decided to do something about it, so Frank used his invented Geometry Chess Symbols (Canada Trademark TMA771400, copyright 1069744) along with Sudoku created the *Frankho ChessDoku* in 2008. *Frankho ChessDoku* is a unique puzzle which combines arithmetic, chess, and Sudoku all in one puzzle and is specially designed for children to solve arithmetic using backwards strategy by following chess moves and logic. In 2009 Frank Ho and his wife Amanda Ho jointly published a workbook.

Frank always has an idea about teaching math that is students should always be encouraged and more importantly be given a chance to THINK, and it means even when they are doing pure computation problems. This is the reason he has created many basic number facts computation workbooks using the idea of integrating math, chess, and puzzles. Math + *Chess* + *Sudoku* = *Fun Frankho ChessDoku*©

The pleasure of working on Ho Math Chess workbooks could be very well described by a famous classical Chinese poem 山重水复疑无路,柳暗花明又一村 (Equivalent English phrase is *seeing light at the end of tunnel.*)

Frank has described the characteristics of Ho Math Chess worksheets in Chinese rhyming sentences (打油诗) as follows. Its meaning mainly describes the magic of Ho Math Chess puzzles.

只见棋谜不见题　　劝君迷路不哭涕
数学象棋加谜题　　健脑思维真神奇

Introduction of CalcuDoku

The original CalcuDoku was invented in 2004 by a Japanese teacher Tetsuya Miyamoto in Japan (3).

Comparisons

The key difference between *Frankho ChessDoku* and CalcuDoku is that *Frankho* ChessDoku uses Frank's invented Geometry Chess Symbols to guide children on the directions of arithmetic operations instead of using "boxes or "cages" as used in Miyamoto's puzzles.

Frankho ChessDoku does not just use chess pieces to replace numbers in Sudoku as seen in some ChessDoku puzzles. *Frankho ChessDoku* invites children to trace chess moves to see the results just as if they were playing chess game by examining the intersections of chess moves and then use the logic of Sudoku to figure out the answers. Both strategies of playing chess game especially the intersections of chess moves and the arithmetic Sudoku logic need to be combined to solve *Frankho ChessDoku* puzzles.

Miyamoto runs a learning centre in Japan and teaches his puzzles to children. Frank and his wife also use their puzzles to teach children from age 4 and up in their Ho Math Chess learning centre in Vancouver, Canada. Both Frank and his wife teach children from kindergarten and up and both of them also teach math contest preparations.

From a student's learning math point of view, *Frankho ChessDoku* offers more powerful learning and mental training advantages over regular Sudoku and also other types of arithmetic Sudoku. The following table gives some comparisons. In addition to be a fun puzzle, *Frankho ChessDoku* is more suitable for students who like to improve their brainpower and also mental math ability.

	Frankho ChessDoku	Regular Sudoku	CalcuDoku
addition, subtraction, multiplication, and division	Can provide 4 mixed operations by following chess moves within one equation with no confusion.	No computations	Only independent and separate +, −, ×, ÷ operations can be provided. Mixed 4 basic operations could cause confusion for young children.
vertical, horizontal, and diagonal operations	The horizontal or vertical operations are provided. The diagonal operations can also be provided. The "jump" operation (knight move) can be provided.	No computations	Only horizontal or vertical operations are provided. No diagonal operations can be provided. No "jump" operation can be provided.
Framed or boxed operations	No framed operation is required since the operation direction is guided by chess moves. Children can always circle operation statements themselves. This flexibility allows intersecting "boxes" with no confusion.	No computations	Since operation is always "boxed" or "caged" with single operation, so no flexibility is allowed for mixed operations. Intersecting frames or boxes would cause confusion.

Math Chess Sudoku Puzzles 一青少年益智棋芸健脑

Frankho ChessDoku 一 何数棋谜算独

© 2007 — 2020   Frank Ho, Amanda Ho   All rights reserved.   www.homathchess.com

Student's name _____ Date _____

Example 1

Rule

All the digits 1 to 3 must appear exactly once in every row and column. The number appears in the bottom right-hand corner is the result calculated according to the arithmetic operator(s) and chess move(s) as indicated by the darker arrow(s).

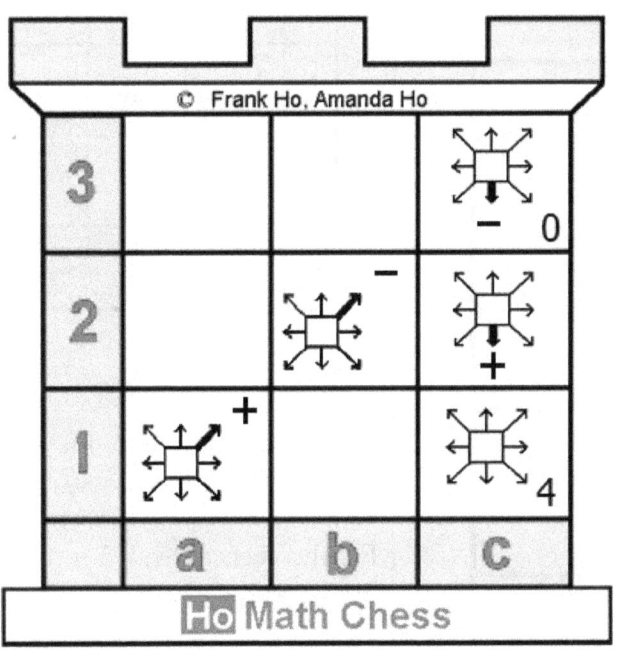

A CalcuDoku is not able to produce the diagonal operation of the above *Frankho ChessDoku*.

The mixed operation $3 + 2 - 1 = 4$ or $2 + 3 - 1 = 4$ is also difficult for children to work on if it happens in the CalcuDoku since it involves two operations at the same time but is very easy for *Frankho ChessDoku* to identify it with no confusion. This deficiency in CalcuDoku means children seem to always be stuck with only one operation at a time with little chance to work on mixed operations. In contrast, Children working on *Frankho ChessDoku* will have plenty of opportunities to work on either single or mixed operations with no confusion simply by following chess moves.

Step 1:
Circle all operations by following chess moves.

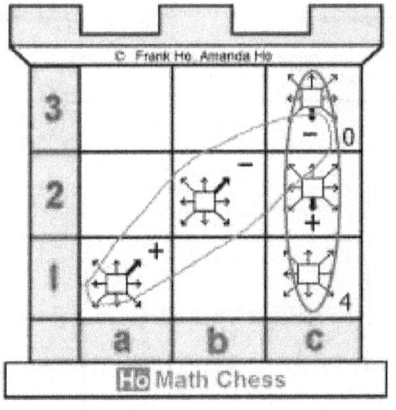

Step 2.
For the diagonal oval, $2 + 1 - 3 = 0$,
$1 + 2 - 3 = 0$.

For the vertical oval, $3 - 1 + 2 = 4$
So, we know c3=3.

The final answer is as follows.

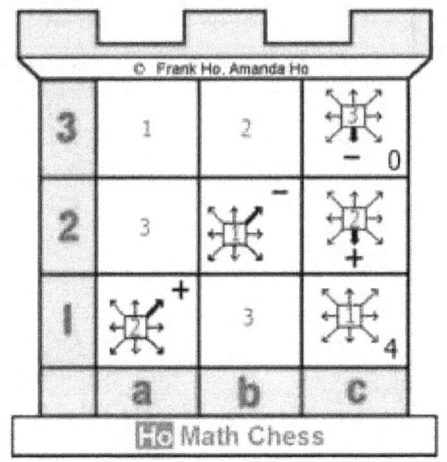

Page 281 of 288

Example 2

A CalcuDoku cannot produce the following "Jump" movement as acting by the chess knight move at c3.

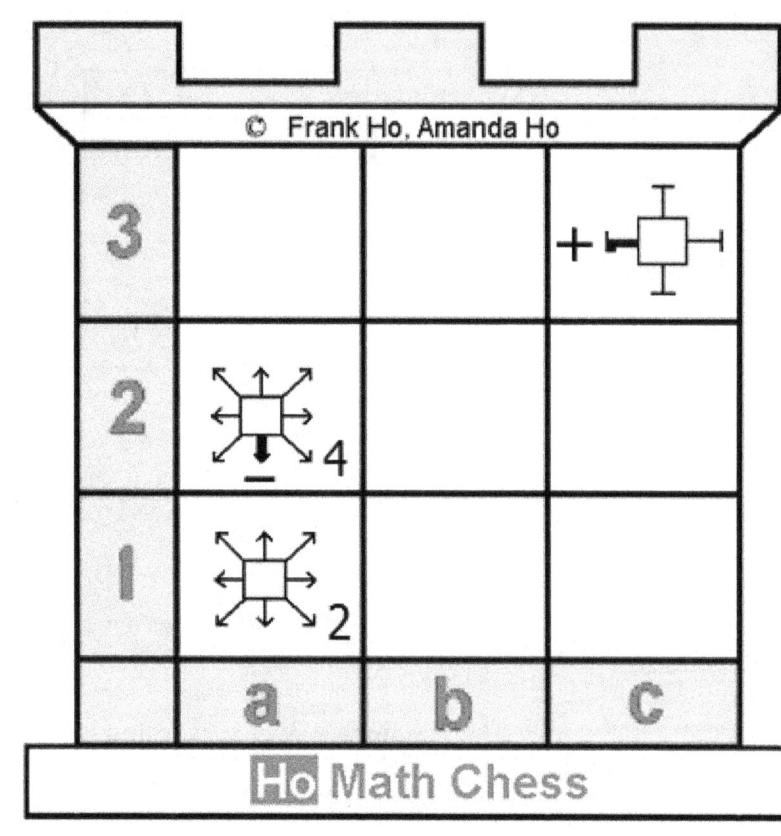

Step 1

Circle all operations.

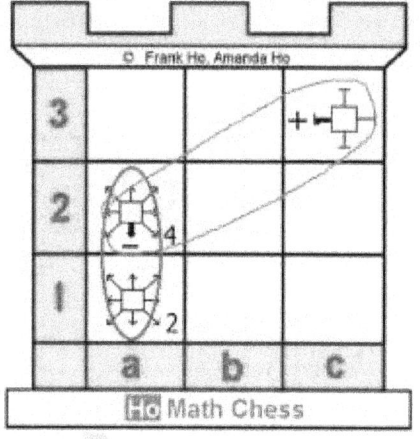

Step 2

For the diagonal oval, $1 + 3 = 4$, $3 + 1 = 4$, $2 + 2 = 4$.

For the vertical oval, $3 - 1 = 2$. So, we know a2 = 3.

The final answer is

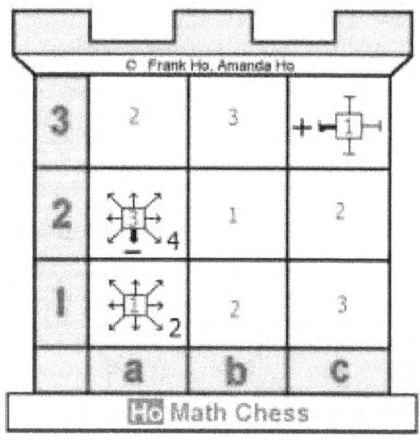

Example 3

The famous Sum and Difference problem can be easily illustrated by using the above *Frankho ChessDoku diagram* with intersection and also can be very easily solved but trying to create it using the idea of CalcuDoku demonstrates confusion for children.

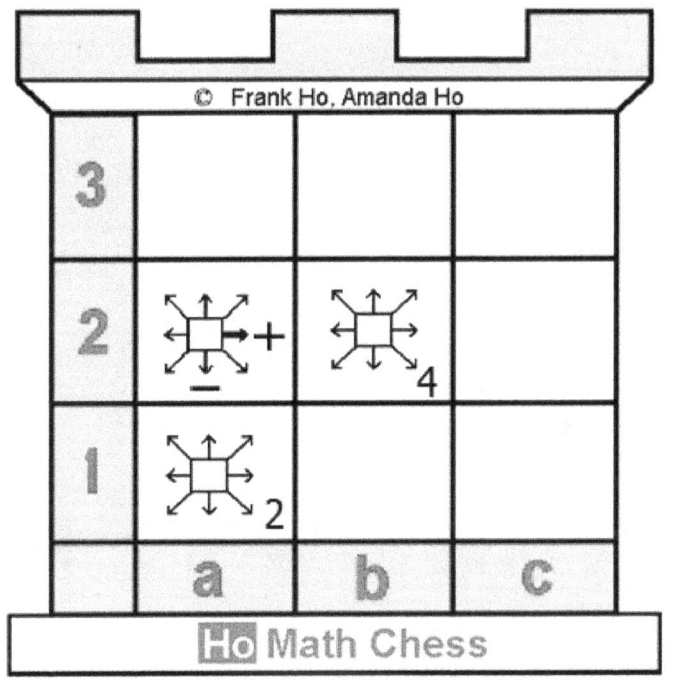

Step 1

Circle all operations.

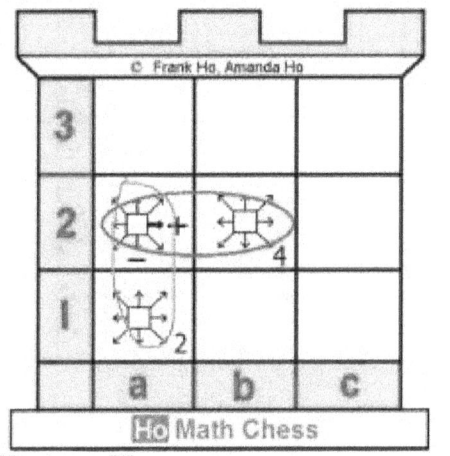

Step 2

Start at intersection a2.
For the horizontal oval, $3 + 1 = 4$, $1 + 3 = 4$, $2 + 2 = 4$.
For the vertical oval, $3 - 1 = 2$
So, we know a2 = 3.

The final answer is as follows:

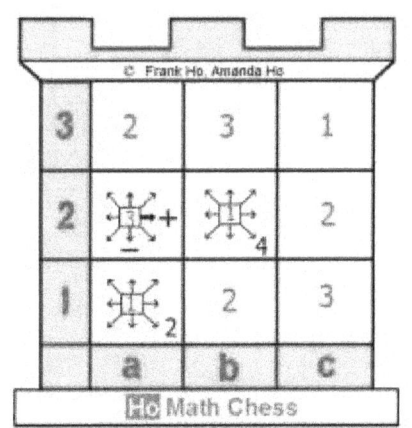

The following are the same problem (Sum and Difference) using the diagrams of CalcuDoku.

The left CalcuDoku diagram causes confusion because we do not know which box is for 4＋ and which box is for 1－. The Venn diagram concept can be easily demonstrated in the *Frankho ChessDoku* but causes confusion in the CalcuDoku.

The left CalcuDoku diagram uses the dotted box but again it still causes confusion as stated above.

Commutative law

The conventionaal way of calculating is in the direction of left to right or top to down, but this rule does not apply to CalcuDoku because as shown below" 2 – " can be expressed as 3, 1 or 1, 3 and it appears to students that the subtraction can be done by exchanging the two numbers and this is in violation of the commutative law. It would have no problem for *Frankho ChessDoku* to handle the subtraction and division operators because the calculation direction is clearly defined by using chess moves.

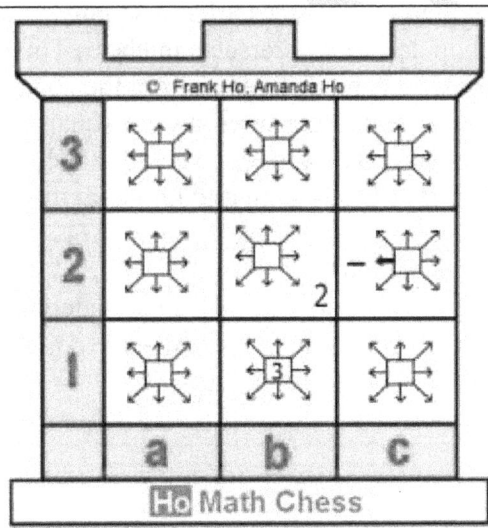

For subtraction operator, the answer could be operated from left to right but sometimes, it could be also from right to left.

The above CalcuDoku does require student to think about how 3 and 1 are to be arranged, so it could present extra challenging for students, but the confusion could also occur when the mixed operators (+, −, ×, ÷) are presented together with no operating directions are given.

The left *Frankho ChessDoku* presents no operation confusion and does not have the confusion of commutative law for children.

Chess strategy and Frankho ChessDoku strategy

Often a chess player would analyze the chess moves and see where each chess piece intersects each other, then decide to take the action of next move. This kind of thinking is also reflected in the strategy on how to solve *Frankho ChessDoku* and the following example demonstrated the transferred knowledge between chess and *Frankho ChessDoku*.

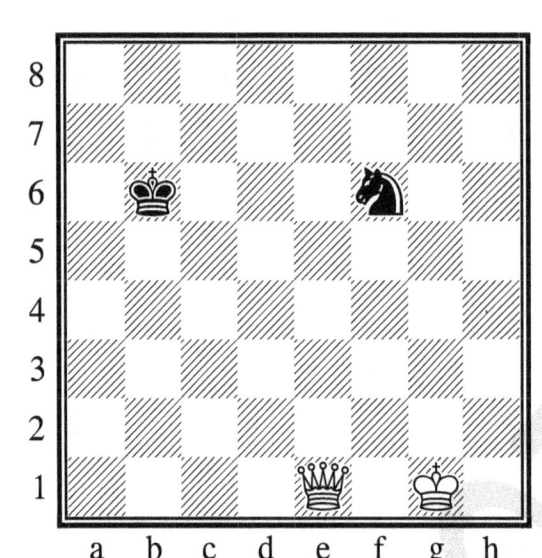

Find a Black move to fork.
Qe1 moves to f2 to fork black king and knight.

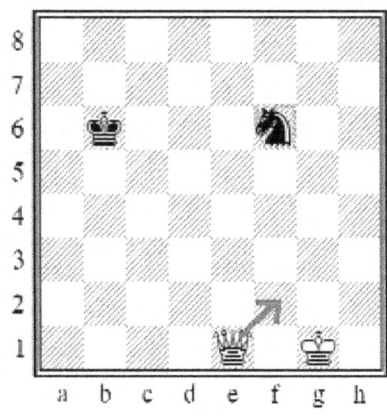

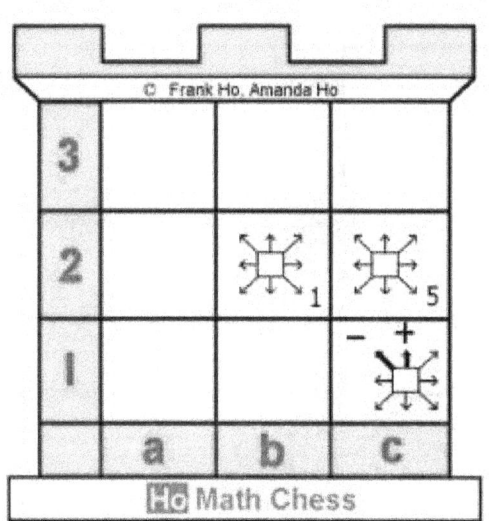

The above c1 intersects with b2 and c2 at the same time so in other words, c1 is a square where bishop and rook intersects in chess. This kind of thinking is no difference from the chess diagram on the left to consider at what square where the queen could move to such that the queen could fork Black king and knight at the same time.

Frankho ChessDoku trains children to watch the intersections of lines and this knowledge could be transferred to benefitting chess play.

Triangular solving strategy for 3 by 3 grid

The simplest 3 by 3 case of *Frankho ChessDoku* can be created by using only one number and one math operator. All other math operations are really redundant.

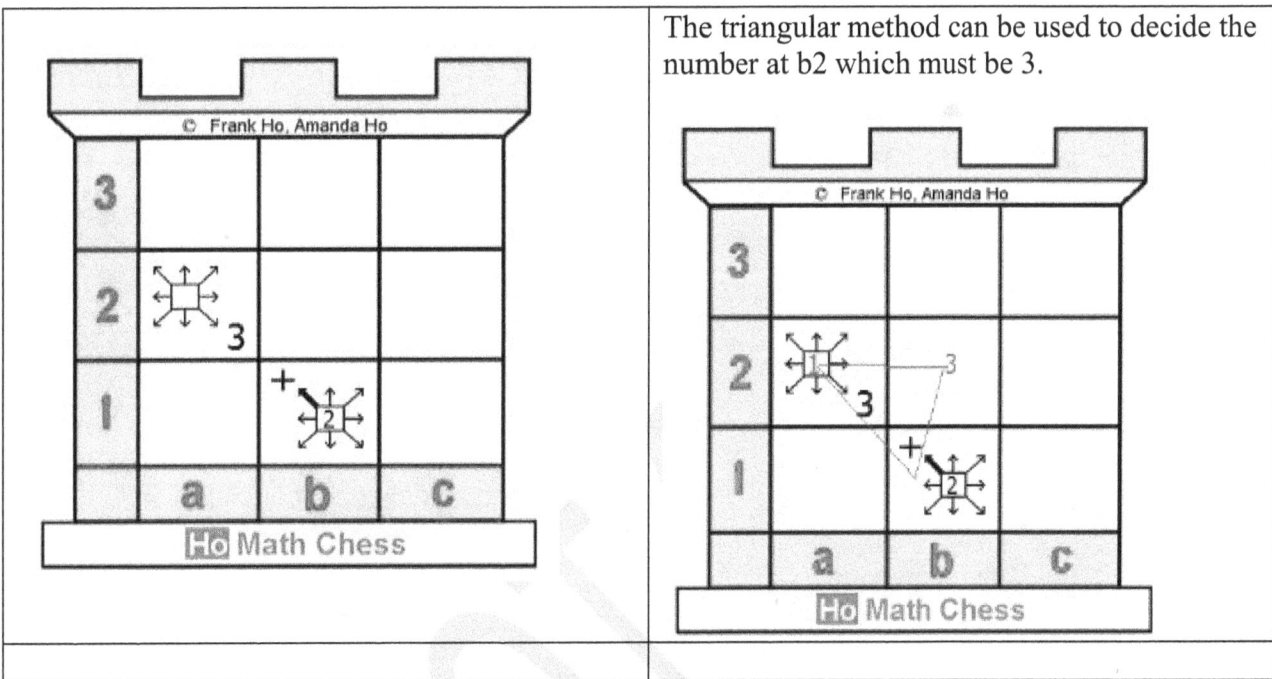

The triangular method can be used to decide the number at b2 which must be 3.

The above diagonal operation cannot be duplicated by CalcuDoku; instead, a horizontal operation could be made. The operation directions in CalcuDoku can be replicated in Frankho ChessDoku but not always the other way around. Frankho ChessDoku is much more flexible in terms of mixed calculations and also trains more visualization.

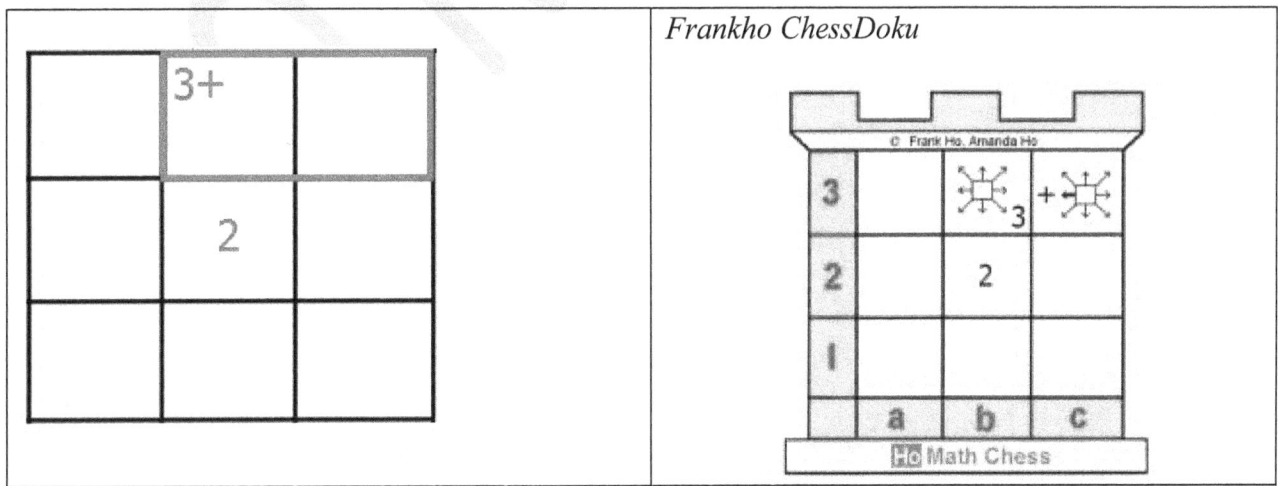

Frankho ChessDoku

References

(1) http://susanpolgar.blogspot.ca/2008/10/ho-math-and-chess.html
(2) http://www.mathandchess.com/releases/release/1441781/17465.htm
(3) http://en.wikipedia.org/wiki/Tetsuya_Miyamoto

www.ingramcontent.com/pod-product-compliance
Lightning Source LLC
Chambersburg PA
CBHW081126170426
43197CB00017B/2770